Reformatio Legum Ecclesiasticarum

Habent sua fata libelli

Volume XIX
of
Sixteenth Century Essays & Studies

Charles G. Nauert, Jr., General Editor

Composed at Northeast Missouri State University
Kirksville, Missouri
Cover Design by Teresa Wheeler, NMSU Designer
Manufactured by Edwards Brothers, Ann Arbor, Michigan
Text is set in Clearface Regular 10/12

The Reformation
of the Ecclesiastical Laws
of England, 1552

◆

James C. Spalding

◆

◆

Volume XIX
Sixteenth Century Essays & Studies

This book has been brought to publication with the
generous support of
Northeast Missouri State University

Library of Congress Cataloging-in-Publication Data

[Reformatio legum ecclesiasticarum. English]
The Reformation of church law / [edited by] James C. Spalding.
   p.   cm. — (Sixteenth century essays & studies : v. 19)
   Translation of: Reformatio legum ecclesiasticarum.
   ISBN 0-940474-20-4
   1. Ecclesiastical law—Great Britain—History—Sources. 2. Church of
England—History—Sources. I.Spalding, James C. II. Series.
KD8624.S6R4413   1992
262.9′8342—dc20   92-9667
                                                    CIP

Contents

Illustrations

NOTE: Illustrations from the *Reformatio* have been reduced by approximately one-third.

James C. Spalding

In Appreciation

James C. Spalding will long be remembered by his doctoral students as "the Graduate Students' Friend." A man of immense integrity, compassion, and knowledge, Jim never viewed his students as cogs in the academic machinery of graduate school. He always took his students seriously, accepting them as they were and as peers. Thus, when talking with Jim, one might learn about his latest research project, about his concern for the Church, about his passion for justice in the world, or his family. One gained from these frequent conversations insightful commentaries upon ideas, events, and movements, all of which provided a glimpse of a great man's worldview and which in turn had a broadening effect upon his students. Jim's worldview integrated knowledge, his personal involvement in myriad activities, and the events of the world into a carefully constructed Christian theological system rooted in the Reformed tradition. This worldview, coupled with his caring concern, touched the lives of all his students and particularly his graduate advisees and their families.

There is a special nature to Jim's theological and historical concerns. Especially well versed in the literature of the Reformation, Jim often highlighted his lectures and discussions with past and contemporary religious thought and practice. One always sensed his profound appreciation for the Biblical witness, and his Christ-centered theology reflected itself in his life and work at the University of Iowa as well as is work in the Church and community.

Jim spent the bulk of his time and energy with his students, helping them to reach their own professional goals. He often nudged students into research that one had the feeling he would like to have explored himself. We learned scholarship from a scholar whose scholarship was shared scholarship. Many of us reaped the benefits of Jim's research and work which he selflessly shared in the pursuit of common academic goals. As a result, Jim's scholarly life continues to thrive and flourish in the students he inspired and befriended, in the significant articles he wrote that appeared in various learned journals, and now in this monograph.

Many of us have said to him often and with utmost sincerity, "Thanks for all you did!" That, of course is an understatement. We do hope this volume, made possible in his honor and bringing to light an area of research in which Jim has worked for many years and produced in this his year of retirement, 1992, will be further testimony of the gratitude and inspiration so many owe to him.

Dan Danner
Richard Hughes
Robert V. Schnucker

February 1992

Tabula Congratulatoria

Hubert B. Brom

James B. Bross

Leo G. Cox

Dan Danner

George C. Field

R. Eldon Fuhrman

Donald G. Good

Ronald S. Gowler

Herbert Harold Hazelip

Bruce J. Horacek

Richard T. Hughes

Donald Lake

Robert E. Page

James A. Reinhard

Charles W. Roundy

Robert V. Schnucker

Monte Thomas Starkes

Paul Taylor

Robert J. Tollefson

Mark E. VanderSchaaf

Godfrey Noel Vose

Preface

This monograph in the Sixteenth Century Essays and Studies series contains a translation of the Latin manuscript entitled *Reformatio legum ecclesiasticarum* (The Reformation of the Ecclesiastical Laws) of England, completed in the year 1552. The original manuscript is extant in 269 folio leaves, with some the leaves blank, which today are preserved in the British Library under the file Harleian MSS.426. This manuscript has here been translated into English working from a microfilm copy and published in this volume. An introductory essay places the manuscript in its historical context.

The Latin manuscript is the product of a royal commission, which had its origins in the lay resistance to some of the features of the canon law. This resulted in a submission of the English clergy in 1532, calling for a representative committee to reconcile canon law with common law and the statutes of the realm. That committee work came to fruition toward the end of the year 1552. The *Reformatio* was then introduced to the House of Lords by Thomas Cranmer in 1553, but it did not receive a serious consideration at the time.

The manuscript is basically in beautiful scribal hands, but it also has all of the blemishes that one would expect from the work of a committee trying to perfect it. There are a large number of corrections and additions in the manuscript made in the handwriting of Thomas Cranmer and Peter Martyr Vermigli as well as some where the handwriting has not been identified. Examples of the handwriting typical of the manuscript are in the text.

John Foxe later used this manuscript, together with another manuscript, now lost, which belonged in a collection of papers belonging to Archbishop Matthew Parker. From these Foxe prepared the first printed edition of the *Reformatio*, published in Latin in 1571. Foxe left identifiable notations on at least thirty folio pages of the 1552 manuscript, and there are probably more of his marks which cannot be identified. In notations he referred at least twice to the Codex of Matthew Canterbury, (Archbishop Parker), but this manuscript cannot now be found. This lost codex could have been prepared in 1563 for the Convocations of that year. On the basis of these two manuscripts, Foxe published the Latin text of the *Reformatio* in 1571 somewhat in haste but with the intention that it be used by the then current Parliament to give a statutory ratification to a reformed canon law. The bibliographical reference is *Reformation Legum Ecclesiasticarum, ex Authoritate primum Regis Henrici 8. inchoata; Deinde per Regem Edourdum 6. provecta. adauctaque in hunc modu, atq; . . .* (London: John Day, April 1571). The Foxe publication, with some corrections, was reprinted in London by Daniel Frere in 1640, and again by the Stationers' Company in 1641.

Edward Cardwell had the 1571 Foxe publication republished in 1850, and a reprint edition of this was bought out in England in 1968. (Edward Cardwell, ed. *The Reformation of the Ecclesiastical Laws, As Attempted in the Reigns of King Henry VIII, King Edward VI, and Queen Elizabeth.* (Oxford: Clarendon 1850). The reprint was published by Gregg International in England.

There have been no English translations in print until now of either the 1552 Harleian manuscript, or the Foxe, or Cardwell editions. The translation offered here is of the 1552 manuscript with all of the textual corrections by Cranmer and Vermigli, and others who had their hands on the text at that time. This is not a translation of the Latin of the Foxe 1571 edition nor of the Cardwell publication of 1850, which is basically a reprint of the 1571 edition, although those texts were consulted. Edward Cardwell believed that the extant 1552 British Museum manuscript was the final document produced in the reign of Edward VI and that the Codex of Matthew Parker represented revisions, reorderings and additions made by Parker and Foxe to the 1552 document.

The most serious study of the *Reformatio* in recent years was by Leslie Sachs in his J. C. D. dissertation of 1982 at the Catholic University in America. He challenged Cardwell's thesis and held that the Foxe publication was based on the final draft in Edwardian days and that the Harleian manuscript was only the penultimate committee draft. He, therefore, entitled his dissertation *Thomas Cranmer's "Reformatio Legum Ecclesiasticarum" of 1553 in the Context of English Church Law from the Later Middle Ages to the Canons of 1603.* (Ann Arbor: University Microfilms, 1982).

By calling it the *Reformatio* of 1553, Sachs underscored his belief that the Parker Codex used by John Foxe but now lost was the final recension presented to the House of Lords by Thomas Cranmer in 1553 rather than the manuscript here translated which Sachs called the penultimate text. The Parker Codex, according to Sachs, was presented to the House of Lords in 1553 and is what John Foxe had printed in 1571. At present this is conjecture. Unless the Parker Codex can be found, it will not be possible to settle this issue.

Of one thing we can be sure, the British Museum manuscript that has been now translated and here published dates from the year 1552 and represents the thinking of the leadership of the Edwardian church at that time. Therefore, in this book we will speak of the translated text as the *Reformatio legum ecclesiasticarum* of 1552, not of 1553. Sach's use of 1553 implies that the Foxe publication of 1571 was the Parker Codex and that this was what was presented to the House of Lords in 1553.

My questioning Sach's theory is based upon the extensive evidence of Foxe's hand on the folio pages of the 1552 manuscript. If Foxe had a complete manuscript of the final recension of the *Reformatio* which had been presented to the House of Lords in 1553, why did he bother to work so hard with the 1552 manuscript while preparing the *Reformatio* for publication? If Foxe had had a clean copy of the "ultimate 1553" recension not now extant why did he not print it was it stood rather than dealing so extensively with the 1552 manuscript with its many corrections so difficult to read?

There are eight titles in the Foxe edition of 1571 that are not in the 1552 manuscript. They were certainly in the Matthew Parker Codex, but there is no evidence that they were present in the manuscript presented to the House of Lords in 1553. The Codex of Matthew Parker must have contained these and other materials. It could have been prepared for the Convocations and Parliament of 1563. It is conjectural on Sach's part to believe that it was a complete "ultimate" manuscript presented to Parliament in 1553. According to Foxe's introduction to the 1571 publication, now translated and contained in Appendix I of this book, Foxe did not present the *Reformatio* as a proposal to be voted up or down as it stood. Modifications were expected by him in a way comparable from the modification to the Forty-Two Articles of Religion in Edward's day into the Thirty-Nine Articles of the Elizabethan Church. I see no reason to believe that Archbishop Parker did not think the same way about the *Reformatio* that he did about the Forty-Two Articles. He was, after all, on the committee that produced the *Reformatio.*

Sachs in presenting his case tended to put a distance between the thought of John Foxe as a proto-Puritan, and that of Matthew Parker as a proto-Anglican, which in my opinion is not justified. Sachs would also put a distance between Parker and Martin Bucer which I believe is unwarranted. Sachs made much of the influence of Bucer on the *Reformatio* but did not believe that the *Reformatio* ever represented the thought of Matthew Parker. However, Parker was a colleague, friend, and disciple of Bucer as much as was John Calvin or Peter Martyr Vermigli. This is not to say that there were no differences of opinion. Of course there were, but basically they all sought to express the same basic position. There is time for such discussion in later articles rather than continuing this forward or cluttering the narrative introduction that follows.

A few comments need to be made concerning problems in the manuscript in its microfilm form and their impact on the translation. Often it is impossible to read what has been lined out because of the width of the lining out stroke and this is so indicated in a footnote. As one would expect, the scribe would make a mistake in spelling or grammar and correct the error or a subsequent editor would make the correction. Some of these are reported in the footnotes. A goodly number of changes were made in the Latin text that when translated, produce little or no change in English. When it can be accurately asserted that the changes are in the hand of Cranmer or Vermigli, it is shown in the translation and the footnotes. A table of symbols has been provided to help the reader recognize the changes made in the 1552 manuscript.

Iowa City, Iowa
February 1992   James C. Spalding

Acknowledgments

This publication would never have seen the light of day without the patience, persistence, and prodding of Robert Schnucker of the Sixteenth Century Journal Publishers of Kirksville, Missouri. His energy and overtime work together with his encouragement have made the book possible.

Several persons were involved in the translation from Latin to English. Above all, major credit for translation should go to Professor Joan O'Brien of Southern Illinois University who spent lonely hours worrying with the various scripts and technical Latin terms of the manuscript in the University of Iowa Library while I was at the Folger Shakespeare Library in Washington, D.C. getting to know the context for the document. Professor Benjamin Hubbard of California State University at Fullerton also did some of the early work. The English translation was to have been smoothed and polished by the late Professor Donald Sutherland, superb medieval historian and specialist in medieval English Law whose untimely death prevented his final reading. That task has been done with great care and insight by Professor Charles Nauert of the University of Missouri, a consummate scholar of Renaissance Latin (the same style of Latin used by Cranmer and his associates in producing the *Reformatio*). They all have my sincere thanks. If there are faults and blemishes in the translation, however, I must shoulder the blame.

My thanks go to the Folger Shakespeare Library for a summer grant to further this study. My thanks are given also to their staff as well. It is a civilized place to do research. Any obscure references in this book can undoubtedly be found in that library.

A number of people have helped with preparing the text for its printed form including my dear wife, Virginia, who proof read and actually came to find these legal propositions interesting. The work of all those associated with the Sixteenth Century Journal Publishers in Kirksville is greatly appreciated.

EDITORIAL SYMBOLS, ABBREVIATIONS, AND NOTES USED IN
REFORMATIO LEGUM ECCLESIASTICARUM

Clearface Regular type: The main body of the *Refamatio* is set in this style of type.

Zapf Chancery type: Emedations in Cranmer's handwriting are set in this style of type.

————————   A line through text indicates it has a line through it in the MS. Explanation for the line is in a footnote at the bottom of the page on which the line occurs.

[   ]   Text enclosed in square brackets is in Peter Martyr Vermigli's handwriting.

<   >   Text enclosed in angle brackets is missing from the Foxe and Cardwell editions.

Fol. 000:   Folio numbers in the outside margins of the text indicate the folio pages of the 1552 MS.

★   The star symbol in the body of the text indicates the beginning of the folio page listed in the outside margin.

[manuscript in Thomas Cranmer's hand — Latin cursive]

Example of Thomas Cranmer's hand

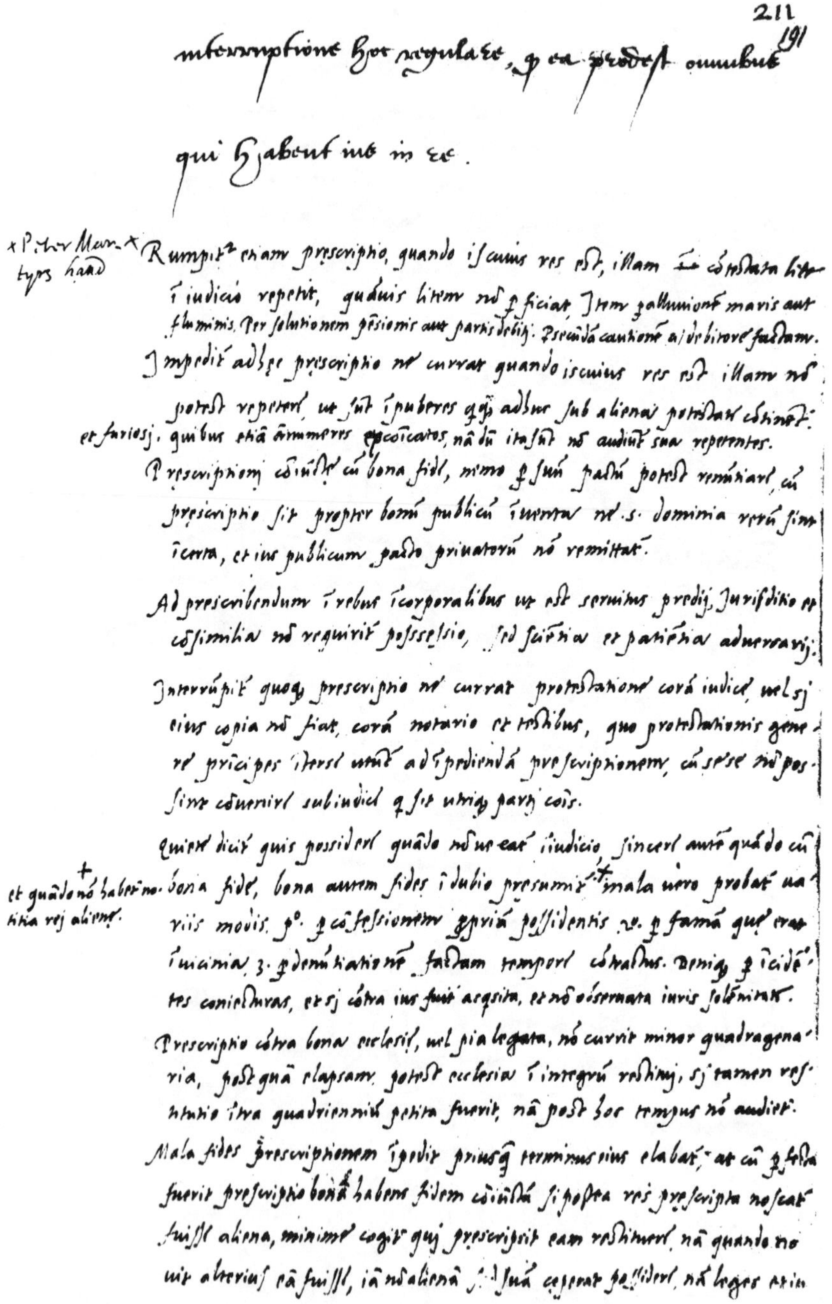

211
191

interruptione hoc regulare, quia ea prodest omnibus qui habent ius in re.

+Peter Mar-+ tyrs hand

Rumpitur etiam prescriptio, quando is cuius res est, illam in contestata lite in iudicio repetit, quamvis litem non perficiat. Item gallumione maris aut fluminis. Per solutionem pensionis aut partis debiti. Per secundam cautionem a debitore factam.

Impedit adhuc prescriptio ne currat quando is cuius res est illam non potest repetere, ut sunt impuberes qui adhuc sub aliena potestate continentur. et furiosi. quibus etiam annumeres excommunicatos, nam dum ita sunt non audiunt sua repetentes.

Prescriptionem coniunctam cum bona fide, nemo per suum pactum potest renuntiare, cum prescriptio sit propter bonum publicum inventa ne s. dominia rerum sint incerta, et ius publicum pacto privatorum non remittatur.

Ad prescribendum in rebus incorporalibus ut est servitus predij, Jurisdictio et consimilia non requirit possessio, sed scientia et patientia adversarij.

Interrumpit quoque prescriptio ne currat protestatione coram iudice, vel si eius copia non fiat, coram notario et testibus, quo protestationis genere principes interesse utuntur ad impediendam prescriptionem, cum sese non possint convenire sub iudice qui sit utrique parti communis.

Quiete dicitur quis possidere quando non vocatur in iudicio, sincere autem quando cum bona fide, bona autem fides in dubio presumitur + mala vero probatur variis modis. 1° per confessionem proprium possidentis 2° per famam que erat in vicinia 3. per denuntiationem factam tempore contractus. Denique per incidentes coniecturas, et si contra ius fuit acquisita, et non observata iuris solemnitate.

+ et quando non habet notitia rei alienae.

Prescriptio contra bona ecclesie, vel pia legata, non currit minor quadragenaria, postquam elapsam, potest ecclesia in integrum restitui, si tamen restitutio intra quadriennium petita fuerit, nam post hoc tempus non audietur.

Mala fides prescriptionem impedit priusquam terminus eius elabatur, at cum perfecta fuerit prescriptio bonam habens fidem coniunctam si postea res prescripta noscatur fuisse aliena, minime cogitur qui prescripsit eam restituere, nam quando novit alterius eam fuisse, iam non alienam, sed suam ceperat possidere, nam leges etiam

Example of Peter Martyr Vermigli's hand

Editor's Introduction

How can a Church better order its life to be effective in ministry? This perennial question was given a fresh answer during the reign of King Edward VI in 1152/53. The English Church, which at that time counted all of the residents in England as its constituency, had been severed from the Church of Rome. Now it had to reorganize its life under the supremacy of the crown. The King and Parliament of England had placed the responsibility for this reorganization in the hands of a select committee of thirty-two people. This committee had first been proposed as early as 1532, at the very beginning of the break with Rome. Twenty years later, after much delay, the members had been chosen and put to work. They produced a document which was designed to revise the canon law of England.

This document, the *Reformatio legum ecclesiasticarum,* was completed in the winter of 1552/53. It was intended to be joined with the Forty-Two Articles of religion with Catechism and with the Second Prayerbook of Edward VI as one of the three symbolic standards for defining the life of the Church of England. These three books corresponded to what were regarded as the three external marks of the true Church: where the Word is truly preached, where the sacraments are rightly administered, and where discipline is maintained.

While the English Parliament and King endorsed the articles and prayerbook as doctrinal and liturgical norms, thereby making them a part of statutory law, the passage of the *Reformatio* was blocked in the House of Lords by John Dudley, Duke of Northumberland, who was virtual ruler of England at the time. The untimely death of King Edward VI and the succession to the throne of his Catholic sister Mary stalled reconsideration of the document until the reign of Queen Elizabeth. During her reign, in 1559, 1563, and 1571, the document was brought to the attention of Parliament and/or to both Convocations. In 1571, the *Reformatio* was printed in Latin with an introduction by John Foxe for use that year in Convocations and Parliament. Thomas Cranmer's son-in-law, Thomas Norton, a member of Parliament, was active then in promoting the document; however, Queen Elizabeth's personal policy concerning the governing of the Church proved to be the stumbling block to the adoption to the *Reformatio* in its then current or revised form.

In contrast, the Articles and Prayerbook, with their status in Edwardian statutes, were adopted again in revised form early in Elizabeth's reign. Those who had created the originals for these books of the English Reformation were also on the committee of thirty-two that produced the *Reformatio*. They had

1

intended the *Reformatio* to be an integral part of the total design for reformation. The document, which is presented here in English translation, describes the discipline and government of the Church of England as intended by the authors of the Articles and the Prayerbook. It was designed to be a normative plan defining how the Church of England would show forth the third external mark of the true Church, the mark of discipline.

Leslie Sachs, in his doctoral study, speaks of the *Reformatio* as describing "the Church that never was."[1] Perhaps this is an apt description, for the Church of England lived on without such a statutory disciplinary and governing norm until it finally completed the reformation of its ecclesiastical laws with full legal sanction in 1969. However, the document deserves attention and remembrance as a creative product of the interchange of Catholic, Lutheran, Reformed, and Anglican ideas before those terms became more narrowly and separately defined. It represents the first and only effort by a major nation in the Reformation era to replace a canon law tradition which had been functioning for at least five hundred years. In this introductory essay, the *Reformatio* will be described in the context in which it was imagined, developed, and written.

THE REFORMATION OF ECCLESIASTICAL LAWS IN ENGLAND TO THE SUBMISSION OF THE CLERGY IN 1532

On May 16, 1532, the Convocation of Canterbury, soon followed by the Convocation of York, which together spoke in the name of the clergy of England, presented to King Henry VIII the *Submission of the Clergy*, which had been adopted only the day before. On that same day Sir Thomas More resigned as Chancellor of England and returned the Great Seal to the King. This submission—together with the resignation of More, the great lay defender of and apologist for the old regime within the Church—marked the end of an era. This date can be defended as the key moment in the reformation of the Church in England.

At the time, the Church of England was still in communion with the Bishop of Rome. Members of Parliament and the King's council, as well as the members of the two Convocations, would have protested their doctrinal orthodoxy in opposition to Lutheranism and Lollardy. Nor was there any great call among these officials for a major modification of the worship of the Church. Concern to reform doctrine and worship appeared only later in the Church's history.

There had been a long-standing call for the reformation of laws that governed the discipline of the Church. The *Submission of the Clergy* in 1532 made it clear that a reformation of canon law should take place. Reformation

---

[1]Leslie Raymond Sachs, "Thomas Cranmer's 'Reformatio legum ecclesiasticarum' of 1553 in the Context of English Church Law from the Later Middle Ages to the Canons of 1603" (J.C.D. dissertation, Catholic University of America, Washington, D.C., 1982: University Microfilms), chap. 4. This dissertation is the most complete study of the *Reformatio* to date.

of the Church in England was to be first of all a reformation of ecclesiastical laws.

The first paragraph in the *Submission* contains the promise that the clergy of England shall

> never from henceforth enact . . . or execute any new canons or constitutions provincial or synodal in our Convocations or synod in time coming . . . unless your Highness by your royal assent shall license us to assemble our Convocation and to make, promulgate and execute such constitutions and ordinances as shall be made in the same; and thereto to give your royal assent and authority.[2]

Having relinquished final authority on future canon law to the crown, *Submission* authors recommended in the second paragraph that a committee of thirty-two persons, sixteen from the houses of Parliament and sixteen from the clergy, should be chosen by the King in order to make a study of the constitutions, ordinances, and canons provincial or synodal enacted earlier. Those canons which the committee found to be in contradiction to any of God's laws or the laws of the realm were to be abrogated and removed. Conversely, those laws that stood up under the examination were to continue in full force. This was to be the task of a royal commission for the reformation of the ecclesiastical laws of the Church. The composition of the committee was to guarantee that no decision could be made on the retention or elimination of a canon, constitution, or ordinance without the agreement of both laity and clergy.

The submission of the clergy and the relinquishing of their independence in the area of canon law is not to be explained simply in terms of the desire of a tyrannical Henry VIII that would force the clergy to acquiesce in policies designed to permit the annulment of his marriage to Catherine of Aragon. Rather, one must look to the House of Commons which had agitated against the tyranny of canon law early in Henry's reign, when the King's marriage with Catherine still held promise. This lay concern found Henry's great matter of the annulment to be a convenient rallying ground.

Lay antagonism to canon law had been earlier focused by the mishandling of the case of Richard Hunne, a London merchant. Hunne, resenting the loss of a petty and rather pathetic suit in an ecclesiastical court, had reacted by filing in a secular court a writ of praemunire against his clerical opponent. The writ was based upon an interpretation of the Second Statute of Praemunire of 1393, 16 Richard II, c. 5, under which a person was judged for prosecuting in a foreign (e.g. papal) court a suit that properly belonged in an English secular court. The penalty was severe, involving forfeiture of property, imprisonment and even outlawry. It had been designed to protect English

---

[2]For the complete text of the *Submission of the Clergy,* see Henry Gee and William John Hardy, *Doctrines Illustrative of English Church History* (London: Macmillan, 1910), 176ff.

prelates from punishment by papal authority for executing judgements of the King's Courts in questions of patronage and also to prevent arbitrary translations of bishops in or from England by the pope without their own and the king's consent. Later, common law lawyers developed the practice of using such writs as a device to institute suits in secular courts to counter suits filed in ecclesiastical courts. They reasoned that all ecclesiastical courts were ultimately papal, and therefore foreign, courts. This assumption became such a problem to the Church in England that in 1447 the clergy petitioned King Henry VI for relief, and for many years thereafter, the use of the writ against Church courts diminished.

Perhaps Hunne's use of the writ of praemunire was considered a frontal attack upon clerical prerogatives. Although the use of praemunire had diminished, the feeling toward its use by some of the clergy was intensely negative. In 1505 Bishop Richard Nix of Norwich wrote to Archbishop William Warham of Canterbury that "if your fatherhood would favor me, I would curse all . . . promoters and maintainers of . . . praemunire as heretics and not believers in Christ's Church."[3] Bishop Ralph Fitzjames, who was considered a reactionary on many matters by his contemporaries, argued that praemunire was to be countered by the charge of heresy.

Bishop Fitzjames' attitude toward praemunire was put into practice with Hunne, who was charged with heresy and imprisoned in the Lollard's Tower of St. Paul's. On December 4, 1514, Hunne was found dead under circumstances sufficiently suspicious to convince a coroner's jury — and modern scholars — that he had been murdered by the Bishop's chancellor, with the assistance of the bell-ringer of St. Paul's and the jailer. As if this were not bad enough, the deceased Mr. Hunne was then judged guilty of being a contumacious heretic and his body was burned so that his heirs would be deprived of his property. The three alleged murderers were protected by canon law courts and were never brought to trial.

Members of the House of Commons meeting in 1515 passed a bill to restore Hunne's property to his family, but the bill was rejected by the House of Lords, which had a clerical majority. Bills designed to remove ecclesiastical liberty from murderers and felons were similarly defeated by the Lords. In May 1514, Pope Leo XI had reaffirmed in the Lateran Council that laymen had no jurisdiction over clergy and that clerics were immune from temporal punishment. In 1512, the House of Lords had been willing to approve, on a temporary basis, an act by which criminal clerics in minor orders became subject to lay punishments for their crimes. When the Lords then did not renew this in 1515, it was seen by many of the laity to be an attempt to protect real criminals from having to face justice.

---

[3]Public Record Office (hereafter PRO), *Anc.. Corr.* (S.C.I.), vol. 64, no. 83 in Michael Kelly, "The Submission of the Clergy," *Transactions of the Royal Historical Society,* 5th Series, 15 (1965): 108.

Even though the Hunne property was restored to the family by executive act of Cardinal Wolsey in 1523, this experience and others less notorious were in the minds of members of the House of Commons when what came to be known as the Reformation Parliament gathered at Westminster in 1529. Then Henry VIII used praemunire as a powerful weapon to bring the Church under royal control. The long experience of common lawyers and the numerous outrages of clerical immunity were used by the king to his own advantage.[4]

In 1523 the venerable Christopher St. German published in Latin a dialogue between a student of common law and a doctor of divinity in which the student went to considerable length to explain to the theologian how canon law differed from common law in England. A second edition appeared in 1528 and a third, undated English edition was published in either 1530 or 1531. The main argument, in St. German's words, is:

> How the lawe of England is grounded vpon the lawe of reason/ the lawe of God/ the generall customes of the realm/ and vpon certayne pryncyples that be called maxymes/ vpon the partyculer customes vsyed in dyuerse Cytyes & countryes/ and vpon statues whiche have ben made in dyuerse Parlyamentes by our souerayne lorde the kynge and his progenitoures/ and by the Lordes spirituall and temporall/ and all the Commons of the realm.[5]

In the second edition, in English, St. German demonstrates knowledge of the *Corpus Juris Canonici,* which had been brought into a standard form through Jean Chappuis and published in Paris between 1504 and 1506. St. German also referred to case books of canon law such as the *Summa Angelica* and the *Summa Rosella* published in 1487 and 1495 in Venice by Georgio Arrivabene. St. German, an expert in both canon law and common law, consistently upheld the latter in case of difference. Part of this has to do with the proposition that canon law has precedence only in spiritual matters and not in temporal matters. Most cases in any court of law at that time had to do with temporal matters. St. German's position is based upon the arguments of Marsilius of Padua, cited frequently by St. German, and the writings of John Gerson and sometimes Pierre d'Ailly. For St. German, when a person was

---

[4]Gee and Hardy, *Doctrines,* 125. Here the text of the statute is given. There was a First Statute of Praemunire, 1535, 27 Edward III, st. 1. The Second Statute is cited above. A fine article on the statute is: F. W. Waugh, "The Great Statute of Praemunire," *English Historical Review* (hereafter *EHR*) 37 (1922); 173-205. See also on the Hunne case, Arthur Ogle, *The Tragedy of the Lollard's Tower* (Oxford: Oxford University Press, 1949), 228-38. Ogle shows the relationship between the laity's attitude toward the Hunne affair and subsequent actions of the Reformation Parliament. For other articles on the Hunne affair see: E. Jeffries Davis, "The Authorities for the Case of Richard Hunne (1514-15)," *EHR* 30 (1915): 477-88; S. F. C. Milson, "Richard Hunne's 'Praemunire'" *EHR* 76 (1961): 80-2; J. Fines, "The Post-Mortem Condemnation for Heresy of Richard Hunne," *EHR* 78 (1963): 528-31.

[5]Christopher St. German, *The Dialogve In English between a Doctor of Diuinitie, and Students in the Lawes of England* (London: John Rastell, [1530?]), fol. 73r-v.

excommunicated in a canon law court for debt, trespass, or other such things, he or she might retaliate with a writ of praemunire against whoever sued. In chapter xxv of the second dialogue, St. German deals with a specific problem where canon law and common law disagree as to who might be the son and heir in case of wills. He flatly states that even though wills are handled in canon law courts, in such cases ecclesiastical judges must take the "'kynges' law as the lawe spirituall."

In his second dialogue as well as in a third treatise, *Here after foloweth a lytell treatise called the newe addicions,* published in the 1530s, St. German develops more fully the primacy of the king acting in Parliament. But St. German did maintain that a statute passed by Parliament that was in contradiction to the law of God (Old and New Testaments) would be null and void. His one example of this was if a law were passed asserting that the king should administer the sacraments, it would be void. St. German, like Marsilius, had no difficulty in seeing a difference between canon law and the law of God.[6]

The second dialogue was more radical than the first in criticism of canon law. St. German took the position that when the two legal systems clashed on any matter involving property, common law should take precedence, even in ecclesiastical courts. The final authority in all temporal matters was the king acting in concert with Commons and the Lords. St. German refrained from taking a direct hand in public policy, even when asked. Yet his ideas took public form in the Reformation Parliament through such members as Thomas Cromwell and Thomas Audley. Even Sir Thomas More could be seen as encouraging such thought during his opening address to Parliament in November, 1529 when he stated that "of all matters of State those concerning ecclesiastical most needed reform." Whatever More intended, members of the House of Commons promptly began to reform those ecclesiastical matters that were of concern to them.

In the first session of the Reformation Parliament, acts were passed which invaded the realm of canon law. These acts dealt with matters that had perturbed laymen in England for a long time. One of these regulated mortuary dues, a cause for which Richard Hunne had been, in the eyes of some, a martyr. Other acts regulated the fees charged for probate of wills, restrained the practice of pluralities, forbade the involvement of the clergy in trade and commerce, put a limit on beneficed clergy accepting chantries, regulated the right of sanctuary, and denied the "privilege of clergy" to low order clerics charged with serious crimes. When such acts began to come up to the Lords from the House of Commons, Bishop John Fisher of Rochester made a comment which was not taken too kindly by some members of Commons:

[6]Franklin LeVan Baumer, "Christopher St. German," *American Historical Review* 13 (1937): 631-51.

My Lordes, you se daily what billes come hither from the common house and all is to the distruction of the Churche, for Godes sake se what a realme the kyngdome of Boheme was, and when the Churche went doune, then fell the glory of the kyngdome, now with the Commons is nothing but doune with the Churche, and all this me semeth is for lacke of faith only.[7]

The bishop's implication that the members of Commons were heretics did not improve relations between the clergy and laity. Already the lords spiritual were in an embarrassing position due to the charges against Cardinal Wolsey. When the lords temporal and the king sided with the Commons against them, clerical resistance to these acts collapsed. At the same time, the House of Commons drafted a document that came to be known as the *Supplication against the Ordinaries*. That early drafts of this document were in Thomas Cromwell's handwriting has suggested to historians that the document originated in the court.[8] However, the evidence makes clear that Cromwell began work on this supplication while a member of Parliament and not yet a member of the King's Council.[9]

Parliament was not in session during the year 1530, and the project was shelved for two years. Meanwhile, the attack upon ecclesiastical courts came from another direction. The new challenge was in the form of a praemunire charge levelled by the King's Bench against the entire clergy of England simply for exercising jurisdiction in the courts of canon law. The whole apparatus of the ecclesiastical courts in England was comprehended by this praemunire accusation as though such courts were an illegal enclave of a foreign power in contradiction to the authority of the English state and its courts. Although this use of praemunire was new and radical in its comprehensiveness, the way had been prepared by the practitioners of the common law. Again, although Thomas Cromwell seemed to have been privy to this action, he could hardly have been responsible for it, since as yet he was not a member of the King's Council. It is probable that the king favored such action in order to put pressure on the pope to resolve Henry's marital problem, but the challenge to canon law was more broadly based than that. In the writ against them, the clergy of

---

[7]Edward Hall, *The Triumphant Reigne of Kyng Henry The VIII* (London, 1904), 2:167. Hall, who was a member of the Reformation Parliament, gave a vivid account of this Parliament in his chronicle; cf. idem 163-71. The concessions and the arm-twisting is obvious. The king probably supported Commons in exchange for their forgiveness of a loan made to him six years earlier. Support of the temporal Lords was obtained through the use of a conference committee chaired by the king with eight representatives from each house.

[8]Philip Hughes, *The Reformation in England* (New York: Macmillan, 1950), 1: 237f. Cf. Gee and Hardy, *Documents,* 145.

[9]G. R. Elton, "The Commons' Supplication of 1532: Parliamentary Manoeuvers in the Reign of Henry VIII," *EHR* 55 (1951): 507-34; and J. Cooper, "The Supplication against the Ordinaries Reconsidered," *EHR* 72 (1957): 616-41.

England who had "exercised, practiced, or executed in spiritual courts and other spiritual jurisdictions" were accused of having

fallen and incurred into diverse dangers of his [the king's] laws by things done, perpetrated and committed contrary to the order of his laws, and specially contrary to the form of the statutes of provisors, provisions, and praemunire.[10]

An earlier charge of praemunire against fifteen of the higher clergy for having aided and abetted Cardinal Wolsey had been dropped in favor of the more comprehensive and inclusive charge so that all the clergy were implicated in being involved in Cardinal Wolsey's misdeeds. The second charge's radicalness is reflected in the Act of Pardon, where a list is given of every possible cleric involved in canon law:

archbishops and other said bishops, suffragans, prelates, abbots, priors, and convents, and every person of the same convents, convents corporate and every person of same convent corporate, abbesses, prioresses and religious nuns and all other religious and spiritual persons, deans and chapters and other dignities of cathedral and collegial churches, prebendaries, canons and petty canons, vicars and clerks of the same and every person of the same, all archdeacons, masters, provosts, presidents, wardens of colleges and of collegiate churches, masters and wardens of hospitals, all fellows, brethren, scholars, priests, and spiritual conducts and every one of the same, and all vicars general of diocese, chancellors, commissaries, officials, and deans rural and all ministers hereafter generally rehearsed of any spiritual court or courts within the said province of Canterbury, that is to say: all judges, advocates, registers, and scribes, proctors constituted to judgements. . . .

Only laity seem to be left off this list, and Parliament then enacted another statute in order to allow lay people the same pardon. The pardon for the archdiocese of York came a year later in 1532. The terms of the pardon were these: besides £100,000 ransom money, Convocation was asked to acknowledge the king as the supreme head of the Church of England. Convocation delicately phrased that acknowledgement by adding the phrase, thanks to Bishop John Fisher, "so far as the law of Christ allows." They also asked the king that

---

[10]Act of Pardon, 22 Henry VIII, c. 15, in: A. Luders et al., eds., *The Statutes of the Realm*, 11 vols in 12 (London, 1810-28; reprt. 1963), 3:334-38.

some clear statement be made as to the actual limits of praemunire. Until such limits were set, the whole system of ecclesiastical discipline was in limbo.[11]

Although the system of ecclesiastical discipline was on unsure footings, the Church in England still felt free to deal with cases of heresy. In August 1531, "saint" Thomas Bilney, whose case had been presented at Convocation earlier that year, was burned at the stake. However, the burning of a live cleric did not seem to agitate laymen quite so much as the burning of a dead layman, William Tracy of Todington, "a worshipful squire" and sometime sheriff of Gloucestershire. Edward Hall, a member of Commons, devoted several pages of his chronicle to Tracy's case and does not mention Bilney.

Tracy's will had been judged heretical by the Convocation of 1531. Thomas Parker, chancellor of the diocese of Worchester, had the body exhumed and burned. If anything was needed to revive the ghost of Richard Hunne, this was it. Although Parker had the warrant of Archbishop Warham of Canterbury, he did not have the warrant of the crown, and he was fined £300 for his omission.[12] Once again the Church, finding itself challenged by the temporality, could be interpreted as striking back with heresy charges. By the time Parliament came into session again in 1532, two more men had been burnt at the stake, and heresy proceedings were in effect against James Bainham, who was a member of the Inner Temple and an acquaintance of some members of the House of Commons. Those who had strong feelings about the problems of canon law had occasion to be aroused.

The famous *Supplication Against the Ordinaries,* polished by two years of editing, came to a Church weakened and uncertain about its own rights of jurisdiction. Some members of Parliament were even more embittered than they had been when they first met in 1529. In this supplication the increasing tension between the spirituality and the temporality was blamed on the turmoil produced by "fantastical and erroneous opinions" coming into England as the result of the publication of "seditious and overthwartly framed books compiled, imprinted, and made in the English tongue in parts of beyond the sea, contrary and against the very true Catholic and Christian faith, and published and sold within this your realm." At the same time there was the problem of the "uncharitable behaviour and dealing of divers Ordinaries, their Comissaries and Substitutes in the spiritual courts of this realm." The members of Commons

---

[11]J. Scarisbrick, "The Pardon of the Clergy, 1531," *Cambridge Historical Journal* 3 (1956): 22-39. This article gives a definitive account of the affair. Scarisbrick made a careful comparison of what the king wanted to have stated and what was finally written. It is clear there was still some "fight" left in Convocation. For the complete text of the petition of the Convocation of Canterbury, see Jeremy Collier, *An Ecclesiastical History of Great Britain* (London, 1852), 9:117f. The Convocation of York under Cuthbert Tunstall raised more of a fuss but to no avail. Freedoms guaranteed to the Church in Magna Carta seemed to be disappearing. Cf. David Wilkins, *Concilia Magnae Brittaniae et Hiberniae,* 4 vols. (London, 1737), 2:745, 762-65; and Hughes, *Reformation in England,* 1: 230-32.

[12]Hall, *Chronicle,* 2:225-27. Ogle, *Tragedy,* 263-65.

were careful to avoid the appearance of condoning heresy. They made sure that the issue was directed to the canon law and its courts.[13]

With such matters taken care of in the preamble of the *Supplication,* the members of Commons then made specific charges in twelve paragraphs, the first two of which are the most important. First, they charged that the clergy, through Convocation, had made and were still making laws and ordinances concerning temporal things, some of which were repugnant to the laws and statues of the realm. The clergy were therefore interfering with areas beyond their proper competence and were doing it without obtaining the consent of the king and of the laity, i.e. Parliament. Furthermore, such laws and ordinances were not available in the English language. As a result, laymen were in danger of censures of excommunication or even of charges of heresy when they had simply been trying to follow the laws of the realm.

In the second paragraph a protest was made against such judicial procedures in ecclesiastical courts as the holding of persons without bail, regarding them as guilty on the basis of two possibly quite prejudiced or characterless witnesses, and the *ex officio* procedure of forcing the accused to testify against himself on the basis of subtle and confusing questions which could trap the lay person into an ignorant answer. Again, it should be noted that the men of the House of Commons were not condoning heresy. They wanted repression of the same but they were opposed to repressive ecclesiastical court procedures.

Matters dealt with in later paragraphs included excessive fees in canon law courts, inconvenient travel to courts beyond the locale of the lay person, and the traditionally vexatious problems of tithes, mortuaries, probates, patronage, number of holy days, the giving of benefices to minors, and the use of clergy in secular offices.

When members of the Convocation assembled after the Easter recess on April 12 and began to discuss the *Supplication,* they were still prepared to do battle with the members of Commons for control of canon law. Bishop Stephen Gardiner of Winchester, who stood high in the circle of leaders close to the king, took the lead in drafting their answer. In reply to the charge that laws were made which were repugnant to the laws and statutes of the realm, it was asserted that the clergy's authorization for making laws came from "the Scriptures of God and the determination of Holy Church" and that the justice of such laws must be judged by those standards. Although the clergy valued the opinion of the king because of his "wisdom, virtue, and learning," they

---

[13]The text for the *Supplication* is found in Ogle, *Tragedy,* 324-30. The text found in Gee and Hardy, *Documents,* 145-53, was an earlier draft and not the final draft presented to the Conyocation of Canterbury.

could not "submit the execution of our charges and duty certainly prescribed by God to the king's assent."[14]

The king delivered the answer to Thomas Audley, Speaker of the House, and others, with the comment, "we think their answer will smally please you, for it seemeth to us very slender." He assured Audley that he would be neutral in the struggle between Commons and Convocation, which was really a struggle between the supporters of common law and those of canon law.[15]

The king also let it be known through his almoner, Edward Fox, that he was unhappy with Gardiner for his stating of the case for the freedom of the Church over against the king. The temporary displeasure of the king toward Gardiner was fateful for the reformation of England, for it almost certainly kept Gardiner from succeeding to the see of Canterbury later in the year. Gardiner's explanatory letter to the king did not help matters at this time. His understanding of the supremacy of the crown and that of the crown were too far apart.[16]

The second attempt of Convocation to provide and answer satisfactorily to the king focused on the distinction between realms of authority. The Church was free to "rule and govern in faith and good manners" and the Church's authority was asserted "to make and ordain rules and laws tending to that purpose: . . . so that before God there needeth not of necessity any temporal power or consent to concur with the same by way of authority." The clergy maintained they could defend this position through Holy Scripture. As a matter of fact, they could also defend this position on the basis of the common law philosophy of Christopher St. German. So long as they stayed in the area of "spiritual" matters rather than temporal, this was consistent with the position presented in *The Doctor and the Student*. Furthermore, the "law of God," according to St. German, which came from the Old and New Testaments, took precedence over either "general customs" or statutory law made by the "king and his progenitors and by the lords spiritual and temporal and all the commons of the realm." It would have seemed then that this second answer was on safe ground. Moreover, to secure this position, reference was made to the book which Henry VIII had "most excellently written against Martin Luther." Surely

[14]Gee and Hardy, *Documents*, 154-76. Here the text for the *Answer of the Ordinaries* is given. The successive compromise answers before the final submission are to be found in Wilkins, *Concilia Magnae*, 3:753, although in the wrong order, and in Francis Atterbury, *Additions to the First Edition of the Rights, Powers, and Privileges of an English Convocation* (London, 1701), 14-31. A thorough discussion of the Convocation of 1532 is the prize essay by Michael Kelly, "The Submission of the Clergy," *Transactions of the Royal Historical Society*, 5th Series 15 (1965): 97-119.

[15]Hall, *Chronicle*, 2:209. Hall commented: "For a truth their answer was very sophistical," and he noted that the answer did nothing toward alleviating the clash between clerics and laity over the law.

[16]J. A. Muller, *The Letters of Stephen Gardiner* (Cambridge: Cambridge University Press, 1933), 38f.

that book is of such nature "that of your honour ye cannot nor of your goodness ye will not revoke."

As an added sweetener to their concessions, the clergy in Convocation promised not to put into practice any acts or ordinances that they should make thereafter until they had received the king's consent and authority, except for matters of "faith and reformation of sin." As to past laws that do not concern these matters, if the king would be so kind as to let them know where there were ordinances contrary to the king's laws and prerogatives, they would revoke them.[17]

Regardless of whether the king actually saw this second answer, it was not satisfactory to him, and on May 10, word came to Convocation from the king through Edward Fox that three articles had to be maintained in their answer to the *Supplication:* (1) that no future constitution was to be enacted by the clergy without the king's approval; (2) that earlier constitutions were to be examined by a committee of thirty-two, sixteen representing the laity in Parliament and sixteen representing the Convocation; and (3) that all constitutions and canons shown to be consistent with the laws of God and the laws of the realm would be regarded as valid and have the king's assent.[18]

Since this was the first definite word of the king's own position and since he seemed to be conceding far more to the Commons' side of the argument than the clergy had expected, a conference of bishops was held to determine strategy, and it was decided to send ten canon lawyers and theologians to confer with Bishop Fisher, who was ill in Rochester. Evidently, word of this mission reached the king, and he was irritated by such an obvious sign that the clergy was preparing to resist him. The next day the king called in a delegation from Parliament, including the speaker, twelve other members of Commons, and eight Lords, and said:

> Well beloved subjects, we thought that the clergy of our realm had been our subjects wholly, but now we have well perceived, that they be but half our subjects, yea, and scarce our subjects: for all the prelates at their consecration make an oath to the pope, clean contrary to the oath that they make to us, so that they seem to be his subjects, and not ours; the copy of both the oaths I deliver here to you, requiring you to invent some order that we be not thus deluded of our spiritual subjects.[19]

Edward Hall, who preserved these oaths in his *Chronicle,* judged that "the opening of these oaths was one of the occasions why the pope within two

---

[17]Wilkins, *Concilia Magnae,* 3:753f.

[18]Wilkins, *Concilia Magne* 3:749. Excerpts are found here. The source for the excerpts comes from Peter Heylin from the official records of the Convocation before those records were lost in the great fire of London of 1666.

[19]Hall, *Chronicle,* 2:211. Hall printed the text of both oaths.

years following lost all his jurisdiction in England." The Act of Supremacy was very near. In the oath to the pope, which was read to the Parliament, there was a section on canon law which must have rubbed salt into common lawyers' wounds: "the rules of the holy Fathers, the decrees, ordinances, sentences, dispositions, reservations, provisions, and commandments apostolic, to my power I shall keep and cause to be kept of others." The concerns of the king and the concerns of the Commons were both touched by such an oath.

After the conference of the experts with the Bishop of Rochester, Convocation attempted a third level of compromise. Their answer had two parts. First of all, Convocation promised "that from henceforth during your highness' natural life. . . we shall forbear to enact, promulgate, or put in execution any such constitution or ordinance, so by us to be made in time coming unless your highness by your royal assent shall license us to make, promulgate, and execute such constitutions. . . ." Perhaps Bishop Fisher had told them, "After all, Henry is mortal, and this too shall pass." They were prepared, if worse came to worse, to throw themselves under the tender mercies of a mortal king rather than submit to the power of a Parliament whose works would have a more lasting effect.

Convocation conceded secondly that since the House of Commons believed that some of the provincial constitutions which had already been enacted were "prejudicial to your highness' prerogative royal," they would submit these "constitutions to the examination and judgement of your grace only." If any were found by the king to be either prejudicial or onerous, they would only be too glad to modify or even to annul them "saving to us always all such immunities and liberties of this Church of England, as hath been granted unto the same by the goodness and benignity of your highness, and of others your most noble progenitors."

Finally, they requested that such constitutions as stood up under the king's examination be ratified and approved by the king so that Church courts might proceed on the basis of these constitutions and canons.[20]

All of this was couched in the most flattering statements concerning the king's "most high and excellent wisdom," "princely goodness," and "incomparable learning far exceeding in our judgement the learning of all other kings and princes." Neither their flattery nor their concessions were adequate, and new drafts of what the king wanted them to agree to reached the Convocation on May 13 and 15. On May 15 the final submission of the clergy was obtained, although the lower house of Convocation had already left due to the proroguing until November 5. According to a study by Michael Kelly, only three bishops of the province of Canterbury submitted unequivocally, three others with reservations, and "a suspiciously vague number of monastic prelates." Kelly's comment is simply that "the epochal decision in the history of the English

[20]Wilkins, *Concilia Magnae*, 3:752.

Church was enacted by a rump Convocation."[21] There is no evidence that the submission was even brought before the Convocation of York.

However inadequately the clergy had been represented in this action, the submission was nevertheless real in its consequences. Henceforth, no new canons would be adopted by the clergy without royal assent and authority, nor would Convocation meet except at the request of the king. The validity of the constitutions and canons then in existence were now left to the judgement of a royal commission of thirty-two men, composed of equal portions of laity and clergy. Such a committee of thirty-two produced the document entitled *Reformatio legum ecclesiasticarum* in the year 1552.[22]

REFORMATION OF THE ECCLESIASTICAL LAWS IN ENGLAND FROM 1532 TO THE END OF THE REIGN OF KING HENRY VIII, 1547

With Thomas More's resignation coincident to the submission of the clergy in 1532, the new Keeper of the Great Seal was Thomas Audley, who had been serving as Speaker of the House of Commons in the Reformation Parliament. He had participated with his fellow M.P., Thomas Cromwell, in composing and editing the *Supplication of Commons,* and he held strongly to the theory of Christopher St. German that the final authority in England on all temporal matters was the king in Parliament.

As a sample of Thomas Audley's understanding of the proper place of ecclesiastical jurisdiction in the realm of England, there is a conversation with Audley which Stephen Gardiner recalled some years later in a letter written to the Privy Council, August 30, 1547. Wrote Gardiner:

> And thus I have heard the learned men of the common law say that if any, although he be deputed by the king, do, in execution of spiritual jurisdiction, extend the same contrary to any common law or act of Parliament, it is a praemunire both to the judge and the parties, although it be done in the Kings Majesties name.[23]

In December, after Parliament came into session again, Audley was also given Thomas More's former position as Chancellor.

Others active in the protest of common lawyers against canon law were also strengthening their position in 1532. Thomas Cromwell, now as Master of the King's Jewels, Clerk of the Hanaper (a fee-receiving department), and Chancellor of the Exchequer, was proving his worth to Henry by the organization of the king's finances. Christopher St. German anonymously published *A Treatise concernynge the diuision betwene the spiritualtie and temporaltie,* and

---

[21]Kelly, "Submission of the Clergy," 117.

[22]Ogle, *Tragedy,* 346. On the creation of the committee, Ogle wrote: "Mercifully, it perished in embryo." It turned out to be an amazingly long-lived embryo!

[23]J. A. Muller, *Letters of Gardiner,* 368.

in which he renewed his attack upon the canon law from the standpoint of common law. To this work Thomas More gave the major amount of attention in his *Apology* of 1533. More felt that St. German was unfair in his attack upon the English clergy, for most of the laws attacked were "laws not provincial made by the clergy here, but the laws usual through the whole Church of Christ, whereof the making may be not laid to them." It was unreasonable, thought More, to be angry with the English clergy, who were bound to keep laws that they did not make.[24]

The problem of "laws usual through the whole Church of Christ" was to obtain only limited interest as a result of the Parliamentary Act in Restraint of Appeals in 1533, which went far to sever the canon law of England from the more universal canon law of the Roman Church. This act declared that "appeals in such cases as have been used to be pursued to the see of Rome shall not be from henceforth had nor used but within this realm." It was stated that as far as the "empire" of England was concerned, the body spiritual thereof had

power when any cause of the law divine happened to come in question or of spiritual learning. . .sufficient and meet of itself, without the intermeddling of any exterior person or persons, to declare and determine all such doubts and to administer all such offices and duties as to their rooms spiritual doth appertain.

Due to the fact that "sundry inconveniences and dangers" have risen and sprung up by reason of appeals sued out of this realm to the see of Rome, in causes testamentary, causes of matrimony and divorces, and right of tithes

the King's Highness, his Nobles and Commons. . enact, establish and ordain that all [such] causes. . . whether they concern the King our sovereign Lord. . ./ or any other subjects. . shall be from henceforth heard, examined, discussed, clearly finally and definitely adjudged and determined, within the King's jurisdiction and authority and not elsewhere, in such courts spiritual and temporal of the same as the natures, conditions and qualities of the causes and matters. . . in the contention shall require. . . .

Anyone who sought to take an appeal beyond England would henceforth fall under the penalties of praemunire. Appeals from lower ecclesiastical courts were to go to the Court of the Arches or Audience of the Archbishops of Canterbury or York as the case might be. The Court of final appeal for any case that involved the king was the upper house of Convocation.[25]

---

[24]Arthur Irving Taft, *The Apologye of Syr Thomas More, Knyght,* Early English Text Society (London, 1930): 162. This volume contains both the *Apologye* and the work by St. German.

[25]Geoffrey R. Elton, *The Tudor Constitution* (New York: Cambridge University Press, 1982) 344-49. Cf. also G. R. Elton, "The Evolution of a Reformation Statute," *EHR* (1949): 44:174-97.

An earlier draft of this document in Thomas Audley's hand concerned itself only with the king's great matter of the annulment, but in a subsequent draft of the *Restraint of Appeals* the matter was enlarged to include any sort of appeal that might come from a canon law court. In this way common lawyers were able to use the king's concern to further their own concern in reforming canon law. The subsequent draft also made mention of the two oaths that bishops had to take which had been so disturbing to the king that he had asked the members of the House of Commons on May 11, 1532, to invent "some order that we be not thus deluded of our spiritual subjects." The final law did not mention the oaths; however, the law did become the foundation stone of the new order. Thomas Cromwell, aided by Audley, both leaders of the King's Council, as well as members of the House of Commons saw to the laying of the foundation by serving as the primary drafters of the act.

The *Restraint of Appeals* was followed by the acts of *Restraint of Annates and Dispensations* in 1534, which cut off all financial payments to Rome. These acts also provided that archbishops and bishops would be chosen by cathedral chapters electing the person nominated by the king. All dispensations and other licenses would henceforth be issued by the Archbishop of Canterbury, under supervision by the Crown.

These acts severing the Church of England from Rome made imperative a program for seriously reevaluating the canon law then current and modifying it in relation to the new set of circumstances. A concrete incentive for change reached the House of Commons in the petition of a citizen of London, Thomas Phillips, who had been imprisoned in the Tower for three years by the Bishops of London on a heresy charge. He had been placed in the Tower of London rather than the old Lollard's Tower of St. Paul's Cathedral by the then Lord Chancellor, Thomas More, who still firmly believing in the suicide and not murder of Richard Hunne, had not wanted a repeat of that late unhappy event. In receiving the petition of Phillips, the House of Commons was once more disturbed by the memory of Richard Hunne, and they saw merit in the petition. However, when it was submitted to the House of Lords on February 7, 1534, it was rejected as frivolous. The House of Commons sent it once again to the Upper House on March 2, and it was turned down *una voce*. The basis upon which Phillips was held was the *ex officio* process of canon law, which was so repugnant to common lawyers.

On March 5,

the Common house went before the king into his palace and the speaker made a proposition to the king to and in the name of all his subjects, desiring his grace of reformation of the acts made by the spirituality in the Convocation against his grace and his subjects in calling many of his subjects to the courts *ex officio* and not knowing their accuser and to cause them to abjure or else to burn them for pure malice, and upon their abominable curses, taking of tithes and offerings contrary to justice, and that they were judges and parties in their own causes. Therefore at that time, it was ordained that eight of the lower house and eight of the higher house and sixteen bishops with other clergy should discuss the matter and the king to be umpire. . . [26]

In this manner they were able to express to the king their feelings about the procedure used under canon law against people accused of heresy, and they reminded the king of the project described in the *Submission of the Clergy* of 1532, according to which there was to be a select royal commission of thirty-two persons to bring the canon law of England into line with the new understanding of the relation of the Church to the Crown.

Parliament then passed two more acts dealing with the reformation of canon law, *An Act for Punishment of Heresy* and *An Act for the Submission of Clergy to the King's Majesty,* both of which cleared the House of Lords and received the king's consent immediately before the proroguing of Parliament on March 30, 1534. The preamble of the first of these acts expressed concern about the ambiguity of the term 'heresy'. Even a learned man could be trapped into such a charge. As a result, Parliament repealed the heresy statute of 2 Henry IV, ch. 15, but Parliament remained much opposed to heresy itself, and it confirmed two earlier acts in so far as their provisions were not repugnant to the present law. There had to be two lawful witnesses to make accusation, and presentments of heresy had to be made by jurors who were substantial citizens. Sheriffs and "other stewards" could inquire into heresy in their courts as they could to any common annoyance and make presentation to the ordinaries. The hearing should be made in open court, and provision was made for a person accused of heresy to be let out on bail.

The most important provision, however, was to make clear to that "great number of the king's subjects having little or no learning" that a man speaking against the "pretensed power or authority" of the bishop of Rome is not in danger of the charge of heresy. Furthermore, papal "laws, decrees, ordinances or constitutions" set forth for the advancement of the pope's "worldly glory and ambition" and which were "not approved and confirmed by holy scripture" were "never commonly accepted or confirmed to be the law of God or man within the Realm." Therefore Parliament ordained that no one could be condemned for heresy for criticizing

any laws called Spiritual laws made by authority of the See of Rome by the policy of men, which be repugnant to the laws and statutes of this Realm or the king's prerogative Royal . . . any whatsoever canon

---

[26] *Letters and Papers, Foreign and Domestic, of the Reign of Henry VIII* (London, 1862-1910): 7:168, no. 399. This is also found in J. P. Cooper, "The Supplication against the Ordinaries Reconsidered," *EHR* 72 (1957): 636. Cooper accurately dates this in 1534.

laws, decrees, ordinances, constitutions or other thing heretofore made or being hereafter to be made to the contrary notwithstanding.[27]

This act, making possible a free discussion of Roman canon law, was a necessary preliminary to the other *Act for the Submission of the Clergy,* which used the 1532 *Submission* in its preamble and had five key provisions, which follow.

The first provision stated that no new canons or constitutions would be enacted by Convocation or executed by the clergy unless "the same clergy may have the king's most royal assent and license." Secondly,

> forasmuch as such canons . . . as heretofore hath been made by the clergy of this realm cannot now at the session of the present Parliament by reason of shortness of time be viewed, examined, and determined by the King's Highness and thirty-two persons to be chosen and appointed. . . .

It was enacted that the king should have the authority to appoint the thirty-two persons at his pleasure. This committee should have the authority to study and examine canons, and the king and the committee acting together should have the power to determine which should be continued.

The third provision pointed out that, in the meantime, no canon or constitution could be carried out which was contrary or repugnant to either the king's prerogative or the customs, laws, or statutes of the realm. Fourthly, no appeals were to go beyond the kingdom as stated in the Act for Restraint of Appeals, but a new determination was made of a court of final appeal within England. If a person felt that he had failed to obtain justice in the archbishops' courts he could appeal to the King's Majesty in the King's Court of Chancery. The final provision renewed the threat of praemunire.[28]

Henry VIII apparently felt no need for promptness in appointing the committee of thirty-two. Whether he was not as anxious as his common-law-oriented parliamentarians or whether this stalling was the king's policy to implement his role as the arbiter between Parliament and clergy is hard to determine.[29] Without the actual appointment of the commission there could be no official re-examination of the canon law of England. This did not, however, hold up a process of unofficial re-evaluation on the part of common law experts. The first problem was identifying the canon law that needed to

---

[27] Luders et al., *Statutes of the Realm,* 3:454ff. The text of the act which was repealed, 2 Henry IV, c. 15, can be found in Gee and Hardy, *Doctrines* 133-37. Phillips, by the way, made a career out of his prison experience and eventually became a keeper in the tower, where he sought to salvage the souls of people to be executed. See Hall, *Chronicle,* 2:284.

[28] *Statues of the Realm,* 2:460f. Cf. Elton, *Tudor Constitution,* 339-41, where most of the statue is reprinted.

[29] Cooper, "Supplication," 640f. Cooper suggests that the delay was Henry's policy to enhance his "Supremacy" in the Church by protecting the clergy from the more radical common law people in Parliament.

be reformed. There was no simple answer. Some order had been brought into the canon law which was universal in the Roman Church with the publication of the *Corpus Juris Canonici* in Paris between 1504 and 1506. As far as that canon law distinctive to England was concerned, there were two important volumes available. One was Bishop William Lyndwood's 1430 codification of and commentary upon the constitutions enacted by the Province of Canterbury in Convocation between 1222 and 1416. This had been printed without the glosses in the 1490s by Wynkyn de Worde, and a magnificent edition with commentary was published in Paris in 1501. The other volume was John of Ayton's commentary, produced between 1333 and 1348, upon constitutions enacted at the legatine councils held under Cardinal Otho in 1237 and Cardinal Octhobon in 1268. This volume also had been published in Paris in 1504.[30]

Lyndwood's *Provincials* and John of Ayton's *Legatines* were canons which had been produced by and for English people. Where there might have been some question as to what canon law pertained to England and what did not, there was no question but what these two books did contain canon law of England. The text of the *Act for Submission of the Clergy to the King's Majesty* has referred to canons and constitutions which had been enacted by the convocations of the clergy of England, not to those which had been formulated beyond England, and these two books were the most obvious source for those English canons which needed to be examined by the projected committee of thirty-two.

Accordingly, in 1534 someone with a common law mentality translated into English the *Constitutions prouincialles/ and of Otho/ and Octhobone,* which was printed by Robert Redman in London. The preface and address of the translator to the reader are revealing and deserve notice. The preface, short and to the point follows:

> Hereafter ensue the Constitutions provincial, and of Otho, and Octhobone, which be not put forth to bind any of our most gracious sovereign lord the king's subjects, but to the only intent that the people of this realm of England should know them, such as they be. For the clergy of this realm (whom commonly we have used to call the church or the spirituality) without the assent of the king's highness, the nobility, and commons of this realm, have never had nor yet have any just and lawful power to make any Constitutions or laws over any of our said sovereign lord the king's subjects. Therefore, such as they

[30]For bibliographical references for the Paris editions of these books, see Georg Wolfgang Panzer, *Annales Typographici* (Hildesheim: Olms, 1963), 7:500, 508. After these Paris editions of the early part of the century, there was a 1534 English translation of both the provincials and the legatines but without glosses. This edition is discussed later in the text. In 1557 the provincials were published again in Latin with a dedication to Cardinal Reginald Pole, legate of the Apostolic See, Archbishop of Canterbury and Primate of England. This edition, like the fifteenth century editions of Wynkyn de Worde, was without the glosses, but as in the 1534 edition, included the legatines.

be so receive and use them, and give lauds and thanks to almighty God, and pray for the translator that he may come to the bliss that shall never cease. So be it.[31]

The translator in his preface addressed himself to a laity which had been left in the dark about canon laws under which they were subjected. His concern was to reveal what had been available only to those who read Latin. This context was expressed in the address to the reader:

I cannot forget, catholic readers, it was so lately done, that when certain English books began to issue from the parts beyond the seas into this realm of England, the prelates and pastors began to watch diligently in every corner to keep their sheep that they should not feed upon them, admonishing us with open mouth to follow our forefathers and to beware of this new learning lately sprung up. And if they suspected that any had tasted thereof he could not avoid but either he must bear or else burn a faggot. Whereupon I began to muse with myself how this might by justice come to pass that such new learning (if it were so new as they made it) might have so old a punishment, I began to divine and search what manner of learning that was and where it was written which our forefathers (as they said) have done. And to say the truth I could not with all the wit I had come to anything certain that I might say, this is it.

As I thus was busied in myself there came one and desired me in his name that might upon my duty have commanded me in his name to take the pains to translate into English the constitutions provincial and the constitutions legatine, which thing at the very first motion I was very desirous to accomplish not only because I should therein do my duty but also, as me therein thought, give a taste unto the laity of the old doctrine, if the prelates called old which they themselves had made which thing I deny not but they might do full well and conveniently. For if Adam be the old man and Christ the new, why may not Adam's doctrine be called the old and Christ's the new?

---

[31] *Constitutions prouincialles / and of Otho/ and Octhobone / translated in to Engllyshe.* (London: Robert Redman, 1534), vi[v]. This was reprinted by J. V. Bullard and H. C. Bell with the title *Lyndwood's Provinciale* (London: Faith Press, 1929). The reprint does not contain the legatines nor the preface nor address to the reader. In the introduction (xxxi), the editors claim that "Lyndwood was regarded as the law which should be enforced, during and after the Reformation until constitutionally altered. The proof is that Lyndwood was printed in English in 1534—the year of the Act which provided the method of dealing with canon law in the future and also gave Lyndwood, until altered, the force of statute law." It is no wonder that these editors omitted the preface for the translator expressly stated that he was not printing the book in English in order "to bind." Furthermore, the Act made it clear that any of these canons which in any way contradicted or were repugnant to the king's royal prerogative, or the customs, laws, or statutes of the realm were null and void. And, there were common lawyers ready to point out where such contradictions were.

Now therefore you that hunger and thirst for old learning come hereunto; put in your forefeet and fill your bellies that you may grow and be like unto them that be the authors thereof. For it becomes every disciple to be perfect in the same wherein his master is perfect. Let me not I pray you spend my labors which I have taken in vain. This one thing I can assure you of, if you will be the disciples of this doctrine and do as it bids you, shall lightly escape all manner of punishment and shame which the new learning hath always hitherto suffered. This doctrine also is gentle to be understood, although it be somewhat grievous to fulfill; it contains no senses anagogical or tropological or hath in it any hid mysteries though it have an eye to hide treasure, but even as it sounds so it means. As for my part I have not sought any praise in the translation, but was contented to set it forth rudely and plainly without any strange terms that it might be as well understood of the unlearned laity in English as it was before of the learned clergy in Latin, which thing I doubt not but I have brought to pass, and therefore fare you well.[32]

Whoever the translator was, he was acquainted with the proceedings in Parliament, for he also printed the oaths to pope and king that Henry had exhibited to Parliament in 1532. Although the translator was interested in common law, he showed more interest in theology than St. German. Christian humanism and a touch of continental protestantism seem to pervade his attitudes.

Shortly after the publication of the English translation of the provincials and legatines, there appeared a critique of these documents from the point of view of common law. This was printed in London by Thomas Godfrey, presumably in 1534, under the title *A Treatise concernynge diuers of the constitucyons prouynciall and legatines*. The treatise was written in the same spirit as were the works of Christopher St. German, who possibly wrote it. Specific canons were examined in thirty chapters and, as indicated in the introduction, were shown to be in contradiction to the king's laws and his prerogative.[33] Also as promised in the introduction, the author showed that some laws were "very troublous unto the people and not so charitable as they ought to have been." The work was intended more as a sampling than a complete investigation of English canon law.

[32]Ibid., ii^v. I would guess that the translator was Richard Taverner who had studied theology at Cambridge and then transferred to Wolsey's newly founded Cardinal College at Oxford. Taverner later studied law at the Inner Temple. At the time of the appearance of this translation, he had just returned from the continent, destitute, and was helped by Thomas Cromwell. This translation is just the sort of job Cromwell might have asked Taverner to do. Taverner had an outstanding career as a translator. Although he supported the Protestant cause, he avoided situations which might have caused him to be charged with heresy.

[33]*A Treatise concernynge diuers of the constitucyons prouynciall and legatines . . .* (London: Thomas Godfrey [1534?]). See chaps. 20, 26, 29. The corresponding constitutions are found in the 1929 edition of *Lyndwoods Provinciale,* 105, 134, 157.

Those constitutions which are presented as laws contradicting the laws of the realm concern issues over which laity and clergy had long been in conflict. These included tithes, patronage, mortuaries, wills and testaments, pluralities, sanctuary, and privilege of the clergy. In several cases, the author points out that any clerical judges who attempted to enforce such laws would be in danger of violating the statues of praemunire.

Sir Thomas More, in his *Apology,* expressed bafflement over the common law critic's concern about canon law processes regarding heresy. More could not think of a case in which a heretic had not been treated fairly right up through his burning. The criticism, however, became more clear in the treatise when the author discussed under the title "Of Heretics and Schismatics" the Fifth Book of Lyndwood in its third constitution which begins *"Nullus quoque."* In this constitution a person was not only forbidden to question an article of faith under penalty of heresy, but also

> none may presume to dispute openly or privily of the Articles determined by the Church as they be contained in the Decrees, Decretals, and our Constitutions Provincial or Synodal, except it be done to have the true understanding of them, or may call into doubt the authority of the same Decrees, etc. . . .or the power of the making of them.

No wonder people had been cautious in criticizing canon law. The critic was walking on the edge of the abyss of heresy. On the basis of such a constitution, this very treatise of 1534 was an heretical book, even though it nowhere questions an article of faith. The critic noted that at this point this constitution was vicious and was defending the indefensible, for of these canons he maintained that "there be undoubtedly many of them that the makers had no authority to make and that also be directly against the king and his prerogative. . . . In their canons and constitutions the clergy had regarded as heretical things that are not forbidden by the law of God. Heresy, he maintained, has to do with a person who has fallen from the faith and the truth found in scripture.[34]

Next to heresy, the matter of greatest concern to the laity in ecclesiastical courts was excommunication, which would severely damage one's credit in the community and could involve imprisonment. The critic pointed out areas in which, if canon law was enforced, a person could be excommunicated for carrying out temporal matters under common law. Furthermore, canon laws were ambiguous about those matters wherein a person might run into the danger of excommunication.

> It is a dangerous thing to fall into the censures of the church, and therefore they would not be given but for great causes. And in such plain and open manner that every man that would with diligence take

---

[34]*A Treatise,* chap. 23, and see Bullard and Bell, *Lyndwood's Provinciale,* 128.

heed to it might know whether he offended in that thing that they were given for or not; but the more pity is the censures of the church be many times extended in such a general manner and in so many causes that no man can well know how to eschew them and that appeareth many times in the constitutions as when men be cursed for breaking of the church's liberties and expresseth not what the liberties be. . . .

It is recited that all they be accursed that do maliciously presume to take away from churches their right or through malice or contrary to justice do intend to break or disturb the liberties of the same and then thereupon the makers of the said law say farther thus whereby say they we perceive all them to be tied in the danger and in the bond of excommunication that obtain letters from any lay court to let or hinder the process of spiritual judges in all such causes as by the verdict of holy canons be known to appertain to the judges of the spiritual court and the said letters are to be understood as it seemeth of the king's prohibitions. And who can have knowledge what pertaineth to the spiritual court by the canons which be so many and so great in number that few can come to the knowledge of them? And these laws be so uncertain that it will be hard for any man to know whether he be in danger of them or not. And where ignorance shall excuse him that is so accursed and where not it is a right great doubt and such things as touch the people so near as such excommunications do would be brought as near as reason could drive it in to a more clear knowledge than they be yet as to me seemeth.[35]

St. German in his *Doctor and Student* recognized the Old and New Testaments as the law of God and therefore superior even to the laws of the realm. However, the author of this treatise was critical of the way in which the clerics twisted the Bible to their own uses. For example, the commandment to honor father and mother was twisted in the canons to refer to the spiritual father or the prelate and the spiritual mother, the Church. This was, for the critic, precisely comparable to the error of those Pharisees mentioned in Mark 7, where they relieved themselves of their obligation to their parents by dedicating their goods to the religious institution.[36]

There was in this criticism of English canon law a strong lay protest against the idea that the Church is to be defined as the clergy and not as the whole people of God. The author criticized a constitution which excluded laity from chapter meetings and other assemblies of the clergy, for he felt that lay persons could be of help. He ascribed the exclusion to the desire of the clergy to protect

[35]Ibid., chap. 15.
[36]Ibid., chap. 5.

their own reputations rather than to promote the welfare of the Church. In another place, he dismissed as nonsense the idea that laity should be forbidden to order or dispose of the Church's goods. If our Lord didn't meddle in temporal matters, neither should his successors, the clergy. This was a proper role for the laity within the Church. Furthermore, in the discussion of the sacraments in the provincials, it was stated that the sacrament of holy orders was only for the perfect and the sacrament of marriage only for the "unperfect." Unperfect, indeed! The author found this to be not only untrue but insulting.[37]

This should be enough to indicate that if Henry VIII had appointed his committee of thirty-two in 1534, and if the common lawyers had gained the upper hand, there really would have been a radical reformation of the canon laws of the Church of England. In November of that year a short session of the Parliament introduced the Act of Supremacy, which asserted that "by authority of this present Parliament" it was enacted that "the King our Sovereign Lord, his heirs and successors, kings of this realm, shall be taken, accepted and reputed the only supreme head in earth of the Church of England called *Anglicana Ecclesia. . . ."*

That this declaration was made by the authority of Parliament was not lost upon the members of that body, as is attested by Bishop Stephen Gardiner's retelling of a conversation in which Chancellor Thomas Audley said to him:

Thou are a good fellow, Bishop. . . . Look to the Act of Supremacy, and there the king's doings be restrained to spiritual jurisdiction; and in another act [Act for the Submission of the Clergy] it is provided that no Spiritual Law shall have place contrary to a Common Law or Act of Parliament. And if this were not, you bishops would enter in with the king and, by means of his supremacy, order the laity as you listed. But we will provide that the praemunire shall ever hang over your heads, and so we laymen shall be sure to enjoy our inheritance by the Common Laws and acts of Parliament.[38]

Implicit in this very act of supremacy was the concept over which a civil war would be fought in England a century later, namely, that it is not the king alone who is supreme but the king in Parliament.

Even though the committee of thirty-two had not been appointed by Henry VIII, he did take action on reform in January of 1535 by appointing Thomas Cromwell to be Vicegerent for Ecclesiastical Affairs. That same year, the executions of Bishop John Fisher and Sir Thomas More for refusing to take the Oath of Succession enjoined by Parliament in November of 1534 broke the will of any serious opposition. In the spring of 1535, the bishops of England turned in the papal bulls authorizing them to be bishops and received commissions in turn under the king's seal. Nothing, however, could symbolize

[37]Ibid., chaps. 1, 2, 21.
[38]Muller, *Letters of Gardiner,* 392.

the new order of jurisdiction in the Church quite like Cromwell's power to exercise the authority inherent in the supremacy.[40]

As early as December, 1534, there had been plans for a visitation under Cromwell's leadership of the universities, dioceses, and monasteries of England. With his new power as representative of the king's ecclesiastical supremacy, Cromwell had the visitations well under way by the summer of 1535. The visitations at the Universities of Oxford and Cambridge were to be of immense consequence in relation to the reformation of ecclesiastical laws for it was then that the study of canon law in the universities was abolished by royal injunction. Not only did the injunctions abolish lectures "upon any of the doctors who had written upon the Master of the Sentences," in favor of lectures upon the Scriptures "based upon the true sense thereof" but they also declared that

> as the whole realm, as well clergy and laity, had renounced the pope's right and acknowledged the king to be the supreme head of the Church, no one should hereafter publicly read the canon law, nor should any degrees in that law be conferred.[41]

Dr. Layton, in his oft-quoted letter to Thomas Cromwell from Oxford, September 12, 1535, mentioned that pages from Duns Scotus were blowing about the great quadrant court of New College and that Duns "is now made a common servant to every man, fast nailed up upon posts in common houses of easement." One can surmise that volumes of canon law likewise became servants of everyone. Layton went on to report, "We have also, in place of the canon lecture, joined a civil lecture to be read in every college, hall, and inn."[42]

This action effectively brought to an end the academic study of canon law as preparation for one of the professions in England. In its place one would have to obtain a degree in civil law, the study of which had two chief functions in England before this time: preparation for the later study of canon law, and preparation for diplomatic services. From this date on, civil lawyers were to function in the ecclesiastical courts of England. Ten years later Parliament passed a statute which maintained that men who possessed the degree of Doctor of Civil Law could carry out jurisdiction in ecclesiastical courts even though they were married, this at a time when the clergy were forbidden to marry. Hence laity could become officials in canon law courts and pursue their careers there.

On September 18, 1535, the bishops of England were inhibited from conducting any visitations of their own as well as prohibited from exercising

---

[40]An excellent study of Cromwell's power as Vicegerent has been made by S. E. Lehmberg, "Supremacy and Vicegerency, A Re-examination." *EHR* 81 (1967): 225-35.

[41]J. E. Mullinger, *The University of Cambridge from the Earliest Times to the Royal Injunctions of 1535*, (Cambridge: Cambridge University Press, 1873), 630. Here is found the text of the injunctions.

[42]Thomas Wright, *Letters Relating to the Suppression of Monasteries*, (London: Camden Society, 1843), 70f.

any of their own jurisdiction that might prejudice visitations under Cromwell. A letter from two of the commissioners, Thomas Legh and John ap Rice, to Cromwell on September 24, revealed the predicament of bishops as they tried to exert their jurisdiction. The bishops were asked by the commissioner whether the authority for the canon law came from the law of God, or the Bishop of Rome, or the king. If they were to say from the law of God, they were asked to demonstrate it from scripture. They, of course, would not have dared to say that it came from the Bishop of Rome. If it came by the authority of the king, they had no reason to complain about the reforms that were taking place. Legh and Ap Rice suggested that when the bishops were given back their powers, they should be given a set of revised canon laws.[43]

Even though the king had not yet appointed his committee of thirty-two to review and revise canon law, Cromwell already had a group hard at work on the task. On October 6, Dr. Richard Gwent, Dean of the Archbishop of Canterbury's Court of Arches, wrote to Cromwell that he, Dr. John Oliver, Dr. Edward Carne, and Dr. John Hughes, all specialists in both canon and civil law, were ready "to declare how far forward we are in these new laws." Three weeks later, another letter was sent in which Gwent reported that he and the others were quite eager to see the king, presumably about their revisions of the canon law. [44]

Another document surviving from these days is an anonymous "Memorandum to My Master" whose author was most probably William Petre, a doctor of civil law, who later served on the actual committee of thirty-two which produced the *Reformatio legum ecclesiasticarum* in 1553. Petre links these early efforts to reform canon law in the days of Henry VIII with the document which was brought into being shortly before the death of Edward VI. In the "Memorandum," the author suggested first of all certain practical steps which needed to be taken to clear up matters in the Court of Arches during the period in which the bishops were enjoined. He urged that everything be done by the king's authority and in his name. He maintained that money matters touching probation of wills should not have come under canon law in the first place, "for by law civil and imperial constitutions the probation to testaments appertained to the prince." Here was an attack on canon law not from the point of view of common law but of civil law.

Tithes were also declared to be a temporal matter and therefore out of the jurisdiction of church courts. They were a special problem, for no cleric in a case involving tithes could pronounce against an ecclesiastic without hurting himself. Cases of defamation should be kept out of canon law courts, for "they be but brabbling and only stuff to get money for advocates and proctors."

---

[43]British Library, *Cotton Manuscripts* Cleo E VI 254 B. M.; the letter is also calendared in *Letters and Papers of Henry VIII*, 9: 137, no. 424.

[44]*Letters and Papers of Henry VIII*, 9:181, no. 549 and 9:232, no. 690.

Finally, in the memorandum suggestions were made with respect to the practical arrangement of the vicegerent's office and its management. Cranmer, possibly foreseeing the role Petre would play, suggested that he should be the Dean of Arches, Canterbury's high court. Cromwell, as vicegerent, made Petre his deputy regarding the probate of testaments and the administration of estates on January 13, 1536.

When a new Parliament was called into being June 8, 1536, there was a curious situation representing a new order. Petre came in on June 16, 1536 and sat beside Archbishop Cranmer to chair the Convocation as deputy for the vicegerent. Later Cromwell occupied the seat himself, and in both Convocation and the House of Lords, Cromwell had the seat of precedence over Cranmer.[45] This continued until Cromwell's attainder and execution in the summer of 1540.

Some urgency was expressed concerning the reformation of the ecclesiastical laws in the last session of Henry's long Reformation Parliament that met from early in 1536 until dissolved on April 4, 1536. A new act was passed concerning the king's appointment of a commission of thirty-two. At this time, the king was authorized to do this "as well before as after the dissolution of this present Parliament," and the thirty-two members of the commission were to have the power to act for " three years next after the dissolution of this Parliament." Considering the preliminary work already done by men connected with Cromwell, both common and civil lawyers, such a committee ought to have been able to finish the job in that time. However, King Henry did not then appoint the committee.

Royal and episcopal injunctions plus visitation articles were put into operation in place of a reformed canon law. The first set of royal injunctions intended to enforce the statutes relating to the supremacy, to obtain assent to the *Ten Articles* which had been produced by Convocation and which represented the first formal attempt at reformation of doctrine, to regulate ceremonies in order to avoid superstition, to provide for the basic Christian education of the laity, to obtain decent pastors in every parish, to secure Bibles in both Latin and English to be available to the public in every church, to raise the moral level of the clergy, to provide for the poor, and to obtain stipends for scholars at the universities. Aside from the matter of the supremacy, there was little to which a traditional churchman could object, for even the Catholic in exile, Reginald Pole, found that he could accept the *Ten Articles*.[46]

In the Pilgrimage of Grace, the abortive rebellious reaction to the reforming activities of the year 1536, there was an effort to restore aspects of the canon

---

[45]*Letters and Papers of Henry VIII*, 9:370, no. 1071. Petre's appointment is found in 10:31, no.88.

[46]W. H. Frere and W. McC. Kennedy, *Visitation Articles and Injunctions of the Period of the Reformation*, 2 vols. (London: Longmans, Green, 1910), 2:1536-38. The text of the injunctions as well as the articles of visitation from this period and that of Edward VI are found here.

law. In the meeting of the "pilgrims" at Pontefract in December of 1536, the first article drawn up, classified the works of St. German, as well as those of William Tyndale and Robert Barnes, with the heresies of Luther, Wyclif, and Hus. Common law advocacy was perceived as allied with Protestantism. Other articles were concerned with the privilege of the clergy, the right of sanctuary, and retaining tithes for church use. They insisted that as far as church discipline was concerned, "the examination and correction of deadly sin belongeth to the ministers of the church by the laws of the same, which be consonant to God's laws." In addition to these laws drawn up by laymen at Pontefract, the clergy involved urged that the study of canon law become once again a proper scholarly discipline at the universities.[47]

The 1538 Injunctions showed a stronger tendency toward Protestantism. Added to the earlier ones was a strong warning against the burning of candles before images and the extolling of pilgrimages or "feigned relics." Preaching was given a more significant role; an attempt was made to root out lingering Romanists; provision was made for improved record keeping; and an effort was made to encourage the payment of tithes. Such injunctions had authority so long as the state enforced them during the particular king's rule, but they lacked the authority that obtained when statutory laws were enacted by king and Parliament.

Indeed, during this period Parliament was producing a number of statutes reforming ecclesiastical laws. Matters of wills, right of sanctuary, tithes, benefit of clergy, and non-residence of priests were regulated to some degree by statutes at this time. After Cromwell's fall but within the reign of Henry VIII, a statute concerning doctrinal matters, *viz.*, the "bloody whip with six strings," made possible a renewed heresy hunt. But even here, Parliament soon passed a statute limiting the punishment of laity to imprisonment. Clergymen could still be burned.

After Cromwell's downfall, the office of vicegerent was left vacant permanently, and the Archbishop of Canterbury once again ranked as leader of the church under the king. From the time of Cromwell's removal to the end of the reign of Edward VI, Thomas Cranmer was to play an increasingly important role in the attempt to reform the ecclesiastical laws of England.

Early in the year of 1544, Parliament renewed once again the act to provide for the nomination of the committee of thirty-two persons to search, view, and examine the old canons, constitutions, and ordinances provincial and synodal. This time no limitation was put on the time of the appointment of the committee so long as it was within the lifetime of King Henry. Furthermore, this commission was to be given a power which it did not have in the earlier statues. They not only could revise the old canon laws in keeping with the laws of the realm,

---

[47]Madeline Hope Dodds and Ruth Dodds, *The Pilgrimage of Grace (1536-1537) and the Exeter Conspiracy (1548)* (Cambridge: Cambridge University Press, 1915), 1:346-85. The "pilgrims," like Reginald Pole, were willing to accept the *Ten Articles* of 1536.

but they could also "set in order and establish all such laws ecclesiastical as shall be thought by the King's Majesty and them convenient to be used and set forth within his realm and dominions in all spiritual courts and conventions.[48]

There is some evidence that Henry VIII did indeed appoint such a committee of thirty-two after the act of 1544, providing for this committee to operate during Henry's lifetime. There is a letter extant from Thomas Cranmer to King Henry on January 3, 1546 in which he referred to the appointment and the activity of a committee for the reformation of ecclesiastical laws:

> And first, where your majesty's pleasure was, to have the names of such persons as your highness in times past appointed to make laws ecclesiastical for your grace's realm, the bishop of Worcester promised me with all speed to inquire out their names and the book which they made, and to bring the names and also the book unto your majesty; which I trust he hath done before this time.[49]

Since the first statute to describe the committee's work of making canon law was the one passed early in 1544, it would appear that the committee was appointed after this statute had passed. The wording of the statute made it apparent that the committee had not been appointed. Cranmer's letter of 1546 suggests that the committee had been active in the intervening two years and had produced a first recension of the reformation of the ecclesiastical laws of England. Nicholas Heath was, at the time, the Bishop of Worcester and was presumably chairperson of the committee that produced this first edition. Since Heath was deprived of his position as bishop in October, 1551, he could not have been a part of the committee of thirty-two which was resuscitated in October, 1551, the committee which actually produced the manuscript that is here translated. However, it is quite probable that some of the suggestions of Heath's committee were in the extant 1552 manuscript.

From the wording of Cranmer's letter it would appear that he was not personally a part of the committee at that time. However, there is evidence that Cranmer did some work on abstracting canons from the *Codex juris canonici* which he felt were in conflict with common law or statutes of the realm. Most of the extracts have to do with passages in contradiction to the king's supremacy, but some of them involve matters of more ordinary ecclesiastical court problems.[50]

There is another piece of evidence extant which indicates that a book of reformed canon law was either completed or nearly completed during the reign

---

[48] Luders et al., *Statutes of the Realm* 3:976, 35 Henry VIII. c. 16.

[49] John E. Cox, ed, *Miscellaneous Writings and Letters of Thomas Cranmer* (Cambridge: Parker Society No. 15, 1844). 415. This is wrongly dated January 24; see *Letters and Papers of Henry VIII*, 21:48, part 1, no. 108.

[50] Ibid., 68-75. John Strype dated this about 1533 and Bishop Burnett about 1544. Burnett is closer to being correct, for it would have to be a time when responsibility for reform of canon law was with Cranmer rather than Cromwell.

of Henry VIII. This is the letter which was printed by John Foxe at the beginning of his published edition of the *Reformatio legum ecclesiasticarum* in 1571, immediately following the preface. This letter was intended for the king's signature when the revised canon law was to be promulgated. The text of the letter suggests that it was a part of the duty of the king in superintending religion to remove customs unserviceable to the Christian Church, to annul regulations that invaded the royal prerogative, to furnish a book in place of the old canon law, and to require his subjects in schools, colleges, and ecclesiastical courts to abide by it.[51] The letter was never signed and such a book has not survived unless it is contained in revised form in the *Reformatio legum ecclesiasticarum* of 1552.

During this period in his reign, Henry was paying more attention to the more conservative Bishop Stephen Gardiner than to Thomas Cranmer. Gardiner in 1546 was serving as Henry's ambassador to Emperor Charles VI. Also, the Council of Trent had begun in December of 1545, and Gardiner had high hopes for it in that the Council was seen as the result of the desires of the emperor and as a program in which the pope was only reluctantly involved. It is possible that publication of a newly revised canon law was held up by Henry VIII on the basis of a letter, which he had received from Gardiner, urging him not to make innovations at this time in the life of the church for fear of upsetting negotiations on the continent. John Foxe in his *Acts and Monuments* quoted from a reply the king made to Sir Anthony Denny in 1546 when the latter brought to him a number of letters to be signed.

> I am now otherways resolved, for you shall send my lord of Canterbury word, that since I last spake with him about these matters, I have received letters from my lord of Winchester, now being on the other side of the sea, about the conclusion of a league between us, the emperor, and the French king, and he writeth plainly unto us, that the league will not prosper nor go forward, if we make any other innovation, change, or alteration either in religion or ceremonies, than heretofore hath been already commenced and done; therefore, my lord of Canterbury must take patience wherein, and forbear until we may espy a more apt and convenient time for that purpose.[52]

It is possible that the extant letter patent which Foxe attached to his edition of the *Reformatio* in 1571 was one of the letters referred to by Henry on this occasion. Denny himself favored the more Protestant side in the contest between Cranmer and Gardiner, and probably reported the king's statement

---

[51]Elwood Cardwell, ed., *The Reformation of the Ecclesiastical Laws, as Attempted in the Reigns of King Henry VIII, King Edward VI, and Queen Elizabeth.* (Oxford: 1850; reprt. Farnborough, England: Gregg International, 1968), xxviii-xxx. This summary of the letter's content comes from Jeremy Collier, *Ecclesiastical History of England,* (London: 1852), 5:139. The full text is in 9:223-25. The letter is found in Appendix 2 of this translation.

[52]John Foxe, *Acts and Monuments,* (London: Religious Tract Society, 1877), 5:562.

directly to Cranmer. If this letter had not been among those to which Denny referred, it is probable that Cranmer did not submit the letter to be signed by the king at this time. He had already experienced the king's refusal to sign letters having to do with less significant matters for reformation such as bell-ringing on Halloween, covering images during Lent, creeping to the cross, and rood-beams in churches.

Thomas Cranmer was realistic about the opposition to reformation concerns in the church and proceeded cautiously, waiting for the propitious moment. That moment for the promulgation of a new book of canon law never came during the reign of Henry VIII, for the king died within a year. Ralph Morice, Cranmer's secretary, told John Foxe years later how hopeful Cranmer still was for further reformation under Henry VIII and even for similar reformation under Francis I toward the end of the reign of both kings, and how that was interrupted by their deaths in 1547.

> I am sure you were at Hampton Court, quoth the archbishop, when the French king's ambassador was entertained there in those solemn banqueting-houses not long before the king's death; namely when, after the banquet was done the first night, the king was leaning upon the ambassador and upon me; if I should tell what communication between the king's highness and the said ambassador was had, concerning the establishing of sincere religion then, a man would hardly have believed it: nor had I myself thought the king's highness had been so forward in those matters as then appeared. I may tell you, it passed the pulling down of roods, and the suppressing the ringing of bells. I take it that few in England would have believed, that the king's majesty and the French king had been at this point, not only, within half a year after, to have changed the mass in both the realms into a communion (as we now use it), but also utterly to have extirped and banished the bishop of Rome, and his usurped power, out of both their realms and dominions. Yea, they were so thoroughly and firmly resolved in that behalf, that they meant also to exhort the emperor to do the like in Flanders and other his countries and seignories; or else they would break off from him. And herein the king's highness willed me, quoth the archbishop, to pen a form thereof to be sent to the French king, to consider of. But the deep and most secret providence of almighty God, owing to this realm a sharp scourge for our iniquities, prevented for a time this their most godly device and intent, by taking to his mercy both of these princes.[53]

This indicates that Cranmer's trust in the eventual protestantization of Henry VIII, not to mention Francis I and Charles V, was as unrealistic as his sober estimation of his opposition within England was realistic. Foxe, on the

[53]Ibid., 5:563 f.

other hand, believed that Henry VIII had the blood of too many martyrs upon his hands for the Lord to grace his reign with a complete reformation.

THE REFORM OF THE ECCLESIASTICAL LAWS OF ENGLAND DURING THE REIGN OF EDWARD VI, 1547-1553

With the death of Henry VIII and the accession of his son Edward VI under the protectorship of his uncle Edward Seymour, Duke of Somerset, the Protestant-minded leadership in the Church of England could continue reform. Thomas Cranmer himself was cautious about the speed at which such reformation should take place. In the same conversation reported to John Foxe by Cranmer's secretary Morice, the secretary recalled that he had asked Cranmer why he did not go forward more rapidly with reformation now that Henry was gone, for the "opportunity of the time" served the cause better in the days of Edward VI. Cranmer replied that, on the contrary,

> It was better to attempt such reformation in King Henry the Eighth's days than at this time; the king being in his infancy. For if the king's father had set forth any thing for the reformation of abuses, who was he that durst gainsay it. Marry! we are now in doubt how men will take the change or alteration of abuses, in the church. . . .[54]

Cranmer sought, therefore, to encourage a reformation, little by little, waiting to be sure that people, at least those with power, were willing to go along with each step before the next one was taken. As a result, for the first few years there was no reformation of doctrine from that set forth in the King's Book of 1534 except for the repeal of the Act of Six Articles. The reformation of worship was done in stages. The document for the reformation of the canon law was not ready until the end of Edward's reign,154 and that proved to be too late.

Yet from the beginning of the reign, through royal injunctions and later through parliamentary statutes, canon law was in fact revised in England. On July 31, 1547, the Royal Injunctions of Edward VI were issued as the basis for the first general visitation of the Church by commissioners of the crown since 1538. In fact, the majority of these injunctions are based upon the earlier royal injunctions of 1536 and 1538. Among the new items added to the earlier ones were those which commanded the use of the new *Book of Homilies* by the non-preaching parsons and the obtaining of Erasmus' *Paraphrases* of the gospels in English by each parish church to be used with both Latin and English versions of the New Testament. Both the *Homilies* and the *Paraphrases* were published the same day as the injunctions, and both had the effect of moving the church in a more Protestant direction. This was particularly true of the third homily, on justification, written by Archbishop Cranmer, which his conservative opponent, Bishop Gardiner, maintained to be in contradiction

[54]Ibid.

to the King's Book. The introduction to the *Paraphrases* by Nicholas Udall and Thomas Key presented a Protestant point of view with which to read Erasmus.[55]

Other publications sponsored by Cranmer at this time presented not merely a Protestant position but also encouraged people to think in terms of further canon law reform. This was true both of the Nuremberg-Brandenburg Catechism, which Cranmer translated into English with additions of his own, and of the *Consultation* of Herrmann von Wied, Archbishop of Cologne. The former was presented as Cranmer's own catechism. It contains a sermon placed in the catechism by Cranmer on the authority of the keys and the use of that authority within the Christian congregation to help to amend the lives of those who live in open sin.

> And although those canons, ordinances and rites which be agreeable to the gospel (and were ordained in time past, to punish such open transgressors and malefactors) are now in our time almost utterly abolished and taken away, yet for this cause we ought not to despise or cast away, the authority and use of the keys.[56]

A need for the revised canon law is here clearly stated.

In the *Consultation* it was held that the "discipline of Christ with the saints" was a part of the third "sign" or mark by which one could discern the true church, along with the marks of preaching of true doctrine and the lawful use of the sacraments. Furthermore, there was recommendation for something akin to the institution of the lay "elder" who would work with the pastor in administering such discipline. The pastor, "with other godly men," were to work with the person in need of discipline, and if they failed they were to present the case to the superintendent [bishop] for the area who would then come to the local congregation and meet with the obstinate one, the pastor, and "others appointed to that office." This body with the superintendent present had the power of excommunication.[57] This type of disciplinary consistory was similar to that developing especially in Reformed (and some Lutheran) churches at that time, but as it is described in the *Consultation* it is within the framework of episcopacy. Such a plan appeared later in the *Reformatio* of 1552. Martin Bucer is probably the source of the idea in the *Consultation*.

When Parliament met for the first time during Edward's reign, in November, 1547, the members of the lower house of Convocation, meeting at the same time, revived the need to get on with the work of the committee of thirty-two

---

[55]Craig Thompson, "Erasmus and Tudor England," in *Extraite de Actes Du Congres Erasme, Rotterdam, 27-29 Octobre, 1969.* (Amsterdam: North Holland Publishing Co., 1971). 50-55.

[56]Thomas Cranmer, *A Short Instruction Into Christian Religion, Being a Catechism Set Forth by Archbishop Cranmer in MDXLVIII: Together with the Same in Latin,* translated from the German by Justus Jonas in 1539 (Oxford University Press, 1829), 201.

[57]Herman von Wied, *A Simple and Religious Consultation of vs Herman by the grace of God Archbishop of Colone, and Prince Electoure, &c* (1548), fols. CCxxv and CII.

for revising the canon laws of England. Under the prolocutorship of reform-minded John Taylor, they petitioned

> that ecclesiastical laws may be made and established . . . by thirty-two persons. . . . so that all judges ecclesiastical, proceeding after those laws may be without danger and peril.

They also sought to be

> adjoined and associated with the lower house of Parliament; or else that such statutes and ordinances, as shall be made concerning all matters of religion, and causes ecclesiastical, may not pass without the sight and assent of said clergy.[58]

When it became clear that it was possible to discuss matters freely which had formerly been prohibited by the Act of Six Articles, the lower house of Convocation voted 53 to 22 that the laws should be abolished which made the marriages of clerks in holy orders null and void. This would indicate that had clergy in the lower house been consulted on reform of the ecclesiastical laws, they would have been as reform minded as the Protestant leadership expressed by Cranmer and others.[59]

In 1547 Parliament itself did not revive the statute for the committee of thirty-two, but it did take up a number of bills reforming specific aspects of canon law. Most important of these was the Act for Repeal of Certain Statutes, which abolished the Act of Six Articles and other statutes concerning heresies going back to the fifth year of Richard II. Statutes prohibiting circulation of books discussing the lively religious issues of the time were eliminated. Also, statutes for permission of communion in both kinds, election of bishops by letters patent only and the abolition of chantries were passed. A bill to permit married men to be ordained passed the House of Commons but failed to pass the House of Lords.

Thanks in part to the adverse turn of fortune for the Protestant cause on the continent of Europe, some of the leading Protestant minds, invited to England by Cranmer, came to join in the English reformation. Peter Martyr Vermigli arrived from Strassburg in December 1547. He was an experienced disciplinarian while still an Augustinian in Italy before he fled the Roman Inquisition in 1542. Like John Calvin, he had been inspired by Martin Bucer's efforts to establish a proper discipline in the churches of Strassburg. Vermigli believed that discipline was one of the three external marks of the Church by which one could determine the true Church. Furthermore, as a lecturer on the Old Testament, he was impressed by the Deuteronomic view of history. He believed that until a nation shaped itself according to proper ecclesiastical

[58]Wilkins, *Concilia*, IV, 15f.

[59]John Strype, *Memorials of the Most Reverend Father in God, Thomas Cranmer, Sometime Lord Archbishop of Canterbury*, 2 vols. (Oxford: 1840), 1:222.

discipline, it was under danger of severe judgment of God. He was installed as professor of theology at the University of Oxford, and he added his plea to Cranmer's original invitation to Martin Bucer to come to England. In this plea, Vermigli emphasized England's need for a leader conversant with Church discipline.[60]

When the Augsburg Interim proved to be unacceptable, Martin Bucer left Strassburg, where his plans for establishing a serious discipline in congregations had come close to fruition before the disastrous battle of Muehlberg. He now applied his talents to further the reformation in England, arriving in April of 1549, and became a professor of theology at Cambridge.

A third important continental Protestant was John Alasco, or Łaski, former Polish nobleman and bishop, friend of Erasmus, and general superintendent of the churches of Emden. Under his leadership, the "Church of the Germans and other foreigners in the City of London" was established formally in the summer of 1550. As superintendent, he had under his direction four ministers of the word, two Dutch and two French. Four elders were elected to assist in maintaining discipline, along with four deacons who were to assist the poor and the sick. This form of government was established under the Bishop of London, consistent with episcopacy. In this case the superintendent acted collegially, functioning with the advice and consent of his presbyters. It is probable that King Edward, the Duke of Somerset, and Archbishop Cranmer saw this church as a pilot project to give guidance in the further reformation of the national Church. Through it, they could see a new kind of ecclesiastical discipline in practice.[61]

In the second session of Parliament, meeting in November 1548, legislation was passed making it possible for priests to marry and abolishing the use of precontracts as a means for the annulment of marriages. Parliament passed new tithe legislation and an act of uniformity to support the use of the First Prayerbook of Edward VI. Members of the House of Commons tried to make it possible for divorces to be obtained in cases of adultery, but they failed in their effort.

During the third session of Parliament, beginning in November 1549, specific legislation was introduced for the complete reform of ecclesiastical laws. At the beginning of the session, Thomas Cranmer and others submitted a bill affecting ecclesiastical jurisdiction which would have given bishops and their ordinaries the power to excommunicate and imprison those who needed discipline within an "immoral" nation. Concurrently, a bill was introduced into the House of Commons which would help to raise the standards for admission

---

[60]Hastings Robinson, *Original Letters Relative to the English Reformation, Written During the Reigns of King Henry VIII, King Edward VI, and Queen Mary, Chiefly from the Archives of Zurich*, 2 vols. (Cambridge: Parker Society Nos. 52, 53, 1846-47), Pt. 2, p. 472. Letter from Peter Martyr to Martin Bucer, December 26, 1548. Hereafter to be cited as Zurich Letters.

[61]Frederick A. Norwood, "The Strangers' 'Model Churches' in Sixteenth Century England," in Franklin Littell, ed., *Reformation Studies* (Richmond: John Knox Press, 1962), 181-96.

to practice law in the ecclesiastical courts. Each bill passed the respective house in which it was introduced but failed after the third reading in the other house.

On January 21, 1550, the House of Commons gave a first reading to a bill which revived the statutes of Henry VIII calling for a committee on the revision of the ecclesiastical laws. A new feature of this bill was that it called for a committee of sixteen rather than the thirty-two of previous statutes. The bill passed the lower house and was taken up by the House of Lords on January 25. There it was amended to include the original number of thirty-two. Cranmer and other bishops opposed the bill in this form, and the bill was passed over the opposition of the eleven bishops who were present. Only William Barlow, Bishop of Bath and Wells, was listed as present but not in opposition. On February 1, the bill in its new form was ratified by the House of Commons, and it became a statute of the realm.[62]

One can only guess at the reason for Cranmer's opposition. Both the more conservative and the more Protestant-minded bishops were opposed to the bill. Is it possible that Cranmer was pushing hard for the passing of his bill on "Ecclesiastical Jurisdiction" which was dying in the House of Commons on the very day he and the other bishops opposed the Commons originated bill? Cranmer may have seen in his own bill a more immediate way to get at the same end: the discipline of the congregations of England through church courts. After all, he had seen three other bills over eighteen years providing for a committee of thirty-two revisers, and nothing had been accomplished yet. Did he think the passage of a bill now was only going to continue the shelving of the project? If this was the case, then Cranmer and the other bishops were voting against the bill "as a protest against its inadequacy and hypocrisy."[63]

The make-up of the committee was changed from the original statute, which called for sixteen of the clergy without specifying their classification. The new statute asked that at least four of the sixteen clergy should be bishops. The original statute asked for sixteen to represent the temporality of the upper and lower houses of Parliament. The new statute asked simply for sixteen from the temporality, of whom four were to be expert in common law.

When the Privy Council considered appointing the committee a year and half later in October 1551, the formula used was that eight of the committee should be bishops, eight should be divines (theologians), eight should be civilians (experts in civil law), and eight should be practitioners of common law.[64] There were no temporal lords on the committee, though their presence was envisioned in the original statute. This was perhaps a fatal error, for the final product of the committee was frustrated by a temporal lord during the reign of Edward VI. On the other hand, at least ten of the final committee

[62]*Statues of the Realm,* vol. IV, pp. 111ff. (1550).

[63]Jasper Ridley, *Thomas Cranmer* (Oxford: Clarendon, 1962), 331.

[64]John R. Dasent, ed., *Acts of the Privy Council of England,* A.D. *1550-1552,* New Series, 3 (London, 1891), 382.

selected had served as members of the House of Commons. A tentative committee of thirty-two was selected by the Privy Council on October 6, 1551, but the letter of commission does not seem to have been completed at that time.

In a paper from that period, which cannot be precisely dated, Edward VI expressed his concern about the reformation of many "abuses." He believed that ministers could better pursue their threefold task of "setting forth the word of God, continuing the people in prayer, and in the discipline." A better ecclesiastical discipline could help to solve social problems such as "swearing, rioting, neglecting of God's word, or such like vices." He noted that some of the bishops were not good examples and were therefore incapable of executing discipline. Some were papist; some were ignorant; some were too old, and others had an "ill name." This could be helped by better appointments in the future.[65]

Those bishops who were considered good examples were the eight bishops selected for the committee of thirty-two. They were Archbishop Thomas Cranmer of Canterbury, Bishop Thomas Goodrich of Ely, Bishop Nicholas Ridley of London, Bishop John Ponet of Winchester, Bishop Miles Coverdale of Exeter, Bishop William Barlow of Bath and Wells, Bishop John Hooper of Gloucester, and Bishop John Scory of Rochester. All of these bishops represented the Protestant cause, and they constituted half the bishops who attended Parliament with any degree of regularity during the later years of the reign of Edward VI.

There are three listings extant of the membership of the committee of thirty-two: 1) Minutes of the Privy Council for October 6, 1551; 2) the Journal of King Edward VI for February 10, 1552; and 3) the commission on the Patent Rolls for February 12, 1552. The last of the three listings is the most official. In these three listings the names of the eight bishops remain constant.[66]

The eight divines selected in October were: John Taylor, prebend of Lincoln Cathedral, soon to become Bishop of Lincoln, prolocutor of the lower house of Convocation during the first Parliament of Edward VI; Richard Cox, Almoner to the king, Chancellor of Oxford, Dean of Westminster, former tutor to the king; Matthew Parker, Vice-Chancellor of Cambridge; Hugh Latimer, popular court preacher and former Bishop of Worcester; Sir Anthony Cooke, Latin scholar, tutor to Edward VI, and member of Parliament; Peter Martyr Vermigli, Italian Protestant and biblical scholar, professor of Divinity at the University of Oxford; Sir John Cheke, tutor to Edward VI, professor of Greek at Cambridge, provost of King's College, Clerk of the Privy Council; and John Alasco, Polish humanist and Protestant, Superintendent of the Church of the Strangers in London.

---

[65] *Literary Remains of King Edward the Sixth.* ed. J. G. Nichols (London, 1857), 397.

[66] *Acts of the Privy Council,* 3:382; Nichols, *Literary Remains,* 397; R. H. Brodie et al., eds., *Calendar of the Patent Rolls Preserved in the Public Record Office. Edward VI, vol. IV, 1550-1553* (London, 1926), 354.

Hugh Latimer was dropped from the list in February 1552, and in his place on the king's list of February 10 was Rowland Taylor, rector of Hadleigh, advocate at the Doctor's Commons and chancellor for the Bishop of London who was listed as one of the civilians in the other two lists. On the Patent Roll list of February 12 was the name of Nicholas Wotton with doctorates in civil law, canon law, and divinity, member of the Privy Council, dean of both Canterbury and York, and active diplomat.

The eight civilians selected in October 1551 were: Sir William Petre, doctor of civil law from Oxford, deputy for Thomas Cromwell in ecclesiastical affairs in 1536, diplomat, Keeper of the Great Seal for Ecclesiastical Affairs since August, 1547, member of the Privy Council; Sir William Cecil, member of Gray's Inn, master of requests, member of Parliament, member of the Privy Council, Secretary of State; Rowland Taylor of Hadleigh as previously noted; William May, Dean of St. Paul's', diplomat, president of Queen's College Cambridge; Bartholomew Traheron, member of Parliament, Keeper of the King's Library, Dean of Chichester, and the one member of the group who could rightfully be called a Calvinist; Sir Thomas Smith, doctor of civil law from Padua, Greek scholar, formerly professor of civil law and vice chancellor at Cambridge, chancellor to the Bishop of Ely, clerk of the Privy Council, Master of the Court of Requests, Secretary of State and diplomat; Richard Lyell, doctor of civil law from Oxford, advocate at the Doctor's Commons; and Ralph Skinner, Warden of New College, Oxford, member of Parliament, rector of Broughton Astley.

King Edward's list of February 10 had only seven listed under civilians, Taylor being listed as a divine and the names of Smith and Lyell dropped. Sir Richard Reade was added, a doctor of civil law from Oxford, advocate at the Doctor's Commons, master of the Court of Requests, and Chancellor of Ireland. On the Patent Roll list the name of Skinner was dropped and Taylor and Lyell restored.

The original October listing of common lawyers included: Sir James Hales, justice of the common pleas, member of Gray's Inn, king's sergeant, counsel to Cranmer, member of the Privy Council, member of Parliament; Sir Thomas Bromley, member of the Inner Temple, king's serjeant, justice of Common Pleas, justice of the King's Bench, member of Parliament; John Gosnold, solicitor at the Court of Augmentations and Solicitor General, member of Gray's Inn, member of Parliament; William Stamford, member of Gray's Inn, member of Parliament, serjeant-at-law, later justice of common pleas, noted for his *An Expocicion of the King's Prerogative;* John Caryll, member of Parliament, serjeant-at-law; John Lucas, master of the request, member of Parliament; and Robert Brooke, recorder for the city of London, member of Parliament, member of the Middle Temple, serjeant-at-law, later speaker of the House of Commons and chief justice of Common Pleas. King Edward's list of February 10 had the name of Thomas Gaudy, serjeant-at-law, in place of Robert Brooke, whose name was restored on the Patent Roll list of February 12, 1553.[67]

It would be hard to imagine a more illustrious committee being chosen at that particular time in England, judging these men in terms of either their past or future influence. The constituencies notably missing were conservative clergy and representatives from the temporality in the House of Lords. Such conservatism as was there would have been among those laymen who found it possible to advance their careers under Queen Mary a few years later. As one looks at the list of names, the distinction between divine and civilian on the one hand or civilian and lawyer on the other is not clear in individual cases.

According to John Foxe, writing in 1571, the original intention was to form four committees of eight, each containing two men from each of the four categories. Then the ecclesiastical laws were to have been divided into four parts, with each subcommittee later reporting its recommendations to the larger committee. If all of these committees met in 1552, evidence of their meetings does not survive. On November 5, 1552, a commission was addressed to one committee of eight—composed of Archbishop Thomas Cranmer, Bishop Nicholas Ridley, Richard Cox, Vermigli, Rowland Taylor of Hadleigh, Bartholomew Traheron, John Lucas, and John Gosnold—to prepare and reduce to writing a draft code of reformed ecclesiastical laws in order to receive a final revision and ratification by the whole committee of thirty-two. This was probably the most important working committee of the four. The minutes of the Privy Council for October 6, 1551, reads: "viii of these to rough-hewe the Cannon Lawe, the rest to conclude it afterwards." On November 11, a letter was addressed to the chancellor to make a new commission for the "first drawing and ordering of the canon laws, for that some of those other than were before appointed by the King's majesty are now by his highness thought meet to be left out." Those left out were Ridley, Traheron, and Gosnold. In their places were named: Bishop Thomas Goodrich of Ely, Dr. William May, and Mr. Richard Goodrich.[68]

Presumably the new code of canon law was roughed out during the winter of 1551 and 1552 by the smaller committee and then later discussed by the larger group. John ab Ulmis wrote Henry Bullinger that a "convocation" began on December 12 "to deliberate and consult about a proper moral discipline and purity of doctrine."[69] It is, of course possible that the committee had earlier drafts going back to the time of Henry VIII. In any case, the subcommittee had something ready for wider discussion within the committee by March, 1552.

---

[67]Sachs, *Cranmer's 'Reformation,'* 234-42. In this appendix, Sachs gives brief biographies of the committee members.

[68]*Calendar of Patent Rolls, Edward VI,* vol. IV, p. 114 for the November 4 and 11 listings. See Appendix 3 for letter.

[69]Robinson, *Zurich Letters,* Pt. 2, p. 444, John ab Ulmis to Bullinger, January 10, 1552.

Peter Martyr Vermigli, writing from London on March 8 to Henry Bullinger in Zurich, expressed his own understanding of what was being accomplished:

For the King's majesty has ordained, that, as the gospel is received in his kingdom, and the bishop of Rome is driven out, the church of England shall be no longer ruled by pontifical decrees, and decretals, Sistine, Clementine, and other popish ordinances of the same kind: for the administration of these laws has for the most part prevailed up to this time in the ecclesiastical court, under the tacit authority of the pope; though many other laws were enacted by which the external polity of the church might be regulated. To the intent therefore, that so powerful a kingdom might not be deprived of this, as it appears, necessary advantage, the King has appointed two and thirty persons to frame ecclesiastical laws for this realm, namely eight bishops, eight divines, eight civil lawyers, and eight common lawyers; the majority of whom are equally distinguished by profound erudition and solid piety; and we also, I mean Hopper, a Lasco, and myself are enrolled among them. May God therefore grant that such laws may be enacted by us, as by their godliness and holy justice may banish the Tridentine canons from the churches of Christ! But as I am conscious we have need of the prayers of yourself and your colleagues in furtherance of so great an undertaking, I implore them with all the sincerity and earnestness in my power. For it is not only necessary to entreat God that pious and holy laws may be framed, but that they may obtain the sanction of Parliament, or else they will not possess any force or authority whatsoever.[70]

Other letters written to Zurich at this time indicated that the reformers in England were more confident of the king's desire for this reformation than they were of Parliament's. Bishop Ridley and Goodrich (who had meanwhile become Lord Chancellor) were named by Martin Micronius as tending to "stand in the way with their worldly policy" and thereby to impede progress.[71]

Progress was so impeded that people became anxious about whether the work would be completed within the three-year deadline. On April 14, a bill for "Continuance of the Act of Thirty-two Persons to endure for Three Years next after this Session" was passed by the House of Commons and sent to the Lords. There it had two readings, but Parliament was adjourned the next day before the bill was approved.

A few months later, Richard Cox in a letter to Henry Bullinger, dated October 5, 1552, gave the Swiss reformer good news about the adoption of the revised Prayer Book in which Cox had played an important role, but at

---

[70]Ibid., 503. Peter Martyr to Bullinger, March 8, 1552.
[71]Ibid., 504. Martin Micronius to Bullinger, March 9, 1552.

the same time he was much concerned that the reformation of the ecclesiastical laws was still not completed.[72]

At the time Cox wrote this letter, Edward VI drew up a memorandum in his own hand entitled "Matters for the Council, October 13, 1552." Under the heading "For Religion" Edward listed "th' abrogating of th' old canon law, and the establishment of a new."[73] Since eight of the members of the committee of thirty-two were also members of the Privy Council (Cranmer, T. Goodrich, Petre, Smith, Cecil, Wotton, Bromley, and Cheke), this does not appear to be too sanguine a hope on the part of the king.

However, shortly a manuscript of a reformation of the ecclesiastical laws was completed, and it is extant in 269 folio leaves which today are the property of the British Library. It is this manuscript which now has been translated into English and published in this volume.[74]

In March 1553, Cranmer sought to obtain the consent of the House of Lords to the *Reformatio legum ecclesiasticarum* during the last Parliament of Edward VI. Already, the Forty-Two Articles of Religion and the accompanying Catechism had been endorsed by Parliament, as well as the Second Prayer Book of Edward VI. These symbolic books, defining reformation of doctrine and worship, continue to live through the Thirty-Nine Articles and the Book of Common Prayer. However, adoption of the third symbolic book, the *Reformatio legum ecclesiasticarum,* which defines the third outward mark of the church, its discipline, was blocked in the House of Lords.

It was John Dudley, the Duke of Northumberland, who brought a halt to the attempted ratification, according to a report from the Imperial Ambassador on April 10, 1553. When the volume of reformed ecclesiastical laws was presented to Parliament by Cranmer, according to this account, the Duke of Northumberland informed him that nothing could be done about it.[75] Furthermore, he told Cranmer that he [Cranmer] and his fellow bishops had better look to their own business, for certain priests were preaching sedition in what they were saying about the nobility and that if the bishops did not correct this, they could be held personally responsible. A rational counterargument to Northumberland could have been that, with a revised canon law, the clergy could be better disciplined in these and other matters. However, Cranmer remained consistent with his career as a church leader prepared to bide his time until a more propitious moment for reform arrived. He thus chose not to press the case for adoption of the *Reformatio*. Perhaps in the face of Northumberland's power he had no other choice. One can only

---

[72]Ibid., Pt. 1, p. 123. Richard Cox to Bullinger, October 5, 1552.

[73]Literary Remains of Edward VI, 547.

[74]Harleian MSS. 426, British Library.

[75]The text of Imperial Ambassador Scheyvfe's notes has been printed in James Gairdner, *Lollardy and the Reformation In England* (London: Macmillan, 1911), 400. Gairdner's translation is on p. 363.

guess at the reason for Dudley's opposition; perhaps the proposed limit upon lay looting of church property played a role.

Leslie Sachs, in his previously cited dissertation, suggests that the *Reformatio* failed because of lay opposition to its clericalism.[76] Insofar as this is true, it is indeed ironic, for the very genesis of the reformation of the canon law had been born of pre-Protestant lay grievances about canon law. This lay concern had been expressed through members of the House of Commons. The failure of the *Reformatio* in 1553 was because of opposition in the House of Lords from one layman, John Dudley, Duke of Northumberland. Richard Cox, in his letter to Bullinger of October 5, 1552, mentioned the opposition of nobility. There may have been others besides Dudley, but we do not know about them. Certainly the modern layperson would be uncomfortable with many provisions of the *Reformatio* as it stands, but there is no evidence of serious lay debate in the House of Commons. Provision had been made that laity with common law training were on the committee of thirty-two. Were the lay and common law concerns not heard on that committee?

There was not a more propitious moment in Edward VI's reign, for the king died soon thereafter. Given the Catholic reaction during the reign of Mary, there was no possibility for these revised canon laws to be enacted until the reign of Elizabeth. Under Mary, statutes were repealed, getting back to canon law as it existed in 1529 before the revision of canon law was suggested by parliamentarians. Cardinal Reginald Pole, as a substitute, brought out a new code of constitutions entitled *Reformatio Angliae ex decretis Reginaldi Poli, Feb. 10, 1556.* It had a stillbirth and was published in Rome in 1562. It was published with a catechism composed by Cardinal Carranza in Spanish and translated into English.[77]

Because of Dudley's opposition and Edward's death, the *Reformatio,* this third confessional book of the Edwardian Reformation, did not obtain the dignity or status of the Forty-Two Articles with Catechism or of the Second Prayer Book of Edward VI. These latter had a more permanent role to play in the reformation of the Church of England through the Thirty-Nine Articles and the Book of Common Prayer. In spite of the Articles and Prayerbook being pushed aside during the reign of Queen Mary, their statutory character gave them a quality that the *Reformatio* did not have.

There is not the space in this short introduction to review in detail the contents of the *Reformatio.* Such a summary review is available in Sach's fourth chapter, "The Church that Never Was."[78] Sach's book could well be read as a companion volume to this present translation. A point that Sachs touches upon passage is worth elaborating. There are two ultimates stated in the

---

[76]Sachs, *Cranmer's 'Reformatio,'* 123, 163, 198, 230.

[77]James Gairdner, *The English Church in the Sixteenth Century from the Accession of Henry VIII to the Death of Mary* (London: Macmillan, 1902), 369.

[78]Sachs, *Cranmer's 'Reformatio,'* 135-77.

Reformatio which can easily come into conflict with each other. On the one hand, "all jurisdiction, both ecclesiastical and secular, is derived from him [the king] as from one and the same source." On the other hand, "so much authority may be entrusted to divine Scripture, that no eminence of any creature may be preferred or equated with it."[79] This twofold commitment to the godly king and the Holy Scripture, two absolutes in the English Reformation, did not originate with the *Reformatio,* but these two commitments are there and there is no resolution of what happens when the two authorities seem to be in opposition. When these are seen to be in conflict in the history of England in the next hundred years, one will be the primary emphasis of some and the other will be the primary emphasis of their opponents. The division that eventually led to Civil War between Puritan/Parliamentary and Royalist forces, and then to State Church and tolerated Nonconformists — and probably also to the later Tory-Whig two-party system — can be seen as having roots in this English commitment to two ultimates. The issue here does not divide laity from clergy, but in time of crisis a deep division cut through laity and clergy combined.

In previous publications,[80] I have pointed out how the *Reformatio* provides for a congregational disciplinary program that parallels other churches in both the Reformed and Lutheran traditions by having elders (seniors) meet with the pastor weekly to decide who needs admonishing, and so forth. This parallels attempts made in Cologne, Strassburg, Geneva (where alone there was success), and even in Lutheran territories such as Mansfeld. This embryo congregational presbytery or church session could apply penalties. As Sachs maintains, this role of the laity seems to be overlaid on a more traditional structure of church officials without giving an indication of how such elders are to be elected or appointed. Perhaps these elders were intended to be an expansion of the numbers and roles of churchwardens who were also entrusted with oversight of morality in the *Reformatio.*[81] The fact that this Reformation understanding of congregational elders involved in discipline seems to overlay the more traditional forms of church office could indicate that some of the forms of the *Reformatio* might have been written in the days of Henry VIII. The doctrine or substance of the *Reformatio* is definitely Protestant. Many of the forms are pre-Protestant. This combination helped form those qualities peculiar to the Church of England.

A more liberal feature of the *Reformatio* from a lay point of view was the provision for divorce in cases of adultery, desertion, even long-though-licit

---

[79]Ibid., 137, 140.

[80]James C. Spalding, "The *Reformatio Legum Ecclesiasticarum* of 1552 and the Furthering of Discipline in England," *Church History* 39 (1970): 162-71; idem, "Discipline as a Mark of the True Church in its Sixteenth-Century Lutheran Context," in Carter Lindberg, ed., *Piety, Politics, and Ethics* (Kirksville, Mo.: Sixteenth Century Publishers, 1984), 119-39.

[81]Sachs, *Cranmer's 'Reformatio,'* 154; Cardwell, *Reformatio*, 93f.

absence (two or three years after return could be expected), capital enmity (incompatibility?), and repeated spouse abuse.[82]

There are statements written in Thomas Cranmer's hand at the end of Chapter 4 in the section on Judgements against Heresies that recommends for obstinate heretics either exile, imprisonment, or punishment "in some other way in accord with the prudent consideration of the magistrate." This certainly should mitigate the charge against Cranmer that he "undoubtedly" advocated the execution of the heretic.[83] It does seem strange that Foxe, with his antipathy to capital punishment for heretics, did not include Cranmer's milder recommendations in his 1571 publication.

In an important provision, responsibility was lodged for the oversight of the poor with the office of deacon,

> so that he should strengthen the weak, release the imprisoned, and comfort the needy; . . . be the father to orphans, a patron of widows, and a solace to all the afflicted and all the wretched. . . .[84]

The diaconate was intended to be a significant position. This does again have a parallel in function with Geneva but within the form of a traditional hierarchical structure for the place of the deacon.

The wide range of subjects listed in the *Reformatio* under Ecclesiastical Jurisdiction included:

> benefices, marriages, divorces, wills, administration of the goods of deceased persons, withdrawal of the legatees, mortuary dues, tithes, offereings, and cases involving other ecclesiastical rights. Also usury and heresies, incest, adultery, fornication, sacrilege, perjury, blasphemy, attack on faith, defamation and verbal abuses, laying violent hands upon a clergyman, accounts of churches and stewards, cases of debt to churches and their ministers, repair and dilapidation of churches, cemeteries, and other ecclesiastical buildings.[85]

There is quite enough here to concern laity and to provide lively discussion between those who wanted to make canon law consistent with common law. Was such a discussion held in the committee of thirty-two? Would such a discussion ever be held?

THE ATTEMPT TO COMPLETE THE REFORMATION OF ECCLESIASTICAL LAW DURING THE REIGN OF ELIZABETH I (1558-1603)

---

[82]See chaps. 1-21, "Concerning Adultery and Divorce," of the following translation.

[83]See p. 79 of this translation. the charge against Cranmer is by Sachs, *Cranmer's 'Reformatio',"* 160.

[84]See p. 140 of this translation.

[85]See pp. 263 of this translation.

Considering that almost half the membership of the Edwardian committee of thirty-two did not survive the reign of Mary, members of that committee took leading roles in the settlement of the government of church and state during the first year of Elizabeth's reign. Even Nicholas Heath, who had been involved in canon law revision in the days of Henry VIII and who was Archbishop of York and Chancellor for Mary at the time of her death, was amazingly cooperative in making for a smooth transition in government even though he was not willing later to serve in church government. William Petre, the civil lawyer, who had come into Henry VIII's government through Anne Boleyn connections, who had been involved in canon law revision in Henry's time, who had been mentor and a close co-worker with William Cecil under Edward, who had served on the Edwardian committee of thirty-two, who had served for a time as secretary for Queen Mary, now again appeared as William Cecil's colleague. Cecil, who had kept a close official relationship with Elizabeth during Mary's reign, now served at Elizabeth's right hand in the transition and reorganization of government. Thomas Smith, John Cheke, Walter Haddon, William May, Richard Goodrich, and Anthony Cooke, all of whom had been associated with the production of the *Reformatio,* also had major positions in Elizabeth's secular government.[86]

Anthony Cooke took primary responsibility in the House of Commons in February, 1559 for guiding through the House of Commons the restoration of the supremacy and the revised Prayerbook. On February 27, 1559, a bill was introduced into the House of Commons, where Thomas Smith also had a seat with Cooke, to revive the committee of thirty-two. After passing the House of Commons, the bill failed in the House of Lords. At the time, there was still a solid phalanx of Catholic bishops in the House of Lords strong enough to prevent the bill's passage.[87]

After the Conference of Westminster at the Easter recess at which Richard Cox and John Scory, members of the committee of thirty-two, debated the Catholic bishops, the commitment of two bishops to the Tower diminished their vote in the House of Lords. With all nine bishops voting no and with Archbishop Heath not using proxies, the Act of Uniformity passed the House of Lords by three votes and the bill was complete on April 29, 1559. The Prayerbook had been reaffirmed. Then on July 19, 1559, a nineteen-member ecclesiastical commission was appointed to manage church affairs which became

[86]Conyers Read, *Mr. Secretary Cecil and Queen Elizabeth* (New York: Knopf, 1955), 63-65, 116, 118, 479n.; F. G. Emmison, *Tudor Secretary, Sir William Petre at Court and Home* (Cambridge: Harvard University Press, 1961); Mary Dewar, *Sir Thomas Smith: A Tudor Intellectual in Office* (London, 1964), 3:296; John Strype, *The Life of the Learned Sir John Cheke,* (Oxford, 1821), 20; Hugh F. Kearney, *Scholars and Gentlemen,* (London: Faber, 1970), 5:40; C. J. Lee, *The Poetry of Walter Haddon,* (The Hague: Nijhoff, 1967), 52-53; William Haugaard, *Elizabeth and the English Reformation:* (London: Cambridge University Press, 1968), 130-34.

[87]Simonds D'Ewes, *The Journals of all the Parliaments during the Reign of Queen Elizabeth,* (London, 1682), 14. *Journals of the House of Commons,* 1: 55, 56, 58. *Journals of the House of Lords,* 1: 566.

known as the Court of High Commission. Of its members, fifteen were lay persons, including Thomas Smith, Richard Goodrich, and Walter Haddon, all of whom had been associated with the *Reformatio*. Matthew Parker, who had not yet been consecrated Archbishop, was one of the clerics. Any six of the commission could act if at least one of seven designated persons were present. The four above-named *Reformatio* veterans were counted among that seven.[88] On June 24, in the absence of a revised canon law, injunctions and visitation articles were issued in the name of the queen which had the force of law during her reign. Many of the Edwardian committee of thirty-two were engaged in giving practical effect to those injunctions.

In 1559 newly consecrated Archbishop Matthew Parker published his *Eleven Articles,* which served as a doctrinal standard of the Church of England until the *Thirty Nine Articles* were adopted. In the *Eleven Articles,* Parker affirmed that the maintenance of ecclesiastical discipline was one of the external marks of the true Church, which at least would indicate Parker favored something like the *Reformatio* in order to define the forms of discipline. Parker's articles for visitations for 1560 also show his concern for the maintenance of discipline.[89]

With new bishops appointed and installed, it was possible to have a meeting of the Convocation when Parliament met in 1562/3. Concern for discipline in the church was expressed in an address to Parliament by Nicholas Bacon, the Queen's Chancellor.[90] It is possible that Archbishop Parker possessed a copy of the *Reformatio* when Convocations met. Perhaps he had the one John Foxe used for his 1571 edition. We have an indication that a revision of the *Reformatio* was a concern of Archbishop Parker during the first Convocation of Canterbury under Elizabeth in January, 1563, and we know that Bishop Edwyn Sandys brought up a proposal to again revive the committee of thirty-two.

Unfortunately, most of the records of this Convocation were destroyed when St. Paul's Cathedral was burned in 1666. However, John Strype found among surviving records a document that began as follows:

General notes of matters to be moved by the clergy in the next Parliament and Synod

I. A Certain form of doctrine to be conceived in articles, and after to be published and authorized

II. Matters worthy of reformation, concerning certain rites, &c. in the Book of Common Prayer

[88]Henry Gee, *The Elizabethan Clergy* (Oxford: Clarendon, 1898), 138.

[89]Mark VanderSchaaf, "Archbishop Parker's Efforts Toward a Bucerian Discipline in the Church of England," *Sixteenth Century Journal,* 8, no. 1 (1977): 85-103.

[90]D'Ewes, *Journals of All The Parliaments,* 60. See William P. Haugaard, *Elizabeth and the English Reformation,* 73.

III. Ecclesiastical laws and discipline to be drawn, concerning both the clergy and laity

IV. To procure some augmentation of temporal commodities for the supply of the exility of small benefices and livings.[91]

These concerns were precisely the concerns of the leadership of the church during Edward's reign, and for that matter, they parallel concerns expressed eighty years later at the beginning of the Long Parliament, when the *Reformatio* was printed once again. Strype was not sure of the actual author of the paper he had found, but this paper was used by Archbishop Parker at the 1563 Convocation for it has marginal notes in his handwriting.

In response to the first note, the Forty-Two Articles became Thirty-Nine Articles, emphasizing more anti-Roman Catholic positions vis-a-vis Tridentine canons and dropping some anti-Anabaptist statements. The article concerning the Eucharist was modified so that both Lutheran and Reformed perspectives on the Real Presence would be acceptable. Sachs in his discussion overdoes the contrast between the *Reformatio's* contrast between the heresy articles where the impanation theory of the presence of Christ was condemned. Luther himself would have condemned a theory which ascribed to a priest a special power to make a change in the bread and wine.[92] The negative decree of reprobation was dropped in the article on predestination. Faithfulness of martyrs and exiles under Mary who held differing though Protestant views was a factor in obtaining acceptance of such change, but some of the changes simply reflected a decade of history. At the same time, a catechism by Alexander Nowell was recommended by Archbishop Parker and adopted. Nowell had been one of the exiles during Mary Tudor's reign who had not left Frankfurt to go to Geneva. Yet Nowell recommended that congregations should choose "elders" or ecclesiastical magistrates, to hold and keep the discipline of the church," working with the pastor in that discipline.[93] This was in keeping with the recommendation of the *Reformatio*.

When it came to liturgy, in the "General Notes" it was suggested that vestments be done away with, that private baptisms be avoided, that organs be removed, and so on. When these were proposed in the form of six articles before the lower house of Convocation, forty-three to thirty-five of those present were in favor of the revisions. However, when proxies were counted,

---

[91]Haugaard. *Elizabeth and the English Reformation*, 346-15. Haugaard recovered two copies of the "General Notes, " manuscript and has filled in some notable omissions of Strype's *Annals*, part 1, 473-84. Cardwell simply copied Strype's material and thus is missing some of the material. Haugaard assumes Parker was opposed to the intent of the "General Notes."

[92]Sachs. *Cranmer's 'Reformatio'*, 144. For a discussion of motives for changes in the Articles, see John Strype, *Annals of the Reformation during Elizabeth's Happy Reign* (Oxford, 1924), vol. I, part 1, pp. 484-99.

[93]Alexander Nowell, *A Catechisme*. (Cambridge: Parker Society, 1953), 218.

it was fifty-nine to fifty-eight in favor of the negative vote. Some of the reform element in the meeting saw this as a reason to prohibit proxy votes in synod meetings. William Haugaard argues that the queen was personally involved in the nullification of these radical proposals.[94]

When the matter of reform of ecclesiastical laws was brought up, it was suggested that a new committee of thirty-two be appointed to review the *Reformatio* as well as other suggestions for developing discipline. Even if we had more records of the Convocation left from the Great Fire of 1666 and knew more exactly what happened, we would not add to the fact that this Convocation and Parliament again fell short of revising canon law.

Although a revised canon law had not been adopted, the doctrine of royal supremacy described in the *Reformatio,* as it was to be practiced under Queen Elizabeth and as it was followed in the Vestiarian Controversy, eventually prompted Thomas Erastus, the Swiss physician in Heidelberg, to write the response which made the term 'Erastianism' a part of the history of Christianity. Erastianism in its historic sense does not describe the *Reformatio* at all but rather the position of those lay people whom Sachs in his study sees as frustrating the passage of the *Reformatio.* Sachs perceives the *Reformatio* as Erastian, using that term in the popular but historically incorrect sense of defining a policy of church control by the state. If that is what it is, many pre-Reformation situations can be called Erastian. The very clericalism which Sachs sees invading secular and lay areas of concern was what Thomas Erastus opposed. The laity identified by Sachs as opposing the *Reformatio,* and not the document itself, are properly labelled Erastian.[95]

To demonstrate Erastus' relationship to the Vestiarian Controversy requires a short narration. The part of the story that is well known was that on January 25, 1565, Queen Elizabeth wrote to Archbishop Matthew Parker, insisting in no uncertain terms that he should obtain uniformity of vestments among the clergy.[96] Although Archbishop Park would have preferred to do otherwise, he had to publish his *Advertisements* enforcing the queen's desire without publicly being supported by the queen's authority.[97]

In the ensuing burst of controversy, a young "hot gospeller,"[98] named George Withers, was called to a conference with Archbishop Parker for having preached an inflammatory sermon in 1565 at Cambridge recommending that the stained glass windows be broken out. Parker withdrew Withers' license to

---

[94]William P. Haugaard. *Elizabeth and the English Reformation,* 284.

[95]Sachs, *Cranmer's 'Reformatio,'* 163, 218.

[96]Queen Elizabeth's letter is found in the *Correspondence of Matthew Parker, D.D., Archbishop of Canterbury,* ed. John Bruce and Thomas Perowne (Cambridge: Parker Society No. 33, 1853), 223-27.

[97]Strype, *Annals of the Reformation,* 525-28.

[98]The term "hot gospeller" is found in Donald J. McGinn, *The Admonition Controversy* (New Brunswick: Rutgers University Press, 1949), 541 where McGinn cites what is presumably Anthony Gilbey's pamphlet, *To my louynge brethren that is troubled about the popishe apparrell. . .* A4v.

preach and Withers left for Geneva.[99] Withers, not knowing Elizabeth's role in ordering Parker to bring the clergy into line, hoped to get support from continental Protestants to protest to Elizabeth about Parker's *Advertisement* and the actions of the bishops in England. Theodore Beza in Geneva was willing to give Withers support, and Beza sent him to Henry Bullinger in Zurich. However, Withers found that Bullinger and his colleague Rudolph Gualter were offended by Withers' painting "in the blackest colours" the English bishops who were close friends of theirs; they were equally offended by Withers' petition to Elector Frederick III of the Palatine in which Withers advised that any overture made by the Elector should blame the bishops and not the queen.[100] Eventually, Withers became a student at the University of Heidelberg while promising that he would not break stained glass windows and in 1568 presented theses toward his doctorate. Among the theses submitted by Withers was one that the Swiss physician Thomas Erastus felt called upon to answer. Withers had maintained

> that in every church that was rightly instituted, there ought to be a Government or Discipline observed, whereby the Ministry, in conjunction with elders for that purpose to be elected, should have right and authority to excommunicate any vicious livers, even princes themselves.[101]

Erastus, originally from Aarau just twenty miles from Zurich, insisted that there was no warrant in the Bible for excommunicating persons who made an outward profession of the true Christian faith. After all, Christ had not debarred Judas from the Last Supper, and Saint Paul had enjoined each person to examine himself, "himself, he says, not others."[102]

> To thrust them from that Sacrament which is of God's institution when they are minded to come, is more than any church or man has a right to do; for none can judge of the heart but God alone. It may chance that some sparkes of piety and remorse may kindle in a sinners soul. . . .[103]

Thomas Erastus would have objected to the *Reformatio* on the same grounds he objected to Withers' thesis, and he would have been amazed to find a scholar in the late twentieth century call the *Reformatio* "Erastian."

From the other side, Withers, with his concern for a more vigorous discipline as an essential mark of the true Church, would not have been satisfied with the *Reformatio*. The proto-Puritanism represented by George Withers and

---

[99]Parker, *Correspondence*. 234, 236, 238.

[100]Robinson, *Original Letters*, Pt. 2, pp. 269-72; 294, 296-305.

[101]Thomas Erastus, *A Treatise of Excommunication*. (London, 1682), A4r.

[102]Ibid., 69.

[103]Ibid., 78.

many others in England (not to mention Beza in Geneva, Gaspar Olevianus in Heidelberg, Andrew Melville in Scotland, and leaders in Netherlands and France) found a strong voice in Thomas Cartwright at Cambridge in 1570, who in his lectures on the Acts of the Apostles, derived from Acts the presbyterian theory of church government as the only allowable form.[104]

Add to this the Northern Rising in 1569 influenced by the Roman Catholics and the pope's excommunication of Queen Elizabeth in 1570 and his interdict absolving her subjects from allegiance to her, and one has the religious atmosphere of the time in which John Foxe, with presumably the encouragement of Archbishop Parker, saw fit to publish for the first time the full text of the *Reformatio legum ecclesiasticarum* of 1552. The Thirty-Nine Articles and the Book of Common Prayer had been approved; should not a body of revised canon law also be approved?

In his introduction to the text (see Appendix I), John Foxe made a strong case for the serious consideration of these laws. He recommended that a common law document paralleling the *Reformatio* ought to be prepared. It was a time within the nation when a consistent body of ecclesiastical and secular law was needed. A strong emphasis upon the godly king, the one absolute of the English Reformation, was presented by Foxe throughout the introduction, and both Henry VIII and Edward VI were given high praise for their role in Church reform. Foxe believed that if Edward VI had lived longer, the *Reformatio* would have become law.

It is not as though Foxe recommended that the *Reformatio* in its current form be accepted without change. He expected and encouraged revision. There were matters in which one could have second thoughts and there was a need for discriminating reflection.[105] Foxe saw by comparing the Book of Common Prayer and the *Reformatio* an inconsistency which needed attention. The problem had to do with what Foxe saw as a conflict due to his commitment to the second absolute of the English Reformation, the Holy Word. The dichotomy of the godly king and the Holy Word is apparent throughout Foxe's "Introduction." The audience to which the publication was addressed were "learned men" in general and members of the Parliament in particular. He hoped for approving voices and votes that would lead to a public authorization of a Reformed canon law.

Archbishop Parker's role in this publication was positive at least to the degree of facilitating Foxe's use of the manuscript. Foxe, in going over the manuscript in preparation for publication, altered the sequence of the chapters; in some instances, materials in the manuscript were left out; in other instances, Foxe included new material. Whether or not there were two manuscripts, as Cardwell argued in the last century, is difficult to determine. It is clear that in

---

[104]A. F. Scott-Pearson, *Thomas Cartwright and Elizabethan Puritanism*, (Cambridge, Cambridge University Press, 1925), 25-43.

[105]Cardwell, *Reformatio Legum Ecclesiasticarum*, 304.

the manuscript translated here Foxe's handwriting is on the original pages and his directions in reordering the sequence of the chapters is followed in his 1571 edition and by Cardwell later. It is also impossible to ascertain whether or not Archbishop Parker or Foxe or both were involved in the resequencing of the chapters or in the additions or deletions. Just as in 1563, when Parker supported the modification of the Edwardian Articles and the Book of Common Prayer, so in 1571, Parker probably believed along with Foxe, that the *Reformatio* should be changed. It was not published with the intent that no changes would be allowed. A revised version would have been consistent with Parker's theological stance which had been powerfully influenced by the writings of Bucer, as had Parker's friends, Calvin, Vermigli, and Grindal. There are striking parallels between Parker and Bucer on church discipline.

Archbishop Cranmer's son-in-law, Thomas Norton, a member of Parliament as well as the translator of Calvin's *Institutes* into English, introduced the reissued *Reformatio* into the House of Commons on April 5, 1571. Norton refreshed the memories of the members of the House of Commons concerning the committee of thirty-two and how their document had finally been "drawn by that Learned Man, Mr. Doctor Haddon, and penned by that Learned Man, Mr. Cheke," and now was printed in a book due to the effort of John Foxe.[106] The result of this effort was that once again a committee was appointed, including members of both the Privy Council and the Parliament, with the charge to consult with the bishops about the *Reformatio*. The one result we know that came from this consultation was a promise of the bishops to deal with a revision of canon law in Convocation.

The consensus of historians of this period is that again it was the opposition of one particular lay person, Queen Elizabeth, who made it clear that she did not want to see Parliament as a primary forum for religious issues. She was not so heavy handed as John Dudley had been. Her father, Henry VIII, through men like Thomas Cromwell and Thomas Audeley, had worked with the members of Parliament holding the common law mentality expressed by St. German that the supremacy for both church and nation involved the king in Parliament. This had been followed in Edward's reign. Elizabeth used this approach with William Cecil's leadership in her first Parliament of 1559 to establish her position, which she later found to be a less than useful understanding. Elizabeth would work with Parliament on secular issues and with her bishops, minus Parliament, on ecclesiastical issues.

William Haugaard interprets Elizabeth's approach to be a move toward letting the church be the church. For example, she had not used a lay vicar as vicegerent as had Henry VIII; she did not use the Privy Council in church affairs as had her half-brother Edward. In the 1570s she could be seen as protecting the church from an intrusive laity in Parliament. In this view,

---

[106]Simonds D'Ewes, *The Journals of all the Parliaments during the Reign of Queen Elizabeth* (London, 1681), 156.

Elizabeth was supporting more, not less, clericalism in the government and discipline in the church. On the other hand, she was protecting the laity from clerical interference in secular life as was implied by a reformed discipline whether in its less radical form in the *Reformatio* or the more radical form represented by Withers, Cartwright, and the Puritan cause, which was soon to focus on the Admonition Controversy. The defeat of the more moderate form of reformed discipline expressed in a traditional church structure as in the *Reformatio* helped to incite the Presbyterian Puritan movement of the 1570s and 1580s.[107]

The lack of reformed discipline within the framework of the church as established provided tinder for the fire of a radical Puritanism. The use of the Court of High Commission together with the leadership of Archbishop John Whitgift and Richard Bancroft in the 1580s and 1590s to put out the fire, would be comparable to the lay intrusion of Henry's vicegerent and Edward's Privy Council, which Haugaard deplores. The Court of High Commission was an ecclesiastical court but with predominately lay membership. It made effective use of the *ex officio* proceedings which were so opposed to the practices of common law.

The bishops fulfilled their promise to the new parliamentary committee on the *Reformatio* in the Convocation of 1571. Canons of discipline were drawn up by Matthew Parker and accepted by the other bishops. They were not presented to Parliament for ratification.[108]

The standing of these canons in law was well expressed in an account by Strype telling of a letter to Parker from Edmund Grindal, Archbishop of York, thanking Parker for a copy of the canons.

> He thanked his Grace for the book of Articles and Discipline. But he stood in doubt whether they had *vigorem legis,* unless they had either been concluded upon in Synod, and after ratified by her Majesty's royal assent *in scriptus;* (fine words, added he, fly away as wind; and will not serve us, if we were empleaded in a *premunire;*) or else where confirmed by act of Parliament.[109]

Parker asked the queen for her *in scriptus,* but she responded by saying that since the bishops derived their authority from the supremacy of the queen, any act of Convocation was authorized by her. How that assurance would stand up in a crucial case of praemunire was an open question. The queen's policy

---

[107]Haugaard, *Elizabeth and the English Reformation*, 333-41. See also, Claire Cross, *The Royal Supremacy in the Elizabethan Church.* (London: George Allen and Unwin, Ltd., 1969), 68-95.

[108]Edward Cardwell, *Synodalia* (Oxford: The University Press, 1917), 111-31. Here one will find the Latin text adopted by the bishops in 1571. An English translation was made soon after their adoption in 1571 and is found in *A Booke of Certaine Canons, Concernyng Some Parte of the Discipline of the Church of England* (London: John Daye, 1571).

[109]Strype, *The Life and Acts of Matthew Parker,* 3 vols. (Oxford, 1821), 2:60.

toward religious issues coming up in Parliament made it fruitless for the bishops to take their canons to Parliament for ratification. As Grindal then perceived and soon was to experience personally, the Church was not exactly set free of lay intrusion by Elizabeth's policy. The canons were something less than enforceable.

Mark VanderSchaaf has made an analysis of the Canons of 1571 and has shown how the canons are in large part consistent with Martin Bucer's views on church discipline and particularly as expressed by Bucer during that time, when he and Matthew Parker were closely associated with each other at Cambridge. Of course, the canons also show some traces of the *Reformatio*.[110]

Of particular interest in the Canons of 1571 is the role of churchwardens who have responsibilities akin to the elders or seniors in the Protestant churches emphasizing the importance of church discipline. In addition to looking after the property of the local churches and maintaining decorum in the services, the churchwardens were to examine the credentials of ministers coming to churches to make sure the ministers had official approval. Once the ministers were in the parish, the churchwardens were to oversee the ministers' moral behavior and to report significant irregularities to the bishop. The churchwardens were also responsible for discipline among the laity, whether the offenses were minor or major in nature, and the churchwardens could initiate the process leading to excommunication. Thus it is that Patrick Collinson can write that in certain regions of England where Puritanism was strong, churchwardens served as "shadow" elders in the Elizabethan church. Robert E. Rodes, Jr., cites Bishop Cooper of the Lincoln Diocese in 1577, recommending that a minister use a group of churchwardens and some other upright parishioners to work in the disciplinary process.[111]

With the death of Archbishop Parker in 1575 and the sequestration soon thereafter of his successor, Edmund Grindal, the generation of those church leaders who were active in the days of Henry VIII and Edward VI was coming to an end. At the beginning of Parliament on January 20, 1580, Queen Elizabeth sent an admonition to the House of Commons that they were "not to deal with matters touching Her Majesty's Person or Estate, or touching Religion." Nevertheless, the House entertained a motion

> . . .made for a Publick Fast, with Prayer and Preaching to be exercised by this House for the Assistance of God's Holy Spirit, to the Furtherance of his glory, the Preservation of Her Majesty, and the better Direction of the Actions of this House.[112]

---

[110]VanderSchaaf, "Archbishop Parker's Efforts," 98-99.

[111]Patrick Collinson, *The Elizabethan Puritan Movement* (Berkeley: University of California Press, 1967), 351. Robert E. Rodes, Jr. *Lay Authority and Reformation in the English Church, Edward I to the Civil War* (Notre Dame: University of Notre Dame Press, 1982), 140.

[112]D'Ewes, *Commons Journal*, 1:115.

Elizabeth quickly showed her "great Mislikng of the Proceedings of the House," by its meddling in the matter of religion, and on January 25, she extracted an abject apology from the House for this "offence," "contempt," "negligence," and "rashness."

There was a discussion about excommunication in the Convocation meeting at the same time in 1580 and in Convocation there was a reference to the *Reformatio,*

> the means that were thought fit to be used instead of excommunication by Archbishop Cranmer, Peter Martyr, Bucer, Mr. Haddon, and others that did assemble for that purpose at that time, were imprisonment and mulct pecuniary.[113]

The *Reformatio* had now become a reference manual rather than a potential working part of the constitution of the Church of England.

During this last period of Elizabeth's reign, the idea of discipline in local congregations under elders and the pastor which was found in the hopes of many Protestants but which came into practice most effectively in Geneva and in Scotland, became identified with the Puritans who wanted to eliminate the "prelatic" bishops in a further reformation of the government of the Established Church in England. However, Richard Bancroft, that nemesis of the Puritans wrote in a tract in the 1580s:

> The Church of England doth holde and defend, that so the substaunce be observed, the Word of God trulye preached, the Sacramentes rightly administered, Vertue furthered, Vice suppressed, and that the Church be quietly and orderly governed. . .the names and offices by which these things are attained doesn't matter.[114]

The man whom Andrew Melville called "the capital enemy of all the Reformed Churches in Europe" displayed a conviction that discipline (virtue furthered, vice suppressed, and the church quietly and orderly governed) was, along with the preaching of the Word and administration of the sacraments, of the very substance of the church. When Bancroft came into a more significant position of power in the Church of England, he saw to it that ecclesiastical discipline played a key role in the formulation of the *Constitutions and Canons of 1604.* The discipline outlined in those canons resembles the form of discipline in all the reformed churches in those sections which concern the churchwardens or questmen who were to be "chosen by the ioynt consent of the Minister and the Parishioners."[115]

---

[113]Cardwell, *Synodalia,* vol. II, 550f.

[114]Albert Peel, ed. *Tracts Ascribed to Richard Bancroft* (New York: Cambridge University Press, 1951), 95.

[115]*Constitutions and Canons Ecclesiastical 1604,* H. A. Wilson, ed. (Oxford: Clarendon Press, 1923), canons LXXXIX, XC CIX, CX.

THE DELAY OF THE DISCIPLINARY REFORMATION

The 141 canons of 1604 had stronger royal backing than the 1571 canons of Matthew Parker since King James I gave the 1604 canons his support *in scriptu* by issuing a proclamation on July 16, 1604, dismissing the concern for further reformation as "fantasices" of the "troublesome spirits of some persons, who never receive contentment either in civil or in ecclesiastical matters." When Bancroft became Archbishop of Canterbury in November 1604, he could use the canons effectively without so much fear of violating praemunire as Grindal had expressed in 1571. The first Parliament under James I insisted that before canons and constitutions passed by Convocation could become law, they had to be ratified by Parliament and in the instance of the canons of 1604, Parliament refused to ratify them.

Many lawyers and judges who served in common law courts supported Puritans and others by insisting that the only laws valid in England were common law and statute law. In fact, Edward Coke had won cases in common law, and published them, in which he saw limits to the royal supremacy based on pre-Reformation ecclesiastical law.[116]

The Canons and Constitutions of 1604 did not have the status of statute law for opposition groups. As a result, when a preacher came to be charged with violating ecclesiastical law he would often cross file in a common law court and be sustained by the latter. This problem was precisely the problem that the committee of thirty-two was supposed to solve over seventy years before with a *Reformatio Legum Ecclesiasticarum*. A considerable coalition of common lawyers, merchants, lords, and parliamentarians came to side with Puritans in their concern for further reform.

Hence, in spite of the Canons of 1604, the poet John Milton could publish a pamphlet in 1641 in which he expressed amazement at the long delay of the reformation in regard to church discipline. Milton was reasonably satisfied that there had been a reform of doctrine. For him, the problem of the English situation was that while the reformation had begun with concern about church discipline rather than doctrine, after more than one hundred years it was still discipline, not so much doctrine, that needed to be reformed. Milton was aware of the attempt of the committee of thirty-two in Edward's reign, but Milton felt that the very makeup of the committee, which had such different "professions" and "ends," ensured that its work would come to nothing. We know that Milton came to appreciate the more liberal views of Martin Bucer on divorce expressed in his *De Regno Christi* of 1551, views that were stated in the canons of the *Reformatio* but which did not become a part of English law until the twentieth century.[117]

---

[116]Rodes, *Lay Authority and Reformation in the English Church*, 108.

[117]John Milton, *Of Reformation Touching Church-Discipline in England: and the Causes that hitherto have hindered it* (London: Thomas Underhill, 1641), 1-11. This treatise has been reprinted in *The Works of John Milton* (New York: Columbia University Press, 1931), vol. 3, pt. 1.

The reformation of the Church of England, as it was progressing under King Edward VI, was normative to many of these of the party of the opposition in church and state. John Pym (the leader of the majority in Parliament during those distressing times which led up to the break between King and Parliament and the resulting Civil War in England in the 1640s) gave an address at the crucial moment in the Parliament of 1629. Concerned with what was taking place in the life of the church under Archbishop William Laud's leadership, Pym cited what he regarded to be normative documents for the doctrine and government of the Church of England. He maintained that heading the list of those documents that give evidence to "what is the established religion of the realm" were the articles set forth in 1552, the catechism adopted in King Edward VI's days, the writings of Martin Bucer and Peter Martyr, and "the constant professions sealed with the blood of many martyrs such as Cranmer, Ridley, and others." He also listed the later Thirty-Nine Articles and "the articles agreed upon at Lambeth as the doctrine of the Church of England.[118]

With such sentiments as these expressed by a person who became a major leader in 1640 and 1641, it is not too difficult to understand why the *Reformatio legum ecclesiasticarum* published by John Foxe in 1571 (even though a bit musty) should have been republished in London in 1640 and 1641. The *Reformatio* had come from that normative period of the first reformation, which had become stuck, and it was part of the unfinished business of any further reformation.

What could be done? Parliament could name another committee. This was exactly what was suggested in a sermon before Parliament by Edmund Calamy, pastor of Saint Mary's, Aldermanbury, on December 22, 1641 at a most critical time in the whole relationship between king and Parliament:

> Now this is the great work that the Lord requireth at your hands, O ye Worthies of Israel: To . . . repair the breaches of God's House, to build it up in its beauty . . . and to bring us back not only to our first Reformation in King Edward's days, but to reform the Reformation itself. For we were then newly crept out of Popery, and (like men that come newly out of prison where they have been long detained) it was impossible but our garments should smell a little of the dungeon from which we came. . . . so it was with us in our first Reformation; it was a most blessed and glorious work like the resurrection from the grave; . . . . And as our Saviour Christ . . . commanded his disciples to unbind Lazarus, and to take away his grave-clothes, oh that you also would command the Apostles of Christ, the faithful and learned ministers of this kingdom to meet in a free National Synod, to inform you about taking away of these grave clothes and eyes-blinding napkins,

[118]Daniel Neal, *The History of the Puritans* (Bath: Toulmin Edition, 1794), vol. 2, pp. 185f.

or whatever else shall be prejudicial to the piety and purity of God's worship.[119]

In two years, that new committee of clergy, lords, and members of the House of Commons had been appointed by Parliament and was hard at work on further reformation. The parliamentary committee came to be known as the Westminster Assembly of Divines. The nation itself was by then involved in the Civil War, testing those old issues of whether the supremacy in both church and state means king alone or king together with Parliament, and in the showdown of absolutes, testing whether the godly king or the Holy Word comes first. Those who made the Holy Word central came also to encounter an authentic Erastianism in the Westminster Assembly. The *Reformatio,* even if it had become law, could not have solved any of those dilemmas.

---

[119]Edmund Calamy, *Englands Looking-Glasse,* Presented in A Sermon Preached before the Honorable House of Commons at their late solemne Fast, December 22, 1641. . . (London: December 22, 1641), p. 46.

First page of Table of Contents in Thomas Cranmer's hand

CONCERNING THE HIGHEST TRINITY
AND THE CATHOLIC FAITH[1]

Chapter 1. Concerning The Christian Faith To Be Embraced
And Professed By Everyone

Inasmuch as the power of ruling and the right of administering laws
has come to us from God, we must begin with him. When his nature
has been defined rightly and in due order, the provision of the remaining
laws will be easier. We have taken care that these laws be applied so
as to strengthen the true worship of God in our realm and to preserve
the holy state of the Church. For this reason, we desire and command
all persons to whom our authority extends in any way to accept and
profess the Christian religion. Those who undertake any thoughts or
actions against it, alienate God from themselves by their impiety.
Moreover, we who are ministers of the divine Majesty have ordained
that all properties and ultimately life itself are to be taken away by
judgement from all those who have committed such a monstrous crime
of impiety, and this is to be binding on our subjects no matter what
their name, place, or condition may be.

Chapter 2. Concerning What Is To Be Believed About The
Nature Of God And Of The Blessed Trinity

All of the children of God, reborn through Jesus Christ, with ★ a pure
heart and a good conscience and a real faith shall believe and confess
that there is one true and living God, eternal and incorporeal, impassible,
of immense power, wisdom and goodness, the Creator and Preserver
of all things both visible and invisible; and that in the unity of his
divine nature there are three persons of the same essence and eternity,
the Father, the Son, and the Holy Spirit; the Father, existing truly
from himself, not begotten or proceeding from anyone else; and the
Son, truly begotten by the Father; the Holy Spirit, moreover, proceeding
from both the Father and the Son. Nor is there to be placed in this
distinction of persons any diversity or inequality of nature, but as far

---

[1]There are two folio pages that precede the main body of the text. The first one
and a half pages consist of a Table of Contents in Cranmer's Hand. This is followed
by a second Table of Contents in Foxe's hand giving the order followed in the 1571
edition of the *Reformatio*. There then follows a blank page with the title of the first
chapter at the top of the page.

as substance or, as they say, the divine nature is concerned, all things are absolutely equal among them.

Chapter 3.   Concerning Christ And The Mysteries Of Our Redemption.

It must be believed, moreover, that when the fullness of time had come, the Son, who is the Word of the Father, assumed human nature in the womb of the blessed Virgin Mary from the substance of her own flesh in such a way that two natures, divine and human, were inseparably conjoined wholly and perfectly in the unity of a person; and because of this, there is one Christ, true God and true man; who truly suffered, was crucified, died, and was buried, descended into hell and rose on the third day, and through his blood reconciled the Father to us, offering himself as an oblation to him not only for original sin but also for all the sins which people have committed by their own will. ★

Folio 2r   Chapter 4.   Concerning The Two Natures Of Christ After The Resurrection.

It must be believed, moreover, that our Lord Jesus Christ, even after the resurrection, is possessed of a twofold nature; a divine one which is immense, uncircumscribed and infinite and which is everywhere and fills everything; and a human one, finite and circumscribed by the limits of a human body which, after it had purged our sins, ascended into heaven and there sits at the right hand of the Father so that it is not everywhere but rather must remain in heaven until the time of the restitution of all things, when he shall come to judge the living and the dead in order to render to each according to his works.

Chapter 5.   Concerning The Three Symbols.

Inasmuch as almost everything regarding the Catholic faith, both as to the most blessed Trinity as well as the mysteries of our redemption, is contained briefly in the three symbols, that is to say, the Apostolic, the Nicene, and the Athanasian, we therefore accept and embrace these three symbols as a compendium of our faith which can easily be proved by the most firm testimony of the divine and canonical scriptures.

Chapter 6.   What Are Canonical Scriptures Of The Old
                Testament.

Moreover, in order that the faithful may not be in doubt about which
scriptures are canonical, from which alone the dogmas of religion and
faith should be made manifest ★ and be confirmed, we have drawn   Folio 2v
up a list of them to be inserted here following that order in the Old
Testament which the Jews use; to wit:

The five books of Moses
    Joshua
    Judges
    Samuel (2)
    Kings (2)
    Isaiah
    Jeremiah
    Ezekiel
    Twelve Minor Prophets
    The Psalms
    Job
    Proverbs
    Daniel, excluding the apocrypha
    Chronicles (2)
    The Song of Songs
    Ruth
    Lamentations
    Ecclesiastes
    Esther
    Ezra and Nehemiah

All of these books which we have enumerated are certainly canonical.

Chapter 7.   Sacred Books Which Are Not Canonical

The books which are entitled the Wisdom of Solomon, Ecclesiasticus,
as well as Judith, Tobias, Baruch, Third and Fourth Esdras, the Books
of the Maccabees, together with the apocryphal parts of Esther and
Daniel are moreover to be read by the faithful and to be recited in the
Church since there is much in them which is of value for the edification
of the people. However, not so much authority should be given to
them that the dogmas of our faith either should or could be established
and constituted from these alone and apart from and without regard
to the other sources of undoubted scripture. ★ Therefore these are   Folio 3r
to be heard and read both with judgement and sobriety.

Chapter 8.   Concerning The Canonical Books Of The New
              Testament.

In the New Testament the church recognizes and admits as canonical
books these which follow:

The Four Gospels, namely, Matthew, Mark, Luke,
John

The Acts of the Apostles

The Epistles of Paul to: The Romans, Corinthians
(2), Galatians, Ephesians, Philippians, Colossians,
Thessalonians (2), Timothy (2), Titus, Philemon,
Hebrews.

Canonical[2] Epistles: James (1), Peter (2), John (3), Jude
(1), Apocalypse.

Chapter 9.   All the Things Which Must Be Believed Are From
              The Canonical Scriptures.

This, therefore, taken as a whole, is Holy Scripture in which we believe
that everything necessary to believe is fully and completely contained,
so much so that whatever is not read nor found in it, nor follows from
it nor is proved from it should be demanded by no one to be believed
as an article of faith. ★

Folio 3v   Chapter 10.   The Authority Of Divine Scripture Is Supreme In
                           The Church.

The Authority of Divine Scripture is believed to be such that no
excellence of any creature whatsoever should be preferred or equated
to it.

Chapter 11.   The Church Can Establish Nothing Contrary To
               Scripture, Nor Should She Force Anything
               Besides It To Be Believed Necessarily.

For this reason it is not lawful for the church to establish anything
which goes against the written Word of God nor can she so expound
one passage so that it contradicts another. Therefore, although the
church is the witness and the guardian and the preserver of the divine

[2] Added in Cranmer's hand.

books, nevertheless this prerogative is in no way conceded to her so that she might either make a decision contrary to these books or establish any articles of faith without the testimony of these books and force them on the Christian people as having to be believed.

Chapter 12. On Going Back In The Old Testament To The Hebrew Codices, In The New Testament To The Greek.

For the rest, if in the reading of the divine Scriptures, there should be anything ambiguous or obscure in the Old Testament, the interpretation of this should be sought from the fount of Hebrew truth, and in the New, the Greek codices should be consulted.

Chapter 13. The Symbols of Faith Are Useful In Interpreting Scripture.

The more important principles of the faith (which we call articles) taken from the most illustrious sacred Scriptures and ★ contained in a brief manner in the symbols are to be kept constantly in mind while expounding the sacred Words lest we should sometimes interpret or define anything contrary to them.

Folio 4r

Chapter 14. What Is To Be Thought Concerning The Councils.

For even though we willingly grant great honor to councils especially universal ones, nevertheless we judge all of them are to be placed far below the dignity of the canonical Scriptures and we also make an important distinction among the councils themselves. For some of them, such as especially those four, Nicaea, Constantinople, First Ephesus, and Chalcedon, we accept and embrace with great reverence. The same judgement we make concerning many others which were held afterward. In them we see and confess that the most holy fathers have established, according to divine Scripture, many things in a most important and sometimes holy way concerning the blessed and most high Trinity; Jesus Christ, our Lord and Saviour, and the human redemption procured through him. However, we do not consider our faith bound by these except to the extent that they are able to be confirmed by the holy Scriptures. For it is obvious that some councils have sometimes erred and have defined things which are contrary to each other, partly in our juridical actions and < even partly in matters of faith. >[3] Thus the councils are certainly to be read with esteem and Christian reverence, but for all that are to be examined according to the pious, certain, and correct rule of Scripture. ★

Folio 4v   Chapter 15.   What Is the Authority Of The Holy Fathers?

Finally, we consider that the authority of the orthodox fathers is in no way to be despised, for much of what they say is outstanding and useful. However, we do not admit that judgement should be made about the sacred Words on the basis of their opinion. For the sacred Words should be the rule and the indicator of all human doctrine for us. Even the fathers themselves were reluctant to grant themselves such an honor and frequently warned the reader that he should admit his own [i.e. the father's] opinions and interpretations only to the extent that he was aware that they agreed with the sacred Words. Therefore, let their authority and respect remain with them but let it yield and be subject to the truth and authority of what the sacred Books teach.

Chapter 16.   Epilogue.

Finally, because it would be a lengthy and obviously truly laborious task now clearly to write down everything which must be believed by the Catholic faith, we judge what we have said briefly concerning the most high Trinity, our Lord Jesus Christ, and the salvation imparted to the human race through him to be sufficient.

Chapter 17.   They Perish Who Oppose The Catholic Faith Or
Fall Away From It.

Nevertheless we are not able to pass over the fact that all of those who are unwilling to embrace the orthodox and catholic faith perish miserably and that those who abandon the faith they once acknowledged and accepted will be condemned even more severely.

Folio 5r   CONCERNING HERESIES

Chapter 1.   Who Are Heretics And Who Are Not

We establish as heretics all those who take any decree of our common faith in a sense other than that which has been determined by Sacred

---

[3]The phrase "even partly in matters of faith" is missing in the Foxe edition of 1571 and in Cardwell's of 1850.

Scripture and who dwell in error such that they in no way allow themselves to be removed from it. Nor in this matter should one wonder whether someone has been the author of error for himself or whether he is following and defining something taken from someone else. But there are those who do not remain in heresy nor defend it but are searching for truth. When they have been fully instructed by legitimate judges, they acknowledge their own fault to themselves and easily allow themselves to be corrected in it. They should not be placed among the number of heretics.

Chapter 2.   How Schismatics And Heretics Differ

Many people confuse schismatics with heretics, but there is a great difference between them. For schismatics do not have a faith different than the rest, but they separate themselves from that common society which should exist among Christians. ★

Thus it not infrequently happens that when they have wandered   Folio 5v
far from the pious practices and offices of others, they at length fall into some heresy. Thus they segregate themselves completely from the accepted community of the good.

Chapter 3.   ~~That which was the first heresy~~Concerning those who reject the authority of Sacred Scripture.[4]

Satan, the chief enemy of the Christian name, has mixed into the saving seed of Divine Scripture sown in the Church of God, such a powerful pestilence of heresies, as if cockles and weeds, that one could hardly count all the inflammations by which the Church has been burning and still is sadly burning. The Devil meanwhile daily accumulates more material of false opinions. Therefore, we by these, our constitutions, will enumerate briefly those heresies of which the present pestilence still presses strongly for the destruction of religion in our times. In which category those are most frightening (and thus will be named by us first) who remove and reduce Sacred Scriptures to the weakness of superstitious men. At the same time they are overconfident in themselves so that *they do not feel themselves held bound* by the authority of Scriptures, but *claim* a certain peculiar spirit from which they say all things are supplied in abundance for whatever they teach and do.[5] ★

[4]The original title was lined out and the new title was written in by Cranmer.

[5]Both of the additions are in Cranmer's hand. The material lined out cannot be read.

Folio 7r   Chapter 4.   ~~Which [Were] Second, Third, And Fourth~~
Concerning Those Who Either Totally Reject The Old Testament Or Totally Require It.[6]

Beginning in the earliest times the filth of the Marcionites, the Valentinians, and the Manicheans, as well as many other similar dregs has been flowing; by whom the Old Testament was repudiated as absurd and evil and not in agreement with the New. In the same way, many of our time are found, among whom the Anabaptists especially must be placed, for whom if anyone cites the Old Testament they hold it to be *already abrogated and entirely obsolete.*[7] They reduce everything contained in it to the ancient times of our ancestors. Therefore, they conclude that none of this material should come down to us. The opposite although equally impious error of others, is that of those who still adhere so much to the Old Testament that they demand of us as a necessity circumcision and certain ceremonies instituted by Moses.

~~The third error then also follows. It is the error of those who think that by the death of Christ such license has been granted to us and such impunity in all matters has been permitted that we are not even bound by those solemn precepts of the Decalogue nor finally by any other remaining holy practices of life which dot the Sacred Scriptures.~~[8]

Chapter 5.   ~~The Fifth [Heresy]~~ Concerning The Two Natures Of Christ[9]

There is a pernicious and widespread error about the twofold nature
Folio 7v of Christ. Some are of the sect of the Arians, holding ★ Christ to be so much of a man that they deny he is God. Others judge him to be so much God that they do not recognize him as a man. And they speak nonsense concerning the body divinely *assumed from heaven and fallen into the womb of the Virgin*[10] which as it were in transit flowed through Mary as though through a canal or a conduit. Some people frequently say this is the very makeup of the body of Christ. All of

---

[6]The original chapter appears to have been lined out by Cranmer and the new title is in his hand in the manuscript.

[7]This phrase inserted by Cranmer

[8]In the manuscript, this paragraph is Xed out. Although Cardwell claims this cancellation is at Cranmer's hand, it is impossible to determine if this is accurate or not.

[9]Cranmer seems to have lined out the first word of the title and inserted the word "two."

[10]Opposite this line, Cranmer has written in the margin "Valentinian."

these errors are to be corrected by the authority of the Sacred Scriptures in such a way that Christ is accepted in his higher nature as God eternal and as the equal of God the Father. In his human nature he truly has a body *made in time not more frequently than once neither from any other material than* the true and sole substance of the Virgin Mary and just like other human bodies circumscribed by its own limits of place. These people *assert that the Word was changed into the nature of flesh which as soon after death* as possible was received into heaven and *again* changed *back* and absorbed into the Divine Nature. Those imitate this madness who give such broad limits to the body of Christ that, they believe it either to be *simultaneously in all* places *or to be abiding in an infinite number* of places. If we were to profess this we would be taking human nature away from Christ. ★ For just as the nature of God assumes this for itself, it permeates everything, so also it is always an attribute of the human that it be circumscribed by certain limits of place.[11]   Folio 8r

Chapter 6.   *Concerning The Holy Spirit.*[12]

For just as those rotten members must be segregated from the body of the church who have such a perverse opinion concerning Christ the head, so also is detestable the impudence of those who with Macedonius conspire against the Holy Spirit, not acknowledging Him as God.

Chapter 7.   ~~The Eighth heresy~~ Concerning Original Sin, Free Will And Justification.[13]

Regarding the sinful downfall contracted from our birth which we call original sin, we must avoid and dispel the error first of all of the Pelagians and also of the Anabaptists among whom there is agreement contrary to the *truth* of Sacred Scripture in this: that original sin *existed in Adam alone and did not come down to his descendants* nor did it bring any perversity to our nature except that from the sin of Adam there is proposed the harmful example of sinning which invites men to imitate and exercise the same evil. And in like manner we must proceed against those who place so much strength and force in the free will that they decide that by it alone without *any special* grace of Christ ★ it is possible   Folio 8v

[11]The sequence of sentences in this paragraph are those of the manuscript. Foxe altered the sequence and Cardwell followed Foxe. All of the changes indicated in the above paragraph are in Cranmer's hand. In the manuscript where chapter 5 ends above, Cranmer inserted a new chapter heading, "Concerning the Holy Spirit," which follows.

[12]This is in Cranmer's hand and it is inserted between the lines showing that what was once a continuous paragraph is now divided by the new chapter heading.

[13]Again this appears to be Cranmer's doing for the new chapter title is in his hand.

for men to lead upright ~~and perfect~~ lives. Moreover, those should not be heard whose impiety attacks the salutary and scripturally founded doctrine of our justification in which it must be held that the justice of men is not to be weighted by the influence of works, < but that it proceeds from faith alone which we have firmly declared in Jesus Christ. Nevertheless, it should always follow in all respect that, since they are justified by faith, they occupy themselves in good works. Sacred Scripture demands these as the necessary fruits which proceed from a true and sincere faith. > [14]

Chapter 8.   ~~The Ninth~~ *Concerning The Innocence Perfection* Of The Justified And ~~The Tenth~~, *Concerning Works Of Supererogation.* [15]

By means of our laws we must crush the pride of those who attribute such a degree of perfection of life to justified men as the weakness of our nature cannot bear. Nor are any persons except Christ able to claim for themselves that surely they are devoid of all sin if they have turned their mind to living rightly and piously. And they want this absolute perfection of conduct to happen in this present life, although it is weak and fragile and inclined toward the destruction of virtue and duty. Then too, the arrogance of those who have introduced certain works of supererogation must be restrained and subdued by the authority of laws. By means of these they think not only that they

Folio 9r are able ★ fully and completely, to satisfy the laws of God, but also that there is something in them over and above that which the commands of God require *so that they are able to gain merit for themselves and to apply merits to others.* [16]

Chapter 9.   ~~The Eleventh [heresy]~~ Concerning the ~~condition~~ *fall* of the justified and ~~The Twelfth [heresy]~~ *concerning the sin against the Holy Spirit.* [17]

They also have a perverse opinion concerning the justified who believe they are not able to fall into sin after they have once been made just. Or if they should happen to do something prohibited by the laws of God, God will not consider those things as sins. Opposite to these in opinion but equal in impiety are they who affirm that any mortal sin

---

[14]All the changes in this paragraph from the insertions to the phrase lined out are in Cranmer's hand. The section at the end bracketed by carets, although in the manuscript, is missing in Foxe's edition of 1571 and that of Cardwell of 1850.

[15]These changes are in Cranmer's hand.

[16]This last phrase was added by Cranmer.

[17]These title changes are in Cranmer's hand.

whatsoever which is freely committed by us after receiving baptism is an act against the Holy Spirit *and cannot be forgiven.*[18]

Chapter 10. Concerning Masses and Purgatory

Exceedingly curious is the perversity of certain persons who expect the forgiveness of sins, but do not believe this to be fully and in every way accomplished by the death of Christ applied to us through faith alone. Therefore they seek to perpetuate other sacrifices by which they may be cleansed, and to this end ★ they employ masses. < They believe that in them a sacrifice is offered to God the Father which without doubt is the body and blood of our Lord Jesus Christ in truth and, as they likewise say, in reality. Its purpose is to obtain the forgiveness of sins, and to procure the salvation as much of the dead as of the living. > ~~Also they give to the masses such broad authority that they consider that the torments of purgatory are sometimes diminished by them and frequently are taken away completely.~~ < In this way they to a great extent detract from that unique sacrifice which Christ the Son of God offered on the cross and most fully presented to God the Father. And the priesthood which is the property of the one Christ, they lower to the miserable level of man. > [19] Truly, Sacred Scriptures reserve only the death of Christ for the cleansing of sins, and they do not lay down any other sacrifice which can have any power in this matter. Moreover, concerning their purgatory, there is indeed not even one syllable to be found in the Holy Scriptures.

Folio 9v

Chapter 11. ~~14. Concerning The Light Of Nature; 15. Concerning Temporal Punishments Of The Damned~~ Concerning The Damnation Of Unbelievers And The Impious.[20]

Dreadful and monstrous is the boldness of those who contend that in every religion or sect which men have professed, salvation for them is to be hoped for if they only strive mightily for innocence and integrity of life according to the light which shines in them infused by nature. Pests of this type are transfixed by the authority of Scripture.

[18]Cranmer added this last phrase to the paragraph.

[19]The material contained between the two sets of carets is not in this chapter of the manuscript but was in Chapter 20, Concerning the Abuses of the Mass. Foxe's marginal note at the beginning of this chapter gives the instruction to move that chapter to this place. Foxe and Cardwell followed this instruction in their editions. It would appear that the phrase that is lined out before the carets was done by Cranmer for the stroke of the line appears to be his.

[20] Cranmer struck the two lines designated as 14 and 15 and inserted his new title.

For there the sole and unique name of Jesus Christ is commended to us so that all salvation should come to us from him. Not less is the madness of those who in this our age again bring forth the dangerous heresy of Origen. It states that surely all men (however much they shall have contaminated themselves with sins) are finally to achieve salvation ~~since they will have satisfied divine providence from the commandment by reason of the greatness of the punishments imposed on them because of their sins~~ *when for a time set by divine justice they shall have paid the penalty for the shameful acts they have committed.*[21] But sacred Scripture frequently declares that the damned are to be passed into perpetual torment and eternal flames. ★

Folio 10r   Chapter 12.   Concerning The Annihilation Or Sleep Of Souls And The Resurrection.

Certain persons impiously philosophize that the souls of men departing from this life, when once they have left bodies behind and up to the final time of the last judgement, are either enveloped in sleep or return to absolutely nothing. But at the time when the day of the last judgement comes, they are again either aroused from sleep or rise again from ruin with their own bodies. Akin to these is the error concerning the resurrection which many (agreeing with Hymenaeus and Phyletus) say to be already finished and concluded. This is because it should refer only to the soul which Christ (who by the mediation of his death has poured forth grace on us) has aroused precisely from the death of sins. But this doctrine of theirs is uneven and truncated. For in such manner as Jesus Christ himself was recalled from death to life with a whole, true and complete body, *with his soul neither perishing nor sleeping,* so too we who are the members of Christ *shall indeed after* Folio 10v *death live.* ★ But then following our head we shall rise with both souls and bodies for that last judgement.[22]

Chapter 13.   Concerning ~~Removal of~~ Magistrates[23]

Would that the wild stupidity of the Anabaptists might be overthrown! They deny that it is licit for Christians to hold the office of magistrate as though on that account Christ had come down to earth in order to abolish the administration of public affairs. For indeed the Holy Spirit has established princes and magistrates to be the ministers of God so that they may impart his favor to those who do well and restrain evil actions with punishments. For if these two should be

---

[21]This phrase was lined out by Cranmer and he put in the new phrase.

[22]The additions in this chapter are in Cranmer's hand.

[23]Apparently struck out by Cranmer

absent in human affairs there would follow the greatest confusion of all things. ~~Therefore in our republic, legitimate public officials of every kind will remain and will take care that human laws as well as and in the first place, Divine laws, are firmly and strictly preserved.~~[24]

Chapter 14. Concerning The Community Of Goods And Wives[25]

There must also be excluded the community of goods and possessions introduced by the same Anabaptists which they promote *to such an extent* that to no one at all does there remain anything which belongs to him and is his alone. In this matter their ★ speech is amazing since they must realize that theft is prohibited by *divine Scripture* and alms giving, which we are to give from our own resources, seems to be praised in both testaments. Neither of these certainly would be possible unless the ownership of goods and personal possessions were left to Christians. Certain Nicolaitans also emerged from the deficiencies of Anabaptism. Certainly the most defiled of men, they argue that the use of women *and even of wives* should be promiscuously spread about among all. Their foul and sinful lust is first of all contrary to piety and scripture, and moreover, violently attacks all civil decency as well as that natural and incorrupt light shining in our mind.[26] Folio 11r

Chapter 15. Concerning Oaths And *Participation In The Lord's Supper.*[27]

Moreover, the Anabaptists do not allow the legitimate use of oaths. In this they proceed contrary to the opinion of the Scriptures as well as the examples of the fathers of the Old Testament, and also of the apostle Paul and even of Christ and God the Father. Their oaths are frequently repeated in the holy books. ★ Then they separate themselves from the body of the church and refuse to come to the Lord's holy table with others, and claim that they are held back either because of the wickedness of the ministers or because of [the wickedness of] other brethren, as if excommunication could be perceived in someone before the church has pronounced against *him*[28] a sentence of excommuni- Folio 11v

[24]Someone (Cranmer?) put a diagonal cancellation through this phrase.

[25]The original title in the manuscript was "19. Concerning community of goods" and "20. Concerning community of wives." These were lined out and the new tile put in.

[26]All of the changes shown in this paragraph are insertions in Cranmer's hand.

[27]Cranmer has struck the numbers 21 and 22 and changed the title to what is above.

[28]This is an insertion in Cranmer's hand.

cation in which it is declared that he is to be avoided like a heathen and a publican.

Chapter 16. Concerning Ministers And Holy Orders

Similar is the madness of those who separate the ordination of ministers from the church, denying that certain doctors, pastors and ministers ought to be stationed in certain places. They do not allow lawful [religious] vocations, or the solemn imposition of hands, but spread the power of publicly teaching to all who, whenever they have a smattering of sacred letters, claim to possess the Holy Spirit; and they employ them not only for teaching but also for governing the church and administering the sacraments. Indeed, all of these practices are clearly contrary to the writings of the Apostles.[29]

Chapter 18. Concerning Baptism[30]

Next, their cruel impiety attacks baptism which they do not wish to be imparted to infants but altogether without reason. For the infants
Folio 12r of Christians belong to God ★ and to the Church no less than did formerly the offspring of the Hebrews to whom circumcision was administered in infancy. And so, baptism should be administered to our infants because they are sharers of the same promise and divine covenant and were received by Christ with the greatest kindness.[31] Many errors are piled up by others concerning baptism which some stupified people look upon in such a way that they believe that from that very external element itself the Holy Spirit emerges and that all his power, and strength by which we are recreated, and grace, and all the other gifts proceeding from Him come into being in the very founts of baptism. In summary, they want our whole regeneration to be due to that sacred will which meets our senses. But in truth the salvation of souls, the renewing of the spirit, and the benefit of adoption, by which God acknowledges us as His children come to us from the divine mercy flowing to us through Christ as well as from the promise
Folio 12v apparent in Sacred Scripture. Also, to be seen as impious ★ is the

---

[29]In the manuscript at this point on fol. 11v, there follow three lines on baptism which are the first part of Chapter 18 Concerning Baptism. This means that the order of the two chapters is reversed with 17 following 18, and that is the sequence followed here. A marginal note in the manuscript acknowledges this reversal. The changes in the chapter are in Cranmer's hand.

[30]The chapter title is inserted between two lines of the text, and it is in Cranmer's hand. The number he inserted is 18 and not 17.

[31]Between the end of this sentence and the beginning of the next, two chapter titles have been lined out and a line has been drawn to link the two parts as one.

crude superstition of those who connect God's grace and the Holy
Spirit so much with the elements of the sacraments that they clearly
affirm that no child of Christians will attain eternal salvation who has
been seized by death before he was able to be baptized. We judge[32] the
matter far differently. For salvation is to be denied to them alone who
despise this holy fount of baptism or who shrink away from it because
of pride or haughtiness. Since such insolence does not belong to the
age of children, nothing can be discerned by the authority of Scriptures
against their salvation. Indeed, on the contrary, since the common
promise includes them, we must have the greatest hope for their
salvation.

Chapter 17. Concerning The Nature Of The Sacraments.

The temerity is ~~contrary~~ great also of those who so diminish the
sacraments that they wish them to be taken as bare signs and only
external tokens as though by the knowledge of these the religion of
Christian men could be distinguished from others. Nor do they realize
how great a sin it is to believe that these holy institutions of God ~~are
emptied out and destroyed~~ are empty and meaningless. For when these
institutions are dispersed among us, faith is strengthened by the power
of the divine Spirit, ★ conscience is built up, and the promise of the   Folio 13r
forgiveness of sins procured through Christ is certified by these
sacraments as though by a certain seal. Moreover, by the word of God
which takes place both the faithful are instructed by the nature of the
symbols used concerning the price of our redemption procured through
Christ, and the Holy Spirit is more abundantly instilled by grace in the minds
of the faithful. Furthermore, the covenant which was made between God
and us through Christ is strengthened so that He is our God and we
are his special people. And we bind ourselves to the abolition of sins
and to undertaking a life of integrity. If these things are correctly
reflected upon, it is necessary that the calumny of those who want to
leave the nature of the sacraments impotent and bare must become
silent.[33]

Chapter 19. Concerning Transubstantiation In The Eucharist
    And The So-called Impanation Of The Body Of
    Christ.

Even in the matter of the Eucharist there has crept in the very dangerous
error of those who teach, preach and argue that by virtue of certain

---

[32]The phrase "we judge" is Cranmer's insertion.

[33]The insertions and cancellations are in Cranmer's hand.

Folio 13v

words which the minister whispers toward the symbols of this sacrament, the bread ★ is changed or (as they themselves say) is transubstantiated into the body of Christ, and likewise the wine into the blood. Because this dogma is indeed opposed to scripture, disagrees with the nature of a sacrament, and so distorts the true body of Christ that either it leads to the divine nature being diffused everywhere, or being mixed together with an apparition or a certain artifice, we wish to get rid of the whole of this papist dream-inducing drug and clearly acknowledge the true nature of bread and wine remaining in the eucharist which the Holy Spirit attests to in evident words. Therefore, we do not allow this sacrament to be raised on high, nor to be carried about, nor to be preserved, nor to be adored; and so we give no more veneration to the eucharist than to baptism and the word of God. Except for the fact that the symbols *of bread and wine* retain the pious and scripturally instituted use of communion, we *do not* wish them to have ~~exactly the same~~ *a greater* estimation than have the bread and wine which are in daily use among us. They are stuck in the same mire who place the substance of bread and wine in the eucharist, but who think that by the power of the consecration applied through the minister the true and natural body and blood of Christ is added and

Folio 14r

mixed together with the natures of the symbols, ★ and placed underneath them, even up to the point that whoever approaches the table of the Lord, be they pious, receive the true and natural body of Christ and his pressed-out blood together with the bread and wine. But in truth because the symbols of the sacraments ~~they are thus joined together and carry the signification of the things and have a certain vivid representation of them, [while] they nevertheless do not contain or express the things themselves in their members and substances;~~ *do not contain within themselves really and, as they say, substantially the things which they signify;* and because it has been determined by Scripture that Christ brought his human nature to heaven nor is he about to descend to earth with it before the time of the last judgement; moreover since this fabricated presence of the natural body of Christ has no greater power for the edification of our religion than that presence of Christ which is perceived by faith *and indeed brings with it many inexplicable questions and false and revolting assertions;* we wish by all means to destroy this absurd doctrine by which the body and blood of Christ sneak into the eucharist and are included in it naturally, and, as they say, substantially. For it is foreign and alien to the sacred writings. Next, it is contrary to the truth of the human nature which Christ assumed and is far removed from the nature of the sacraments.

Folio 14v

Finally, it is the common bilge ★ of the many superstitions brought together into the church of God.[34]

Chapter 20. Concerning Marriage[35]

From the very beginning of the Church there has been a large group
of heretics which shunned marriage as a filthy and impure thing, and
they either completely banished it from the assembly of the faithful
★ or if it were permitted because of our weakness, they thought that   Folio 15r
nevertheless it should in no way be repeated. Since their opinion was
in violent disagreement with the rule of piety which is obvious in the
sacred writings, it has been rejected with an old censure of the church,
time and time again. But the devil has proposed something else in
place of this impiety, undoubtedly so that all who profess the solitary
life, or are involved in the administration of the church might lose the
faculty of contracting marriage for all time. Since this evil custom of
theirs is opposed to Sacred Scripture, we wish it to be completely
abolished and held by no one.

Chapter 21. Concerning The Roman Church And The Power Of The Roman Pontiff.

We must keep in check by the bonds of law the insanity of those who
think that the Roman Church was established on such a rock that it
has neither been in error nor is capable of erring, although many of
its errors can be repeated by most people's past memory, and even
our own, regarding in part that which should shape our life ★ and in   Folio 15v
part those things by which the faith should be established. Wherefore,
intolerable is the error of those who wish the universal church of the
whole Christian world to be held together by the rule of the Roman
bishop alone. For we so define the church which can be perceived
that it is the coming together of all faithful men in which Sacred
Scripture is honestly proclaimed, and the sacraments, at least in those
parts which are necessary, are administered according to Christ's
instruction.

Chapter 22. Concerning Predestination.

On the fringe of the Church many live with wild and dissolute customs.
Since they are overly curious about the matter itself, carried away by
extravagance and directly at odds with the spirit of Christ, they always

---

[34]The insertions and deletions in this paragraph are in Cranmer's hand.

[35]At the end of chapter 19, at the top of folio 14v, the first five lines are Xed out.
The notation in the margin in Cranmer's hand indicates this section and the following
eleven lines are to be transferred to the earlier chapter 10 where they are found in this
translation.

affirm in sermons predestination and rejection or, as they customarily say, reprobation. Thus, God in his eternal plan has decided with certainty about salvation and ruin, and hence they seek a hiding place from their own evil deeds, crimes, and perversity of every kind. And when pastors condemn their shameful and dissipated life, they place the fault of their crimes on the will of God and with this defense consider ★ the reprimands of their faults to have been refuted. And so, in the end, by the devil's influence, they are flung headlong into a pit of desperation or they lapse into a kind of relaxed and easy security of life, *without either repentance or awareness of their crimes*.[36] These two abuses appear to have a different nature but the same result. Instructed by the Sacred Scriptures, we in truth propose such a doctrine on this matter that an attentive and accurate notion regarding our predestination and election is upheld. Regarding these the decision was made by the will of God before the foundation of the world was laid. Therefore, this attentive and serious notion which we have spoken of in regard to these matters, delights with a kind of sweet and joyful consolation the souls of the pious men inflamed by the Spirit of Christ who feel keenly the subjection of the flesh and of the bodily members, and who strive upward to the affairs of heaven. For this notion confirms our faith in the eternal salvation which will come to us through Christ, kindles the most intense flames of love for God, marvelously prompts the giving of thanks, leads us most quickly to good works, and keeps us very far from sins, O because we have been chosen by God and made ready by his Son. ★ This singular and excellent condition demands of us the greatest soundness in behavior and the most excellent perfection of virtue. Finally, it diminishes arrogance in us so that we do not believe that through our powers things are accomplished which are granted by the voluntary beneficence and infinite goodness of God. Moreover, we consider that no one is able to bring about cleansing of his own faults in this situation. For God brings about nothing unjustly and does not ever impel our reluctant wills to sinful acts. For this reason, everyone should be admonished by us that in actions to be undertaken they not make reference to the decrees of predestination, but adapt the overall plan of their life to God's laws. And let them consider the promises *to the good* and the threats to the wicked *generally*[37] put forth in the Sacred Scriptures. For we ought to go forward in devotion to God by those ways and abide by that will of God which we see opened up in the Sacred Scriptures.

Folio 16r

Folio 16v

---

[36]This change is in Cranmer's hand.

EPILOGUE

A great vile medley of other heresies could be heaped up, but at the time we have only wished to name those which in these times of ours are spread abroad most powerfully through the Church. All the faithful are bearing witness in the name ★ of God and our Lord Jesus Christ Folio 17r in order to draw to themselves very far away from these most pestilent opinions. And we are also demanding vehemently from those who administer church and state that they take care, as far as they can, to have those heresies taken out by the roots and completely thrust out of our kingdom.

CONCERNING JUDGEMENTS AGAINST HERESIES

Chapter 1.   Under Which Judges Heresy May Be Investigated

A judgement regarding heresies is fashioned in four manners: by investigation, or accusation, or evangelical denunciation, or restriction. He who becomes a defendant either by accusation, investigation, or evangelical denunciation because he has either affirmed, defended, preached, or taught some heresy will plead his case before *his* bishop or archbishop. An appeal, nevertheless, is granted to the defendant from the bishop to the archbishop and from the archbishop to our royal person. And if the case is brought down to the defendants [?], we want three bishops to be employed who are most learned in the knowledge of sacred scripture, and [we want] to be joined to them, two doctors of civil law, outstanding in respect to experience and knowledge of the law, so that by them the whole case can be treated with reason and in [due] order. Those indeed *who are not bishops* and have the privilege of [that] position, and are called exempt, will plead their cause before either those bishops or archbishops within whose dioceses their exempt position has stood.[38] ★

Chapter 2.   The Manner Of Proceeding Against Heretics   Folio 17v

First, however, as often as the crime of heresy is charged through an inquisition, whether infamy has been fully established against the defendant, or the defendant has made no objection to the charge, howsoever much he afterwards denies that those points apply to him, still, unless he exhibits suitable bail bond, as would be required by

---

[38]The sequence of the sentences in the manuscript was altered in the 1571 edition so that the sentence beginning "Those indeed. ..." followed the sentence ending "... bishop or archbishop." and the sentence beginning "An appeal. ..." became the last sentence in the chapter. The insertions and deletions are in Cranmer's hand.

law, he can be detained in prison in the meantime by the bishop until the case comes to an end. ~~If indeed he confesses his error and says that he is ready to abandon it, he should be dismissed, but with this caution, that if he has harmed or corrupted anyone by his speech or doctrine, he should make amends to them according to the judgement of the ordinary, lest the contagion of error should creep in and spread outward among the people.~~[39] Beyond this, if one who has been called to trial by an authorized judge on account of a crime of heresy should disregard [the summons], and if with insolence of mind he was not present at the [assigned] time, let him first incur the punishment of excommunication. Thereupon, as soon as it has been possible for the ordinary to make investigation and to apprehend [the man], let him be thrown into prison until he has interposed an abundant bail bond, as would be required by law.[40] When, indeed, the crime of heresy proceeds through inquisition or ★ evangelical denunciation, it should be handled summarily, without the solemn preparation of matters pertaining to trials.

Folio 18r

Chapter 3.   *Bringing Heretics To Their Senses* [41]

And since in trials all things are debated on both sides and either the defendant is convicted or he himself confesses the crime, he should first be warned to cease from error. But if he promises that he will do so, he will bind himself to it by oath. Thereafter, *at the discretion of the judge,* he will bring forth the fruits of penitence, and so at length, he will be dismissed. Nevertheless, there is this proviso: that he should repair, as far as he is able, the scandal to his brothers (if there has been any); and, *lest the contagious error spread,*[42] that he should publicly confess in those places where he spread the error that he has been turned against the heresy. But if he tenaciously clings to his heresy, let him be sent away for a while to men gifted in learning so that they can recall him to the [true] way. And if, by their persuasion, he gives up his opinions, he can, after an oath has been interposed that he wishes to give up the heresy, be set free. We always repeat that condition set down before: that he should certainly give definite signs of his penitence and should instruct his brothers through contrary doctrine on those points where before he had infected them with heresy.

---

[39]It is hard to determine who struck out this section of the manuscript but the stroke is similar to that made by Cranmer.

[40]A chapter title has been lined out here and then a line drawn to include the next sentence into chapter 1.

[41]Added in Cranmer's hand.

[42]The insertions are in Cranmer's hand.

Chapter 4.   Obstinate Heretics

Those, indeed, who accept neither warning nor [sound] doctrine in
any ★ way but have absolutely persisted in heresy are first to be   Folio 18v
declared heretics by the judge and thereupon to be inflicted with the
punishment of excommunication. When this decision has been carried
out, if within the space of sixteen days they have withdrawn from the
heresy, let them first publicly exhibit clear indications of penitence.
secondly, let them solemnly swear that they will never revert to that
heresy. Thirdly, let them make public satisfaction by contrary teaching,
and, when all these measures have been fulfilled, let them be pardoned.
But before that, let a strong and serious exhortation be directed to
them to disassociate themselves completely after that time from the
present error as well as from all other heresies. When indeed the error
has settled so far within and is so deeply rooted that the defendant
cannot be bent to the truth even by the sentence of excommunication,
then since all other remedies have been used, let him finally be sent
away to the civil magistrates to be punished. [or let him be driven into
perpetual exile, or be sunk down to the unending darkness of prison,
or let him be punished in some other way in accord with the prudent
consideration of the magistrate, as seems most conducive to his
conversion.][43]

Chapter 5.   T̶h̶o̶s̶e̶ ̶W̶h̶o̶ ̶A̶b̶j̶u̶r̶e̶ ̶H̶e̶r̶e̶s̶y̶ On Judgements Against
Heresies[44]

He, indeed, who has obligated himself by oath to repudiate a heresy
should first profess that he abhors completely that heresy which is
the concern of the present discussion. Next, he will publicly affirm
the contrary opinion, ★ and he will openly testify that he follows and   Folio 19r
firmly holds to all things in this matter which the holy and universal
church of God follows and holds by the authority of the sacred
scriptures, and that he will never again relapse[45] into heresy from
which he has now desisted.

---

[43] The phrase set between the brackets has been added to the manuscript and is
in Vermigli's hand.

[44] The title originally appeared at the top of folio 19r but wrote in the new title
at the bottom of folio 18v.

[45] In the manuscript the word "rediturum" is written above the word translated
"relapse." The hand appears to be that of Vermigli.

Chapter 6.   How Heresy Ought To Be Proven

And because the crime of heresy causes great fierceness [in people] and the highest abuse, a man cannot be fully convicted by ill-repute only, nor by other semi-complete (as the law puts it) and shortened examinations of that kind. But, nevertheless, these very things have such power that they bring home to the defendant the necessity of clearing himself. If this clearing, certainly, cannot be properly fulfilled by the defendant, then he ought to be condemned immediately for the [heresy] itself.

Chapter 7.   How The Iniquity Of Judges Should Be Punished

Just as heresies must be absolutely excluded from our domain (as far as is possible), so we must with the greatest effort be on guard lest anyone be called into the danger of so horrible and odious a crime Folio 19v without just ★ cause. Therefore, if a judge, whether because he hates someone or in order to get money or to show abuse to him, has unjustly brought against [him] this case of heresy and has established legal proofs against him by the fault of the judge, let the punishment be taken from him by the decision of a higher judge.

Chapter 8.   How A Decision Is To Be Arrived At And How
Witnesses Are To Be Questioned

When the crime of heresy is recognized, let the judges in arriving at a decision take counsel of a few theologians and legal consultants who have already carefully examined all the proceedings of the case. Also it is fitting that the witnesses who will be summoned be examined by the judges themselves unless it happens that illness or another just cause has impeded the judges. If they themselves are by chance impeded, let them substitute for themselves two honest men to whom the duty of investigating the testimony can be safely committed.

Chapter 9.   What Is To Be Done When The Verdict In A Case
Of Heresy Is Pending And The Defendant Has
Fled

If the case in a heresy dispute is pending and in the interim the defendant slips away to another place where the former judge cannot Folio 20r continue to conduct the trial, ★ the judge will demand, either through a sheriff or through the prefect of the town in that area, where the defendant is going about (whom they call a mayor) that he take care to return the defendant to him and to the appropriate law court. Then the mayor or sheriff, when he has understood the judge's directive written in the judge's own hand and fortified by his seal, will immediately provide that the defendant be apprehended, and will dispatch him to the proper judge. But if the mayor or sheriff neglects to do so, he will immediately be judged[46] excommunicated because of the very matter which he neglected, and separated from the Church.

Chapter 10. What Should Be Determined In Respect To Those Who Have Confessed Or Been Convicted.

In the case of one who has confessed the crime of heresy or been convicted in such a way that the sentence of the judge has turned out against him and been pronounced: if he has not appealed nor received a concession during the time for an appeal, nor has made satisfaction for the crime in the opinion of his own judge *no pardon will help him, but*[47] from that time he has been made infamous by his very insolence. Nor may he at any time be accepted for the duties of a public officer, nor for ~~giving~~ *counsel*,[48] nor for giving testimony. ★ He will not even have the right to make a will. Beyond this, however, whatever business he has with others, he would indeed be compelled to respond in judgement to all of them but no one of them to him. For we have determined that the crime of heresy is public. For since the religion of God common to all is violated, it seems good for the punishment to be inflicted publicly on him. Folio 20v

Chapter 11. The Penitence of Church Ministers

If it should happen that ministers of the Church are the defendants in a heresy case, and if when convicted in the case they have submitted to the sentence and afterwards they put aside the error and return to their senses; nevertheless by common law they will not return to their former position in the Church. For ministers of the Church should have a sound reputation not only among the members of their own household but also among outsiders. Although it is right that the matter should proceed by common law in this way, nevertheless if circumstances occur in such a way that the Church would be very much stripped of good ministers, or if the cause of quiet and concord demands it, we permit this to the ecclesiastical judge: that he may allow those who repent of their errors to return to their offices and positions ★ in order that the necessities of the churches may be helped Folio 21r

---

[46]The word "videbitur" in the manuscript was lined out but this appears to be the correction of a scribal error.

[47]This is an insertion in Cranmer's hand.

[48]The word "giving" has been crossed out in the manuscript so that "a counselor" is a possible translation.

and peace may not be impeded. Nevertheless, in this matter we wish this to be adhered to: that they not ascend to a greater position in the Church than the one they previously held unless the greatest necessity unable to be met in any other way has demanded it. ★

Folio 22r

CONCERNING BLASPHEMY[49]

Chapter 1.　In Which Matters Blasphemy May Be Involved

Of every class of sins none is more horrifying, nor is God our Lord more vehemently disdainful of one or caused greater insult, nor does the sharp spear of vengeance turn more quickly against any sin than the crime of blasphemy. [It happens] when, turning against God with the most conceited manner of contempt or carried away in a fervid attack of fury against him, we pour forth abuse either against him or against those things which pertain to his most divine majesty. And the difference between blasphemy and heresy is that blasphemy contemptuously and wrathfully hurls insults against God while heresy erroneously and ignorantly takes up false opinions.

Chapter 2.　How Blasphemy Should Be Punished

Therefore, let it be established by us that this accursed unholy act of blasphemy, as soon as it has been legally established, not be tolerated by the bishops in any way but be constrained by means of the same
Folio 22v　penalty with which the persistent insanity of heretics is punished. ★ And not without cause, since the wrath of God so blazed up against this madness of blasphemy in ancient times that to subdue and overwhelm the one guilty of this crime a gathering of the people and of the entire multitude took place so that by means of a public stoning the crime might thus be stamped out. And God himself bears witness by the public calamities which he often brings about that in them he is taking revenge for the shameful act of blasphemy.[50] ★

---

[49]The manuscript originally had a section titled, "Blasphemy, in which." The "in which" (quibus) was then crossed out. The chapter title was then written, possibly in Cranmer's hand, "In Which Thing It May Be Involved." Then, perhaps when the "quibus" was cancelled, the word "blasphemy" was added making the chapter read as it does here.

[50]At this point in the manuscript, at folio 23r, there is a table of contents written in what might be John Foxe's hand showing in some instances the reorganization of the chapters that was made for the 1571 edition and subsequently reproduced in the nineteenth century Latin edition of Cardwell.

CONCERNING OATHS AND PERJURY

Chapter 1. Distinctions Regarding Oaths

As oaths which contribute to the glory of God or the help of our brothers have been allowed to Christians (provided they are taken in judgement, justice and truth), that kind of levity in swearing ought to be completely removed from our souls and our discourses which is bantered about in our familiar daily conversations. For in the latter instances, reverence for God is diminished and perjury easily committed. For this reason, those who have been contaminated by a perverse manner of swearing and cannot be frightened from it by warnings ought to be coerced by a just punishment because they are contemptuous of the name of God and of divine matters.

Chapter 2. The Penalty For A Rash Oath

He who has heard any person at all swearing rashly or without just cause should immediately admonish him to put twelve pence (*denarii*) on the next Sunday into the common treasury which they call the poor box. Also, let him put the money in the box at that place where the crime[51] of swearing was allowed to happen. And if the guilty person has neglected to do this, his name ★ should be referred to the ordinary Folio 24v by the man who heard him. The ordinary will call the person to himself and prescribe for him a penalty for the fault to be fulfilled publicly. Nevertheless, he will not be freed from the fine of twelve pence.

Chapter 3. ~~The Form Of Public Penance And Of Lawful Oaths~~ The Form Of Public Penance[52]

This will be the public penance for one swearing rashly: he shall stand with head uncovered before the pulpit in a higher place than are the rest of the people for as long as it takes to recite the homily on Sunday. When it is concluded he shall immediately confess from that same place that he vehemently repents of his rashness by which, in swearing without cause, he abused the very sacred name of God.

[51]Here in the manuscript a redundant "crimen" in the ablative case has been underlined. It would appear that the word should have been struck due to scribal error.

[52]The new title is not in Cranmer's hand. The hand most closely resembles that of Foxe.

Chapter 4.   The Form Of A Legitimate Oath[53]

Now we desire that a legitimate oath be taken in these words and no others: May God so help me through our Lord Jesus Christ.

Chapter 5.   What Perjury Is

That we may be more easily able to avoid the crime of perjury, its nature will first have to be explained by us. Next it will have to be made clear how grave the offense to God is in perjury. Perjury then is a lie confirmed by an oath or a violation of a valid oath. Now he Folio 25r perjures himself who knowingly and with an oath ★ designed for deception cheats someone, or who willingly violates a licit oath, or who in swearing so completely complicates his words that the meaning of the oath is not understood. Against such fraud we always wish to hold this rule: a person should be believed to have sworn that which the person to whom the oath was given understands in the common usage of those who speak.

Chapter 6.   Judges Who Demand An Oath

The crime of perjury is very grave. For in the first place it is contrary to a precept of God. Next, God is made use of thereby as the witness to something false. Finally, an oath by which truth, a factor very greatly necessary to human society, ought to be confirmed is distorted to support lies. Since, therefore, one sins so vehemently by acts of perjury, judges should not be hasty in demanding oaths especially because subsequent acts of perjury clearly follow from oaths.

Chapter 7.   The Penalty For Those Committing Perjury

If clerics who knowingly and willingly have uttered oaths regarding licit and honest matters have afterwards broken pledges which they could have kept, or have confirmed by oath things which when they Folio 25v swore they knew to be false, then let ★ them first be expelled from the grade of clergy in which they stand. Also, let them be deprived of benefices, as they are called. Let them not only be without the present ones but let them be perpetually excluded from all those which they might be able to obtain. A layman who has been convicted of the crime of perjury will, if it seems to the judge that his resources can bear it, contribute ten pounds to the poor box in the place where the act of perjury took place. Also, he will testify in a public confession

---

[53]This chapter title is inserted between the lines of what was a single chapter as indicated in the lined out original title for chapter 3. The new title is in Cranmer's hand.

before the church that his misdeed displeases him. If indeed the actions of the convicted defendant are not such that the fine can come to ten pounds, let him then publicly acknowledge his crime in the presence of the church, and let him stand before the pulpit with bare head and feet during the whole time in which either a homily dealing with perjury is delivered or a sermon is preached. Moreover, let him endure all these things together in the above manner for three Sundays in succession and he will place into the poor box as much as his resources will be judged able to bear. Yet, the ecclesiastical judge will have power so that by reason of circumstances he may in his wisdom either reduce the prescribed penalty or add to it. Meanwhile, we strongly command our judges themselves that they not connive in this horrible crime of perjury whose bounds or limit men do not discover. ★ But, Folio 26r if anyone of them has been negligent of those things established by us in this area, we already declare to them beforehand that this shameful carelessness of theirs will incur our utmost hatred. Truly it seems that we ought to add most equitably that whoever has knowingly given cause for perjury shall be laid hold of with the same penalties to which before we subjected those convicted of perjury. In summary, moreover, let this apply to all who are convicted of the crime of perjury: they shall be held in disrepute; they shall not be allowed to give testimony; and an oath shall never be brought to them after the time of the perjury, unless perhaps it is a burdensome oath in which they themselves would make their own case poorer. Finally let whoever has injured a brother another through perjury [54] be forced to make full satisfaction to him for the injury.

Chapter 8.   Legitimate Oaths Which Are Not To Be Declined

Nevertheless, we do not wish that men be alienated from every kind of oath because of these penalties of perjury. Therefore, if anyone has been ordered by legitimate authority to swear or to respond to an oath which has been uttered, he shall not refuse the judge who rightfully demands it. But, if by chance he has determined to refuse, he will be reckoned obstinate in the matter and will sustain the penalty of excommunication if he is over fourteen years of age and of sound mind. ★

---

[54]The cancellation and new material is in Cranmer's hand.

Folio 26v   Chapter 9.   ~~Breaking Faith In Ecclesiastical Causes~~ *Breaking Faith*[55]

Faith is the firmest bond of human society. For this reason, men ought to be constrained by law in keeping faith. Therefore, if pacts or promises should not remain firm and should not be fulfilled which were agreed upon either by those who have sworn faith or those who have not sworn faith or those only giving assurance of truth in earnest, then we wish those who have sworn falsely by their own faith in this way first to be laid hold of by means of arbitrary penalties from ecclesiastical judges; secondly, let them be forced to make full satisfaction to those persons who have been deceived by their faithlessness.

Chapter 10.   What The Exceptions Are To Faults Of Perjury
And Of Breaking The Faith

Certainly the preceding laws should admit of two exceptions. The one is that those should not be considered perjurers or breakers of faith who have carried out all the most important matters so as to keep their oath and their trust, yet are hindered for a reason of some sort which they are unable to avoid. Indeed, it will be enough for them to prove their good will and effort to the judges. Nor are those to be considered breakers of the faith or perjured from whom in an undeliberative and unthinking way promises about evil or disgraceful

Folio 27r   or impossible things ★ suddenly slip out, or if the promises were proper at first and in the course of time have degenerated into this absurdity. Still this has been laid down and maintained, that he who knowingly and willingly swears or promises a disgraceful or unjust thing or a thing which cannot be done, is indeed not to be held for this crime if he does not fulfill the things sworn. On the other hand he will give to the ecclesiastical judge just compensation for his rashness.

Chapter 11.   Of What Kind General Oaths And Promises Ought
To Be

In brief, he who swears or promises that he will uphold statutes or customs of churches, chapters, universities, or of whatever places or societies of this sort, cannot be compelled by the authority of such an oath or promise to undertake matters of a harmful type, or matters which cannot be accomplished. For the soul of one swearing or

---

[55]The words were cancelled by someone. The stroke of the line matches that of Cranmer.

promising cannot have any honest regard for such perversity. On this account, it is determined that in the conclusions to such oaths and promises this be added: "I will keep these things in all their parts in which they agree with the Sacred Scriptures, with the civil and ecclesiastical laws of this kingdom, and insofar as my powers will allow."[56] ★

CONCERNING PREACHERS

Folio 32r

Chapter 1.   The Nature Of The Office Of Preaching And How
It Should Be Received

Because the office of preaching is extremely necessary to the people of God, the Church should never be deprived of it. Nevertheless, that office should be provided for with utmost care so that no one is accepted for such a noble duty unless he brings with him to that position piety and suitable learning. That this can be better known, we wish to interpose the authority of the bishops on behalf of those who are to be prepared as preachers in the churches. Nor do we permit anyone to accept his office of preaching or place himself in it unless he has been called to it by the legitimate power of them whose concern it is. In this regard, we wish there to be such care by the bishops that they do not approve indiscreetly all of whatever sort who boast that they are inflamed by the spirit of God. Rather, let them consider and weigh the life and erudition of those men so as to be able to know from that whether their spirits originate from God.

Chapter 2.   Preachers Must Guard Against Errors And Books
Of Errors

Those to whom the power of preaching is granted should be extremely
★ vigilant lest they spread abroad in the church either errors or useless   Folio 32v
inquiries, new sayings which are the inventions and contrivances of men, or finally any other ferment of superstition: expressly, moreover, the pamphlets of the Anabaptists, condemned by public authority in our entire kingdom or [the pamphlets] of any others whom they call separatists; or volumes already disapproved or which will hereafter be disapproved or either teach in any manner or relate or make known the names of those [separatists] so as to confirm some part of that doctrine about which they publicly preach.

[56]Folios 27v to 31v are missing. At the top of folio 32r is Foxe's hand with the instructions to go to folio 168, Iuramento Calumnie. This is the section in the 1571 edition which precedes "Preachers."

Chapter 3.   Of What Sort The Behavior And Learning Of
Preachers Ought To Be

Preachers, the teachers of life, should have such a pleasing and
moderate disposition that they never contend bitterly among themselves,
nor hurl abusive language at one another. But, if by chance there is
someone among them who has made known publicly in a sermon an
unholy doctrine, he should be admonished to acknowledge publicly
his error. But if he refuses to do so, let the judge lay hold of him with
the penalties of a heretic unless he has given up his opinion and is
also taking care that where he sowed this very destructive doctrine
some sound and pious preacher is there overcoming his heresy so that
the people who are taking in the poisonous error may not withdraw
Folio 33r ★ from the true and common faith. Let preachers sharply rebuke the
wickedness of vices, but let the oration so proceed against those vices
that they do not show forth separately and specially the hidden offenses
of any man. Nor let them cite anyone by name as guilty before the
public unless someone has been so troublesome that he has been
contemptuous of the preceding ecclesiastical warnings. Let the manner
of speaking of preachers also be clear and intelligible, not obscure
and puzzling. And let them not willingly involve and entangle their
words in such a way that they can be twisted just as well to either
side [of a question].

Chapter 4.   To Whom The Office Of Preaching Properly
Pertains

In the office of preaching, archbishops should have first place. Let
bishops, deans, and whoever have been established in posts of honor,
as they call them, follow. Not only should these persons be in this
most sacred occupation, but the same power should also be granted
to pastors and parish priests in their flocks, unless just reasons are
present for which their bishops have indicated silence for them.[57] ★

---

[57]In the manuscript there follow three chapters that are crossed out, chapters 5,
6, and 7. In the margin of chapter 5 in Cranmer's hand is the note "Let this be put
under the title, Divine Offices, or Cathedral Churches." This instruction was not carried
out in the 1571 Foxe edition. Chapter 6 has a marginal notation from Cranmer "Let
it be placed in the title Universities." This is also missing from the 1571 edition. What
was originally chapter 7 in the manuscript has Cranmer's marginal notation "Put under
the title Divine Offices." This chapter is also missing from the 1571 edition. These
chapters have been translated above and follow with the designation 4a, 4b, and 4c.
The chapters are found in Cardwell's edition of 1850, Appendix, 331.

Chapter 4a. What The Order Of Sermons Is In The Colleges Of A Cathedral

For all sacred assemblages, it seems very much in order to us that, as far as possible, a sermon be delivered. Therefore, we command that in all cathedral churches on every Sunday, either the bishop himself or the dean or some one of the prebendaries deliver a sermon. In the same way, on each feast day let someone of them either preach to the people or at least recite a homily.

Chapter 4b. What The Order Is In Universities

In the universities let there be a sermon on each Sunday and feast day in the University chapel, as they call it, unless when on the legitimately appointed day a sermon which is also solemn is set forth separately in some college. And these sermons will be accomplished partly by the bachelors of theology, partly by the doctors of the same discipline, partly by the heads of the colleges who, as heads, have indeed been duly called to preaching. However, because the cathedral at Oxford is a parish church, each of the canons employed there will deliver sermons to the people four times in the space of a year. And in the universities we do not give to bachelors or doctors of theology, to canons or heads of colleges the freedom ★ to employ substitutes to satisfy those duties when it is their time to preach, unless illness has stricken them or a clearly necessary absence is calling them away and has called them away.

Chapter 4c. What The Order Is In Towns And Villages

Let sermons also be executed throughout the towns and villages and practiced in them, or in those which are sometimes without them, let there be a clear and distinct reading of a homily which, if the time has not been taken up with a sermon, we wish to have a place in all the churches of our kingdom on each Sunday and feast day. We further add that each year in whatever parish, no matter how small, four sermons shall be executed.

Chapter 5. The Calling Together Of Preachers By The Bishop

That the fruit of preaching may be more plentiful and a greater consensus exist among the preachers, let the bishop at certain times every year gather together all preachers to whom he has given the special privilege, that is the special and peculiar power of preaching throughout his entire diocese. Let him communicate with them about

[their] sermons and learn from them what the vices are in those places
Folio 34v which ★ they most often frequent so that by a kind of common
conspiracy of preachers, wickedness may be restrained, and piety
promoted.[58]

Chapter 6.   Those Who Should Be Present At Sermons

Because the special character of Sabbath worship consists in gaining
knowledge of Sacred Scripture, we wish those who are unwilling or
neglect to be present at sermons to be struck with ecclesiastical
penalties, unless sickness impedes them, or a necessary journey, or
other exercises of piety or other business of this kind which absolutely
must be undertaken at once. In this connection the prime duty should
be that of the nobility and the leaders of men so that by their most
illustrious and ~~excellent~~ honored[59] example they may encourage the
zeal of the common people and of their inferiors. Next, we command
on account of the great need to establish discipline in this matter, that
magistrates, judicial officers, chiefs of cities and the rest of those who
are distinguished by any jurisdictional title whatever be present at
sermons, unless an important matter, and one which by all means
should not be neglected, detains them.

Chapter 7.   What Should Be Determined About Those Who
             Raise An Outcry During A Sermon

If there are any people of such rudeness that, while the preacher is
Folio 35r still speaking ★ from the pulpit, they wish to raise an outcry, or
interrupt him or rail at him[60] in some manner, they are to be separated
from the Church and separated from communion with it until they
openly acknowledge the crime and have returned to their senses. In
the same way, whoever either by aimlessly walking about, or by
inopportunely chattering, or by walking out of the sacred assemblage
in such a way that contempt of the sermon or of the preacher can be
detected or who knowingly and willingly turns the people's attention
away from the sermon in any other way whatsoever or disturbs them,
will pay the merited penalties for this kind of wicked frivolity. Let
them make satisfaction in the matter to the Church since they have
offended it by their very perverse example.[61]

[58]It needs to be noted that frequently Cranmer has written a "running head" at
the top of each page. That is the case here and on numerous preceding pages.

[59]This change is made in Cranmer's hand.

[60]This interlining is in Cranmer's hand.

[61]Folio 35v is a blank page with the title "Preachers" at the top. Folio 36r is a
blank page with the title "Concerning Matrimony" at the top. The chapter does not
begin until folio 37r.

CONCERNING MATRIMONY

Chapter 1.   What Matrimony Is

Marriage is a legal contract, inducing and effecting a mutual and perpetual union of a man with a woman, by the order of God, in which each surrenders to the other power over his body, for the purpose of begetting offspring or of avoiding harlotry or of controlling life by means of reciprocal obligations. For, from henceforth we do not want marriage to take place by any promises or contracts, words, and agreements of any sort unless it has been celebrated with this formula, which we have ordered to be appended here.

Chapter 2.   How Marriage May Be Contracted[62]

To start with, whoever is the minister of the church, on three Lord's Days, or at the least on three holy days, shall announce publicly before the people in the church the coming wedding. Then the bridegroom and the bride will station themselves openly in the front of the church, and openly engage in those ceremonies and rites which our regulations concerning divine matters require in this circumstance. Moreover, we give so much authority to this formula that if any ceremony is spoken or performed ★ in any way contrary to this, marriage cannot exist in this case. But all things of this kind are preparations or certain beginnings for marriage, but marriage itself is not contained in them. And And so[63] both persons are free and unbound and one cannot demand any right of marriage from the other until they have employed the lawful ceremonies of marriage and have given and received mutual fidelity before the Church with the prescribed words.

Chapter 3.   How Seducers Of Women Are To Be Punished

On the other hand, the loathsome sensuousness of those who take advantage of the innocent simplicity of girls and women and besiege their chastity by promises and enticements, until they finally violate their bodies most shamelessly, ought not to be free from heavy punishment. For when they deprive them of the treasure of their chastity, which is more precious than all other riches and goods, it is just that they should receive a greater punishment than thieves whose wickedness is in external matters. Therefore, we enjoin them to be

---

[62]The word "How" was inserted in Cranmer's hand to replace a lined out word that now cannot be read.

[63]The change is in Cranmer's hand.

driven out of the church by the weapon of excommunication; and
Folio 38r these men are not to return to these women unless they marry ★
those whom they formerly abused as harlots. But if by chance this
cannot be done, the judges shall inventory their goods, and after
careful examination will confiscate a third portion from them for the
women who have been contaminated by their lust. But if their goods
should not bear this partitioning, they will be fined to support at their
expense any offspring. And moreover, they will have as many penalties
imposed upon them as the ecclesiastical judge will consider is sufficient
to remove the offense to the Church if their crime has become known
to the people.

Chapter 4.   Marriage Is Not Valid Without The Consent Of
              The Parents

Since it is in accord with Holy Scripture, piety, and justice that
marriages are condemned and are considered void when either children
or orphans contract without the knowledge and consent of either their
parents or guardians, we enjoin that neither children nor orphans ~~take~~
marry wives or husbands unless the authority of those in whose power
they are shall have intervened. But if they ~~have married~~ *have done this*,[64]
we decree that such a wedding is not valid at all and relapses into
Folio 38v nothingness. ★ But if parents or guardians have failed to provide
honorable conditions for marriage or if they have been too harsh and
bitter in proposing these conditions, appeal should be made to the
ecclesiastical magistrate, and we want these parties to plead their cases
before him in difficulties of this kind and the whole case to be settled
by his justice.

Chapter 5.   What Might Be The Age, The Time, *And The*
              Place, Of Marriage[65]

It follows that we must set a fixed age at which marriages may be
concluded and that we must point out the times they ought to be
withdrawn. Therefore, a girl when she has completed the 12th year,
can accept betrothal to a man; a man when he reaches his 14th year
may accept betrothal to a woman. We do not, in any way permit that
participants in a wedding shall be younger than these ages. But no
times have been excluded for the celebration of marriage provided
they are of such a kind as to conform to the ceremonies included in
this law of ours. It is always pleasing that this be kept at the place

[64]The changes in this paragraph are in Cranmer's hand.
[65]This was inserted by Cranmer

or, as people call it, the parish so that the marriage is performed in that place in which either the bride or the bridegroom is a resident. And, if any minister shall join them in marriage in any other place he will incur the punishment of excommunication. ★

Chapter 6. Concerning The Prohibition of Marriage Folio 39r

When the bridegroom and bride have come together in the church so that they may be joined in marriage, if anybody puts himself forward at that time and announces a reason, or says that he could announce one, why they cannot be joined in marriage, let him promise to make this claim good within the following month. Let him [also] promise that he will make full satisfaction for all the preparation made for celebration of the marriage, and for that purpose he shall obligate not only himself but also on his behalf some wealthy person as sureties. Only then shall he be heard, and the marriage shall be postponed for a whole month. Nevertheless, since this postponement can sometimes be a bad deception and fraud, so that in the meantime there might be an occasion for a new marriage, in order to avoid all clever deception, let his precaution be taken in the law itself, namely that while the controversy regarding the former marriage is pending, they will await for the whole month the outcome of that case, and they will not turn to any other new marriage in the meantime. If they have broken this decree of ours by their levity, we condemn and revoke every new marriage of this kind and the person who was accused of this defection will undergo the penalty of excommunication until he shall have given satisfaction to the person to whom he has been unfaithful. ★

Chapter 7. Concerning Impediments of Marriage[66] Folio 39v

The nature of these [marriages] has been weakened by some permanent injury so that they cannot be participants in sexual relations at all, and in such a way that this is concealed from the spouse. Although there was mutual consent and the marriage proceeded with all the rest of the ceremony; still a true marriage cannot exist in a union of this kind; for the other party is deprived of the blessing of bearing offspring and also does without the enjoyment of a spouse. But, if this bodily defect is known to both parties and nevertheless mutual consent concerning marriage continues, the marriage may proceed because no injury can be done to those who are willing. The same principle applies to people whose bodies are enchanted and weakened by evil arts. Since the fruit of marriage is removed from them, the

---

[66]In the manuscript, the title originally was "Que morbi matrimonium impediant," but someone cancelled "morbi."

marriage itself must be withdrawn. In addition, a marriage will be dissolved if it is not made clear to the one party concerning the other who the party was, or of what condition he was. But in this place, we understand condition to involve a state of liberty or of servitude. ★

Folio 40r **Chapter 8.   Difficulties Which Do Not Hinder Marriage**

We permit marriage for the deaf and dumb, who are sound of mind, since they can make known by signs between themselves their desire and agreement; but the insane, unless they have certain intervals of sanity, in which they might still manage their affairs with reason, are to be kept completely from marriage. With those who are not of the Christian faith, marriage to Christians is not to be arranged. For since it is proper for Christian children to be brought up in the Christian Faith, there is great anxiety that that could not happen unless both parents are Christians. But if it happens that those who are already husband and wife are of different religions, these persons are not to be heedlessly separated, but they are to keep together for as long a time, in harmony with the doctrine of Paul with respect to Christian charity, as the person who is of a foreign religion will continue living and cohabiting with the other one.

Chapter 8a.   What Must Be Done In The Absence Of A Spouse[67]

If by chance either spouse is absent for a long time from the home
Folio 40v and nothing can be known for certain concerning ★ his life or death, the deserted person shall go to ecclesiastical judges and after explaining the case will receive a two or three year period from them in which to await the missing person. If the person diligently sought in this period meanwhile is nevertheless not found nor anything about his life is discovered, if the deserted person seeks a new marriage, the judge should allow it. If the former husband returns subsequently, he will not, however, recover his wife unless he shows that there were such great difficulties that he could not return more quickly or send back word of his condition.

---

[67]This chapter has been designated 8a because in the manuscript it has been crossed out but in a marginal note, Cranmer wrote that the chapter is to be moved to another place. In Foxe's hand in the margin is the notation: "This is considered in the title 'On Adultery and Divorce.'" The chapter as it appears in the manuscript is translated above although its substance is later found in Chapter 9 on Adultery and Divorce.

Chapter 9. Marriage Is To Be Allowed For All

Since marriage is a lawful and devout custom, and prevents the disgrace of many shameful things, we want it to be able to be repeated as many times as there is need, provided that it is done properly. We do not keep any persons of any condition, rank, or age whatsoever from marriage; nevertheless we give counsel to those Christian women who are aged and very much advanced in years, and also we encourage them zealously that they should not want ★ to join in marriage with Folio 41r young people both because they cannot have children from them; and also because there might be manifold and great perversity in their wantonness.

Chapter 10. Polygamy Is To Be Avoided

However, we want polygamy to be done away with by our laws, and we think it right that in a marriage there should be only one sole spouse, for in this way was marriage established by God in the first place. And so if anyone has taken more than one wife, he must send away all the latest ones and keep only the one whom he first took in hand, (if she wishes to acknowledge him as husband); but to the others who will be turned out, he shall grant a dowry to each one, and he will make amends to the church in addition, subject to whatever punishment the judge will reckon suitable for such an enormity. Then too, the worthlessness of women will be penalized by punishment if knowingly they delivered themselves to the same man and if any fault of theirs can be apprehended in this misdeed.

Chapter 11. Marriage Cannot Be Abrogated Because Of
Disputes And Quarrels

Once a marriage has been already concluded and consummated, if such quarrels, disputes, insults, controversies, ★ bitterness, abuses, Folio 41v debaucheries, and depravities of many kinds boil up so that the married couple do not wish to remain in the same household, and other duties of marriage are not discharged mutually, they shall be subject to ecclesiastical penalties, and they shall be forced into the same household, and they shall also be called back to the honorable and pious mutually shared duties of the marriage, provided no such incidents have occurred on account of which it would be legally permissible to seek divorce.

Chapter 12. Marriages Are Not Valid If Contracted By Force And Fear

Briefly we want to apply this to all marriages, that if force and fear compelled a marriage, provided they were so extreme that they could overwhelm men of firm character, in accord with the teaching of the civil law, by all means such a forcible wedding is to be dissolved and is to be held as null. Although these problems can afflict a marriage only with great difficulty, if it possesses all the lawful ceremonies and is wholly perfected in that form which we established above, nevertheless if force and fear rush in for any reason, it is allowable for a marriage oppressed by them to be utterly dissolved. ★

Folio 42r ### Chapter 13. That Mothers Should Nourish Infants From Their Own Breasts

An excessively easy and attractive custom has become very much fixed in the custom of wives to remove their offspring from their own breasts and send them away to wet-nurses. Since this practice relies for the most part on no probable causes but is done because of a sort of lax indulgence of their own bodies so that they can spare themselves and may avoid the honest and natural burdens of child-rearing, and since this inhuman and in fact inhuman laziness, to call it by its proper name, brings with it the cause of many evils, we are of the opinion that it belongs to the duty of our preachers to encourage mothers not to desert in any inhuman way the offspring whom they brought into light nor deny the benefit of their breasts to those on whom they conferred a little bit earlier the benefit of their womb and viscera.[68]

Folio 44r
★CONCERNING DEGREES PROHIBITED IN MARRIAGE

Chapter 1. There Ought To Be No Marriage Between Persons Who Are Not Legally Eligible

Since marriage is a legal union between a man and a woman, great caution ought to be applied lest persons enter into marriage against legal right and divine law, and such persons are united in its bonds as divine laws do not want to be admitted to the society of a union of this kind. For if this should happen, incest would contaminate our kingdom and the churches distributed throughout it. Then it would

---

[68]In the manuscript at this point there are three blank pages with the title "Concerning Marriage" at the top of each one.

be necessary that these same persons, corrupted by their heinous union, would incur the greatest hatred of God.

Chapter 2.   What Consanguinity And Relationship By
              Marriage Are

There are many grades of consanguinity and affinity in which marriage cannot exist. But first in order that these very headings may be understood, consanguinity is understood in those who were begotten by the same elders by whom we were begotten, or those descended from us through propagation of body and blood. But affinity proceeds by means of the marriage of male and female. Moreover, these two headings of consanguinity and affinity have been brought together ★ in such a way that first divine laws and then civil laws have noted   Folio 44v certain grades in each category in which marriage should not be entered into in any way.

Chapter 3.   What Kind Of Divine Law There Is In Prohibition
              of Marriage

God has set down a fixed law of these grades in Leviticus chapters 18 and 20; we and all our posterity must be bound by this law. For the precepts of those chapters were not peculiar to the commonwealth of the ancient Israelites, as some imagine it, but they have the same weight of authority as our religion bestows on the Ten Commandments so that no human power can decide anything contrary to them in any way. And so the Roman Pope appropriates this power to himself, irreligiously and they hurt their own consciences greatly whoever seek such dispensations, as they are called, in this matter either from the Roman Pope or from any other person. Nevertheless, this rule in these chapters of Leviticus must be carefully observed, namely in that place by no means all persons who are not legitimate are specified by name. For the Holy Spirit there designated obviously and clearly only those persons from whom ★ similar distances of intervening grades and   Folio 45r differences can be inferred and discovered between them. As for the sake of example, since a mother is not given to a son as a wife, it follows that a daughter cannot be given to her father. And, if it is not lawful for a paternal uncle to have his brother's wife in marriage, then neither may a marriage be contracted with a maternal uncle.

Chapter 4.   Rules To Be Observed In The Law of Leviticus

Therefore, in order that all mistakes may be avoided, we must enumerate and mention the remaining persons who are in equal limits of relationship *united with those people* of whom sacred Scripture makes open mention. In this matter we want two rules to be earnestly considered; one of these is that whatever places are assigned to men we understand that the same have been allotted to women, assuming always that the degrees of proportions and relationships are equal. The second rule is that man and wife are judged to have one and the same flesh between them, and thus where anyone touches anyone on Folio 45v a degree of consanguinity, ★ it will touch his wife by the same grade of affinity because it is also valid on the contrary side by the same reasoning. And if we will hold to those limits, we will not *judge more persons to be excluded by law* than the sacred Scriptures ordain, and we will maintain untouchable and inviolate those relationships concerning which God gave us commandments.[69]

Chapter 5.   An Enumeration Of Persons Prohibited In
Leviticus

In Leviticus the persons regulated are specified by these names: mother, step-mother, sister, daughter of son, daughter of daughter, father's sister, mother's sister, wife of father's brother, daughter-in-law, wife of brother, daughter of wife, daughter of son of wife, daughter of wife's daughter, sister of wife. But persons whom Leviticus omits are these: mother-in-law, grandmother, and those who are above her in a direct line, since all of these seem to us to be in the place of mothers. And on the other hand the daughter of a great-granddaughter and those who are below and are begotten from them, since through them they have the resemblance of daughter, we ought to keep away from them. There are to be added the daughter of a brother, the daughter of a sister, and those who are begotten of them in a direct descending line, the wife of a son of a brother, the wife of a son of a sister, the Folio 46r daughter of a wife's brother,★ the daughter of a wife's sister, *the wife of a maternal uncle,*[70] the sister of a wife's father, the sister of a wife's mother, the son of a husband's brother, the son of a husband's sister, the husband of a father's sister, the husband of a mother's sister, the husband of a brother's daughter, the son of a step-son, the son of a step-daughter.

Chapter 6.   What Must Be Considered In The Preceding List

And those degrees preceding the former law have a double consideration. For in the first place, not only do they possess such an

---

[69]The changes in the paragraph are in Cranmer's hand. In both instances the words lined out cannot be read.

[70]The insertion is in Cranmer's hand.

ordering in legal marriage as we have already set forth, but they have the same place in ~~every~~ [the] ~~natural~~ *unlawful*[71] union of bodies. For a son cannot according to this law take his mother as a wife, and he cannot have his father's concubine by the same law and the father ought not to touch in any way the son's wife, hence he ought to remove himself from her whom his son has abused. For this reason, a mother ought not to be united in marriage with the husband of her daughter nor also with the man who wronged her daughter. ~~And the case of many similar persons is the same.~~[72] The second precaution is that not only are ★ those whom we have mentioned separated while their husbands still survive but also the same is perpetually valid even when they are dead. For just as it is terribly disgraceful in life for a father, a brother, *a paternal uncle,* or a maternal uncle to dare to dishonor their wives, so after their death, their *marriage* has equal disgrace *if concluded with them.*

Folio 46v

Chapter 7.   Spiritual Association Does Not Hinder Marriage

Since a spiritual association, as it is commonly called, is not introduced in the sacred Scriptures, and is not supported by any sound and stable principles, it ought not to impede at all the course of marriage.[73] ★

CONCERNING ADULTERY AND DIVORCE

Folio 48r

Chapter 1.   That Adultery Ought To Be Severely Punished

So heinous is the guilt of adultery that it is attacked by a suitable commandment of the Decalogue; and also, under the ancient divine laws promulgated by Moses, it was punished by the culprit's being publicly stoned to death by the people and buried beneath the stones; while finally by the civil law also it was punished with death. It follows therefore that a crime so hateful to God and visited by our pious forefathers with a punishment specially appropriated to it, ought not to be passed over by our Ecclesiastical Judges without the most condign punishment.

---

[71]This change is in in Cranmer's hand.

[72]It might be assumed that Cranmer lined out this sentence but there is no evidence to support that assumption. The lined out sentence might have been done by the scribe or some other person. The rest of the changes in the chapter are in Cranmer's hand.

[73]There follow in the manuscript two blank pages with the heading "Concerning Degrees Prohibited in Marriage."

Chapter 2.   How Ministers Who Have Been Convicted Of
Adultery Ought To Be Punished

Let us begin with church ministers, whose lives ought to be characterized by especial rectitude. If, therefore, any one of them be convicted of adultery, fornication, or incest, if he has had a wife of his own, all his goods and property shall pass to her and to the children, whether born of her, or the lawful fruit of any previous lawful marriage. Should he, however, have neither wife nor children of his own, all his property shall, at the pleasure of the judge, either be Folio 48v divided among the poor, or applied to some other works of piety. ★ In the next place, should he have held any benefice, he is, after being convicted of adultery, incest, or fornication, to lose it as of and from that time, and to have no power of receiving any other. Furthermore, he is either to be condemned to perpetual banishment, or to be consigned to the darkness of the dungeon for life.

Chapter 3.   In What Manner The Layman Is To Be Punished

The layman convicted of adultery is to restore his wife's dowry to her. He is also to give up to her the half of all his goods. Furthermore, he is either to be condemned to perpetual banishment or committed to prison for life.

Chapter 4.   In What Manner Wives, Either Of Ministers Or Of
Laymen Are To Be Punished

On the other hand, wives, whether of laymen or of ministers, if the crime of adultery be proved against them and the judge give his decision against them, shall be deprived of their dowries and of all benefits which might accrue to them from the property of their husbands, either under any law of our realm, or by custom, or contract, or covenant; and shall, moreover, either be condemned to perpetual banishment or imprisoned for life.[74]

Chapter 5.   The Innocent Party May Lawfully Contract A
Fresh Marriage

When one of the parties has been convicted of adultery, the other, Folio 49r being ★ innocent, if desirous, shall be allowed to proceed to a fresh marriage. For the innocent party ought not to suffer for another's crime to such an extent that celibacy should be forced upon him against his will, and therefore, the innocent party is not to be considered

---

[74]This is a replacement by Cranmer for a word that now cannot be read.

guilty of adultery if he bind himself by a fresh marriage, since Christ, himself, excepted adultery as a reason.[75]

Chapter 6.   The Desirability Of Reconciliation

Since in matrimony there is the closest possible union, and the highest degree of love that can be imagined, we earnestly desire that the innocent party should forgive the guilty and take him back again should there seem to be any reasonable hope of a better way of life; and although this forgiving disposition cannot be learned from any external laws, nevertheless Christian charity may often guide us to it. But, should it be impossible for the guilty party to be allowed to be admitted to a higher condition, no fresh marriage is permitted him.

Chapter 7.   No One May Abandon His Spouse Of His Or Her
             Own Free Will

It is a serious matter and brings with it a grievous disturbance of the family when a wife is separated from her husband. ★ Wherefore, with Folio 49v respect to adultery, no one may put away his wife of his own authority and take another, unless an ecclesiastical judge shall first have duly examined the whole case and given his decision. But if anyone should dare to do this, he is to lose all right of action against his wife. Whenever the judge convicts either husband or wife of adultery, he must give notice to the other, the guiltless party, of his freedom to proceed to a fresh marriage; but with this reservation, that he shall fix a certain time in which the injured party may, if desirous, return to his former marriage partner, and if he should refuse to do this, on the expiration of the period, he may then contract another marriage. And we explicitly decree that this period which the judge shall grant shall be limited by the space of a year or six months.

Chapter 8.   Desertion A Ground For Divorce

When either of the parties deserts and withdraws from the other, if the absent party can be found, advice, exhortations and penalties are to be employed to compel him to return to his marriage partner that they may live harmoniously together. If he cannot in any way be induced to adopt this course, he is to be considered a contumacious person in the matter and a scorner of divine and human laws, and for that cause he is to suffer perpetual imprisonment; and the deserted party ★ may claim from the ecclesiastical judge the right to contract Folio 50r

---

[75]The words that were lined out and those then substituted for them by Cranmer appear to only a stylistic change that involved word order.

a fresh marriage. But when the absent person cannot be found, or his whereabouts ascertained so that in this crime no place may be left for light and heedless behavior, then it is our will that the absent person be first summoned to appear by name, according to the form of legal procedure known as *viis et modis,* and if, on this being done, no appearance is entered either by him personally or by anyone acting on his behalf and willing to plead his cause, then the judge shall grant him a stay of two or three years, during which the absent party may come forward. On the expiration of this period if he does not appear himself and adduce just causes for so long an absence, the deserted person shall be freed from the bonds of matrimony and, if desirous, allowed to marry again. But if, when the proceedings are at an end, and a fresh marriage has taken place, the deserting party should, when too late and after the expiration of the two or three years, come forward, he is to be thrust into the darkness of the dungeon for life, and the second marriage shall be entirely legal.

Chapter 9.   The Unduly Protracted Absence Of The Husband
A Ground For Divorce

When the husband has not deserted, but has military service or his business as a merchant or some legitimate and honorable reason of this sort for traveling abroad, and has been absent from home a long time and nothing is certainly known either about his being alive or Folio 50v dead, the judges shall grant to the wife, ★ if indeed she should ask this from them, a space of two or three years during which she is to await her husband's return. Should he not come back during the whole of this time, and if it should be impossible to obtain any information as to his being alive, although the most diligent inquiry has been made in regard to this in the meanwhile, it is right that the liberty to contract a fresh marriage should be granted to the wife, but with this condition, that if in course of time the first husband should return, the wife is to take him back to her, provided he can prove that his having stayed so long abroad was not by his own fault. For unless he should be able to explain so serious and lengthy an absence by some full and sufficient reason, he is to be imprisoned for life and have no right of return to his wife, and she is to continue legally in her second marriage.[76]

Chapter 10. Deadly Hostility A Ground For Divorce

If deadly hostility should arise between husband and wife, and become inflamed to such an intensity that one attacks the other, either by treacherous means or by poison, and should wish to take his life in

---

[76]The two insertions in this chapter are in Cranmer's hand.

some way, either by open violence or by hidden malice, we ordain that, as soon as so horrible a crime be proved at law, such persons should be by law separated by divorce in the courts: for the person does greater injury to his marriage partner who attacks health and life than the one who separates himself from the other's society, or commits adultery with another. For there ★ cannot be any sort of fellowship Folio 51r between those who have begun, the one to plot and the other to dread mortal harm. When therefore, they cannot live together, according to the teaching of Paul, it is right that the marriage should be dissolved.

Chapter 11. The Crime Of Ill-treatment, If Prolonged, A
Ground For Divorce

Should a man be violent to his wife and display excessive harshness of word and deed in his dealing towards her, as long as there is any hope of improvement, the ecclesiastical judge is to reason with him, reproving his excessive violence, and if he cannot prevail by admonitions and exhortations, he is to compel him by making him give bail or by taking sureties that he will not inflict any violent injury on his wife, and that he will treat her[77] as the intimate union of marriage requires. If however, the husband cannot be restrained, either by bail or by sureties, and refuses to abandon his cruelty by these means, then he must be considered his wife's mortal enemy and a danger to her existence. Wherefore she, in her peril, must be helped by the remedy of divorce, no less than if her life had been openly attacked. On the other hand, however, the power given by the law is not abrogated, of restraining wives in whatever ways are necessary, should they be rebellious, obstinate, petulant, scolds, and of evil behavior, provided that the husband does not transgress the limits of moderation and equity. Both in this and in the above-mentioned offenses, it is ★ our will that this Folio 51v principle should be followed, that parties thus set free, if desirous, may contract a fresh marriage, while those convicted of the previous crimes are to be punished by perpetual exile or imprisonment for life.

Chapter 12. Slight Disagreements, Unless Permanent, No
Ground For Divorce

If trifling disagreements or grounds of offense creep into marriage, the words of Paul should act as a check upon them, namely, that either the wife should be reconciled to the husband, a result which ought to be sought after by all ordinary and extraordinary methods of penalties and exhortations, or she is to be debarred for the future

---

[77]This phrase is interlined in the manuscript in the scribe's hand and it appears to be the correction of an omission.

from a fresh marriage, a penalty which we decree to be equally binding on the man.[78]

Chapter 13. Incurable Disease Does Not Annul Marriage

If by chance either of the parties shall have contracted any incurable disease for which no alleviation can be found, the marriage will nevertheless hold good in spite of all difficulties of this kind. Seeing that this, above all, ought to be the principal and distinguishing advantage of matrimony, that mutual troubles may be soothed and alleviated by mutual acts of kindness on the part of the marriage partners.

Chapter 14. In What Manner The Defendant Is To Be Supported During the Lawsuit

Folio 52r Since cases involving charges of adultery, poisoning, ★ mortal treachery and ill treatment frequently entail serious controversy and are of very great length, and the man is in the meantime to maintain his wife by a seemly and fitting allowance, account being taken of the rank and circumstances in which she is.

Chapter 15. The Penalty For False Accusation

The sensual desires of many men have a craving of this character, that they pursue a succession of fresh marriages and long for a constant change of wives. Wherefore, they will devise slanderous charges of adultery and other crimes of that kind against the innocent, unless the punishment for their offenses is made sufficiently severe to act as a deterrent. Therefore, if a man shall charge his wife with adultery or poisoning, and if subsequently the case fail, then the half of his property is to be assigned to the wife. Nor shall he in any circumstances have any right of selling, dividing, bequeathing, exchanging, giving, or alienating that property unless the wife consent thereto. And on the other hand, if the wife shall prosecute the husband for adultery or poisoning, mortal injury or ill-treatment, and lose her case, in the first place, she shall forfeit her dowry, then she is to be deprived of all emoluments which would legally have accrued to her from her husband *unless the husband is of his own accord willing to make*

---

[78]The change made in this paragraph is in Cranmer's hand and is a stylistic change since in the next line, "hortationum" has been cancelled.

some provision for her;[79] finally, their marriage between them is to be maintained intact, as it was before.[80] ★ If it is not the husband or wife Folio 52v who accuses the other, but some other third party from outside accuses one of them, and his case breaks down, the ecclesiastical judge is, at his own discretion, to inflict some heavy and exemplary punishment on him, and he is furthermore to give satisfaction to the party to whom he did the wrong. Lastly, such slanderers may neither return to the Church nor may they be admitted to the Sacraments, unless they have, as far as in them lies, restored the reputation of that person whom they have discredited by calumny and falsehood, and shall have done penance in proportion to the crime. And we decree that these penalties, under this heading, shall be common to all, whether laymen or clergymen.

Chapter 16. The Penalty Of The Husband Who Incites His
                Wife To Adultery.

If the husband shall have been in any way the inciter or instigator of his wife's committing adultery, she, indeed, shall be convicted of adultery, but the husband shall also be declared guilty of procuring, and neither shall be released from the bonds of matrimony. *And this, we decree, is to be understood of the wife likewise.*[81]

Chapter 17. What the Penalty Is To Be When Both Parties
                Are Equally Guilty of Adultery

If the person who has been convicted of adultery should be able to prove the same crime against the other marriage partner, and prove it before that party has proceeded to a fresh marriage, the equal guilt of each party shall involve equal punishment, and the former marriage between them shall remain valid. ★

Chapter 18. What The Penalty Is To Be For The Harborers Folio 53r
                And Abettors Of Adultery

To be sure, those ought not to escape the vigilance of the ecclesiastical judges, who are the harborers of adultery, or who in any way promote the disgrace of it by their help, action, or advice; in which class are, for example, those who wittingly lend their houses to adulterers, or

---

[79]This phrase has been written in the margin in the manuscript but in the hand of the scribe and thus appears to be a correction of an omission by the scribe.

[80]A chapter title has been cancelled at the bottom of this page, 52r, and a line has been drawn to united this folio to the next one. It would appear this is because at some stage two chapters were joined.

[81]This addition is in Cranmer's hand.

a place of whatsoever description, and who are intermediaries of messages, letters or presents of any sort. Wherefore, we decree that all such dregs of humanity who encourage the uncleanness of adultery in whatever respect, must be restrained by ecclesiastical penalties and also by the pronouncements of the judge.

Chapter 19. The Separation *a Mensa et Thoro* To Be Abolished

It was formerly customary in the case of certain crimes to deprive married people of the right of association at bed and board, though in all other respects their marriage time remained intact; and since this practice is contrary to the Holy Scriptures, involves the greatest perversity, and has introduced an accumulation of evils into matrimony, it is our will that the whole thing be, by our authority, abolished.

Chapter 20. How Incest And Fornication Of The Laity Are To Be Punished

Incest, especially that which involves the closest degree of relationship, Folio 53v is ★ to be visited with the penalty of imprisonment for life. Then fornication and indiscriminate licentious lusts of every kind are to be checked by great severity in the punishment, so that they may eventually be completely rooted out from our kingdom. Therefore, the ecclesiastical judges must take vigilant care that they visit with excommunication whatever persons of whichever sex have been involved in sensual associations of an impure and dissolute character, unless after timely warning they repent. And even though they have themselves amended their ways, they are nevertheless to be compelled publicly to make atonement to the church. Moreover, they must place ten pounds in the box set apart for the poor of their own church, or if their means are insufficient, they ~~assign~~ *must place* there as much of their goods as can conveniently be spared.[82]

Chapter 21. How An Illegitimate Child Is To Be Maintained

A child born of adultery or of mere fornication, to use the common term, is to be maintained at the father's expense, if indeed, he can be discovered. But if he cannot be found, the mother herself is to support her offspring at her own expense.[83]

---

[82]This change in Cranmer's hand.

[83]At the end of Chapter 21 in the manuscript there follow two pages that are blank but with the chapter's title "Adultery and Divorce" written in at the top.

★ CONCERNING THOSE TO BE ADMITTED TO ECCLESIASTICAL BENEFICES

Chapter 1.[84]

As the condition of the republic quickly deteriorates when it is managed by men who are stupid and infamous and burning with ambition, so the Church of God in these times of ours labors under a heavy burden because she is committed to the oversight of those who are altogether inept in the undertaking of such a distinguished office. In this matter, there has been much deviation from those formulas of blessed Paul which he prescribed for Timothy and Titus. Therefore, we must find some prompt remedy for such an extraordinary injury to our churches.

Chapter 2.   Diligent Investigation To Be Made Of Ministers

All who partake of the priesthood in some way are to be investigated and thoroughly examined in accord with the custom and precepts of the laws so that the bishop does not inconsiderately lay hands on someone and share in crimes not belonging to him. Nor is anyone to be admitted to church administration unless he has first been properly examined. ★

Chapter 3.   The Office Of Patrons

Moreover, we instruct patrons of ecclesiastical benefices that laying aside all considerations of kinship or any other matter, they have regard for those who are willing and able to carry out in all its parts this sacred office to which they are to be admitted. For the priestly offices have not been brought to patrons so that they might diminish them or take plunder from them, but so that those offices might find peace and *security* under the patron's protection.[85]

Chapter 4.   The Penalties Of Delinquent Patrons

It is a matter of grave importance to patrons that, in the bestowal of benefices, they do not by any agreement whatever shamefully and greedily seek to avert their duty by keeping back any buildings or by appropriating tithes, or by contaminating themselves through any shameful acquisition ~~of this kind as was discussed by us in that chapter which was entitled "On The Proper Conferring of Benefices.~~[86] But if

---

[84]There is no chapter title in the manuscript.

[85]This was inserted, but it is not clear if it was done by Cranmer or someone else.

[86]The cancellations are clear in the manuscript, but there is no way to determine if it is the work of Cranmer.

Example of an edited page

there has been any agreement of this kind contrary to our laws, the patron will lose the right of bestowal for that period of office. Thereupon, he who was about to exercise the right of bestowal will lose the benefice designated for him because he has accommodated his will to a dishonest transaction. Also, he will be excluded from all other benefices which he has been able to obtain. ★

Chapter 5.   Benefices Are Not To Be Left Vacant And Are Not   Folio 59r
                   To Be Conferred Before They Are Vacant [87]

Benefices should not remain vacant for long. Therefore, unless in the space of six months after they have become vacant the patrons have designated new ministers for them, they will certainly forfeit the very right of designation for that time. Nevertheless, we do not wish there to be excessive haste in bestowing benefices and do not allow patrons to make anyone confident of acquiring one of them by any guarantee, written, pledged, or contracted, before the benefices are vacant. For agreements of this kind bring a great amount of detriment with them. Therefore, those who give any such hope about benefices that are not vacant will lose the right of bestowal for that period of office, and those who have aspired to benefices not yet vacant will certainly not be received to them afterwards and will also be removed from all others.

Chapter 6.   Upon Whom The Right Of Appointment By A
                   Patron Devolves[88]

As often as a patron loses the right of appointment, it should pass over to the bishop. If, in the space of six months, the bishop has neglected to install someone suitable in the vacant benefice, the right will be transferred to the archbishop. If in six months, from the time he was informed, he does not exercise his right, we ourselves will assume it. But if six months elapse ★ from the time we knew of the   Folio 59v
matter and we have not bestowed the vacant benefice, the patron's right will devolve again upon him. The matter should thus revolve in the same manner with those persons whom we have named succeeding themselves in order until some one of them carries out the right of bestowal within the designated time.

[87]This phrase was inserted in Cranmer's hand.

[88]The original title read: "To Whom The Right Of Appointment Is Given." The changes made above are in Cranmer's hand.

Chapter 7.   The Summoning of Commissioners

Because we have stated that the doctrine and the uprightness of those who will participate in the priestly office should be thoroughly examined, let the bishop himself first of all choose certain commissioners. Then, because this special care should belong to archdeacons, we do not wish to interfere with their right, but leave this entire business of legal inquiry to be arranged and handled by them. There is, however, this proviso, that they should summon to themselves colleagues whom the bishop has designated as commissioners, whose venerable integrity of conduct has been observed

Folio 60r ★ and in whom knowledge of Sacred Scripture is joined with experience and with skill in governing churches. Also, it is desirable that the bishop himself, if possible, take part in the business of legal inquiry from the very beginning, for this one office is the highest and greatest of all, and in it the condition of the churches is in a special way made firm. For this reason, if the presence of the bishops is demanded in greater and lesser affairs of the churches, it is by no means fitting that it be lacking in this certainly principal duty.

Chapter 8.   The Oath Of Legal Inquiry Is To Be Placed First

We do not wish to proceed to the legal inquiry until an oath has been required of the petitioner so that he may respond truly and sincerely to all matters which have been sought from him in so far as they pertain to the present legal inquiry. Thereupon, all parts of his life will be carefully examined and his doctrine deeply gone into lest perchance he labors under ignorance or under perverse or corrupt knowledge. ★

Folio 60v Chapter 9.   What Is To Be Sought With Respect To Doctrine

Moreover, in so far as the doctrine of those men who are to be involved in the supervision of churches is concerned, we wish the investigation to proceed principally along such lines that their opinions regarding the Catholic Faith and the most sacred mystery of the Trinity may be thoroughly investigated to the extent that belief is necessary in those matters. In the next place, [inquiry should be made into] what kind of faith they have concerning the books of Sacred Scripture, which are called canonical, and into how much authority they place in Scripture. Then let them proceed to matters of controversy, especially the more recent ones of our time. In all, let them explain singly through all its parts the catechism in which the key points of religion are briefly discussed.

Chapter 10. That An Inquiry Should Be Made About Whether
They Are Heretics

Since it should also be known clearly whether they are infected by
any false doctrine, there will have to be an inquiry into what they hold
concerning all those matters which we have taken care to have placed
in the chapter entitled "Heresies." And let those be rejected who, in
the judgement of the commissioners, have not correctly and suitably
responded to these questions or who are lacking in the knowledge of
Sacred Scripture. If, truly, these matters have been determined favorably
for these men, then at length the inquiry should proceed to the
remaining matters. ★

Chapter 11. What Commissioners Will First Require   Folio 61r

The commissioners should certainly first inquire of him [the petitioner]
whether he is willing to conform himself to those precepts of blessed
Paul which are contained in these words to Timothy: "You must be
truly vigilant, labor in all things, do the work of an evangelist, fulfill
your ministry." For in this way, he will always administer with
constancy, as far as his powers will bear, the church to which he will
be appointed; and, at length, let his duty which he ought to exercise in
the priesthood, be declared to him clearly and openly.[89]

Chapter 12. That It Is Necessary That There Be One Benefice
For One Minister

When many benefices all fall to one minister, it is necessarily the fact
that they give less correct and complete satisfaction to each one and
less provision can be made for learned men, who are still needy and
for whom no provision has been made. [Therefore], let the
commissioners seriously inquire of the candidate whether he has at
present any benefice. Should he confess that he does, he shall not
obtain the second one which he is seeking from them. Otherwise, we
wish the benefice to be vacated beforehand, as if its possessor has
died and it will be the patron's right and duty to designate someone
else in his place. ★

Chapter 13. That The Privileges Of Pluralities, As They Are   Folio 61v
Called, Are To Be Abolished

Hereafter, we wish that no one be allowed the privileges by whose
authority many benefices are able to cumulate to one minister.

---

[89]Here Cranmer changed the word order, but this does not change the meaning
in translation.

Nevertheless, we do not want this law of ours to deprive those who heretofore have sought permission to administer several benefices, so that they would be unable freely to enjoy the privileges they had acquired.

Chapter 14. Those Things To Be Considered Causes Of An Absence

Whoever has been either burdened by age or much weakened by the incursion of illnesses so that he is not capable of discharging his office, or whoever has any other just reason for a certain temporary absence, to be approved by the bishop, on account of which he has to be away from his benefice for some time, will nevertheless have to make provision for the interim by putting an upright and praiseworthy vicar in his place. The bishops should also be extremely vigilant that no one, in consideration of anything whatever, deceitfully and craftily should remain absent from his benefice longer than necessary. ★

Folio 62r ### Chapter 15. At What Time The Benefice ~~Should Be Resided In~~ *Should Be Assumed.*[90]

Because it has previously been established by us that one should remain in his benefice except when certain temporary privileges have occasionally freed some, ~~as we have already shown,~~[91] it should also be added that, when someone is appointed to a benefice by a letter of the ordinary after the inquiry has been completed, he should enter into his benefice within the two months next following unless sickness or some compelling necessity, with which he must comply, detains him. But if someone has done otherwise, he will both lose his present benefice and be removed from all others.

Chapter 16. The Office of Prebendaries[92]

Those who formerly enjoyed ecclesiastical benefices free from cares, as they themselves explained and also declare, were accustomed to have a certain immunity from all duties. We, however, have learned well that all who live by the ~~revenues~~ *fruits* of the church ought to care for the services of the churches. Therefore we give to canons as well as to prebendaries whose duties in the churches are not decidedly

---

[90]This change is in Cranmer's hand.

[91]It is not clear who cancelled this phrase.

[92]In the margin by the first line of the chapter, Cranmer has added this notation: "Those two chapters [16 and 17] will be better deferred to the heading 'Prebendaries.'" The changes that are in the chapter are in his hand.

different from each other, this duty: that they support the churches
by teaching, by preaching, by comforting those afflicted by sickness
or adverse circumstances, ★ by sharing together the remaining offices Folio 62v
of piety, or by whatever other legitimate and correct means the bishop
and dean of the church have prescribed.

Chapter 17. That A Five-year Absence Is Granted To
Prebendaries

However, we grant to those who are admitted to prebends or to
canonries or to benefices free from set duties, a period of five years
so that they may apply themselves to doctrinal studies in the
universities. There is the additional stipulation that each year they
write to the bishop as well as to the entire fraternity letters which are
called articles in which they give a faithful account of their lives, their
customs and their progress in doctrine. However, when the period of
five years is spent, they are compelled to enter again their benefices
or ecclesiastical offices.

Chapter 18. The Family of Ministers

After inquiry has been fully made concerning the life [of the ministers],
their religion, their learning, their intention of administering the
benefice and of remaining in it, let the inquiry, nevertheless, descend
also to their family and birth. And although they are not oppressed
by the debauchery of their parents or the adultery of a son as far as
the immortality of the future life of heaven is concern, nevertheless,
God, because of certain immense ★ and powerful hatred of debauchery Folio 63r
and adultery and shameful lust, harshly afflicts in the meantime the
children begotten in vice, bruises their successors and, in the Old
Testament, on account of the same kind of impurity[93] in fathers,
removed sons from the administration of the holy churches of the
Church.[94] Following the example of the divine severity, we prohibit such
sons as are begotten in vice from contact with ecclesiastical duties;
unless it happens that certain extraordinary men emerge possessed of
exceptional talents which shine forth in them to such a degree that
the prior sordidness of their origins is obscured or is compensated for
by the excellence of their virtues, or unless there is the greatest
shortage of ministers in the church.

---

[93]In the manuscript this word is interlined, but it seems to be more of a correction
of a spelling error than a new word.

[94]This change is in Cranmer's hand.

Chapter 19. That The Illegitimate Sons of Patrons Are To Be Removed From The Care Of Churches

The impudence of certain patrons is so great that they obtrude their own children, conceived in adultery and debauchery, into those churches over which they hold the right of designation. Since these [children] are untimely witnesses to their fathers' inordinate passions, rather than suitable ministers for the churches, and since such noteworthy and habitual conduct of theirs conveys a certain authority to sinners, ~~we wish them to be altogether expelled from this kind of ecclesiastical benefices~~ *we wish that all bestowals of benefices of this kind be invalidated and that the patron be deprived of the right of bestowal for that period of office.*[95]
★

Folio 63v ### Chapter 20. That Ministers With Any Bodily Defects Whatever Are Not To Be Prohibited From Benefices

Offensive bodily defects, which formerly excluded men from assuming ecclesiastical duties, will not hereafter have such significance that, because of them, of whatever kind they may be, a learned and upright man may be removed from the administration of a benefice. Nevertheless, attentive consideration will have to be given to those [defects] which either take away completely the faculty of carrying out an ecclesiastical duty or clearly bring it to nought, as blindness takes away the office of reading to which Paul urged Timothy. Again, if a minister's tongue so falters or sticks, or has been so greatly injured by some calamity or other that he cannot be understood by his people when preaching, the greatest fruit of his own ministry necessarily perishes. Furthermore, if a minister is too distorted in appearance or has such a contemptible and repulsive spirit that men shrink from conversation and social intercourse with him, and thus he is unable, publicly or privately, to impart counsel or solace to the needs of others, we see that almost all the things are missing in him which pertain to his office. Therefore, they who have these large and frightful bodily Folio 64r detriments which are so imprinted that ★ the unimpeded administration of sacred matters cannot proceed from them, may by no means attain the dignity of managing benefices. But lesser defects, even if extensive, will not hinder them from benefices, nor need they redeem their deformity with money.

---

[95]The addition and cancellation are in Cranmer's hand.

Chapter 21. The Age Of Ministers

Next comes [the question of] age, which is not to be overlooked in the ministry of the church, since maturity of years conveys authority, and the rashness of adolescence can hardly be appropriate to employment in such holy duties and to the seriousness [involved therein]. Therefore, we wish that the age of thirty be required for bishops, [cathedral deans and archdeacons][96] in whom there ought to be the greatest perfection of character; twenty-five for parish priests, as they are called; the same for prebendaries if indeed any [pastoral] care of a specific group of men has been entrusted to them; and they ought to enter upon the work of preaching and communicating the sacraments as often as either the bishops or the presiding officials commit these offices to their care. Therefore, we wish that those men be sent away to the universities for the sake of study. For they should bring with them learning and every other ability before they enter upon ecclesiastical duties. ★

Chapter 22. The Age of Free Prebendaries   Folio 64v

In those freer and more exempt prebends which do not have the care of a designated flock, young men can be employed who have completed their twenty first[97] year, if the commissioners have observed that the remaining [requirements] have been correctly provided for in them. They can also be allowed to take up residence at the universities for the sake of doing additional studies in Sacred Scripture *if they are deacons.*[98] But that separation ought to be limited, by all means, to a five-year period. *After that period, unless they are ordained to the rank of presbyter, they will be deprived of the prebend already obtained and forced by ecclesiastical censures to restore the fruits they had gained from it in former years.*[99]

Chapter 23. What Kind Of Diligence Is Required Of
Commissioners

The commissioners themselves ought to fulfill their duty with great vigilance and with the utmost assiduity and integrity. But if anyone of them has acted crookedly and, either for profit or for favor, has departed in this entire inquiry from the law of prescribed formulas, not only will he answer concerning the matter to Christ, the highest

---

[96]This is a marginal insertion and the hand might be that of Vermigli.

[97]"First" was added by Vermigli in the margin as an insertion.

[98]This phrase was added by Vermigli as an insertion placed in the margin.

[99]This last phrase was added by Cranmer.

Folio 65r ★ judge, but also, when he has been required, he will be forced to come under the judgement and censure of the bishop.

Chapter 24. The Form Of The Oath For Ministers

Finally, when the whole investigation is finished, if the person seems to be suited for assuming a benefice, he will be bound by oath to fulfill those matters which follow. In the first place, that he will persevere in the received faith and the true religion for his entire lifetime and that he will always hold fast to the pious institutions; that he will not acknowledge the monarchy and the tyranny of the Roman pontiff; that he will revere and venerate the King of England as the supreme head on earth, after Christ, of the English Church; next that he will show his reverence, faith, and submission to the bishop, insofar as all his commands are honest and holy; that he will diminish in no respect the rights of the Church committed to him; moreover, that he has given no gift beforehand nor will do so afterwards, and that no agreement concerning a gift has been made or will be made, either by himself as giver or by any other party as his procurator or vicar, with regard to the present benefice of which he is now taking possession; and if anyone, concealing that fact, has attempted anything of this kind, that, as soon as he has knowledge of it, he will report it to the bishop, and, by his decision, will give up the acquired benefice; but also that he will not then burden his church with new or increased pensions; finally, if it happens that he has not as yet been admitted to holy orders, that within the following six months, he will become a deacon and then will become a presbyter with the year following, *or as soon as he has completed his twenty-fifth year, if it happens that he as been admitted before that time to a freer prebend, as we said above.*[100] ★

Folio 65v ## Chapter 25. Those Who Rush Into And Seize Rashly Upon Ecclesiastical Benefices

And lest some rash person rush into and seize an ecclesiastical dignity or benefice, we wish that whoever has taken possession of some ecclesiastical benefice without the authority of the ordinary and without his authentic signature will not only be removed from the benefice which he unjustly invaded, without any hope of recovering it, but also that he will not be able to obtain any other hence forward. Also, as

---

[100]This last phrase was added by Cranmer.

his insolence requires, he will be excommunicated and suspended from the ecclesiastical ministry.[101] ★

CONCERNING COMMERCE IN ECCLESIASTICAL OFFICES IS TO BE PUNISHED

Folio 68r

Chapter 1. ~~Commerce In Ecclesiastical Offices Is To Be Punished~~ *There Should Be No Commerce In* Ecclesiastical Offices[102]

The excellence of laws is in vain unless the shameful and monstrous avarice of certain men who twist the soundness of the law to their own purposes is restrained by the sure bonds of penalties. For, since our forefathers made the excellent decision that a plentiful income be supplied to ministers of churches from those places to whose guidance they have been appointed, in these recent times such greed is discovered among many patrons for collecting wealth everywhere that they recall some small part either to themselves or their families from their own benefices at the time they invest them.

Chapter 2. How Manyfold Is The Commerce Of Ecclesiastical Offices[103]

Certain men themselves collect the entire incomes of benefices and by stipulation set aside for themselves or their families all the profits from them, bequeathing to the ministers *of the church* certain designated pensions which are ~~also~~ much smaller than a consideration of the benefices demands. Others, acting a little more moderately, reserve for themselves by stipulation only land of the kind which can be valued and is called glebe in the vernacular. Some take ★ homes and buildings   Folio 68v

---

[101]This entire chapter is written in Cranmer's hand. Following this chapter and written in Foxe's hand, is a notation that states: "Missing here are six chapters: 1. On renunciation and rejection of benefices; 2. On the exchange of ecclesiastical benefices; 3. On purgation; 4. On demolition [of buildings?]; 5. On alienation and renting of benefices; 6. On election, etc. in which are contained 39 chapters. You will find this in the codex of Mat[hew Archbishop of] Cant[erbury] fol. 58." And then a second notation, "On demolitions, alienation, renting, see at the end of this codex. These things are added in the printed book."

[102]The changes in the chapter title were made by Cranmer.

[103]This title was lined out and then in Cranmer's hand is the notation, "stet." The insertion found in this chapter is also in Cranmer's hand and perhaps it was his hand that cancelled the word "also."

which were customarily granted to ministers. Almost all the rest either collect an annual pension from the unfortunate ministers, or deduct tithes which they owe from the very consideration of the lands, or they undoubtedly bring about in their benefices some snare, apparent or hidden, to such an extent, that there are almost none who freely confer upon ministers of churches complete and undiminished benefices with a universal right to all privileges.

Chapter 3.   Stipulations Inserted Into Sacred Duties Are Not Valid[104]

Therefore, so that there can be some lessening of previous difficulties, we wish and command that, whether benefices or some other ecclesiastical dignities are [in question], they be granted freely and that nothing in them be taken away for any reason. Also, [regarding] whatever has been stipulated or agreed upon in any way between the patrons themselves and those who are to have possession of benefices or dignities, whether it is transacted between those men alone or has been arranged stealthily through others, and in which both parties insert into the [transactions] their own efforts, we give instructions [as follows]: all matters of this kind stipulated and agreed upon either by the men themselves or by others in their behalf, and which are either already arranged or will be arranged afterwards, are to be abolished by the authority of the present law and reduced to nothing.

★

Folio 69r   Chapter 4.   Of What Type The Examination Of Stipulations Should Be

It is also ordered, as often as anyone presents himself to the ordinary, that before he has been admitted by him to any ecclesiastical dignity, the ordinary make an inquiry about him, and that, as far as he is able, he search out and thoroughly investigate whether there have been any stipulations or agreements of such a kind as were set forth previously. And we wish that in this matter an oath be required by the ordinary from him who is seeking to be admitted, and not from him only but from whatever others whom he [the ordinary] believes to have knowledge of anything in this affair. The ordinary is to seek after the truth in this matter not by oaths alone, but by all other correct and legitimate means.

---

[104]The title of this chapter was lined out and then above it Cranmer has written "stet."

Chapter 5.　The Ordinary May Decide Upon A Judicial
　　　　　　　Clearing From Probable Conclusions

When the ordinary is unable to arrive at a full and perfect proof of
unjust stipulations, and yet, from the progress of the matter, either
he himself has a probable suspicion on his own that something is
wrong or surmises it from the credible testimonies of others, he is
not to admit the person offering himself until [that person] has legally
cleared himself by means of the canonical regulations.

Chapter 6.　The Type Of Penalty For Those Who Make
　　　　　　　Stipulations

If the ordinary has come to know for certain in any way ★ that anyone　Folio 69v
has acquired either a benefice or any other ecclesiastical dignity through
unjust promises, he will first summon to him either the patron or the
patron's vicar as well as the man himself who has been provided[105] with
either a benefice or an ecclesiastical dignity. Thereupon, when by plain
arguments he has proven and been convinced by their traffic, let him
immediately remove the person provided[106] with the benefice or dignity
from the position into which he had insinuated himself in devious and
perverse ways. For when he takes to himself the defilement of simony
by putting a price on sacred matters, he should not only be without
his present position, which was seized through a criminal act, but also
will not partake thereafter of any benefices or dignity or ecclesiastical
office.

★ CONCERNING THE CELEBRATION OF DIVINE　Folio 70r
OFFICES[107]

Chapter 1.　The Times When Divine Services Are To Be
　　　　　　　Celebrated In Cathedral Churches And Colleges

In the principal churches, called cathedrals, and ~~concerning the times
of divine services celebrated in cathedral churches and colleges and~~[108]
in collegiate churches, we wish the divine services to be performed
daily after the manner which the order of the days will demand, either

---

[105]This change is in Cranmer's hand.

[106]This change is in Cranmer's hand.

[107]The word "offices" was added by Cranmer.

[108]In the left margin opposite the cancellation in Foxe's hand is the notation, "An
objection must be raised."

on the eves of feasts or on feasts. For this reason, it is determined that the prayers called matins are to be recited at any suitable time before noon, with the addition of those which have been prescribed for the communion service. That solemn supplication, called the litany, is to occur every Wednesday and Friday. Likewise, in the afternoon the prayers of vespers are to be employed.

Chapter 2.   Who Should Be Present At Divine Services

All whom they call canons and clerics, who indeed are sustained by the outlays of the churches, are to convene for the appointed prayers in the morning as well as the afternoon and are to be present at them daily, unless they are able to offer a just excuse for an absence. But the rest who have not been present are, by the decision of the deans *or in their absence, their vicars,* [109] to be punished with a fine. Nevertheless, on the eves of feasts we by all means spare the studies of those who for the sake of learning have stationed themselves in the colleges of the universities. Yet we instruct all those very same men to be present on all weekdays for the sacred services, unless they have been absent on account of the duty of preaching. ★

Folio 70v ### Chapter 3.   The Administration Of Holy Communion On Sundays And Feast Days

On Sundays and the feasts of churches which are called cathedrals, we command that there be this order in the divine services: after the completion of morning prayers and the recitation of the supplication which is termed the litany, let the communion follow. And so as to facilitate the procedure, we exhort in the name of God and vehemently beseech through His glory that first the bishop himself, if it is possible for him to be present, then the dean and the archdeacon with the canons themselves and all the rest of the clerks, who are *sharers* [110] in the goods of that church, in like manner assemble themselves for communion with the minister, in order to invite others to the same service by their example and to be able to be known by this sign, since they themselves are true and living members of Christ and of the Church. ★

[109]This insertion is in Cranmer's hand.

[110]This word written in Cranmer's hand replaces a cancelled word which is the same as that written by Cranmer.

Chapter 4.   The Time Of Sacred Sermons   Folio 71r

However, we certainly abolish all sermons before noon in these churches
lest anyone be legitimately absent from his church when these occur.
But let the time from two until ~~four~~ three[111] in the afternoon be devoted
to sermons, and let it be immediately followed by evening prayers.

Chapter 5.   The Reading Of Sacred Lessons And The
              Chanting Of Psalms

In reciting of the divine chapters and in the chanting of Psalms the
ministers and clerks should carefully consider the fact that not only
should God be praised by them, but others also should be led to the
same worship by their exhortation, example, and observation. For this
reason, let them pronounce the words methodically and distinctly, and
let their chanting be clear and connected so that all things may attain
to the feeling and understanding of the hearers. Therefore, it is
determined that the vibrato and elaborate music, which is called
fashionable, be removed. It causes such disturbance to the ears of the
multitude that it is often impossible to hear the very language of those
speaking. Furthermore, the hearers themselves are to have a part in
the work together with the clerks and ministers. They will chant
certain small parts of the divine services, the first of which will be the
Psalms. The Creed will be added and the *Gloria in Excelsis,* the Ten
Commandments of God ★ and other special points of religion of this Folio 71v
kind which have the greatest importance in our common faith. For
with these pious exercises and inducements of the divine worship, the
very people will be aroused and will possess a certain feeling for Prayer.
If this amounts to nothing but to listen quietly, the mind will be chilled
and dulled in such a way that it will be able to form no ardent and
serious thought about divine matters.

Chapter 6.   The Order To Be Observed In Urban Parishes

In the same way, in cities with established parishes the whole order
will take place on Sundays and feast days which was previously assigned
for collegiate and cathedral churches, as they are called, except that
the duties of preaching will be attended to in the time before noon,
if possible, or at least a homily will take the place of the sermon. Then
the Lord's Supper will be taken. However, in the afternoon a sermon
will be instituted in cathedral churches only, or in suitable places of
this kind, to which we wish everyone from all places to assemble.
Therefore, in the morning let the ministers of the parish give their

---

[111]The change is in Cranmer's hand.

people a strong reminder so that they may prepare themselves for it. But, in very crowded and populous cities where the number of parishes is great, the distance between them is immense, and there are dense Folio 72r crowds of people, ★ we dispense from the afternoon sermons in that place on account of the location of the parishes and the abundance of men.

Chapter 7.   The Taking Of The Lord's Supper

It will be common to all churches that, *unless some grave cause demands otherwise,*[112] the Lord's Supper will be taken only on Sundays and as a certain appropriate memorial of the Lord to those attending. And we do not indeed *allow* it to proceed at that time unless a suitable number of those who will be partakers of the Lord's Supper present themselves. *In fact, those who are to receive Communion*[113] should gather on the day before in the presence of the minister so that he can take the time to examine their consciences and so that he might deal with them if they have done anything unjustly or of suspect nature in which there has been some general offense to the Church. Then let him explore their faith so that he may correct their ignorance or terrify their insolence or strengthen their doubtfulness. For no one ought to be admitted to the Lord's most sacred table whose faith is not in all respects perfect. Therefore, if anyone of those who are preparing themselves for the Lord's table wavers in any aspect of religion or has Folio 72v been wounded in his conscience, let him have free ★ admittance to the minister, and let him take from him consolation and relief from his sickness. And if he has made himself acceptable to the minister, let him be absolved from the crime, if that is needful.

Chapter 8.   What Is To Be Done When The Lord's Supper Is Lacking

If the Lord's table has been without the proper number of guests, it is preferable that there be no table rather than a solitary one. But the minister will sharply rebuke the ungrateful and impious negligence of the people in that they have removed themselves from the use of the most precious and health-giving Sacrament. And he will teach that it is not in any way fitting that he alone sit at the banquet instituted for many, but that these extraordinary delights for souls have been left by the Lord to a particular Christian community of all the devout. But, if they despise this most divine food of the mind with an enormous

---

[112]This is an insertion in Cranmer's hand.

[113]This change and "allow" are in Cranmer's hand. The words lined out cannot be read.

crime or desert it with horrible ingratitude, the fact remains, that very great and shameful wickedness is theirs, not his own, that everything has been furnished in abundance by him in order that this celestial food might be provided, that he has felt extreme anguish in that their barbarous and unholy insensibility or contemptuousness has put off a banquet so holy and necessary, and that he is entreating them with the greatest effort to consider Sunday as by no means to be neglected. Beyond this, let him earnestly commend to them the cause of the poor so that they might alleviate their needs. ★

Chapter 9.   What Is To Be Done In The Time After Noon   Folio 73r

Let the minister give the first hour of the afternoon to an explanation of the catechism, and let him spend either the whole hour on this matter or something more than that, if it seems advisable, provided it is not a hindrance to the sermon which the people will expect in a cathedral church; for it is completely unacceptable that it be passed over or forsaken. Let either the pastor himself or his vicar deal with the catechism, and let him apply great care to it; for the frequent inculcation of the catechism has the highest benefit and an extraordinary usefulness in the Church of God. We wish not only that it be committed to memory by young boys, but that it also be grasped eagerly by adolescents so that they may be instructed in the compendium of religion, and by their presence, do honor to the devout constancy of boys. When the catechism has concluded, let baptism follow immediately, if any boys have been prepared for it.

Chapter 10.   The Conduct Of Talks And Penance Follow
              Evening Prayers

When evening prayers are finished, which are to be attended by all after the sermon in their particular churches, there will be an assembly. Let the principal minister, whom they call the pastor, and the deacon, if by chance they happen to have been in attendance, or in their absence the vicar of the minister and the elders, undertake with the people an accounting ★ of the funds set aside for pious uses as to how these Folio 73v funds can most properly be employed. And let penance be reserved for the same time. For those should be recalled to an acknowledgement of their sins who have done some public act of perversity which has caused a general offense to the church; and they should make public satisfaction in order that the church may be strengthened by their salutary correction. Then the minister will withdraw and take counsel with some of the elders as to how the remainder, whose morals are said to be depraved and [in whom] a shameful life is detected, may be accosted by sober and virtuous men with a certain fraternal charity in accordance with the precept of Christ in the gospel. If they have set themselves straight by the admonitions of these men, God is to be earnestly thanked. But if they have persisted in crime, they are to be apprehended with that harshness of penalties which we see in the gospel was prepared for their insolence.

Chapter 11. How Excommunication Is To Be Carried Out

When, however the thunderbolt of excommunication is hurled, first Folio 74r the bishop should be approached and his opinion discovered. ★ If he has consented and has added his authority, let the formula of excommunication be carried out before the whole church so that, as far as possible, we may reintroduce in this matter the ancient discipline.

Chapter 12. The Religious Observance For Country Churches

In country churches on the mornings of feast days we wish a homily to be woven into the communion services. The afternoon will be taken up with catechism which we want even those who are older to attend. The explanation of the catechism we assign to the vicar. The principal minister, however, whom we call the pastor, will preach to the people immediately after catechism is concluded. That finished, evening prayers will follow, and finally administration of penances and of the *money*[114] which was publicly collected will be added.

Chapter 13. Sacred Functions Are Not To Be Performed In Chapels

Folio 74v Except in the case of a very special and burning necessity, ★ we do not want the sacraments to be administered in chapels, nor the rest of the divine service to be carried out in them. For the result would thus be that men would desert their own churches and leave them in solitude. Yet, it is most suitable to the fellowship of our faith that the individual sheep be called aside to their own proper pastors and that all the helps of piety and of divine worship be sought from them individually.

Chapter 14. Communion Will Not Be Celebrated In Private Homes

The Communion service will not be provided separately in homes. For it often happens that in the corners of private dwellings errors and

---

[114]Cranmer here corrected a scribal error.

pestilential opinions are whispered; and it thus comes about over and over again that the Lord's most sacred Supper, which is a witness and a sign for them of love, union, and charity, loses when it is removed to the recesses of private dwellings, not only all peculiar and innate power, but also by means of the monstrous crime of men degenerates into an occasion of strife and discord. ★

Chapter 15. What Should Be Maintained In The Case Of The   Folio 75r
              Sick And In The Families Of Nobles

Nevertheless, we are unwilling that the Lord's Supper be denied to the sick and to the extremely weakened who strongly demand it. Leaders also and persons of honor who have in their buildings plentiful and abundant throng [of people] and for whom it is not permissible, since they are busy in a public occupation, to move about in the ordinary churches, will be allowed to take to themselves the Supper of the Lord at home and there carry out every remaining function of the sacred services with a resident minister. There is a proviso: that this privilege not impede the service of a pastor of the common Church.

Chapter 16. Which Services Are To Be Commonly Observed In
              All The Churches

Principally, however, a diligent caution should always be adhered to in every class of churches, and also in the families of noblemen and then in all the places where the divine services are performed, lest anything proceed contrary to the precepts and formulas of that book written in our common tongue which we have ordered to be the proper and excellent judge and master of all divine worship. Whoever has sinned in this matter will, by the decision of the ecclesiastical judges, sustain penalties equal to the magnitude of the crime. Certainly if[115]
★ any other times suitable for divine worship occur, excepting these   Folio 75v
which we have set down, they should be employed in visiting and consoling weak, sick and afflicted persons of whatever kind and in other charitable works of this sort. Let the education of servants, the labor of penance, and the exercise of reading be put in the same category with these. And in sum let there be in all such a participation in feast days that all may turn aside to meditation upon and conduct of sacred and divine matters. ★

---

[115]A redundant "que" was cancelled at the end of this page.

CONCERING SACRAMENTS[116]

Chapter 1. What Is A Sacrament

A sacrament, as we understand that word in this place, is a sign exhibited by God which is able to be seen; by it the grace of Christ, accomplished for us by his promises and merits, and the pardon of sins, expressed by the very words of the promises, are shown forth [to us.] This has a two-fold power in our souls. For, firstly, the acceptance of these external signs and of the powers properly attributed to them recalls to our minds the price of the salvation regained for us and causes us openly to make profession of it. Next, it also sharpens and stirs up faith and adds strength to it. Moreover, it plans mutual charity among us and diffuses in our minds the fear of God. Finally, it stimulates us to a sincere and upright life. In former times circumcision was of this nature. Now baptism and the Eucharist have taken its place.

Chapter 2. What Should Be Sought In A Sacrament

For the accomplishment of a sacrament, three conditions ought to occur. First, it is an evident and clear sign which can be discerned manifestly. Second, it is a promise of God which is represented to us Folio 76v by an external sign ★ and is clearly confirmed. Third, it is a command of God by which an obligation is required of us, partly of doing these things and partly of commemorating them. Since these three conditions occur by the authority of the Scriptures only in baptism and the Eucharist, we place these two only as the true proper sacraments of the New Testament.

Chapter 3. What Is Baptism

Baptism is the sacrament by which our second generation, external to us, is shown forth by the aspersion of water, and pardon of sins is granted, and the power of the Holy Spirit is infused as was comprehended by the words of divine promise proposed in baptism, that there should be a more upright and perfect faith in us. Moreover, while we are being submerged in water and again are emerging from it, first the death of Christ for us and his burial are commended, and

---

[116]In the upper left hand corner of fol. 76r written in John Foxe's hand is a notation that reads: "This title On Sacraments is found in the codex of Matthew [Archbishop of] Canterbury and follows right after the title On Blasphemy." This does not affect the translation but it does indicate that there might have been a second copy of this manuscript and it does help in explaining the different order of titles found in the 1571 edition published by Foxe.

then his resurrection and return to life; so that we recall by these memorials of death and life and openly testify that sin submerged in us lies dead and buried and instead that the new and ★ salutary Spirit Folio 77r of God revives and blooms in us and, when the body has been dipped externally in the external waters, that our souls have been inwardly cleansed of the uncleanness of sin and are raised pure and cleansed to the eternal and celestial shores.

Chapter 4.   What Is The Eucharist, What Fruits It Has

The Eucharist is the Sacrament in which men eat food from bread and drink from wine, men who sit as guests at the holy table of the Lord. The grace of the Holy Spirit is sealed by the communication of this bread and wine among them, and the pardon of sins which they attain from that which they understand in faith and perceive as the holy body of Christ transfixed to the cross for the sake of our salvation and as the blood poured out for the removal of our sins, as the very promises of God openly say. Then also they are instructed by these illustrious signs, which can be openly discerned and they are brought to confess that Christ nourishes them and remains in them; and they themselves in turn have been placed in Christ. In addition, they learn that their union ought to be very great with other faithful ★ men of Folio 77v all ranks; since all are members glued to one and the same body of Christ. Moreover, since there is neither need for transubstantiation for all these things, nor of that presence of the real body of Christ which people used to imagine, but rather these curious inventions of men are first of all against the human nature assumed for our sake by the Son of God, and secondly they are at odds with divine Scriptures, and in addition they conflict with the whole rationale of the sacraments; we have seen to it that these frivolous dreams, as it were, have been justly cut out and thrown into oblivion, especially since, from these ideas, a great and pernicious horde of superstitions was brought into the Church of God.

Chapter 5.   Who Must Be Admitted To The Table Of The
              Lord

We want no one admitted to the table of the Lord until he has professed faith in the church. ★

Chapter 6.   Imposition of Hands Must Be Retained   Folio 78r

In instituting the ministers of the churches, such as deacons, priests, and bishops, the ceremony of the imposition of the hands should be retained; since a mention of this occurs in Sacred Scriptures and it has been the consistent practice in the Church.

Chapter 7.   That Weddings Should Be Solemnly Celebrated

We have decreed that the solemn rites of marriage should be placed before the eyes of the whole church with the greatest gravity and fidelity; if any of these things which we have sanctioned for these rites is absent, the ceremony shall be immediately considered null.

Chapter 8.   When Confirmation Ought To Be Held

We give to our bishops the task of confirming those who have learned the catechism; in these times of ours especially this ought to be observed since infants cannot themselves, at the time when they are baptized, profess their own faith and will. Therefore the time of their confirmation will be most suited for this. ★

Folio 78v Chapter 9.   Pastors Ought To Visit The Afflicted

Pastors of churches should diligently visit the weak, the afflicted and the sick, and can avail much for them by prayers and consolations and sustain them in their most difficult and dangerous times.

Chapter 10. Procedures In These Matters

We have included in one book which treats properly of ceremonies of our churches the formula of all these offices. We wish the administration of each individual matter to be derived from this.[117]

Folio 80r # ★CONCERNING IDOLATRY
AND OTHER CRIMES OF THIS KIND

Chapter 1.   What Vices Must Be Avoided In The Church

The cults of idols, magic, divination, choice by lots, and superstitions should be entirely avoided and exterminated; if anyone contaminates himself with these crimes, he should pay the penalty at the discretion of ecclesiastical judges and if he repudiates these penalties, he should be ejected from the church by the thunderbolt of excommunication; in order that we may abstain more easily from these crimes, we will define them separately one by one.

[117]Folio 79 is missing in the microfilm copy.

Chapter 2.   What Is the Cult Of Idols?

Idolatry, as we commonly call it, is a certain cult in which not the Creator but a creature of something invented by man is adored.

Chapter 3.   What Is Magic?

Magic is an agreement or alliance struck with the devil and his ministers, kindled by songs, prayers, marks of similar means of impiety which concerns either the investigation of future events or the acquisition of certain things which we have sought. ★

Chapter 4.   What Is Divination?   Folio 80v

Divination is the prophecy of secret things, foreseeing by the instinct of a certain evil and impious spirit and connected with auguries, auspices, and omens and other depraved levity of this kind: a curious disposition also marks the fault of these people who profess that they know the ways and events by an appearance of figures delineated by the precepts of astrology, as they wish it to seem, by the appearance of things moved either by secret means or some other cause, then also by the appearance of actions undertaken in every life.

Chapter 5.   What Is Fortune-Telling By Lots?

Fortune telling by lots is understood when hidden things are revealed through lots of any kind or some coming end of present acts is presignified.

Chapter 6.   What Is Superstition?

Superstition is the cult related to God, setting out from a certain immense human eagerness or a fixed propensity of the mind which people commonly call good intention and always has its origin from the natural capacity of man separately without the authority of divine Scriptures. ★

Chapter 7.   The Duty Of The Pastor In These Crimes   Folio 81r

Pastors should diligently warn people so that they may flee from these evils as from certain most grave pestilences of the Christian faith, and so that they may not allow themselves to be bound ever by any respect for any of these things, whether it be money for example, or pleasure, or honor or health, or knowledge of abstruse matters, or some other depraved affection that resounds in their minds or disturbs them. For [such persons] allow themselves to be bound by the impulse of evil emotions, by the chains of the devil, and to fall away from the most sweet liberty of the Christian religion.

Chapter 8.   Who Ought To Be Punished Because Of These Crimes

Moreover, we announce the most serious punishments not only for those who use curious and pestiferous arts but also for those who question such evil quacks concerning their activities, or who
Folio 81v accommodate any work of theirs by any means to their causes. ★

Chapter 9.   The Loss Caused By These Skills Must Be Paid

If anyone receives any loss by means of their evil arts, any loss in grain, fruit, buildings, livestock, or any of their goods, they may be
Folio 83r compelled to make the fullest restitution.[118] ★

FORMULA FOR RECONCILIATION OF THE EXCOMMUNICATED[119]

First of all at that time which was decided by the ordinary, the defendant will approach the church and stand outside the gates, absolutely with all that disposition of body which the legitimate judge has ascribed. But the pastor will approach from the other side and will address him in the full gathering of the church thus.

"Dearest brother N. in Christ, do you wish to confess your sin before God *and in the sight of this Church to bear witness*[120] so that we may understand that your mind has been alienated from the depravity in which you were previously held, and so that we may again gather you into the fellowship of our church from which you had previously been turned away by your singular perversity?" And the defendant should answer: "I very much wish and strongly ask that I be called back by God's kindness and yours as soon as possible to my former condition whence I evilly and sadly fell." *Then*[121] the pastor should lead him into

---

[118]At the end of this section of the manuscript is a note by John Foxe indicating the title "On Preachers" was to come next according to the codex in possession of the Archbishop of Canterbury and in fact this was the order Foxe followed in the 1571 edition.

[119]Folio 82 is blank but with the chapter title at the top that is the same as this chapter. There are no chapter headings in the manuscript.

[120]This insertion is in Cranmer's hand.

[121]This is an insertion in Cranmer's hand.

the church and should deliver this speech to the whole assembled multitude.

"Brothers, before your eyes we have brought this defendant and we have, as is appropriate for our office, placed in your presence this defendant, your brother, who is prepared to acknowledge publicly before you the deformity of his sin, by which he has offended the Lord our God and this his holy church, so that he may prove clearly to us that his senses have been reformed and the infamy of his moral life has been corrected. Although this act should bring no shame to him, still ★ he will greatly magnify the glory of God and the state of our Folio 83v Church. For this reason, therefore, he shows himself in order that he may again be joined with you before God and in order that he may again cherish the brotherly relationship recently interrupted. My role in this is that I should repeat from Sacred Scripture first what ought to be decided separately and properly concerning the crime of the present defendant; then what common thought ought to be undertaken by all of us in regard to our common weakness. First of all, the authority of Sacred Scriptures teaches us two things about sin: the first is that we all without any exception are pushed into the prison of sins; the other is that our chains are borne for this purpose, not so that we might forever lie bound in them but that the immense and infinite mercy of God the Father, because of Christ, might be made manifest. By these thoughts we can easily understand what we ourselves can think about our offenses and then about the offenses of others and what ought to be our attitude towards them. For that fellowship of sinning which previously was said to pertain to all teaches us in this respect, that our whole very nature, indeed by itself, is always borne toward every kind of evil deed. Therefore, offenses of others ought to seem deserving of compassion to us and it is not fitting to accuse fiercely or to despise haughtily brothers who are either limping in their duties or rushing to ruin: but this is rather the part of Christian union that we have no less sorrow in the downfall of brothers, no matter how tremendous and capital, than if we ourselves had fallen.

But, rather we ourselves contemplate our weakness and fall in the fall ★ of brothers and we should make our common complaint Folio 84r concerning this, tearfully, with common voice before God our Father. For if truly we think this within ourselves, that the nature of all men conceives the same of sin, we will never inveigh against others harshly in a matter in which we see that we could be involved; no, rather we will gently and submissively give thanks to God that we have not ourselves slipped into so great a crime and we will ask for the constancy of our innocence by most vehement and ardent prayers. And since indeed *we* are slaves of sin dedicated to miserable servitude ~~we should~~

~~not only acknowledge them among ourselves but also should tolerate and put up patiently with each other~~ *we should forgive them as we share penitence and pray together.*[122] For if we were to do otherwise, we ourselves would speak in testimony against ourselves, in that we would accuse him of fraternal wickedness of which we were similarly guilty, [lit.: in regard to which our depravity was similarly delinquent]. But, since we are wallowing in the banquet of sinners to such a degree that we cannot be extricated from it by any excellence or perfection of our works, but only from the gratuitous mercy of God the Father, because of Christ relief comes to us, so that his name should be kept in the greatest fame and everlasting glory because of this. Our reward for piety and duty ought to be mature and our respect for the singular mercy of God ought to be timely since God has embraced us so firmly in his most beloved son and heir, Christ, that he has transferred all the penalty of our sins onto him and has delivered him to his most harsh torments. If we in our crimes judge ourselves and do not seek excuse for our impious deeds, ★ we deflect the fault and the harshness of divine laws onto God; but rather we should flee to those treasuries of mercy which God the Father has founded in his son Jesus Christ, and we should adhere to him alone forever and should demand firmly and sincerely his salutary and propitious favor with unanimity of purpose.

Folio 84v

For he weighs the intention rather than numbering the words. And if in the intimate recesses of the mind we have derived a true earnest sorrow and we ourselves have withstood our iniquity with the great fidelity and when we have fought this and have made prayers with fixed hope to regain his mercy, God is at hand immediately, even before he is invoked; he offers himself to our embrace and he turns his attention to us before we can plan our petitions in any way. But rather, he pours this healthful and necessary awareness of sins into our minds and he himself placed on his shoulder those taught by this learning and carries them to his most blessed sheepfold, and he exults more over one person finally recalled to health which he has regained by true knowledge of sins and correction of morals than over just and perfect men who previously were slaves in his kingdom.

Therefore, since these things are so, beloved brothers, and since there has been placed at this time in your midst ★ your brother-defendant, who wishes to acknowledge the vileness of his sin before you and wishes to pray for his penalty from our Lord God, common Father in your presence, a presence which he venerates and reveres as the most holy church of God, and since he suppliantly asks that by submitting this defection of his he can find a way to your

Folio 85r

---

[122]This deletion and new wording is in Cranmer's hand.

communion and can arrive at his own higher place of fraternal rank among you, you as Christians for your part ought to remember mercy, and ought to join your sins with the sins of this accused brother of ours present [before you], and ought to judge them to be a perpetual habit and similar to our offenses. But, the humiliation of this brother of ours and his self-deprecation should break our arrogance of mood and lessen our obstinacy. As he has in a way deserted and fled himself, confused and stricken by the shame of his crimes, so your memory of your crimes and shame at them should be the same before God. Then when you attend public, open confession of the crimes of this defendant and you estimate that this confession has been made in the best faith, you should throw him on your shoulders following the example of Our Lord God the Father and should sustain his broken members shattered by the gravest ruins of his sins with the clement lenience of fraternal love; for thus lightening the burdens of our sins by our mutual acts of mercy, we will preserve in an outstanding manner that new golden law of Christ who binds us to sanctify love among ourselves.

Your prayers should set out to God the Father with the prayers of this defendant, your tears ★ also should go with his tears, and thus Folio 85v finally receiving in your mind a sure promise of divine favor because he wishes to impart immense, infinite mercy to us because of Christ, we all, along with this accused brother of ours, may expect pardon of sins, and receiving the accused brother to ourselves piously and dutifully, we all may bear witness to this by our efforts as well as we can. In order that this may be brought into greater light and be discerned more easily, we should accept and acknowledge him as a most beloved brother and as a member of our common body in Christ, by introducing the reason as grace; and in order that our inner feeling should be better witnessed in this recovered member of our body, we should also acknowledge him by public prayers and congratulations and finally even kisses. But you, my brother, first and before all else descend into yourself and, consulting God as your witness and judge, examine carefully your mind in all its parts; realize that you are standing before God, not just appearing before men, and think of the fact that you are handling these matters not just in this age with men but in heaven principally with Our Lord God the Father.

Certainly indeed, my brother, however much we wretches may be confused, God will not be laughed to scorn. Therefore, see to it vehemently again and again that you do nothing in this most holy business craftily or secretly. We are external witnesses of your submission ★ which we have seen. But God enters into the secret Folio 86r inner hidden recesses of your mind and he will avenge most seriously any perfidy he finds in you. Therefore, my brother, magnify the glory of God as much as you can; and you will do this most fruitfully, if you vehemently and seriously detest the baseness of your vices and utterly abhor all memory of them. For this is the greatest splendor of divine glory, that we ourselves who are casting away and rejecting ourselves implore the favor of God through the most holy name of Christ his Son. And, this is the one outstanding light of divine goodness: that although all other things have been spurned and despised, we are saved by the sole gratuitous mercy of God the Father; may God the Father grant this salvation to you and to all of us also, and may there be everlasting honor to Him with the Son and the Holy Spirit. Amen"

When the pastor has finished this speech, the defendant within sight and earshot of the surrounding church will pronounce clearly and distinctly the words which follow:

"Eternal God, Author and Father of all things, you have prepared the heaven and earth and everything shining within these already from the beginning for the glory of your name and the use of our life, so that we might always have the greatest place of your honor and praise and so that we might direct all our actions to your most holy will. But I, most loathsome and offensive sinner among all sinners, recoiling from this plan of yours which is so holy and healthful, have violated your most divine majesty most gravely by my great perversity. To my immense loss and danger, because of the blot of my sins, I have infected Folio 86v and contaminated that most pure garment of innocence ★ in which you had covered me by the sacrament of baptism through Christ; next I have utterly and recklessly thrown away that garment from me, and I have wickedly disjoined myself from the church to which I was united by the force of baptism. Thus it happened that I was pushed into the miserable servitude of sinners and I could expect from your majesty nothing except horrible punishment and everlasting destruction. But, however, because of the great trustworthiness of your promises by which you announce favor and pardon to all, no matter how criminal and wicked, who presents the merits of Christ with fixed faith and rely on these [merits] always, and have great sorrow because of their crimes and sigh and grieve upon remembering them, I gladly profess, acknowledge, detest, and abhor my sin before you, my Father, and before these brothers of mine, located in this present church of yours.

"Therefore, spare me, Lord God, have pity on my utterly miserable and afflicted condition; I call on your infinite immense mercy. A most vile sinner, I call on your mercy that is greater than every thought [of it], O God and Father, because of your Son, my savior Jesus Christ who was driven to the atrocious and disgraceful death of the cross to atone for the common sins of all because of a certain incredible love of the human race. Have pity on me, have pity on me, I say, the most abject and sorrowful and evil sinner, and pour forth the great strength of your Spirit on me hereafter so ★ that I may always cherish your _{Folio 87r} name with everlasting remembrance of your kindnesses and so that I can bear witness to you and spread abroad publicly and privately the praise of your clemency, with a constant integrity of actions and duties."

When he has recited these words, he should stand erect and, being moved to some higher place from which he can easily be seen and heard, he should say clearly and openly the following:

"O brothers, I confess, I confess that I have incredibly offended by my most serious sins my God especially, then you all also, and I confess that I am thus most unworthy in every way to be assumed into your church again and to be numbered among the members of the most precious Body of Christ; since I have rejected and abused the most holy commands of my heavenly Father most evilly and sinfully and since I have profaned as much as I could by my great evil the holy blood of my Savior, Christ, by which I was snatched from the jaws of hell, I have offered to you, brothers, a license for sinning and an example of impiety."

Then he should uncover his own sins of which he was accused and after exposing this, he should proceed with the ordained speech:

"Therefore in this evil way of living of mine, I myself am painful to myself and this ruin that results from my evil deed is indeed intolerable to me in every way; and so I call you all to witness through the immortal God that no one should be led by my most corrupt example to this present evil deed of mine or to any other of this kind. No, rather it is fitting ★ that you should be deterred by my misery _{Folio 87v} from contaminating yourself by a similar shameful act. Then I suppliantly ask you, through the great love of Our Lord Jesus Christ, through his most harsh endurance of death on the cross by which he freed the whole human race from the chains of the devil, that you pardon this present crime of mine in which I foully defiled the most eminent society of your Church. Then, I greatly ask you also to count me among your number in your mercy despite whatever perversity I had."

Then the pastor should question the assembled church thus:

"Brothers, do you wish to pardon the fault of this defendant who is now reviving, this fault by which he offended this gathering of yours and by your common prayers to commend his case to God the Father, that He may show mercy to him, and so that what we do here on earth, he may be willing to confirm likewise in heaven?" The people should respond: "We are willing."

Again the pastor should question thus:

"Do you wish to receive this defendant into your assembly and subsequently to consider him in the number of the dearest brethren?" The people should respond: "We are willing."

Then the pastor should thus address the defendant, who is kneeling:

"Dearest brother, since you have professed in the company of the whole church that you have the greatest, deepest sorrow for your sin Folio 88r and were therefore moved in your inmost feelings; ★ in addition since you have undergone the punishment of ecclesiastical discipline tranquilly and submissively; then since you have asked pardon of your crime from God *and have asked your brothers the same submissively and suppliantly,*[123] vehemently urging them not to use your example in order to be negligent but rather to gain insight in order to live morally; finally since their charity has yielded pardon to you and has placed you again in their society; (Here the pastor, touching the head of the defendant, should begin thus) I, before this church whose administration is committed to me, release you from the punishment of your sins and the bonds of excommunication, through the authority of the power of God, Jesus Christ, and the Holy Spirit, with the consent of the members of this church here present and also with the approval of the ordinary; I restore to you again your former place in the church and your full right."

After these things are finished, the pastor should embrace the defendant and acknowledge his brother with a holy kiss and should raise him with his hands and should lead him in the middle of the church near a table prepared for communion, singing in the meantime the *Te Deum* or *Gloria in Excelsis* or whatever seems most appropriate; and the choir should answer continuously in alternating verses. At the end the pastor should add: "May the name of the Lord be affected with praise." The people should respond: "From this time for all eternity." Prayer should follow with these words:

"We give thanks to you, most gentle Father, that you have recalled this brother of ours from the broad way which descends to eternal Folio 88v destruction in good time by your singular mercy and ★ that you have furnished him the salutary spirit of repentance which is the way to eternal life, so that emerging from the pestilential swamps of the devil, he will migrate into the sweetest pastures of Jesus Christ our Saviour and will be received into his flock from which he previously most dangerously strayed. Therefore, may your name be in everlasting

---

[123]This insertion is in Cranmer's hand.

honor, may your praise be spread always by our constant commemoration, may your glory be cherished and frequented by our offering of continuous prayers, not only in all your remaining infinite goodness but especially towards this brother of ours whom you have led back onto the path to our common joy and exultation so that we might receive the greatest joy from this salvation regained through you, through the salvation of him who formerly brought us the greatest sorrow by his most calamitous downfall. Therefore, we ask you that these prayers poured forth on behalf of [our] brother may come to you, and that you yourself may wish to be the weight and strength in these, so that he with us and we along with him may conform our whole life to your will in fear, faith, hope, love, and in the comprehension of your remaining commands so that we may always acquiesce in the perpetual veneration of your name. Hear us, O God Father, hear us. Grant your Holy Spirit to us your servants because of Jesus Christ who lives and reigns with you in the unity of the Holy Spirit God."

When the pastor has ended the last prayer, he should turn to the defendant now clearly reconciled and should strongly urge him to not fall again into the license of sinning, showing how dangerous are second falls in which, by authority of Scripture, worse extremes are necessary than with the earlier offenses; ★ and from this he should ⟨Folio 89r⟩ require public profession of the defendant that he himself has firmly decided within himself, how he demands and asks God that he help him, that he himself show the most diligent and greatest caution not to incur again the wrath of God and not to wander from his most holy precepts so far that a public gathering of the faithful should again be necessary for him. Then also, he will ask God and will demand the common prayers of the church for this so that God will confirm this beginning and will strengthen him in Christ.

As often as someone is thrown out by excommunication from the church because of the magnitude of sins and the authority of the judges has been used for this, and again he has been received into this communion by that formula which preceded, and he has been freed from crime, he should see to it that at the fixed time prescribed the ordinary should be informed of his reconciliation and he should send that synography signed with the public seals; on this synograph the pastor himself should subscribe first, or his vicar, and some of the most grave and reputable men in he church who were involved in the undertaking, partly so that the reconciliation itself may be better attested, also so that [the penitent] may feel along with the others the shared joy because the matter has been done in a pious and Christian mannter.[124]

★CONCERNING THE CHURCH AND THE MINISTERS AND THEIR DUTIES[125]

Chapter 1. Concerning Sacristans

The sacristans of a parish should be provided with a stipend. It will be his task to instruct all the children of the parish in the alphabet and catechism in the vernacular tongue when they are brought to him so that children may begin to know what is to be believed, how to pray, and how to live well and blessedly. However, anyone who refuses to do this and neglects this duty of his over a two month period should be removed after he has been twice warned by the bishop or the ordinary of that locality. Also, if the parishioners withhold the usual stipend or give a subtracted or diminished stipend, they should be compelled by the bishop or the ordinary of that locale by means of ecclesiastical censure to furnish it. Yet, if the sum of the stipend seems too small to the bishop, it will be his duty by his own free choice to make it more bountiful from the assets of the parishioners, taking into account the parish's wealth. And, it is also his task to keep the church clean, and to take care of the holy Bible and the Paraphrases and the other books of the church so that they be neither torn nor marred; [it is his job to toll] the bells by which people are called either to sermons or to public prayers, or when ever they should pray for conduct of a soul, or any time a grave reason, or the necessity of human accidents requires; to see that the vestments and chalices and whatever other ornaments are assigned for sacred uses be kept clean and shining; and to warn at the proper time the church wardens of anything that is worn out by age or accident or any other necessity that it must be changed; to furnish the water for baptism; to prepare the bread and wine for celebration of the sacred banquet of our Lord; and constantly to assist and dutifully help the pastor as much in the celebration of the marriage ceremony as in the care and visitation [of

---

[124]In the lower left margin on folio 89r, John Foxe's writing indicates that the next title in the Archbishop's codex would be "On Judgements."

[125]A blank folio 90 precedes this chapter but with the same chapter title at the top of the page as found in this chapter title.

the sick] and in funerals and all other sacred functions. If he be found
too little ~~studious~~ diligent[126] in performing these duties, ★ it will be   Folio 91v
the task of the parish priest and the wardens either to call him back
to his duty or to substitute another in his place ~~after one as well as
an alternate admonition~~ after twice warning him.[127] And it will pertain to
these same people, i.e. the parish priest and wardens, when an office
of this kind is vacant, ~~to choose a suitable man for it~~ to hire a suitable
man for the job.[128] If they cannot agree in the selection, let the matter
be determined by the judgement of the bishop.

Chapter 2.   Concerning the Stewards Or Keepers Of The
Churches And Vessels

The stewards of the parishes will procure all of the necessary equipment
for the church by purchases, and will give these things to the sacristan
~~that there is certainty~~ in such a way that it be entirely provided that nothing
detrimental happens to the church's possessions. They will impose
order on the people of God in such a way that when public prayers
or sermons of the word of God or sacred readings are held in the
church, and that while our injunctions or those of the bishop or
whatever statutes or mandates are being recited, or sacraments of the
Lord are being administered, absolutely no noise may be heard in the
assembly from persons walking about, reading, praying, or talking
aloud, or in any other way making noise. But if anyone dares to shout
out at the preacher in the church or to oppose the ministering presbyter
or ~~does not fear to disturb~~ to impede any order instituted by us in the
church, it will be the task of the wardens to throw him out of the
church ~~and the [right of] return to the church is not granted to him
unless it is restored by the bishop~~ and he may not be allowed entrance to
the church except by the bishop. But the bishops ought to curb unyielding
persons of this sort with some ecclesiastical censure as if by a bridle
bringing them to a great gravity and modesty of behavior and ~~to punish with
censure~~ to bind the wardens with ecclesiastical ★ punishments if they do   Folio 92r
not do this. Wardens will be chosen by a majority of the parishioners
and around Christmastime each year will offer to the pastor and the
parishioners, an account of the receipts and expenditures. And since
they are in charge of the furnishings of the church, whatever they have
received from those who preceded them in this office they should hand
over fresh and undiminished to their successors. And ~~if when the
accounting is rendered they have church money~~ after the accounts have

---

[126]This substitution was made by Cranmer.

[127]This change was made by Cranmer.

[128]This change was made by Cranmer.

been completed, if any ecclesiastical money remains in their possession, they should be compelled by ecclesiastical censors to give satisfaction *restore* all this before the next Easter. *The man who refuses* the office of warden imposed by the parishioners will pay ten shillings the first time, twenty the second, forty the third, to the works of the Church,. When called to some ordinary visitation, if they have not gone and performed their duty, they will be punished at the discretion of the visitor.[129]

Chapter 3. Deacons

The deacon will be the patron of the poor so that he should strengthen the weak, release the imprisoned, help the needy; and he will be the father to orphans, patron of widows, and solace to the afflicted and all the wretched as much as he can. He will also diligently hand over the names *of the poor* to the parish priest so that by his advice the whole church may be moved and see to their need, in order that *brothers* who were born of the same heavenly Father and redeemed by the same

Folio 92v price ★ *may not wander around at large* begging. Let them constantly assist their pastors by whom they have been adopted in sacred prayers and ministries *duties.* They will recite to the people the daily readings from the Word of the Lord and they will preach if any necessity occurs, and will administer the sacraments, provided the bishops or ordinaries grant them this permission. Bishops should not promote them to a higher office unless it be demonstrated by the presbyters of the church that they have performed their duties carefully.[130]

Chapter 4. Presbyters

In the presbyter, character should shine out as described by Paul in Timothy 3 and in Titus 1. They should continually feed the flock of God entrusted to them with the word of life and they should constantly entice the flock to *genuine*[131] obedience, both to God and to magistrates *of dignified rank,*[132] and they should constantly invite all Christians to mutual goodwill. They should not be drunkards or gamesters, or bird catchers, or hunters or sycophants, or idlers, or proud; but they should diligently incline to the study of Sacred Scripture and the preaching of the Word and prayers to the Lord on behalf of the church. No one should have a papist shaving or tonsure on his head. No unmarried presbyter should allow a woman younger than sixty to dwell in his house, unless it be his mother or his father's sister or his mother's

---

[129]All the changes in this chapter are made in Cranmer's hand.

[130]All the changes in this paragraph are in Cranmer's hand.

[131]This is an insertion in Cranmer's hand.

[132]This is an insertion in Cranmer's hand.

sister or his sister. Every presbyter should have his own holy Bible not only in ★ English but also in Latin. His clothing should be proper Folio 93r and dignified as befits a minister, not a soldier, in accord with the decision of the bishop.[133]

Chapter 5.   Archpresbyters Or Rural Deans

Let every deanery have a rural archpresbyter who is ~~to be named by the bishop or the ordinary~~ *placed in charge by the bishop or the ordinary of the church.* But, his office will be on a yearly basis. He, as if in a watchtower, will constantly watch over the presbyters, deacons, stewards and sacristans so that each may perform and discharge his duty. He should *investigate* idolators and heretics, practicers of simony, procurers and prostitutes, adulterers and fornicators, those with two wives simultaneously or two husbands, magicians and sorcerers, calumniators and blasphemers, sodomites and drunkards, breakers of last wills and perjurers, violators of our injunctions or those of the bishop. And, he should have the authority of summoning to himself and examining those suspected of these crimes. He should give over in writing to the ordinary of that place or the bishop within ten days every accusation that *has arisen* whether by public reputation or proven or suspected by testimony of witnesses. But, whoever refuses to come to him when summoned by a deputy shall be punished as contumacious, at the discretion of the bishop. He will ensure that the will of the bishop, made known to him through letters, is immediately made known to all the churches of his deanery with as much speed as possible. Otherwise he will be ★ punished for contempt. In about the Folio 93v sixth month of his office, he will inform the bishop or the ordinary of the place how many meetings have been held in his deanery in that space of time.[134]

Chapter 6.   Archdeacons

The archdeacon should be next after the bishop and his vice minister of the Lord[135] ~~but~~ without violation of the rights of the dean which ~~pertain~~ to the cathedral church. And in addition, he should be a presbyter and in perpetual residence so that those who are in subordinate offices shall diligently perform their duty. Therefore, they should be the bishop's eyes. They should reside in the archdiaconate, should preach, perform pastoral duties, and conduct visitations. If they do not do these things and do not give the bishop a ~~reasonable~~ just reason, then

---

[133]The words "in accord with" and "of the bishop" are underlined in the manuscript.

[134]The changes in this chapter are in Cranmer's hand.

[135]The words "his vice minister of the Lord" are underlined in the manuscript.

~~they should be compelled~~ *they should be driven to these duties* by him through censure and ecclesiastical punishments. He will travel through his archdiaconate twice each year or once at the least; not only will he admonish the archpresbyters and all those other lesser ministers of their duties, but also he will seek an accounting from them first of destruction of churches and buildings, and of distribution of the treasury of the poor, and of the accession and disposal of church goods. However, whatever offense exists either in these matters or in those which are *referred* to investigation by the archpresbyter ~~he will punish~~ *will be corrected* by ecclesiastical censures. If he himself does not conduct himself properly, he must be chastised by the bishop in accordance as he deserves. The Archdeacon, also within twenty days after his

Folio 94r visitation has been completed, will refer ★ all quarrels of the people, all ~~transgressions~~ *offenses,* all errors of lesser ministers, finally the whole series of his own actions to the bishop so that through him, as it were through the organ of the eye, the bishop may see what is right and what is wrong through the whole diocese. And among other things, it will be his duty to indicate diligently to the bishop what parishes there are in the diocese, where the wretched, the needy and the sick are not provided for, just as has been recently decreed in the laws of parliament; *so that* they can be more sharply incited to the performance of their duty sedulously and more diligently by the warnings not only of the ordinary but also of the preachers.[136]

Chapter 7. Cathedral Churches

The cathedral church should be the seat of the bishop. The statutes of the founders, received long ago, will be kept pure and intact as long as they are not contrary to the word of God, and are not at variance with our constitutions on religion, either published or to be published. Let it be the right of the bishop to make visitation here, to correct vices of behavior, to punish evildoers and openly ~~to deprive~~ *to throw out of office* those who openly resist.[137]

Chapter 8. Deans

Deans also, since they are allotted among clerics full dignity and an *honored* place in the church, should be presbyters, serious men, learned and outstanding for their great prudence. They should rule cathedral

Folio 94v churches in accordance with their constitutions; ★ they should be in

---

[136]All the changes in this chapter are in Cranmer's hand with the exception of the underlined words in the first sentence. Cranmer might have underlined these but there is no evidence he did or did not.

[137]This is a change in Cranmer's hand.

charge of the college of canons and of the other clerics of the principal church, and they should not allow discipline to slip. With the greatest diligence, they should see to it that the sacred rites are performed in their church with due order and care, so that all benefits may be done with order and with ~~decent~~ *becoming* dignity ~~for edification~~ *for the benefit of the brethren.* As the archdeacons are *abroad,* so they should be at home, i.e., in the cathedral church, helpful to the bishop and his canons and clerics, that is, its two most useful and necessary members. Therefore, the deans ought not to be absent from the church without the greatest and most urgent cause, which must be approved by their *own* bishop.[138]

Chapter 9. Procurators

It will be the task of the procurators not only to be involved with the ceremonies of the cathedral church and to review them *in turn in accordance with* the constitutions of the college, but also to see to it that the interpretation of Sacred Scripture ~~be held~~ *be undertaken* in their college by a learned man and skilled theologian and that this ~~at least~~ should be *done* at least three times a week. They should survey this function themselves personally, or if they have brought anyone to it, they should furnish them twenty pounds a year whether from the common revenues of the college or from the income of the individual prebends; or if this seems more convenient, they should permanently assign one prebend for this task. The dean likewise, and the procurators should deliver a sermon in the cathedral church every Sunday *and no* cleric of the cathedral church, ~~provided he is present~~ *if he is at home,* should have permission to absent himself from this or from the theological lecture ~~under penalty of.~~ *But, if he is absent, a money penalty* of one month's stipend *should be exacted* unless he has proved *the cause of his absence* to the dean or, in his absence, his vicar.[139] ★

Chapter 10. On The Rank And Dignity Of Bishops In The Church   Folio 95r

Since bishops hold the first place among the other ministers of the church, they ought to rule and nourish the lower ranks of the clergy and the whole people of God with such sound teaching, grave authority, and prudent counsel so that they may rule over their faith, that they may show themselves truly to be the servants of the servants of God,

---

[138]The changes in this chapter are in Cranmer's hand.

[139]The changes made in this chapter are in Cranmer's hand. In a note at the bottom of folio 94v, Cranmer has written, "In this place should be added chapters 16 and 17 from the section 'On Admission To Ecclesiastical Benefices.'"

and they should know that ~~rule~~ *authority* and ecclesiastical jurisdiction was conferred on them chiefly for no other reason than that as many men as possible ~~should grow rich [in Christ]~~ *could join* Christ through the bishop's ministry, and ~~hard work~~ *efforts* that those who are already Christ's should grow in Him and *be built up,* and if some should fall away that they should be led back to the Shepherd Christ the Lord and should be renewed through saving penitence.[140]

Chapter 11. Obedience To Be Shown To Bishops

Since all the church ought to pursue peace and ~~to be as eager for unity as they can, therefore...to the bishop~~ *incline to harmony as much as is permitted,* not only the dean, archdeacon, archpresbyter and other ministers will obey *the bishop* who is placed in charge of the church, but also all the members of Christ committed to his care ~~will obey him so~~ *will accommodate their will to his* so that they ~~will most eagerly obey and defer to~~ *most readily obey his will,* both in those matters which teach the word of God and in those also which dictate concerning Christian discipline and our ecclesiastical laws.[141]

Chapter 12. The Various And Multiple Duties Of The Bishop

The bishop should hand down in his church sound teaching of the
Folio 95v word of God ★ especially through himself b**u**t also through others, with as great diligence and care as he can. He should confer holy orders at the appropriate time. He should not lay hands on anyone either because of bribery nor rashly. He should appoint suitable ministers for ecclesiastical benefices; but he should remove unworthy ministers when grave causes and ~~their evil living~~ *perversity of morals* demand this, and he should throw them out of the administration of the church. He should hear the testimony and quarrels of the church concerning its pastors. He should settle disputes that have arisen between ministers and churches. He should correct vices and ~~corruptions~~ *evil habits* by ecclesiastical censure. He should prescribe ~~injunctions~~ *edicts* for a better way of living. He should excommunicate those who persistently and stubbornly make opposition, but he should receive penitents back into grace. He should visit the whole diocese ~~also every triennium~~ *every third year* as much in exempt places as in those that are not exempt ~~because of cases that arise.~~ He should receive the usual collections and at other times as often as it seems best. He should visit *because of new events which may occur.* Let him be free to do so provided that he does it at his own expense and does

---

[140]All changes in this chapter are in Cranmer's hand.

[141]All changes in this chapter are in Cranmer's hand.

not impose new burdens of stipends or collection on the churches. He should have synods yearly at established times. It should also be his concern ~~youths already instructed in catechism or if there is need, [persons]~~ of more mature age *to confirm those instructed in their catechism* at a fixed time of the year. Also, he should approve wills. Finally, let each and every thing be of concern to the bishops which are their concern from the Command of God, and which our Ecclesiastical laws have entrusted to their knowledge and judgement.[142]

Chapter 13. The Family Of The Bishop[143]

As it is necessary that the bishop be endowed with serious and holy habits, so also it is necessary that his family ★ be serious, modest and holy. ~~Because~~ *As much as* domestic *duties* allow, the family of the bishop should be eager for the word of God ~~as it may be~~ *since it can be* useful to the church of God in various ways. For from his home, ~~a Trojan horse~~ *as from a treasury,* men ~~should be drawn forth~~ who are put in command of ecclesiastical ~~ministries~~ *offices.* Certainly, they could learn dogmas of the faith properly and solidly, if the bishop is the man that he should be, and they could ~~gain for themselves no little experience~~ *gather great knowledge* of how to rule the church from his example. But let him beware of raising idle, vain, impudent or dice-playing children. For if he does not know how to be in command of his own home, how will he care for the church of God. Let him have chaplains in his circle who are preachers, who not only disseminate Sacred Scripture, ~~preach the Word of God by supplementing the parish priest when such is lacking or neglected~~ *remedying the neglect and idleness of country folk,* but also prepare others in the family to undertake this task *as much as each one's talents allow.* This indeed is one plan, among others, of relieving such a great paucity of good, faithful ministers of the Church. Thus was the home of Augustine *established,* and that of other fathers who governed the people of Christ in a holy way. Let the wives of bishops be by no means light-minded, idle, ~~vain~~ *devoted to pleasures,* or ~~sumptuously decked out~~ *too ornately dressed.* For pious men are offended in a wondrous way by such things and impious [men] ~~petulantly~~ *insolently* insult evangelical doctrine because of such things. What ~~is said about~~ *has been put down in regard to* wives pertains also to their sons and daughters. ~~And what we have said in this decree~~ *Indeed, what we take up in this present decree* concerning the wife, children and family of

Folio 96r

---

[142]All changes in this chapter are in Cranmer's hand.

[143] The Latin "familia" is here translated "family" but one should also think of the term "household" since the Latin implies not only the bishop's wife and children but also all servants, students, clerical officials, and others who live together in the same household.

the bishop, ~~we wish to develop in proper proportion~~ *we wish to pertain equally* to deans, archdeacons, canons, parish priests, and other ministers of the church. In summary,~~let them release~~ *let them forbid* all price, arrogance, luxury, ~~vanities and absurdities of all kinds~~ by which their preaching and authority could be *diminished too greatly*.[144] ★

Folio 96v **Chapter 14. The Colleges Committed To The Care Of The Bishop In Academia**

In addition, some bishops have certain colleges of scholars committed to their ~~protection~~ *defense* and care. Therefore, it is necessary that they watch over these as carefully as possible; for there also the church has another seminary for its ministers. Therefore, let them see to it *diligently* that *there be salutary masters in Sacred Scripture who uphold sound doctrine,*[145] and that they *disseminate* this doctrine among the fellows of the college while repressing and coercing especially obstinate enemies. For if they do this, and *on the other hand* defend, *support,* and help those who are eager for evangelical piety, in a short space of time the colleges will be well purified. The bishop should not allow the theological lecture in these colleges , if there is any such there, to be discontinued. He should not allow a prelector to be admitted to it who either professes other doctrine or is of shifting and ~~doubtful~~ *unfixed* opinion. He should examine whether an adequate number of theologians is maintained in the college. He should inspect at intervals which ones of them contribute greatly and which are lazy, so that he may know which and how many ministers he can have ~~at hand~~ *ready* when the needs of the church demand.[146]

Chapter 15. Residence Of Bishops

The bishops ought not to be absent from their dioceses or ~~places of duty~~ *churches* for any reason unless an ecclesiastical reason or the greatest need of the nation calls them away. And when they ~~sit~~ *preside* in the cathedral church, it is not suitable that they should ~~conduct the sacred things~~ *carry out their sacred duties* on Sundays in their own chapels or that they should be present in the chapels. Rather, they Folio 97r should go to the cathedral church; there either they themselves ★ should preach or they should hear the preacher, and they should either administer the sacraments in communion themselves or they should

---

[144]It would appear that all of the editorial changes in this chapter are in Cranmer's hand.

[145]Something was lined out and the substituted phrase put in as printed above. Due to the line through the words, it is not possible to translate the Latin.

[146]The changes in this chapter are in Cranmer's hand.

partake with others. For thus, the services will be conducted with more solemnity in their presence, and their presence will embellish the holy gathering.[147]

Chapter 16. Appointing Of Coadjutors

As bishops ought to appoint coadjutors to lesser ministers when *they can no longer administer the church* either *because of incurable* illness or *because of old age,* so also *coadjutors should be given* [by the archbishop] to bishops for the same reasons ~~the archbishop~~ provided our [the king's] consent is granted. Just as the bishops themselves in their diocese ~~purge from their ecclesiastical benefice~~ *remove unworthy* ministers if grave causes *demand,* so they themselves should know that they will have to be deposed by our authority and removed from the church if ~~they have taught corrupt things~~ *they have handed down* and stubbornly defended *corrupt doctrine,* or if ~~they are scandalous~~ *they have offended the Church by disgraceful and dissolute behavior* and after being warned have not come to their senses.[148] ★

Chapter 17. Archbishops

Folio 97v

The archbishops themselves also *should know* [149] that all the matters laid down, in reference to bishops, pertain also to them. In addition, it is their ~~? to ordain~~[150] *duty to place* bishops in their province when they have been elected by us [the crown]. In order that the archbishop may better understand the condition of his province, he will go around and visit his whole province once if he can. As often as it happens that some episcopal seats are vacant, he will fill the *places* of the bishops not only in the visitation but also in the collation of benefices, and in all other ecclesiastical functions. But even where there are bishops, whenever the archbishop notices that they are ~~remiss~~ *slower* or more negligent in performing tasks, and especially in correcting vices, than is intolerable in *officials*[151] of the Lord's flock, he will first warn them paternally; but if he does not succeed *by warning,*[152] let him have a legal right ~~to provide remedy for their negligence~~ *to put others in their place.* He will also hear and judge quarrels and lawsuits of those who

---

[147]All the changes are in Cranmer's hand.

[148]All the changes are in Cranmer's hand.

[149]This replaces something that cannot be read in the manuscript.

[150]This replaces something that cannot be read in the manuscript.

[151]This word is inserted in Cranmer's hand.

[152]Two words in this chapter are insertions by Cranmer, "officals," and "warning." "Among themselves," which follows four lines below, might be correction of a scribal error where "inter se" replaced "interesse."

appeal to him. If bishops of his province quarrel or bring litigation *among themselves* in reference to anything, let the archbishop be the judge and the one who settles matters between them. Let him hear and judge accusations against bishops of his province. Finally, if any contentions or suits arise between the archbishops themselves, these will be examined and settled by our [the crown's] judgement. Let it be the task also of the archbishop to convoke provincial synods at our bidding.

Chapter 18. Synods

If it happens that a serious case should ~~appear~~ *arise* at some time in the church which cannot easily be settled without the counsel of many bishops, then the archbishop to whose province this case pertains will

Folio 98r summon his bishops to a provincial council. ★ None of them ~~shall decline~~ *shall refuse* to come unless he is prevented by ~~an adverse condition~~ *ill health;* and if he is burdened by sickness, he should send another ~~for himself~~ *in his place* who will both excuse his absence and respond and decide for him on the matters to be discussed. But, these provincial councils should never be called without our [the crown's] will and command.[153]

Chapter 19. Synod Of Any Bishop In His Diocese

A bishop should have a synod in his diocese in which he can discuss with his presbyters, parish priests, vicars and clerics those matters which must be decided upon or changed according to circumstances. ~~For a synod is a gentle medicine for correction~~ *For a synod is indeed the most appropriate medicine for correction*[154] of neglect and for removal of errors which are disseminated from time to time among the churches by the devil and evil men. Through synods of this kind, unity and affection between the bishop and his clergy will be increased and preserved. For the bishop will know and converse with his clerics more personally; and they will hear him face to face, and *when the nature of the case demands it,* they will question him.[155]

Chapter 20. The Time And Place Of The Episcopal Synod

Every year a synod will be set by the bishop. He will take care that the set day be indicated to all pastors who are in the countryside

---

[153]Changes in this chapter are in Cranmer's hand.

[154]The words replaced by Cranmer are so heavily lined out that they cannot be translated.

[155]The words replaced by Cranmer are so heavily lined out that they cannot be read.

through the deans ~~rural~~ stationed in the rural districts, but in his own city he will entrust the ~~publication~~ promulgation of the date through the preacher of the cathedral church and through an announcement fixed to the doors ~~and that at least a month before hand~~ a whole month before the synod should begin. But, he should be free to set whatever date for this that he chooses after the second Sunday of Lent. Nevertheless, he should see to it that parish priests and vicars can return quickly enough that they will not be absent from their people on Palm Sunday. The bishop should choose a place in his diocese, which he judges will be most convenient, ★ for all who are coming together. None of the clergy will have permission to be absent from the synod unless the bishop himself approves the excuse. Let the bishop in particular be present and, as is fitting, preside over the synod. If a very grave cause should compel him to be absent, the archdeacon shall preside in his place.[156]

Folio 98v

Chapter 21. Form For The Holding Of A Synod

The clergy should come to the place chosen by the bishop on the appointed day, and in the morning should convene in the church at the seventh hour. First, the prayers which are called litanies will be intoned with solemn rite in the middle of the church. Then ~~the archdeacon~~ the bishop himself, if he is present, will preach. He will exhort [them] in the mother tongue unless otherwise for a legitimate reason. After the sermon, communion will be celebrated. After this has been done, the bishop with all the clergy will proceed to some inner room. All the laity will leave except those whom the bishop has asked to remain. All will take seats according to rank. The matters which seem ~~more~~ especially pressing will be taken up with the utmost gravity and greatest peace.[157]

Chapter 22. Matters To Be Handled In The Episcopal Synod

If any ~~impious~~ corruption of true doctrine has crept in, it shall be exposed. In the Scriptures, matters which are explained falsely to the ~~scandal~~ detriment of souls shall be satisfactorily treated according to the ~~resemblance~~ harmony of the orthodox faith; and matters, which perhaps disturb consciences because they are not understood, shall be faithfully examined and set forth. If any impious and superstitious ceremonies have ~~crept in, they shall be abolished~~ slipped in, they shall be removed. Ecclesiastical quarrels and controversies shall be heard and resolved ~~can be done in relation to the time~~ insofar as time allows. Inquiry shall

---

[156]The changes in this chapter are in Cranmer's hand.

[157]The changes in this chapter are in Cranmer's hand.

be made as diligently as possible as to whether the ~~as regards all the sacred offices~~ *rites of all the sacred offices* are practiced ~~things are done in the churches~~ *in the churches* according to the form prescribed by our

Folio 99r laws. ★ In summary, whatever seems to pertain to the ~~edification~~ *advantage* of the people of God should be treated with sound faith and unmatched diligence. The presbyters will individually be asked concerning *questions involving controversial matters*. The bishop ~~shall hear~~ *will collect* patiently the opinions of the more learned, and he will not allow those speaking to be rashly interrupted by any of those assembled until they have finished speaking: for, as the apostle says, God is not a *God* of confusion but of peace.[158]

Chapter 23. Concluding the Synod

The bishop should not allow the synod to be extended or *prolonged* for many days but should bring it to an end *as soon as possible,* because it is not helpful either for pastors or flocks to be separated from each other *for a long time.* Therefore, he will give judgement concerning cases and quarrels which can be defined in that short period of time. Others which need longer though, either he will judge at his own

Folio 99v tribunal at another ★ time or he will indicate what he has decreed through his archdeacon when he sets out to evaluate the diocese in the month of September. Concerning questions which pertain to doctrine and ceremonies ~~he will make publicly known~~ *he will* partly *set forth* canons *publicly* at that time and will partly entrust them *to be publicly set forth* by the supervising archdeacon when he makes his visitation. Lesser ministers will observe, as valid and enduring, his decrees and opinion, whether published by him at the synod or, *made known* through the archdeacon at visitation. If they think there is an unjust or absurd decree among these, they should bring it up ~~to the archbishop~~ *to us.* It will be his task to confirm or to correct the decree or opinion rendered by the bishop, *but in such a way that* ~~the parts that the archbishop did not change~~ *that the parts that we did not correct* shall ~~will have~~ *retain* their vigor and strength. Thus, the bishop in the synod by promulgating decrees and opinion will urge the clergy to care and [have] solicitude for the flock entrusted to them and will bid each of them to return to his *churches* in peace and in the Spirit of the Lord.[159]
★

---

[158]The changes in this chapter are in Cranmer's hand.
[159]The changes in this chapter are in Cranmer's hand.

CONCERNING WARDENS OF THE CHURCH Fol. 100r

Let the following be the duties of church wardens: namely, to obtain
and administer the goods of the churches, their rights, debts, and
legacies; to denounce to the ordinary of the place, adulterers,
fornicators, the incestuous,[160] usurers, detractors, fortune-tellers, heretics,
practicers of simony, perjurers, and others known for their evil
reputations who hang around in the parish or who are offensive there
and who brawl or fight in the church or cemetery, also[161] those who
habitually do not wish to take part in divine prayers, sacred worship,
or divine mysteries on Sundays[162] and holy days without having any
legitimate impediment; even to exhort others to be silent who make
a tumult in church during divine services or who repeatedly disturb
the sacred mysteries either by conversation or by loud noises. If they
have not quieted down at their urging or at the urging ★ of one of Fol. 100v
them, they will see that this be reported to the ordinary of the place
within a month either personally or through a letter endorsed by, or
with the signature of, either the rector or the vicar. If these offenses
are thus reported by the wardens, and proved in a legitimate manner,
we wish that they be punished without delay with penalties imposed
by the judgement of the ordinaries.

In addition, under the care of the wardens shall be the chapels,
the mansions, and houses belonging to the rector, the vicar, the
prebendary or the master of a college or hospital; he has the task of
reporting ruinous conditions and the squandering of other things, also
deficiencies, and the negligence and errors of curates or ministers to
the ordinary of the place. It is also the task of the wardens to repair
the nave of the parish church, the tower, the bells, the books, and
other equipment of the church and words of Holy Scripture inscribed
on the walls as often as necessary by using the money of the church,
or to see to it that these things are done.★ It is also his task to Fol. 101r
surround the cemetery with a proper enclosure. If the church's money
is not sufficient to accomplish these tasks, wardens may, with the
agreement of four eminent parishioners chosen by them for this
purpose, impose a tax collected from each parishioner proportionate
to their property. The wardens must oblige themselves, before others
beyond the day appointed by them, to pay a just portion. If the
parishioners delay paying this tax or if they obstinately refuse and
have been reported by the wardens to the ordinary of the place, they

---

[160]This word is underlined in the manuscript and perhaps this indicates cancellation.

[161]The hand that made this change cannot be identified.

[162]The text shows a word lined out that appears to have been misspelled.

Fol. 101v shall be compelled by the ordinary, through ecclesiastical censure, to pay this tax together with moderate expenses. ★ The money deposited in the pauper's chest through the liberality of the pious, shall be faithfully distributed among the poor of the parish, or for other pious usages as necessity dictates, at the feast of the Lord's Nativity and at Pentecost, and at other times if need be, by the aforesaid wardens acting on the advice of the rector, the vicar, or the parish priest, and of four other persons selected by them [the wardens] for this purpose from the leading persons of the parish. The wardens when summoned by the ordinary to visitations, synods, and chapter-meetings, in order to render account of their administration, if that shall be necessary, and to report the sins committed in the parishes in which they reside,

Fol. 102r shall not refuse to appear in person. ★ But if wardens show themselves negligent in denouncing or correcting problems or in doing any other things which pertain to their duty, and through evidence of the deed, public rumor, or report by any trustworthy person, it shall be evident to the ordinary of the place that something in the parish must be corrected or reformed, the [~~ordinary~~ bishop][163] himself, by virtue of his office, even though he is moved thereto by no person, can, if he wishes, correct and reform it, after first of all punishing the negligent wardens by a monetary fine to be paid to the poor-chest of that parish at his discretion. In the chapels beyond one mile distant from the parish church, we want wardens chosen and equipped in the same way and

Fol. 102v ★ form. They should be able to exercise equal power as in parishes in all respects and will be subject to similar penalties. We want chapels that are closer to parish churches than one mile to be brought under the church's jurisdiction, and all their goods to be converted to the use of the parish churches, unless the inhabitants are unable to attend the parish churches very often because of floods.[164]

Fol. 104r

★ CONCERNING PARISH BOUNDARIES

If ~~a dispute among~~[165] there is a boundary dispute in an ecclesiastical court, this will be settled by an ecclesiastical judge with the aid of

---

[163]The word "bishop" has been put in by a hand that appears to be that of Peter Martyr Vermigli.

[164]What should be folio 103 is missing from the microfilm copy of the manuscript.

[165]The cancellation in the first line of the manuscript and a cancellation in the second line not shown above appears to be nothing more than a scribal correction.

witnesses and other lawful proofs. In order that parish boundaries may always be known to all, we decree that each year with the wardens and four other men nominated by the wardens, should go around the whole parish in Pentecost week, looking over the limits and boundaries and observing the present old boundaries of each parish and recording this *in the book which they shall cause to be written and shall put it for safekeeping in the chest of the church.*[166] If the minister, or one of the aforesaid persons, is contumacious or disobedient to this our decree, as soon as this becomes known to the visitor or any ★ other suitable judge, he will be fined ten pounds to be paid to the common chest of the church. Fol. 104v

We permit churches to be joined and annexed to neighboring churches if they cannot support a suitable minister because of a shortage of funds. This shall be done by the bishops of the places with the consent of the patrons, subject at his own valuation *to our own tithe,*[167] which is to be paid by the church to which it is annexed. If the patron of the church which is being annexed does not want to consent to the proposed union, he can share with the needy church a sufficient amount of his patrimony to sustain a suitable rector or vicar; and he should be compelled to this by the local ordinary. ★

We wish very broad, spread-out parishes, in which the greater part, or at least a great part, of the parish is known to be farther than four miles from the parish church, to be divided and separated by the local ordinaries and to be assigned to several rectors or vicars as seems most advantageous, always provided that the tithe assessed to the church is first paid to us and that the rights of the church's patron are maintained.[168] Fol. 105r

★CONCERNING SCHOOLS[169]

Fol. 106r

Chapter 1.   Schools In Cathedral Churches

In order that knowledge of the Word of God be preserved in the church, a thing that can hardly be accomplished without mastery of languages, in order that rudeness not creep in *ignorance not reign* among our people and especially among the ministers of the church, and that learning which is the gift of the Holy Spirit, be spread as widely as

[166]This insertion is in Cranmer's hand.

[167]This change is in Cranmer's hand.

[168]There is no folio 105v in the microfilm copy.

[169]The scribe of this section is the same as the one who wrote the earlier portions of the manuscript. The portion on the responsibilities of wardens was in a different hand.

possible, and finally in order that more fortunate talents may ~~be encouraged and fostered by the teaching of letters~~ *be nourished and grow through the study of letters,* we wish that each cathedral church, through our whole kingdom, have a school *so that* boys who have *already* learned the first elements in public schools, ~~may learn under the direction and care of the great school~~ *through the efforts of their teachers,* may then *become learned.* It will be the responsibility of the dean and the chapter to see that twenty pounds be given to the schoolmaster each year either from the common church revenues or from the income of their own prebends; or if this cannot be accomplished, some particular prebend should be earmarked for this so that all of its income be given to the school teacher. *Although* he ~~shall demand nothing as payment~~ *may not receive any pay* from his pupils, he is not prohibited from taking whatever the rich offer him; but *he may not take anything at all* from the poor especially since we have decreed that this institution should be preserved in the churches for the express purpose of *relieving* their plight.[170]

Chapter 2.   By Whom The Schoolmaster Is To Be Chosen

Examination and admission of the schoolmaster is a responsibility of the bishop, although perhaps in some churches hitherto this may have been decided otherwise. In examining the schoolmaster, the following should be especially observed: the man should be orthodox in evangelical doctrine, of good moral character, of serious way of living *purpose,* and skilled in grammar and humane letters, literature, and of sound enough health as to be able to endure the rigors of teaching.

Fol. 106v ★ If the bishop sees any of these qualifications lacking, or if at first they seem to be present, but later the bishop *realizes* the man's character is faulty and marred, the bishop will not admit the man to the office of teaching when he is presented *to him* or he *will remove* him if he has been already admitted.[171]

Chapter 3.   School Visitation

Twice a year the ordinary of the place will examine the boys' progress in their studies and at that time will exclude those whose talents are too limited for letters. He shall not allow books that are not suitable to be taught but will prescribe more useful ones. He will accuse a

[170]"Although" was interlined in Cranmer's hand. The remainder of the changes in Cranmer's hand to the end of this paragraph virtually have no impact upon the English translations, i.e., if the original Latin is used or the changes, the English remains basically the same.

[171]Cranmer inserted "realizes." The changes throughout are all made by Cranmer and they do not change the meaning in the English translation.

teacher suspected of sloth or ~~negligent in diligence~~ *too much truancy* before the dean, or in his absence, before the vice-dean and two procurators. But if he does this twice ~~without results~~ *with no results,* he will remove the delinquent the third time.[172]

Chapter 4. The Schoolmaster's Degree Of Judgment In Running The School

The teacher will keep the plan of teaching which he judges to be most suitable for the ~~talents~~ *minds* and ~~well-being~~ *character* of the students. He will have as many lessons as he thinks are useful. He will divide the classes according to the condition and ~~success~~ *progress* of the students. ~~As concerns hours, both of teaching and of examining [and?] practicing style, and doing drill, he will do those things which he thinks are more conducive to the instruction and education of the youths.~~ The rest of the teaching, questioning, repeating, the style of exercises, the times, he will so divide as the plan of learning and students' talent seems to demand.[173]

Chapter 5. What Textbook Must Be Retained

We also command that in each school no other sort of grammar be adopted for use than the one already formerly proposed and approved by us. ★

Chapter 6. On Learning Catechism Before All Else   Fol. 107r

Immediately after the ~~teaching~~ *mastery* of the first rudiments, each pupil should learn the Latin catechism and should not be promoted to a higher grade until he can answer the catechism questions.[174]

Chapter 7. Morning And Evening Exercises In School

As soon as the assistant teacher or the schoolmaster arrives at school in the morning, all the pupils will recite together in a loud voice in the vernacular the twelve ~~points~~[175] of faith, the Lord's prayer, and the Ten Commandments, and at the end of each commandment they will say the *Miserere Domine* and will cherish these things in their hearts. They will do likewise at night before they leave school.

---

[172]The changes in this chapter are in Cranmer's hand.
[173]The changes in this chapter are in Cranmer's hand.
[174]The change in this chapter is in Cranmer's hand.
[175]Here Cranmer replaced "capita" with "articulos."

Chapter 8.   Care Of Students On Feast Days

On Sundays and feast days, boys should come to school in the morning and then the schoolmaster will lead them to church. They will remain there under his custody until the sacred rites have been finished. The same procedure will be observed in the afternoon, when the students must go either to catechism or to vespers. Thus, care will be taken to see that boys do not absent themselves rashly from divine services and they do not make noise in church or run around during services. ★

Fol. 107v   Chapter 9.   Age Of Admission To School

Boys should not be received into school younger than eight or older than fourteen.

Chapter 10.   Conditions Of Admission

No boy should be received into school who cannot read English and who cannot recite from memory the English edition of the Catechism and who cannot write his own name with his own hand. Likewise, a boy who does not have an English New Testament may not be admitted; for the schoolmaster should see that the boys train themselves in Scripture each Sunday for a year. The same procedure will be followed after the year in New Testament written in Latin. And, other regulations concerning schoolmasters and the education of boys are to be found in the statutes of the cathedral church, if there are any such there, provided they do not contradict these laws of ours. ★

Fol. 108r   CONCERNING UNIVERSITIES AND ESPECIALLY
HEADS OF COLLEGES

Chapter 1.   [No Title Given]

Founders should see to it that henceforth heads of colleges are priests are clergy and that they honor cherish the as regards the true religion, and promote and increase sound doctrine in all ways possible. Every year each of the heads shall preach in the principal church of the university at some time.[176]

---

[176]The word "henceforth" was inserted by Cranmer. The other changes in the chapter are also in his hand.

Chapter 2.   On Retention Of A Just Number of Scholars In
The Colleges

The number of scholars prescribed by the statutes should not be diminished; but if at some time, because of difficulty caused by loss of income or some other very great necessity, the maximum cannot be retained, still the full and entire number should be kept in the theological faculty without reduction.

Chapter 3.   Neglect Of Scholars Should Be Checked

If those who are appointed to theology or other types of teaching have neglected both their public lectures pertaining to their own faculty and the private ones of their own college, they should be deprived of part of their annual stipend according to the decision of the head of the college, unless they were hindered by bad health.

Chapter 4.   On Admitting Theologians To Graduation

When theological scholars are to be made either bachelors or doctors, they should be ~~examined~~ questioned diligently concerning the principal ~~turning points~~ controversies in religion and should not be admitted to these degrees unless they are able to ~~accept and subscribe to the principal propositions~~ acknowledge a legitimate, true understanding of the principal propositions both orally and in writing.[177] ★

Chapter 5.   That Those Who Have Parish Assignments   Fol. 108v
Should Not Remain In Schools

Those who have obtained benefices, to which care of souls is attached, ~~should not be tolerated~~ remain in universities and colleges since their presence is required[178] in shepherding the flock entrusted to them. Still, since the first fruits must be paid by them with respect to the first year when they were fellows in the colleges, from then on they should receive only so much compensation as would be given to them in order to meet their expenses for the whole year[179] if they had been in the college. But, if those who have obtained prebends without the care of souls are compelled to pay the first fruits, they will be able to live for the first year at the expense of their own college. But then they are compelled

---

[177]The changes in this chapter are in Cranmer's hand.

[178]Here the changes made by Cranmer involve only word order and not the meaning as expressed in English.

[179]This change is in Cranmer's hand.

to serve their churches,[180] unless perhaps ~~they should have got permission~~ they have obtained permission from the bishop and chapter to remain for some time at the school, as it has been specified previously in the chapters[181] on admission to ecclesiastical benefices and on prebendaries. At this time they will live at their own expense and will not receive ~~support~~ payment[182] from the colleges since they have been provided for from elsewhere.

Chapter 6. Helping Poor Scholars

Care must also be taken to see that from legacies for pious causes and from special alms, something regularly ~~is paid out~~ is distributed[183] to poor students, especially to those who have applied their efforts to the church's ministry and who have nothing except the stipend of their college which is often very slight. Since if their studies are not cherished and aroused by these means, they will easily ~~turn their studies~~ turn their wishes to other ends and the church ~~will lack suitable~~ will be without suitable ministers.[184] ★

★ CONCERNING THE CRIME OF FORGERY

Chapter 1. What Is The Crime Of Forgery And When One Is Committed

A crime of forgery is an imitation of the truth which is committed with evil deceit, and is joined with damage of a brother and is committed both in words and in writing. All matters which are considered in court and in public use must be fixed and firm. First of all, those who give false testimony fall into this crime; then also those who are led by gain either not to give testimony or to give it.[185]

---

[180] It is impossible to read all that has been cancelled by Cranmer, but it would appear that the meaning remains the same in the original as well as in the new material put in by Cranmer.

[181] Cranmer here replaces "Chapters" for a word that is illegible in the text. The preceding change is also in Cranmer's hand.

[182] The last change in his chapter is in Cranmer's hand. Almost all of the changes in this chapter result in little change in the English translation.

[183] This change is in Cranmer's hand.

[184] The remainder of the changes in this chapter are in Cranmer's hand. Folios 109, 110, 111 are missing from the microfilm copy.

[185] A chapter heading is lined out between the end of this paragraph and the beginning of the next paragraph.

Also, falling under the same crime are those who, in order to suppress or conceal the truth, have changed or in any way tampered with, concealed, broken apart, burned, or removed of their own accord or have damaged seals of any writings of this kind, whether they have destroyed the writings themselves or tampered with them in any way. This applies to wills, last wishes of men, codicils, deeds, documents, contracts, or any other proofs of this kind from which certainty could be gained in court. And ★ not only the authors themselves are Fol. 112v defendants but also those are held who have described, signed, recited and introduced, sent to court writings that were adulterated or in any way altered, or who have procured the writing of such matter or have agreed that it be done, provided they have done this knowingly and with malice. Also, those are held who by malice, in any way, have defiled citations, prohibitions, decrees, edicts, acts or writings whether of civil jurisdiction or of ecclesiastical, or who have corrupted their signatures and seals or have injected false ones in place of true. This crime of forgery also adheres to those who put names on the writings of absentees as though they had been present, or who twist, distort or change with malicious trickery the names themselves. Likewise those who send or divulge false letters or false edicts in the name of judges, either civil or ecclesiastical are held guilty. The crime of forgery also pertains [to those] who open other people's letters by breaking or removing the seals in any way, although they belong perhaps to private citizens, and either read them themselves or cause or permit them to be read by the enemy of the writer; provided they do this knowingly and with malice. Those also are guilty ★ for this Fol. 113r crime who share any documents left in their care with those who represent the opposing parties, unless they have done this with the consent of the judge or of the person who deposited the documents and whom they are serving. The case of these persons is the same and equal in fault for those who explain and unravel a will that has been closed or in some way obscure, if there was a fraud, and if they had no right in revealing the matter so that they could do this justly. This pertains in the same way to those who in any way corrupt account books, especially those of merchants, or who destroy any pages from these. Notaries and scribes also are participants in this crime when they supply witness to documents who were ignorant of all the documents which are treated, if they have done this knowingly and with evil trickery. They, similarly, are at fault who lie when begging or seeking anything from the princes or who are silent about truth necessary for the present case.

Therefore, all such underhandedness to the princes seems to have this most just punishment, namely, that they should be without all those things which they have acquired, not by truth but by lying and pretense. Next, all are involved in this crime who, although they know that letters, documents, contracts and whatever other writings ★

Fol. 113v of this kind are vitiated and tampered with, nevertheless keep these same things in their possession and do not destroy, nor burn nor in any way eliminate them; in fact, they do not even affix any note by which they can be set aside. For loss from these things often comes down to posterity. Finally it is just that those be numbered in this group whose greed is so insatiable and open that they divide the same solid and entire estate and sell it piecemeal among several men.

Chapter 2.   How Defendants And Suspects Of This Crime Are Brought Together

Therefore, the judge will call together these men, and similar ones against whom an accusation of forgery can be brought in one of the following four ways, through inquisition of course, or accusation, or exception, or denunciation. The judge will see to it that a person who is clearly suspected of forgery is apprehended, and once apprehended will not free him until there is a clear judgment concerning the truth.

Chapter 3.   Penalties For Convicted Men

Those who have been accused and lawfully convicted, if they can be sought out and found, will undergo ecclesiastical penalties duly

Fol. 114r pronounced by the decision of the judges. ★ Then, they will be deprived of profits and gains which had come from the corrupt writings or writings distorted in any way, and deprived of anything coming to them in the future as well as those also which have already come to them. In addition, they will be compelled, as far as their means allow, to make full satisfaction to all persons whose condition has been worsened in any way by their fraud. They will also be infamous, will be removed and expelled from offices and benefices, if they have any, and will never be eligible for offices and benefices from that time at which they were convicted and condemned for this type of crime. And if they were ministers, it is necessary that they be excluded from the office which they perform in the church.

Chapter 4.   What Must Be Decreed In Regard To Corrupt Writings

Since we have said what must be done to forgers, it follows that we should see what must be decided about the writings themselves. Since they are corrupt and tampered with, we do not wish them to be of moment or influence or to be introduced into court. Indeed, also precaution must be taken so that if there was any sentence brought by judges on the authority of false witness or writings that had suffered violence, this same sentence should be revoked and taken back and be considered null and a ★ new pronouncement be made, which is Fol. 114v congruent with the rule of truth and justice.

Chapter 5.   Fraud And Evil Trickery Are Considered, Or Seen,
             In Crimes Of Forgery

Sometimes it can happen that someone, not with evil trickery nor knowingly but ignorant and personally deceived by another, might innocently take up a false document as true and make use of it. If this should happen and the man who used the document can prove his innocence in this matter to the judge, we wish him to be completely freed from this crime which can never exist unless fraud and evil trickery exist together there.

Chapter 6.   How The Fault Of A Scribe Caused By
             Negligence Should Be Punished

It also happens that when some document is copied from the archetype or, as they commonly call it, the original, a scribe, because of negligence and lack of care, errs and puts down something other than what was placed in the original. But, if the scribe defends and establishes the fact that this was done with no fraud or evil trickery, he will not be condemned of forgery, but, nevertheless will pay the penalty of negligence which the judge assigns. Indeed, it was necessary that he be careful in this matter so to diligently match his writing with the first copy. Moreover, that writing in ★ which there is such an Fol. 115r error cannot command any trust.

Chapter 7.   Seals Of Universities And Societies Without The
             Consent Of The Head And The Majority Of The
             University Are Not Valid

Seals of chapters, churches, universities, hospitals, and other societies of this kind will not be affixed to any diploma or document of any kind unless the head is present or consents and unless also the greater part of the canons or fellows either of the college or of whatever university it may be in whose hands the authority of executing acts rests at that time, agrees with the head. Those who act otherwise in this matter or cause such action shall be punished severely at the discretion of the ecclesiastical judges, and we want removed as false and worthless any documents or diplomas or writings of any kind that were not attested as we have commanded. And if perchance there was any loss brought to the estate of anyone through these documents, full satisfaction shall be made for this by those who either signed them themselves or brought it about or gave consent to the signing of writings otherwise than was previously decided by us.[186]

Fol. 116r   ★ CONCERNING STRIKING CLERICS

Chapter 1.   By What Penalties Force Against A Cleric Should Be Punished

Whoever has knowingly laid violent hands on a cleric, unless he is willing to make satisfaction for this according to the decision of ecclesiastical judges and unless he is willing to do penance suitable for such an atrocious crime, will be subject to excommunication. And we do not allow him to be relieved of this until he has performed fully a penance, to be imposed at the discretion of his ordinary.[187]

Chapter 2.   Exceptions In This Case

Since every honorable means of maintaining safety ought to be preserved, if anyone in legitimate self-defense or in the service of justice proceeds to the use of force against a cleric, whoever has offended against the words of higher law,[188] if he has disclosed to his ordinary that force was used for these reasons which we have given, we wish him to be completely free and dismissed without penalty. Also, let there be equal punishment of clerics if they have laid violent hands on laymen.[189]

---

[186]The following five pages in the manuscript are blank. This note written by Vermigli at the conclusion of chapter seven states: "On witnesses and their testimony, see folio 179."

[187]This is a change made by Cranmer.

[188]This phrase might have been lined out by Cranmer. The stroke of the line is similar to others identified with Cranmer.

[189]At the bottom of this page 116v, in John Foxe's hand is the note: "On prescriptive rights, see folio 138." Folios 116v, 117, and 118 are not in the microfilm copy.

★CONCERNING WITNESSES
AND THEIR STATEMENTS

Chapter 1. When Witnesses Must Be Examined Before A
Contested Suit

The problem must be considered as to whether proof must be made through witnesses in the principal case, and whether in the accessory and preliminary case. If in an incidental and accessory case (cases are of this kind which arise out of opposed dilatory exceptions, from declinatory exceptions of the trial and also certain peremptory exceptions such as the exception of [legal] agreement on the judged matter, the limitation of a suit through oath) there is no need to await the [formal] testimony of the suit because such controversies prevent judgement from being made on the principal question unless there is first agreement on them, agreement which is impossible if the proofs are not brought forward. Therefore, it is necessary ★ that witnesses be admitted to prove such exceptions before the testimony of the suit on the principal case which has been made. But in the principal case, the proof of witnesses is not regularly admitted unless the suit has been contested; for prior to the contesting of the suit, it cannot be determined what is the principal controversy between the litigants. Therefore the judge would be inept if he would allow the proof of this matter to occur concerning the controversy of which there was not yet sufficient agreement. Sometimes, however, even the witnesses of the principal business are received before the trial of the suit; but this happens only because of special reasons and because of some benefit of the law; so that if anyone would fear the extended absence or death of those who have knowledge of the matter which might be relevant to the controversy, he ★ can see to it that their testimonies be written down for posterity in a public instrument; or if the suit has already been initiated, he can see to it that they are examined by a judge, provided the suit has not yet been contested. However, wherever this has happened, it is necessary that the testimony of the witnesses be signed and, as soon as possible, be announced to those who anyone feels will be their adversaries in this case; and the testimony should not be made public until a year has elapsed after the reception of such witnesses or until the suit has been contested so that there be no apparent fraud for them to have been unaware that the witnesses were received in regard to this matter.

Chapter 2.   Delay In Producing Witnesses

That party which has the burden of proof can seek a delay for itself
Fol. 120v from the judge in order to produce ★ witnesses; and the judge is
bound to give the delay to the party allowing a sufficient amount of
time, according to the distance of the witness's residence from the
residence of the judge. And while the time of the granted delay is
pending, the defendant can bring to the judge, from one to three
times, the names of those whom he is going to produce as witnesses;
this is not allowed a fourth time unless the defendant swears that
chicanery is involved.

Chapter 3.   Articles Of Proof

After the names of the witnesses have been given to the judge, the
articles of testimony, to be given, must be shown simultaneously.

Chapter 4.   Summoning Of Witnesses

But the man producing witnesses should see to it that they are
Fol. 121r summoned by the judge, and that a fixed time is established ★ for
them to give their testimony. For those who push themselves in of
their own accord to offer testimony to the judge, are considered
suspect. Still even unasked witnesses suffice for the credibility of the
business.

Chapter 5.   Summons Of The Opposite Party

However, not only the witnesses, but also the party against whom
they are being produced must be called to hear, and see that the
witnesses are produced after a general clause of summons has been
added. This is because whether the witness comes or not, still the
judge will proceed in the case as much as he can according to law.
And at the same time a copy of the articles which the one who produced
the witnesses showed to the judge, must be given to the opposite
party; so that if he wishes, he can pose his own questions. ★

Fol. 121v Chapter 6.   Questions

Questions moreover can be asked both concerning the credibility of
the person and the circumstances of the business. The interests,
habits, wishes, fortunes, *age, relationship,* conditions *of his whole life*[190]
are relevant to exploring the credibility of the person. How the witness

---

[190]This phrase and the one preceding it showing a change in the manuscript, were
interlined in what appears to be Cranmer's hand.

gained knowledge of this affair, whether he himself was involved in the business or heard of it from others, why it was done, and what it was, when, where, with what intention, and with what plan, all these pertain to the circumstances of the business.

Chapter 7. Delay To Receive Questions

However, in like manner, a delay can be sought by the party against whom the witnesses are produced in order to draw up questions. However, the judge ought not give a copy of the questions to the party Fol. 122r ★ who is producing witnesses so that the party may not instruct the witnesses from these how to respond.[191]

Chapter 8. Protestation In The Delivery of Questions

Also a party can declare at the delivery of the questions that he wishes to admit the witnesses produced only so far as his right of rejecting their persons and statements by means of other witnesses may be reserved. For unless someone made protestation about the rejection of the witnesses before their testimony is made public, it is not heard afterwards unless he swears that he was not induced by any malice or deceit aimed at protracting, to make such a rejection, and that now is the first time that he discovered his reason for objecting to the witnesses.

Chapter 9. Oath Of Witnesses

However, it is required that witnesses offer an oath before they give any ★ testimony because an unsworn witness, no matter how Fol. 122v conscientious he may be, is not believed to the detriment of another person. They shall swear that they will tell the whole truth that they know concerning the matter about which they are swearing, with no admixture of falsity; that they for both parties will tell the truth which they know pertains to the business, even if not asked; and that they will not give testimony for money or love or hatred or fear or any other motive. Nevertheless when both parties, in turn say, that the witnesses need not swear, they should be believed even without having taken an oath. We wish the oath of the witnesses to extend to the whole case and even any[192] interrogation of a legitimate, specifically for ★ one article.   Fol. 123r

---

[191]Cranmer replaced "necnon" with "non."

[192]Cranmer's change in the Latin text makes no change in the meaning of the English translation. He replaces "quantacunque" with "quaecunque."

Chapter 10. There Should Not Be Oaths On Holidays

Witnesses should not take an oath on holidays since it concerns process of law and a judicial act. But sworn witnesses can be examined at any time because the examination of witnesses is not a judicial act, but happens separately and in a secret place so that the witnesses may be freer to give testimony. For testimony is considered of no value when it is spoken openly before all.

Chapter 11. Delegation Of Examination

Moreover the judge can either examine the witnesses himself or delegate this duty to another; but he to whom the judge committed the examination of witnesses cannot in turn delegate it to another because he seems to have been chosen because of his diligence. ★

Fol. 123v ## Chapter 12. When Witnesses Must Be Rejected

We wish witnesses to be admitted to give testimony, even if there is objection against their person, unless excommunication is the basis of the objection to them or the opponent brings prompt proof of his opposition to the witnesses' testimony.

Chapter 13. Witnesses Should Be Compelled By The Judge If They Refuse To Come

If any witnesses refuse to come when requested, they must be compelled by the authority of the judge since he who tries to suppress the truth is scarcely less delinquent than the one who gives false testimony.

Chapter 14. Those Who Can Not Be Compelled To Be Witnesses

Fol. 124r Witnesses should not be called rashly for a long ★ journey and much less should soldiers be called from their standards for the sake of offering testimony. But for this we command that the custom of each province of our kingdom in regard to the calling of witnesses be observed.[193]

---

[193]The last sentence in the manuscript is lined out and in Cardwell's edition of 1851, it states this was done by Cranmer but there is no internal evidence that Cranmer in fact did this. It could have been done later by another person just as well.

Chapter 15. A Trip Should Be Made To Both Nobles And The Weak ~~Through~~ For Their Examination[194]

If witnesses were constituted in some greater dignity, or were held down by some natural, inevitable impediment so that they cannot come to court conveniently or suitably, then the judge should go to them or should entrust their examination to a good man.

Chapter 16. Duty Of Witnesses

The duty of a witness consists in this especially, namely that he should expose the truth concerning matters well known to him. ★ We Fol. 124v therefore prohibit any witnesses who are of any status, condition, or name from assuming to themselves the duty of judging, or from deciding anything about any crimes or from even making inquiry unless at the command of that judge, who ~~through these laws of ours~~[195] is known to have jurisdiction in this case in which they are trying to bring action under penalty of contempt.

Chapter 17. Who Must Be Prevented From Testifying

We wish the following to be prevented from testifying: all those condemned of any notorious crime, the leaders of domestic enemies, those who are subject to commands by reason of a father's or a master's power, also parents and those who take the place of parents, ★ those below legal age and those who are demented, those openly Fol. 125r seeking profit, agents and solicitors of cases for those cases in which they are known to have made solicitations, unless both parties consent, also those who try to give testimony in their own behalf; these are completely forbidden to give testimony. However, those suspected of crimes, merchants, upright and honorable in other respects, friends, women, relatives with whom marriage is not forbidden by divine law, those who have previously given testimony against the other part, can be admitted to testimony. But, a good judge can easily determine on the basis of credibility, dignity, morals, gravity, and constancy of the witnesses, and of the seriousness of the matter under controversy what he either should believe ★ or ought to consider as not proven Fol. 125v by them.

[194]This is a scribal correction of "per" for "pro."
[195]This is lined out in the manuscript.

Chapter 18. Testimonies Of Certain People Ought To Be Rejected

Those who have given false or changeable testimonies or have betrayed the case of one of the parties, and those who are judged to have received money for giving testimony or not giving it, not only will lack all credibility but also will be duly punished by the judges, and will make satisfaction to the offended party.

Chapter 19. Those Who Must Be Rejected From Testimony

A participant in a crime and a person less than 20 years old ought not to give testimony in criminal cases; nor one who previously in a similar case is proved to have given testimony against him. Procurators, Fol. 126r lawyers, ★ and others carrying on business of some kind should not be admitted to testimony in behalf of their masters. But if the opposing party wishes to use their testimonies, they are compelled to speak the truth which they know, after putting aside their office.

Chapter 20. Witnesses Concerning A University

Individuals from some university can be witnesses in the case of the university if it is not a matter principally concerning the right of the witness himself, or if it is a matter of his own individual advantage and not of the goods of the university.

Chapter 21. When Domestic Witnesses Can Be Admitted

It has been discovered by experience that some persons, either because Fol. 126v of boredom ★ with their previous marriage or led by hope of a second, more prosperous marriage, bring charges of adultery against their spouses. Therefore, the judge should be prudent in this situation and should not allow himself to be easily imposed on, nor should he believe those who labor under some suspicion or who have not alleged some probable and conclusive explanation of their statements. But, when from the nature of the act itself, witnesses are not usually offered, credence can be given to members of the household who are honorable and deserving of belief in other respects, unless the good name and blameless life and honorable manner of living, of the accused party, counterbalances. ★

Chapter 22. If One Has Once Approved The Person Of A Fol. 127r
Witness, He Presumably Always Approves Unless
A New Exception Emerges

One who approves the person of a witness in one act approves of him
in every other unless a new reason for weakening his position arises.
Therefore, one cannot oppose the person of a witness whom he has
once produced unless some new reason emerges; still it is permitted
to oppose his statements.

Chapter 23. In Someone Else's Case Several Witnesses From
The Same Family Can Be Brought Forth

There is nothing to prevent several witnesses even from the same
family from being able to be produced in a matter involving someone
else.

Chapter 24. The Witness Of Some Writing Ought Not Be
Rejected Because Of A Crime Committed Later Or
Discovered Later

If anyone of the witnesses of a testament or indeed of ★ some other Fol. 127v
document was considered free from or alien to all crime by the common
estimate and opinion of men at the time of the completion of the
material at which the testimony itself is written down, his testimony
ought not be tainted because of some hidden crime or some offense
detected, laid bare or committed later; and nothing should be detracted
from his credibility unless the testator survives three months after the
revelation of such a crime and has taken steps to ensure that another
[witness] was submitted in that man's place.

Chapter 25. Those Who Have Done Penance Can Be Restored
To Credibility As Witnesses

But since we always prefer, because of our concern for subjects that
they gain some advantage ★ rather than to drive them into despair, Fol. 128r
if any criminal renounces his crime sincerely, and has performed
worthy penance for it by judgment of the church on behalf of the
same and has returned to a more temperate life, we have decided that
then the capacity for giving testimony should be restored to him.

Chapter 26. To What Witnesses Credence Must Be Given

It is proper to show faith in sworn witnesses and not in written testimonies: still one must believe those witnesses who conclusively or presumptively prove the matter under consideration.

Chapter 27. It Is Not Permitted To Produce Witnesses Too Often On The Same Or Contrary Articles

One who has produced some witnesses and has dealt with the matters covered by the testimony, or in a sense has gone into the same matters Fol. 128v once or several times, ★ shall not have permission to produce either the same or other witnesses on the same matters or directly contrary articles.

Chapter 28. When Witnesses Can Be Repeated

Witnesses must be fully examined and must not often be called away from their businesses. However, if either by deceit, or by negligence of the judge, they have not been examined in the proper manner, it ought not to harm the party rightly suing or proposing articles, for the same witnesses to be called back. But, if by the fault or negligence of a party some defect is detected in the words of the witnesses, no help will be given to that party, nor may witnesses subsequently called back, whether by action of the judge or at his request, be of advantage to him in any way. ★

Fol. 129r ## Chapter 29. Punishment Of Witnesses Who Give False Testimony

If anyone, after this, is so unmindful of his duty that, influenced by some blind affection, he was apprehended in giving false or much altered testimony, he will be punished extraordinarily at the discretion of the judge whom he offended in this respect. And under penalty of contempt, we wish[196] all our ministers always[197] to be prompt and ready in regard to the requests of the aforesaid judges in the execution of penalties of this kind inflicted, or to be inflicted on false witnesses.

---

[196]Cranmer's change of "volumusque" from "volentes" really does not alter the translation.

[197]The word lined out is "futuros" and by leaving it in, the translation is not substantially changed.

Chapter 30. When A Witness Should Be Held To Render An
Account Of His Statement

A witness in all acts perceptible by bodily senses ought ★ to render Fol. 129v
an account of his statement only if he is asked. But, in matters not
subject to the senses in this way, he ought to render an account even
though not interrogated.

Chapter 31. Witnesses Outside Of Court

The judicial statement of a witness is not overturned by his contrary
extrajudicial statement; but this will detract much from his credibility
unless the same witness can give some just reason as to why he gave
such varied or contradictory testimonies.

Chapter 32. Expenses Must Be Paid For Witnesses

As often as witnesses are called away from their business ★ to bear Fol. 130r
testimony, we wish this to happen at the expense of the party producing
them, who will bear their expenses from the time they begin their
journey until they have returned to their dwellings.

Chapter 33. Witnesses With Counter Arguments Must Not Be
Disapproved By Others

Witnesses rebutting the rebuttal witnesses must not be admitted lest
it happens that the business be protracted longer than is fair if
permission were granted to produce fourths against thirds, and so on.

Chapter 34. Statements Of Witnesses Must Be Interpreted
According To The Customary Mode Of Speaking

The statements of witnesses must not be interpreted sophistically, but
rather must be interpreted benignly, and especially according to
common usage and manner of speaking of the witness himself. ★

Chapter 35. When The Statement Of One Witness May Be Fol. 130v
Supplemented By The Statement Of Another

Also the statement of one witness may be supplemented by the
statement of another who gives fuller testimony; and he will receive
the interpretation from that fuller statement according to its deserts
according to old laws[198] provided it is agreed that they are trying to
testify about one and the same deed.

---

[198]This is lined out in the manuscript.

Chapter 35b. Witnesses Who Absolve Are To Be Preferred To Those Who Condemn[199]

Since our laws are more inclined to absolve than to condemn, we wish that if some witnesses make for the good reputation or innocence of someone, while on the contrary others [make for] his bad or harmful reputation, those who have made for his innocence shall be preferred, provided that otherwise the witnesses are equal. ★

Fol. 131r ### Chapter 36. Inconstancy Of The Witness

Witnesses who vacillate against the credibility of their testimony must not be heard.

Chapter 37. A Party Can Interpret Its Own Obscure Intention

If witnesses testify with clarity about some matter which may have been obscurely presented by a party, still the party can interpret its intention so that the statements of the witnesses may be helpful to that party.

Chapter 38. Witnesses Ought To Testify On Behalf Of Each Party If They Are Required To

Witnesses ought to testify on behalf of each party if required either by the judge or by the party who did not produce them, although they receive their expenses from the party principally producing them.

Chapter 39. Examination of Witnesses

The service of the notary, and not his industry, seems to be preferred Fol. 131v in the examination of witnesses. Thus they ought to write ★ the statements of the witnesses according to the order of the judge, even extensively, just as each one spoke, since in the words left out more efficacy is sometimes found than in the words that are transcribed by certain notaries.

Chapter 40. Single Witnesses

Single witnesses prove nothing. So the ancients did not permit an oath to be administered, even when evidence was lacking, to the person producing such witnesses unless this sort of singularity tends to one and the same end. We also approve of this.

---

[199]In the manuscript this chapter is crossed out. In the Cardwell edition, it reappears as chapter 46 in this section and it also reappears as chapter 46 in the manuscript.

Chapter 41. Variety Of Witnesses

If, however, any witnesses testify concerning ★ a certain amount that Fol. 132r
is owed, some make it larger and some again smaller, a sufficient
number agrees on a certain amount, the judge can believe them if
there is nothing else that detracts from their credibility.

Chapter 42. Testimonies Concerning Knowledge And Belief

Although witnesses often are so unpolished and ignorant as not to
distinguish between assertions of truth, for example, "I know," and
words which testify nothing of necessity, such as in "I believe," "It
seems," "I recall," still we do not wish credence to be given to witnesses
of this kind if they themselves when warned by our judges about the
nature of these words, a procedure which we always want to be
followed, have not rendered suitable testimony. But in those cases ★
in which old laws have wished credence to be given to testimonies of Fol. 132v
this kind, we have decided that the same [credence] should be given.

Chapter 43. Witnesses Examined Before Arbiters

When witnesses have been examined before arbiters, it is not necessary
that they stand before a judge, if they are living, but the judge can
ask that they be examined again if he wishes; but if they are dead,
[sic] further examination is not required but their testimony must
stand as if they had been received before the judge, subject,
nevertheless, to the right of objecting to their persons and their
statements.

Chapter 44. How The Judge Will Judge From Many Witnesses

If all witnesses are of the same honesty and reputation, and the nature
of the business and also the impulse of the judge agrees with these,
then all the testimonies must be followed. ★ But, if certain of them Fol. 133r
have said something else, although in an unequal number, what suits
the nature of the business must be believed and what lacks the suspicion
of enmity or favor; and the judge will strengthen the impulse of his
mind from the arguments and testimonies which he has found to be
more suitable to the problem and closer to the truth; for it is not
necessary that he have regard for the multitude but for the genuine
credibility of testimonies and for the testimonies in which the light of
truth is more present.

Chapter 45. When A Variation Of Witnesses May Not Be Harmful

If witnesses are found sometimes inconsistent in circumstances which are not essential (a matter to which unsophisticated men do not normally give great attention), but are in agreement on the substance of the matter under discussion, full credence *must be given*[200] to them. For not every inconsistency must be rejected, but only that which contains in itself a certain contrariety and incompatibility. *Diversity*[201] of narration is not at all harmful when the same things are being said.

Fol. 133v ★

Chapter 46. Witnesses Who Absolve Are To Be Preferred To Those Who Condemn

Since our laws are more inclined to absolve than to condemn, we wish that if some witnesses make for the good reputation or innocence of someone, while on the contrary others [make for] his bad or harmful reputation, those who have made for his innocence shall be given preference, provided that otherwise the witnesses are equal.[202]

Chapter 47. The Number Of Witnesses

Although the maximum number of witnesses had been defined by certain laws, *still*[203] we confine this license to a sufficient number, as the judges may determine, ★ and they shall allow to be called only that number which they think to be necessary, lest a superfluous multitude of witnesses be dragged out by unrestrained power for the sake of disturbing people. But, where a [specified] number of witnesses is not required, two witnesses will suffice for proof.

Fol. 134r

Chapter 48. The Judge Can Impose Silence On The Witnesses And Can Change The Order Of Articles In The Examination

It is the job of the judge to investigate all things and to extract the truth by a full inquiry. Thus, we permit him to impose on the witnesses by a religious oath that they should not disclose their statements to fellow witnesses or any others, and that he can examine witnesses,

---

[200]This is the last word on the page and has been added by Cranmer's hand and seems to be the correction of adding a word that was left out by the scribe.

[201]A spelling error was corrected here.

[202]See earlier footnote No. 199 where the original location of this chapter is discussed.

[203]This was inserted by Cranmer.

without observing the order of articles, on all matters as seems expeditious to him.

Chapter 49. Where There Is Danger To A Soul, The Oath Can Be Exacted

If the acts have proven nothing, the judge can exact an oath ★ from Fol. 134v
the principal party wherever it is a matter of danger to a soul.

Chapter 50. Copy Of Testimonies Must Not Be Denied To The Parties[204]

The judge after disclosure of the witnesses should make a copy of the testimonies if the parties request it and he should retain the original. And, it is the job of the judge to set for them a terminal date by which they should refute the published testimonies or uphold them; but when this period ends, if they have neglected to do this, then there will be no opportunity for them to do so.

Chapter 51. Publication Of Testimonies

After the witnesses have been examined, that party most interested in knowing the testimonies can ask the judge to publish them. But in order for this to be done properly, the parties must be summoned to hear the testimonies published. But the publication will happen thus if either the judge himself or a notary public recites the testimonies open in the presence of the parties, or shows openly the sheet on which these were written down and testifies in loud voice that this contains ★ the testimonies of the produced witnesses, faithfully transcribed, Fol. 135r
which the party at his request wished to be published.[205] Afterwards, the judge will set for the parties a terminus within which they may receive copies of the testimonies and another terminus within which they may dispute it if they wish.

Chapter 52. The Producing Of Witnesses After The Publication Of Testimonies

Although the parties are not regularly allowed to produce yet other witnesses after the publication of testimonies, still the judge, by reason of his office, can interrogate anew already examined witnesses, not only after the publication of the testimonies but even after the

---

[204]This change appears to correct a grammatical error and is in the hand of the scribe.

[205]"And" has been replaced here by "or" in the first change in the chapter and in the second, it appears that the correction is of a scribal error.

conclusion of the case; he can do this concerning a matter which he does not seem to have made clear enough in his summation if knowledge of it appears necessary or useful for understanding the case. And if the judge should not do this on his own, the parties can ask the judge to do so.

Chapter 53. When Proof Is Admitted After Disclosure Of The Witnesses

Fol. 135v Again, if anyone wishes to prove anything after the disclosure ★ of the witnesses which is known to be inherent in their former articles as to the necessity of the deed and proof, this is by no means permitted to him. But, if anything unexpected, which no one could easily think up was proved by the opposing party, something which greatly harms the cause of the other party, we think it is not unreasonable that this be rebutted by the harmed party, if he can, despite the disclosure of the witnesses. Also, in matrimonial cases it had been decided formerly in favor of persons so that the disclosure of witnesses should not prevent the introduction of other witnesses; and we moderate and temper this in such a way that the disclosure in these cases should not harm if those witnesses produced after the disclosure were superior to any exception and were such as would be free of any suspicion and were deservedly credible. Otherwise the judge either should not admit them, or will be able to show that they have the credibility which he wishes. ★

Fol. 136r Chapter 54. Neither Witnesses Nor Statements of Witnesses Can Be Refuted After the First Assignment To Hear The Sentence[206]

If anything contrary to the truth is detected or his person can be reprobated in any way, we permit this to be proposed up to the first assignment to hear the sentence[207] whether anyone protested against them or not.

Chapter 55. The Duty Of The Judge In Examining Witnesses

Moreover, it pertains particularly to the office of the judge to examine witnesses diligently on circumstance of the business one by one so

---

[206]The word "sentence" is not in the original manuscript, but was added in the Foxe-Cardwell editions.

[207]In the manuscript "sententiam" replaces "futurum," which was struck out by Cranmer.

that he may add anything which was omitted by chancely the parties or their lawyers, in conceiving the articles and interrogations.[208]

★CONCERNING PRESUMPTIONS[209] Fol. 138r

Chapter 1. What Is A Presumption

A presumption is a conjecture of something collected from various circumstance.

Chapter 2. Rash And Probable Presumptions

A rash presumption proceeds from a mere suspicion and rests on no vestige of deed. But a probable presumption clings to traces of a deed, although it does not remove doubt by itself, but only induces belief.

A probable presumption added to the assertion of at least one witness or some partial proof causes full belief. But, a rash one must be utterly rejected.

Chapter 3. Violent Presumption

A violent presumption is one which relies on such open proofs ★ that Fol. 138v what is contended to be the situation seems to follow in a sense necessarily from them. The judge will not limit his mind to one type of proof; and so in cases which cannot be directly proved by their own nature, he will be able to be brought to pass sentence by presumptions. We are taught that the judge can bring sentence from violent presumptions by the example of king Solomon, who, hearing the case between the two women and discerning the true mother from the natural love of the one towards the child and the hatred of the other, judged that the child should go to the mother who shrank from its division. ~~Third Book of Kings, chapter 3.~~[210] But, the judge should see to it that the violent presumption by which he was moved ★ to bring Fol. 139r sentence should be written down in the acts so that it may appear as the foundation of the sentence that was passed.

---

[208]The word "by" was inserted by Cranmer. The next page in the manuscript is blank, but there is a notation by John Foxe as follows: "Concerning custom, see folio 160." Folios 136v and 137r-v are missing from the microfilm copy.

[209]All chapter headings in this section are in Cranmer's hand.

[210] This was cancelled in the manuscript by someone.

Chapter 4.   Proof Of Sexual Union Through Presumption

No one should doubt that sexual union is proved by extremely strong presumption if a male and female, alone with one another, both nude, were found lying in the same bed. In proving the sexual union of male and female, proof of facts related to this should suffice provided, however, the credibility of witnesses is added. A woman whose husband will notify her, not unreasonably, that she should not speak with the man whom he suspects, nor associate with him secretly, will be regarded as an adulteress if she spurns her husband's warning. ★

Fol. 139v Chapter 5.   Who Must Be Considered As A Father

One is presumed to be the son of the man in whose house and from whose wife one is born, even though the wife perhaps had intercourse with another man at the time of conception, unless the lengthy absence of the husband, or his poor health, or another just cause persuades otherwise.

Chapter 6.   Presumption Of An Evil Mind

The man who does anything against the prescriptions of the laws is always presumed to have bad faith. An evil mind is always presumed in the sin of one caught red-handed. Therefore, one who when he has harmed someone, says he did it in jest is considered as guilty unless he can prove his innocence.

Chapter 7.   Presumption Of A Good Mind

Internal motivations are presumed from exterior actions. Therefore you should understand that the mind of a man is good and upright if you see him devoted to virtues, especially simplicity and modesty.
Fol. 140r ★ From anyone's past life we can know what we may presume about his subsequent behavior, because a consideration of the past instructs us about the future.

Chapter 8.   A Man Who Is Silent About Accusations Of Crime
                Should Be Suspected

If anyone should be silent about accusations which were brought against him or proposed in court for response, he offers a probable presumption of some weight that he does not have a defense.

Chapter 9.   One Who Seeks Subterfuges Is Presumed To
Have A Bad Cause

Whoever tries to avoid judgement by delays should always be presumed
to have a bad cause.

Chapter 10.   When Ignorance Should Not Be Presumed

No one is thought to be unaware of acts which are done publicly and
which anyone ought to investigate. ★ What comes to us at a distance   Fol. 140v
cannot escape the notice of neighbors; for although things are presumed
to be better known to neighbors than to people at a distance, the
former especially are believed.

Chapter 11.   Reputation Or Gossip

Common, well circulated stories about someone induce a serious
presumption.

Chapter 12.   Presumption Of Continence

One who was continent in youth is not presumed to be incontinent in
old age; and this is especially the case if he was devoted to the study
of divine letters and was especially renowned for this kind of learning.

Chapter 13.   Presumption From Habit

Anyone is presumed to be of such a kind as he is habitually found to
be.

Chapter 14.   It Is Presumed That No One Wishes To Squander
His Possessions

It is presumed that no one wishes either to squander or to waste his
own goods.

Chapter 15.   It Is Presumed That The Will Is Not Changed
Unless It Is Proved

Anyone is presumed to remain in the same will as it is agreed he once
had. Thus, one who asserts that his mind has been changed ★ ought   Fol. 141r
to prove it.

Chapter 16. The Sentence *Of A Judge*[211] Is Presumed To Be Good

The presumption must always be in favor of the judge's sentence because of his religion unless the sentence is suspended by appeal.

Chapter 17. The Presumption Favors Writing

The presumption favors written evidence, unless it is proved that one thing was done and another thing was written.

Chapter 18. Presumption of the Law and *De Jure*

Presumption is not of such great import that it cannot be struck out by contrary proof. We think it can be removed unless it is a presumption of law and from law, rather than concerning only the confession of the man whose advantage deals with the case.

Chapter 19. Equal Presumptions Mutually Weaken One Another

Two presumptions of equal power clash with one another mutually and the greater surpasses and entirely vitiates the lesser.

Chapter 20. Presumption of Infirmity Is Removed Through Act

It is a matter of manifest law that the presumption of infirmity is removed through the exercise of an act not compatible with infirmity.
★

Fol. 141v Chapter 21. The Judge Will Judge From Circumstances[212]

If the proofs of the defendant and advocate rest only on presumption, it is the role of the judge to base his judgement on a diligent consideration of the circumstances. As when a man asserts that he has had intercourse with his wife but she denies this, and several matrons who inspected her body agree with her, the judge will easily determine on the basis of opportunity for intercourse, delay, length of time spent together, the age of both, and the credibility and experience of the matrons what actually happened.[213]

---

[211]This appears to be a scribal change. The title began with the nominative case of "iudex" and then put it into the genitive.

[212]This entire chapter was written by Cranmer.

[213]At the bottom of this page, John Foxe has written "Concerning defamation, see folio 268." Folios 142r-v and 143r-v are not in the microfilm copy.

★ CONCERNING TITHES[214]

Chapter 1. Tithes Must Be Paid

Since Our Lord Jesus Christ himself sanctified this law, namely, that those who sow the teachings of the Gospel among men should reap their livelihood from their teaching labors; and from the witness of the same Lord that the workman is worthy of his pay; then also, the divine law that does not allow the mouth of an ox at work threshing to be bound; we must repeat the example of divine clemency and vigorously see to it that neither excessive avarice of our men, or neglect, bring it about that the ministers of our churches not be provided with a just and suitable income from the fulfillment of their sacred duties.

Chapter 2. How Predial Tithes Should Be Paid

Therefore, let it be decided by virtue of our authority that each and every subject of ours at specified and legitimate places and times should put aside a tenth of all the things produced from their estates for the ministers, whether it be hay or whatever kind of grain from whatever places, whether it be saffron, or hemp, or flax, ★ or oil, or fruits of trees, or other profits arising from farms of any kind; for always, whatever computation or terms these commodities have, a tenth of all of them should be set aside fresh and whole from the very things themselves, with the same appearance it had when formerly collected from the farms and should be presented to the ministers, with the exception of strong, tall trees which are twenty years old and are reserved for buildings or better purposes and are not being prepared for the fireplace. A tenth of income from mills, a tenth of turves cut, of stonecuttings and all other opportunities of this kind should be put aside for ministers. Similarly, a tenth of pasturage or any other land into which horses, draft animals, bulls, oxen and any other breeding animals have been put should be taken out for the ministers. A tenth will also be derived from pregnant animals in whatever broods or offspring; and in this number for example are cows, pigs, lambs, horses, swans, hens, geese, doves, rabbits, deer, fish, bees and other animals of equal status. The produce of these same animals, butter, cheese, milk considered in its own nature when it is not put into butter or cheese, wool, or wax. We wish a tenth of all these fruits, no less than from the animals themselves, fully and in each case to be put

---

[214]In the upper right hand corner of this page, folio 144r, in Cranmer's hand is this: "This is finished by us, but must be ? again by D. Haddon."

aside for the use of the ministers without any trickery or craftiness.
★

Fol. 145r   Wherefore, we wish the whole law of tithing to be prescribed from each and every profit and opportunity of the landed estates, to be received according to the plan and form prescribed in the Parliament, which was held in the second and third year of our reign. Also, we want the whole law to proceed with the same means and punishments as were defined in the thirteenth chapter of the aforesaid parliament. This decree of Parliament and its single words and sentences, will have the present firm and inviolate authority to resolve the problem of tithes, no less than if it had been inserted at this time; unless perchance there is in those decrees something which manifestly is at variance with these present laws of ours. But since those decrees of Parliament do not embrace in themselves all the formulas for presenting tithes, and many doubts occur in the daily problem of tithing concerning which nothing has been determined in Parliament, we have seen to it that this next section be added in order to reduce conflicts.

Chapter 3.   How The Annual Tithing Of Animals Is To Be Paid

If six calves only fall to the lot of anyone, or fewer than six, he should Fol. 145v pay two pence for each calf as tithing; if he has seven, ★ he will put aside one for the minister, and the minister in turn will pay back the six pence to the person from whom he received the calf for the sake of restoring the balance. In the same way, when a man has eight calves, one will be removed for the minister: but the minister again will compensate the overpayment by four pence. But, if nine calves are found, the minister will receive a calf and offer only two pence. But, if the minister prefers to await a full benefice of tithes and does not want to profit from his own right until the lawful number of ten calves has been completed, he will bear the proper delay in some way, as had been decided in civil court in many cases; that is, when the time of the lawful number arrives, with one or two exceptions, he will take from the remaining ten calves his choice, the one which he wishes. And we wish to follow the same plan in regard to fowl, horses, and similar animals. But concerning lambs, swans and other animals within the same price range, for each one a penny will be given back and forth, when there are less than ten involved. But, with regard to other smaller animals, which have such a meager life-span that tithing of them cannot be initiated according to a set plan, local custom should be upheld. Anyone who has transferred ownership of such animals before paying tithes on them should give a tenth of the price to the Fol. 146r minister. However, when the possessor has killed animals ★ for the

use of his family or has lost them by accident, then he will pay the
minister as tithing only as much as local custom demands.

Chapter 4.   The Manner Of Division Of Tithing

If by chance it happens that horses, cows, and animals of that kind
which bring about the tithing right with regard to our preceding laws,
migrate from the fields of one parish to another, we want there to be
an equitable division of the tithes between the ministers of those places
in which the animals were pastured, according to a fair estimate of
the times spent in both pastures. But in this law of partition we do
not want any of the sheep to be taken from the shepherd as tithing,
unless they have remained for thirty days in that man's parish. But if
the boundaries and limits of the parishes in which the animals wander
are unfixed and it is not clear to which place the right of tithing
should be paid or that the time for collecting the tithes there is no
agreement that just satisfaction had been made to the other parish in
which the animals formerly were, then it is fitting for the tithe to be
adjudged to the minister of that place in which the animals were at
the lawful tithing time. However when two or more parishes share
common pasture land in which there are few animals or if there are
vast tracts for public use ★ which we call in our language "waste Fol. 146v
grounds" for which there is no right of property for a specific parish,
or when such is the community of pastures of neighboring parishes
that by mutual interchange the right of pasture goes back and forth
at certain times of the year in accord with a certain good natured and
convenient regard to one's own vicinity, then the right of tithe shall
be separated to that place in which the possessor of the animals lives.

Chapter 5.   How Tithing Of Alienated Produce Should Be
              Regained

Many people disperse their calves, lambs, sheep, and other produce
among their children, relatives and clients before the legal tithing time
arrives in order to avoid and elude the tithing. Since it is unjust that
the minister of our churches be cheated by their craftiness, we give
the ministers liberty in this kind of unjust division of tithes, either to
seek by law fresh tithes from the dividers themselves, or to seek tithes
from those who received the produce from the dividers.[215] ★

---

[215]At the bottom of this page, folio 146v, there is a crossed out chapter which
reappears as chapter 7 on folio 147r and will be given at that place.

Fol. 147r Chapter 6.   Commodities Which Come From Sacred Rites ★

All the offerings, produce and profits which usually come to ministers of the church from the rites of matrimony, churching of women, ~~thanksgiving of women after childbirth~~ *child-bearing*,[216] funerals and from the goods of the dead, and from any other religious duties, provided they are not contrary to the book of ceremonies of the Church, to local custom, and to the prescription of the constitutions previously accommodated by us to these matters, we wish these to be given to the ministers with the greatest faith. And, whoever are delinquent in making this kind of satisfaction should be punished by the ordinary for their avarice until they have performed their duty fully.

Chapter 7.   The Law Of Vicars

Since the vicar dwells in the parish and he attends to its care, he should receive tithes, offerings, pensions, perquisites, ecclesiastical gains of every kind which he can rightfully claim, either from the original basis of his office, or from a contract, custom, or benefit of time, which they call prescription. And in addition, we give him all things in general which he has acquired without contention and controversy in the period of ten years before the publication of these laws of ours. Neither the pastor or anyone else may prevent him from possessing these things. Then let him till his lands, if he has any that are suitable for farming, and he will not present any tithes from them either to the pastor himself or anyone else. ★

Fol. 147v Chapter 8.   When The Minister Of The Church Cannot Be
                          Supported From The Provisions Of The Church

When the pastor cannot conveniently take care of his needs because of the paucity of income, whether this happens because of the evil avarice of those who take tithes away from him or make deductions from them or because the tithes and produce are so small that, even if payment were justly made, they could by no means support him, then the bishop shall impose both his fatherly concern and authority in the face of the pastor's difficulties of such a kind so that proper care can be taken for them and their families. This can be accomplished if the bishop imposes a requirement on all the pastors in the form of their giving tithes and other produce justly. But, if even this is not enough, he should persuade the men of the parish in proportion to

---

[216]It is not clear who made this change.

their abilities, that they voluntarily contribute from the means which they have as much in addition to their tithes as seems to be necessary. And if these means are not effective, some third means should be found of joining several small parishes in the neighborhood into one body and one church so that the pastor can well nourish and support his family. ★ But if the ministers who are needy be vicars, then the ~~bishop~~ should urge those who possess church goods ~~by whatever right~~ *for any reason* ~~by the means that seem best~~ *to find some way* ~~to take away~~ of supporting sufficiently the needy vicar and this family.[217]

Fol. 148r

Chapter 9.   Collecting Tithes In Another Parish

If anyone should set a fixed place to collect tithes in someone else's parish or should claim a fixed portion of tithes for himself by lawful prescription, we order him not to dare to take over any other place to collect tithes under that pretext, and not to take other tithes in that parish.

Chapter 10.   Tithes Must Be Paid To The Parish, Not To A Chapel

If by chance a chapel is situated within a parish, offerings, tithes and other ecclesiastical gains shall not be diverted to the chapel but will flow into the parish. If, however, some other arrangement has been made in proper form, it is just that the faith of the agreements be upheld.

Chapter 11.   Places Free From Tithes

No one should be compelled to pay tithes for fields, farms, and any land whether they are possessed by hereditary right or for some other just cause, if such places are free and immune from tithes by laws, constitutions of this realm, lawful privileges, or prescription and just agreements, provided proof of this matter is clearly made to an ecclesiastical judge. ★

Chapter 12.   The Custom Of Compensation Must Be Retained

Fol. 148v

Where it is local custom that other things are given in place of tithes, it is acceptable that this custom be maintained (if there is just compensation for the tithes.)[218]

---

[217]These changes are all made in Cranmer's hand.

[218]The phrase between the parentheses was underlined in the manuscript.

Chapter 13. To Whom Predial Or Personal Tithes Should Be Paid

Predial tithes, that is, tithes which are owed because of estates or farms, will move into those parishes within whose territory the estates or farms lie. But personal tithes, that is, tithes that ought to be levied because of individuals, and all offerings will go into those parishes in which the donors live and participate in divine services and the sacraments, unless by privilege or long-standing practice it is done otherwise. However, when there is disagreement about the boundaries of the farms, concerning which parish they belong to, the bishop shall divert the income of the tithes to that church to which he justly believes they lawfully belong.

Chapter 14. Personal Tithes Must Be Paid According To The Custom Of The City Of London

It is a great indignity that annual tithes are furnished to ministers of churches by poor, hard-working farmers, ★ while affluent merchants and rich men of science and the crafts offer almost nothing to the needs of the ministers, especially since they have no less need for the ministers' services than the farmers. Therefore, as from equal work equal reward should follow, we have decided that merchants, cloth-makers, and other manufacturers of every kind, and all who receive money from learning or any skill shall pay tithes in the following manner: for their homes *of course*,[219] and lands which they enjoy and for ~~from those~~ *their revenues*[220] for which they do not pay predial tithes, but in each year they will give a tenth part of their annual salary.

Fol. 149r

Chapter 15. How Proprietors Should Pay Tithes

But if a merchant, or artisan, or any business man or one who supports himself by science or skill has a right of property either in his home in which he dwells or in the surrounding land which he uses for his business, art or skill, we wish this plan to be initiated with them, namely, that the minister on one side and the possessor on the other should each choose arbiters, and the arbiters shall fix the worth of the house and lands and what the value is. The minister will receive a tenth of this amount from the possessor. And if by chance no agreement can be reached by the two arbiters, the ordinary of that church will assign a third responsible man, one experienced in

---

[219]It is impossible to read the word lined out in the manuscript. The new word is in Cranmer's hand.

[220]This change is in Cranmer's hand.

controversies of this nature. What seems proper to him shall be followed in this matter.[221] ★

Chapter 16. Tithes Of Both Kinds Must Be Paid

Moreover, although merchants, artisans and others whom we have mentioned bring their personal tithes in the form we have outlined, still they will add those [tithes] of the former kind which people call predial [farm tithes]. For if they are masters of farms, sheep, cows, or other such goods which pertain to our above-mentioned laws of tithing, we wish them to make full satisfaction to the ministers for these.

Chapter 17. A Lawsuit About Tithes Shall Not Proceed Between Ministers

Since ministers of the churches ought to be joined together in the closest bonds of charity, and enjoy a peaceful and tranquil life, it is a great disgrace for them to contend among themselves in the basest disputes, and also with large expenditures over the income from tithes. Therefore, in order that the stain of behavior of this kind and the pernicious examples of discords may be removed and ended, *we do not allow in any way this litigation about tithes*[222] to exist between ministers; and no one of them may receive tithes from another of them with respect to ecclesiastical income.

Chapter 18. The Custom Of Not Paying Tithes Should Be Invalid[223]

Since tithes should be paid according to every human law without any diminution and are owed everywhere to the pastors of our Lord Christ, and since because of unpaid tithes in many places the care of souls falls to those who have so little money that they can scarcely support themselves, therefore it happens that few pastors are found who have moderate or any skill in Holy Scriptures. Since among other matters

---

[221]There is no folio 149v or 150r. in the microfilm copy.

[222]Although this phrase is interlined in the manuscript, it appears to be the scribe's hand.

[223]In a notation in John Foxe's hand is this: "This chapter found in the codex of Matthew [Abp. of] Canterbury had been omitted here." Thus at the bottom of the page, Foxe has copied in what he claims was missing. Whether or not this chapter was part of the manuscript Cranmer worked with is not known. The nature of the chapter suggests it might have been added after the time of Cranmer, perhaps during Archbishop Parker's time.

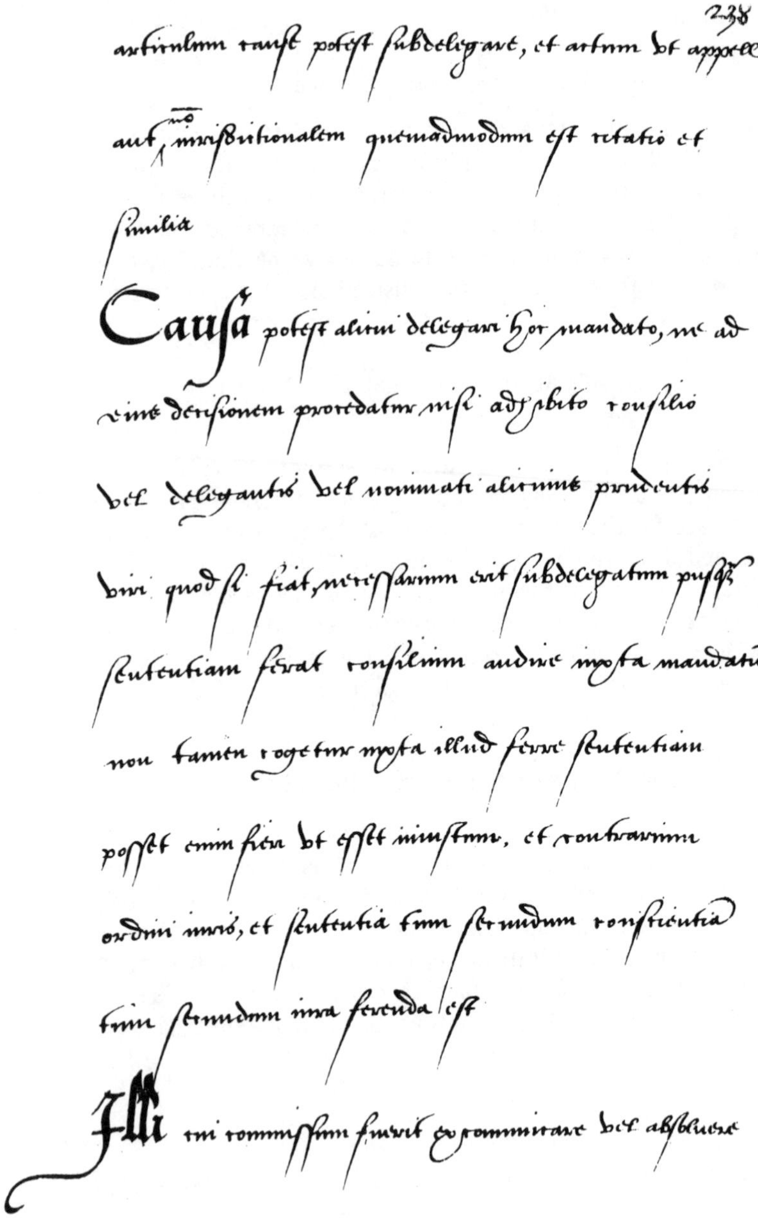

238

articulum causae potest subdelegare, et actum vel appelle

aut non iurisdictionalem quemadmodum est citatio et

similia

Causa potest alicui delegari hoc mandato, ne ad

eius decisionem procedatur nisi adhibito consilio

vel delegantis vel nominati alicuius prudentis

viri quod si fiat, necessarium erit subdelegatum priusquam

sententiam ferat consilium audire iuxta mandatum,

non tamen cogetur iuxta illud ferre sententiam

posset enim fieri ut esset iniustum, et contrarium

ordini iuris, et sententia tum secundum conscientiam

tum secundum iura ferenda est

Illi cui commissum fuerit excommunicare vel absolvere

Example of one scribal hand used

pertaining to the salvation of the Christian people, the food of the Word of God is acknowledged to be especially necessary, and since the mouth of a threshing ox ought not to be bound, and the one who serves at the altar ought to live from the altar, we ordain that despite any standing custom, full tithes of each thing should be paid, and we nullify any existing custom to the contrary. ★

Chapter 19. Pensions

Fol. 151r

Since pensions, which are given to those who cede to others their *benefices,*[224] usually nourish the laziness and avarice of those who wish to share in the gain without working, we will not allow this kind of drone to feed on the efforts of others. We, therefore, do not allow any annual payment of this kind to anyone unless because of his sickness or old age such a plan is necessary. When these impediments occur, the proper bishop of those places shall be consulted. He shall decide on the amount of pension he thinks is just; the successor shall pay this with very great faithfulness. But as long as age and health can bear it, we do not allow any minister at all to retire from the ministry. Otherwise, no income from the parish he has left will accrue to him by law of any kind. Since vicars are intimately involved in the labors of a parish, and for the most part have slight incomes to support themselves and their families, it is right for them to be exempted from paying pensions of any kind. Therefore we ordain that no pastor, patron, or any other person hereafter exact from them anything at all in the name of an annual pension. ★

★CONCERNING VISITATIONS

Fol. 151v

Chapter 1.   The Purpose Of Visitations Of Church

Archbishops, bishops, archdeacons, and, finally, others whose concern it is and who have the right to set ecclesiastical law shall visit their churches and inspect them and celebrate the solemn and customary gatherings in them opportunely so that the people committed to their care may be healthfully, and in proper order governed by their pastors, and so that the state of the churches themselves may be rightly preserved by the assiduous and pious services of the ministers.

---

[224]This appears to be a change made by Cranmer.

Chapter 2.   The Information To Be Sought In Visitations

Moreover, the following matters should be especially looked into in the established assemblies of this kind: whether Sacred Scriptures are diligently and carefully handled; whether the administration of the sacraments is proper and correct; then what is the quality and strength of ecclesiastical discipline; and finally whether the formulas of public prayers are maintained rightly and at the proper times; and whether all other matters involving the ministry of churches are rightly conducted.

Chapter 3.   Form Of Visitation

So that these [visitations] may proceed most easily, it seems good that the whole multitude shall come together in some one place as is Fol. 152r customarily done ★ and after the oaths of the syndics and other customary witnesses have been taken, crimes of persons of every kind should be diligently investigated which pertain to ecclesiastical law; and when these have been fully understood, [the offenders] shall pay the penalties provided by the laws, and a severe punishment shall be imposed on them.

Chapter 4.   What Must Be Furnished And By Whom

Next, care will have to be taken to see that those enjoying ecclesiastical benefices repair and restore all houses in their possession with the following exception: we wish the renewal and repair of the higher places in the churches, called chancels, always to be referred to the rectors themselves rather than the vicars. But, the care and repair of the remaining parts of the churches will be left to those dwelling in the parish. and it will be their responsibility that they should support at their common cost as sacristan the person whom the pastor of the church thinks suitable for this task. In addition, they will watch out for the upkeep of the cemeteries everywhere, the thorough cleaning of vessels and ecclesiastical implements and the keeping of them in their proper places. ★ And the syndics whom they call wardens will give each year an accounting of the church property entrusted to them and will deliver to their next successors the balance in the treasury whole and undepleted.[225] ★

Fol. 152v Chapter 5.   The Punishment Of Negligence In Syndics

Also, [the visitor] must check whether there is just and careful handling of matters entrusted to the safekeeping [of the officials]. Whoever has

[225]These sections were lined out by someone.

disobeyed or has not performed his duty in all these cases set down above should incur the punishment of excommunication or be punished at the discretion of the ordinary.

Chapter 6.   Just Payment For The Visitors

Moreover, since labor should not be without reward, if the archbishop visits and surveys his province, the bishop his diocese, or the archdeacon the churches proper to his duty, or others, by whatever title of ecclesiastical authority they are called, visit and survey their churches, and hold there the customary and usual gatherings and provide the other lawful rites of visitation, they should enjoy all the benefits which pertain to the administration of public business of this kind. And there should be no lessening in this type of payment of those [benefits] which were customarily given to such visitors either by general consensus or by custom or by any other legitimate procedure. Also to facilitate progress in this situation, if any persons neglect or are unwilling to release pay of this kind such as the office of visitation demands, those who undergo the labors of visitation will have the power to set aside revenues from the benefices and to impede all remaining use ★ and even to employ other ecclesiastical penalties until Fol. 153r the offenders make full satisfaction to them.

Chapter 7.   Privileges Of Exempt Places Must Be Moderated

Since we see that liberties and ecclesiastical immunities[226] often afford licentious security for sinning, we wish that bishops have the authority to inspect all colleges, societies, and assemblies that exist in their dioceses no matter what privileges they are protected by, and to assign penalties for transgressions, not only at the regular times of visitations but at all other times, when the magnitude of the crimes demands it; and the archbishop will have the same power in his province.

Chapter 8.   The Source From Which Punishment Of
             Transgressions In Colleges And Gatherings Of
             The Kind Ought To Emanate

Moreover, whenever this prerogative is this particular right or prerogative is granted to anyone in order that he may have the power of judging on his own in some college or assembly of any kind and in order that he may have the power to use this right taking cognizance of offenses of coercing evil doers, still it should be done in such a way as not to

---

[226]There is a marginal notation here in the manuscript that is not clear in its meaning nor can the hand be identified with surety.

hinder the discipline of the archbishop or the bishop. Therefore, for this reason we impose restraints in such a way that if this man ~~finds~~ reveals the crimes first, he has the right to impose punishment for them unless the defendant avoids this by appeal. But if the

Fol. 153v transgressions are brought first ★ to the bishop or archbishop and they have begun to investigate the case, then it is appropriate, that it remain in their jurisdiction. And indeed it is appropriate that this caution be upheld in judging single controversies involving crimes in such a way that ~~as regards~~ other-rights of immunity and customs remain inviolate and safe.[227] ★

Fol. 154r

CONCERNING TRIALS

Chapter 1.   What Is A Trial[228]

A trial is making plain a dubious case by legitimate documents.

Chapter 2.   If The Defendant Confesses, There Is No Need Of A Trial

Why is there need to bring a case to trial if the defendant makes it clear and incontestable by his confession? In that case a trial must not be sought since the defendant confesses that which was principally proposed against him. The opportunity for proof must be enlarged rather than restricted so that the truth may become clear in all cases.

Chapter 3.   Kinds Of Trial

Whether trials are offered, therefore, through witnesses, pleadings, documents, indictments, or reputation, a prudent judge, to whom we judge much, must be attributed in regard to this, will easily decide after weighing the circumstances of events and persons to what degree each should be

Fol. 154v believed. [229] ★ For the judge ought not bind himself to one type of trial, but will estimate from the just opinion of his mind what he should either believe or should regard as unproven to him since he understands that many things often are convincing when taken together, but do not have credibility when taken separately.

---

[227]The changes in this paragraph are in Cranmer's hand.

[228]It needs to be noted that the numbering system used in what follows is not found in the manuscript. The chapter titles, however, are in Cranmer's hand and the editor has assigned numbers to these insertions.

[229]This insertion is in Cranmer's hand.

Chapter 4.   Trial Must Not Be Allowed Unless The Defendant
             Is Present Or Is Absent Through Contempt

But although faith must be put in the judge and not in the party, we,
nevertheless, do not want any kind of trial to be allowed or employed
against anyone unless he himself is either present or absent through
contempt.

Chapter 5.   Trial Must Be Held In The Courtroom And Before
             The Judge

Trial must be held in the presence of the judge and in court, not out
of court, and not in the presence of a notary or a notarial official.

Chapter 6.   Trial Concerns The Plaintiff Not The Defendant

If the plaintiff does not offer proof, the defendant must be absolved
even if he presents nothing, unless such presumptions[230] ★ should   Fol. 155r
arise against him that they can transfer the burden of proof to him.
For still it is not fitting that when the plaintiff clearly shows that he
cannot prove what he has charged, he should bind the defendant to
the necessity of showing the contrary, since by the nature of things
there is no proof for denying a deed. Still, we wish the old mode of
making proof to be observed in negatives that are restricted in place
and time.

Chapter 7.   Contrary Proof

If sometimes contrary proofs are produced by one and the same party,
they ought to derogate mutually from one another, and deservedly.
But, if perhaps contrary proofs are alleged by diverse parties, and
proofs of this kind are offered by those proposing, one must adhere
to the strong proof. But, if there is no agreement on this, the defendant
must be favored unless ★ the welfare of the state, the salvation of   Fol. 155v
souls, or the nature of the case persuades otherwise.

Chapter 8.   Proof Is Incumbent In Common Judgements On
             The Defendant As Well As On The Plaintiff

In common judgements, the plaintiff is as responsible for proofs as
the defendant, and the one will win who has brought better and more
efficacious proofs. But if all things of this kind are equal, judgement

---

[230]At the bottom of this page, folio 154v, four words are cancelled but this is
because they are the first four words of the following page.

will be for the person in possession [of the greater proofs] unless the preponderance of the case persuades otherwise.

Chapter 9. After Disclosure It Is Not Permitted To Adduce Contrary Proofs

If some proofs of a certain impediment have been disclosed, even in a matrimonial case, the other party shall not be allowed to adduce or produce contrary proofs at any time.

Chapter 10. In Every Judicial Act Either A Notary Or Two Witnesses Must Be Present

In receiving proofs and in all other judicial acts, the judge ought to Fol. 156r employ a notary public ★ or two honorable men in his place through whom we require that all things which are transacted be faithfully written down; so that if any controversy arises later concerning the pleadings, this may be removed completely through the public and common originals themselves.

Chapter 11. Proof Is Incumbent On The One Affirming, Not The One Denying

As a creditor who seeks money is compelled to prove the amount, so again the debtor who affirms the payment ought to furnish proof of this. For the proof is incumbent upon the man who affirms, not the one who denies.

Chapter 12. There Is No Proof From Matters Alien To The Case

But proofs, whether necessary or presumptive ought to bear upon the matter under consideration. But they prove nothing which is foreign to the case or controversy.

Chapter 13. Accusers Ought Not Bring Into Court A Matter Which Cannot Be Proved

All accusers should know that they ought to bring that matter to Fol. 156v public notice which is strengthened by suitable *witnesses*[231] ★ or which has been drawn up with very open documents or indubitable judgements for proof and, which has been made evident by arguments clearer than light.

---

[231]This is the last word in the last line on the page and is in Cranmer's hand. It appears to supply the required noun to bring sense to the sentence.

Chapter 14. Synodal Witnesses

We retain the old force and ancient authority, nevertheless, for synodal witnesses and other proofs, which have arisen from great and strong suspicions.

Chapter 15. Each One Is Held To Prove That He Has Fulfilled
A Duty Enjoined Upon Him

As often as anyone is held to do something from a duty enjoined upon him, he himself ought to prove that he has faithfully fulfilled his duty of this kind, and the burden imposed on him, or that he was not the cause why he did not fulfill it.

Chapter 16. Public Records

We consider the registers and public records to be more powerful than witnesses.

Chapter 17. A Defendant Can Undertake The Burden Of Proof
On Himself

The defendant[232] can assume the burden of proof on himself and can teach about his right, although he is not bound to this by any law.
★

Chapter 18. The Defendant Ought To Prove His Exceptions   Fol. 157r

The man who says or objects that something was done through trickery must himself give an explanation of the trickery. Also, in all exceptions the defendant shall take upon himself the role of being the accuser, and is required to verify the exception, just as the plaintiff is required to verify his accusation. If he announces he has changed his mind, he must prove this.

Chapter 19. No One Should Be Admitted To Prove Those
Matters Which Do Not Help The Case At All

No one ought to be admitted to the proof of that matter which, even if proven, has no relevance lest the parties be burdened with pointless expenses, and the suits be delayed longer than is just.

---

[232]In the manuscript the second word "enim" has been struck through making a stylistic change that does not affect the translation.

Chapter 20. When Confession Must Be Preferred To All
Proofs

Fol. 157v All proofs ~~indeed~~[233] ought to yield deservedly to the confession ★ of a party. Therefore, if he confesses something contrary to the documents, witnesses, or sentence introduced or brought in his favor, he will always obtain place, despite contrary proofs, unless the danger of a soul is involved in the case, or laws prohibit a confession of this kind, and unless the confession favors the cause of the one confessing.

Chapter 21. Proofs Are Valid Even If No Designated Term Has
Been Set For Proving

Proofs are not considered spurious, although they are found to have been made without assignment of some limit, or if no delay has been granted for proving it.

Chapter 22. Proofs Entered Into For One Purpose Are Valid
For Another

~~For~~[234] We judge it is just that proofs entered into for one purpose Fol. 158r are valid for another purpose between ★ the same persons.

Chapter 23. A Person Alleging Ignorance Of A Statute Is Not
Easily Believed

One alleging ignorance of a constitution or statute must not be believed unless he brings forth proof of his ignorance or probable presumptions. In such cases the judge, after considering the circumstances of the matter and the person, can delay the oath for full proof by the one alleging ignorance.

Chapter 24. Proof Through Oath

When something pertains to conscience alone, proof through oath is admitted.

Chapter 25. Sometimes Negative Statements Must Be Proven

Proof is necessary from that party which says his opponent has been prohibited from some right by a special law or constitution. Likewise, Fol. 158v if anyone should deny that something ★ has been rightly done, the response must be that he himself must show proof.

---

[233]This was lined out by someone.
[234]This was lined out by someone.

Chapter 26. The Proof From Antiquity

In proving boundaries and ancient matters, rumors, and witnesses concerning what was said and heard, ancient books guarded and found without any suspicion can lead [the judge] to a limited belief, so that he may rightly pass sentence in favor of the man who thus proved his case, unless stronger proofs of the other party require otherwise.[235]

Chapter 27. The Acts Of The Court Must Be Faithfully Kept

The acts [of the court] induce full proof. Therefore, we wish that each and every thing should be faithfully written down, closed in the usual manner, and transmitted to the judges of appeal, ★ who require or Fol. 159r demand this, so that they may gather from them whether there has been proper judgement by the lower judge.[236] ★

★ CONCERNING POSSESSIONS Fol. 160r

Chapter 1.   [No Title is Given][237]

The burden of proof is not incumbent upon the possessor, namely, that the possession belongs to him, since when a plaintiff is deficient in proof, right of property ought to remain with the possessor.[238] In the law of possession, he will be considered superior, and the victor who can prove more ancient possession, especially if that possession was justified by some title, unless the other party introduced better, more efficacious proofs, justifying his possession. One possessing another's goods, although perhaps he may not have a just cause of holding the possession, is

---

[235]Here Cranmer divided the chapter and created chapter 27. The notation for this is found at the top of folio 159r.

[236]Folio 159v is not in the microfilm copy.

[237]Between the conclusion of the section on Trials and this new section on Possessions, the manuscript has a paragraph that has been crossed out. Its translation is as follows: Pursue the possessions which you say belong to you by means of a trial; for the burden of proving that they belong to him does not fall on the person who has possession; the [underlying] ownership will remain with him while you continue in possession during the trial.

[238]This first sentence is found at the very top of folio 159v and is in Cranmer's hand. It was to take the place of the section that was crossed out and translated in footnote 237.

not compelled to restore them, except to the person who fulfills his intention.

However, if someone has obtained possession of someone else's property by fraud or violence, that possession not only will not profit him, but burdens him with [the need for] a strong proof if he himself should later claim that the thing is either his or owed to him.[239]

CONCERNING CUSTOM[240]

Chapter 1.   What Custom Is

Custom is a certain right instituted by habits which is taken in place of law when law is deficient, a certain right initiated, continued, and established either by the habits and usages of the whole people or by the decision of the majority, and having the authority of law. For such right comes from unwritten tradition which practice has approved. For lasting habits approved by the consensus of the users, take the place of law.

Chapter 2.   Custom Is Not Valid Against Reason Or Law

Although the authority of long-standing custom and practice is not to be despised, nevertheless, it is not of such power that it can overcome Fol. 160v reason, ★ or that it ought to provide a precedent for legislation or for positive law.

Chapter 3.   Custom Is Not Valid Against Divine Law or Natural Law

Although sins are so much the graver as they keep an unhappy soul bound longer, no one of sound mind thinks that any custom which in this respect should rather be called a source of corruption, can derogate at all from divine or natural law, whose transgression endangers salvation. For any custom, no matter how old and common, must entirely defer to truth, and usage which is contrary to truth must be abolished.

---

[239]At the end of this chapter in Foxe's hand is the notation, "Concerning the credibility of documents, see folio 194."

[240]It should be noted that the chapters are not numbered in the manuscript, although they are distinctly separated from each other. The numbers have been put in for the convenience of the reader.

Chapter 4. Statutes And Customs Of The Cathedral Church
Must Not Be Changed Without Consent Of The
Bishop And The Chapter

Because[241] novelties often beget ★ discord, it seems sensible to decree   Fol. 161r
that no bishop without the consent of the chapter can change statutes
or old customs of the cathedral church or make new ones; likewise
no chapter without the bishop. But, if they have acted otherwise, the
actions should be decreed to be void unless the statues and ~~prior~~[242]
customs of this kind are at variance with the Word of God or the
edification of the church.

The Custom Of Not Paying Tithes Is Invalid[243]

Since by all human law tithes must be paid without any diminution,
and are owed to the pastors of Christ our Lord throughout the earth,
and since on account of unpaid tithes such a slender income is left
for those who have [pastoral] care of souls that they cannot be suitably
supported by it, and hence it happens that few pastors are found who
have a modest mastery ★ of sacred letters; and since among other   Fol. 161v
things which pertain to the salvation of the Christian people, the
nourishment of the Word of God is known to be especially necessary,
and [since] the mouth of the ox employed in threshing is not to be
bound, but he who serves the altar ought to live from the altar, we
ordain that, any custom to the contrary notwithstanding, a full tithe
of all things shall be paid, and we decree that every custom to the
contrary shall be void.

---

[241]The Latin originally read "Propterea quod," which has been cancelled and replaced by "Quia." Either form would be translated "because."

[242]"Prior" has been inserted by what appears to be Peter Martyr Vermigli's hand.

[243]It should be noted that this title was treated under the section of the manuscript dealing with tithes. This is so noted by a marginal note written by John Foxe and the manuscript has a vertical line down the left margin of the text, perhaps put there by a scribe to call this to the attention of the reader. At the very end of the section on folio 161v, Foxe has written, "Concerning prescriptions, see fol. 208."

Fol. 162r ## CONCERNING THE CONTESTING OF A SUIT

Chapter 1.   What Is The Contesting Of A Suit[244]

The contesting of a suit is the foundation of judgement; for truly the suit exists precisely in the contesting, and is concerned with it, and arises from the suitable response of the defendant whether to a charge or to petitions, either given in writing or put into writing by command of the judge; and the contesting of the suit does not have regard for the incidents or secondary issues, but the principal fountain-head of the controversy. And, since the procedure must be in the form and shape of judgement, if there is an omission, the litigants are vexed by empty labors and expenses.

Chapter 2.   Confession

When the defendant confesses after the charge had already been brought, the suit has been contested from that confession, if indeed the judge can progress to bring sentence since the confession has been made: but, if on the contrary the confession should precede the bringing of the charge, then the contesting of the suit is not made and sentence is not brought, but the judge ought only to command the defendant to pay what he owes within a fixed time.[245] If anyone should respond to the charge of petitions by sending ahead a protest by which he affirms that he does not intend to contest the suit through those Fol. 162v responses, ★ the suit will not be contested.

Chapter 3.   Contestation Of A Suit Does Not Require The
Presence Of The Plaintiff

The contesting of a lawsuit can take place even in the absence of the plaintiff, provided a written charge has been furnished or petitions have been drawn up in writing which the judge can propound to the defendant for response in the trial. For if a response follows by which the things sought are either affirmed or denied, or involving allegation of an intention contrary to the action that is to be contested, the action shall be contested, even though the plaintiff may be absent. In the response which is required for contesting a suit, it does not matter whether the defendant makes response by stating what he believes, or by stating what he knows as the truth.

---

[244]The manuscript does not use numbers in designating the various parts of this section. They have been put in for the convenience of the reader. The titles of all of the sections are in Cranmer's hand.

[245]The first sentence of this chapter was added by Cranmer and is in his hand in the manuscript.

Chapter 4.   Why A Lawsuit Is Contested

The contesting of a suit is required in trials for the following reason, that thereby it may be made clear what is ★ the issue between the Fol. 163r parties concerning the principal matter, which cannot come about unless there is both question and response in intelligible and clear words. Hence, we want all ambiguities and unclear points to be removed by the judge.

Chapter 5.   The Defendant Shall Give A Clear Response In
            The Contesting Suit

If the accused replies to the petitions that he neither admits them or denies them, since this is just as if he did not reply at all, he ought to be urged to [make] *some clear response.*[246]

Chapter 6.   The Defendant Shall Respond To The Various
            Petitions One By One

Since many things are sought in the written charge, the defendant is not permitted to deny all of them at once in general with a single response, for in that way a decision may be easily avoided, and there would not be a resolution between the plaintiff ★ and the defendant Fol. 163v on the suit, and the judge could not dispose of the case with a just sentence. For, it often happens that in a multitude of petitions some are true and some are false, and in these cases we wish the defendant to respond separately to each, since they cannot be resolved by one and the same response.

Chapter 7.   An Insolent Man Brings Prejudice Against Himself

Through the insolence of not appearing, the contesting of a suit does not take place. But a man will be considered insolent either by confessing or by denying inasmuch as it tends more towards his own injury.

Chapter 8.   Delaying Exceptions Hinder The Trial Of A Case

Delaying exceptions do not contest the suit absolutely; rather if the exceptions are proved, at least for a time, they prevent the suit from being contested ★ because they do not concern the principal business Fol. 164r

---

[246]Cranmer inserted this phrase, and although there is an obvious change in the Latin, its carryover into the translation is nonexistent. Cranmer exchanged "aliquod responsum" for "quid respondendum."

of the controversy, about which the contesting of the suit ought to be properly made.

Chapter 9.   Peremptory Exceptions Likewise

Certain peremptory exceptions prevent the suit from being contested, such as the exception of transaction, of judgement made, and of suit completed. Therefore, the judge ought to acknowledge, and pronounce at the beginning of a case on delaying exceptions, and those peremptory ones which impede the contesting of a suit. But, other exceptions beyond these just enumerated do not prevent the contesting of the suit, if they are raised as objections.

Chapter 10.   Witnesses Are Not Admitted Before The
               Contesting Of a Suit To Prove The Principal Case
               But To Prove Delaying And Peremptory
               Exceptions[247]

Fol. 164v Witnesses can be admitted before the contesting ★ of a suit, not indeed in regard to the principal point of the whole case but to prove or disprove delaying and peremptory exceptions which impede the contesting of a suit.

Chapter 11.   Witnesses Can Be Admitted For Perpetual Record
               Of The Matter Before The Contesting Of The Suit

Although by common rule witnesses ought not be received before the contesting of the suit, still if there should be fear of their death or prolonged absence or if there is danger, when the business is complicated and involved, that they would forget the events and order of events, the old and infirm will be received for testimony, and those whose long absence or forgetfulness is suspected, even when the suit Fol 165r has not yet ★ been contested, provided, however, that the party has been summoned. If this party cannot be present, it will be necessary that his own advocate should meet his adversary at the time assigned to him by the judge, by counting from the day on which he first will be able to appear, or else for him, when it is possible, to renounce the admission of such witnesses. If he neglects to do this, the testimonies that are received will not be valid.

---

[247]This chapter heading, squeezed between the lines of the manuscript, is in Cranmer's hand.

Chapter 12. In What Cases Witnesses Should Be Admitted For The Principal Case Before The Contesting Of The Suit

Witnesses can also be admitted in reference to the principal point of the business without the contesting of the suit when it involves the election of prelates, or postulations, provisions, ranks, ★ minor Fol. 165v dignitaries, duties, collegiate churches, prebends, or any ecclesiastical benefices, tithes, usuries, and notaries,[248] to which we add also matrimonial cases. For, we simply permit proceedings summarily in these cases without the form and shape of a trial. ~~Also, contestation of a lawsuit is not required when witnesses are examined in order to create a permanent record, which is sometimes done when someone fears that some danger or damage for himself will be created unless what happened is confirmed by witnesses while it can be done~~[249] In criminal actions when the crime is not notorious, witnesses must not be received unless ★ the suit was contested when the person involved Fol. 166r is most gravely endangered in these actions.

Chapter 13. When The Contesting Of A Suit Is Not Required

The contesting of a suit is not required when the action is not against a specific person, but is only concluded before the judge; as whenever the usefulness and injury of others is involved; likewise, when the case is purely spiritual and is handled without inconvenience to anyone, in interlocutory sentences and sentences of censure but not in manifest questions, in all notorious and summary processes, and when the right of trial is directed to public good. If anyone had demanded a contesting in the ★ investigation of crimes and was prosecutor of this, the Fol. 166v contesting of the suit should be held, but if the judge ex officio should be moved spontaneously, there will be no need of contesting the suit.

When contesting the suit is not required, we wish that the first action that is customarily done after contestation of the suit, for example, exception to witnesses and other things of that sort, should entirely exclude delaying exceptions, which the contesting of the suit customarily excluded, and should altogether have the force and effect of a contesting of the case also in other matters. ★

---

[248]The manuscript has "notorii." If this is not a scribal error for "notarii," it could refer to letters of information filed with a king or a magistrate of high rank.

[249]This section of the manuscript is crossed out but there is no way to determine who did the crossing out.

Fol. 167r Chapter 14. Or When It Should Be So Inscribed Concerning The Contesting Of A Suit

Whenever, in any cases that pertain to our ecclesiastical forum, formal charge but only a simple petition drawn up in acts is required, we have decided that the contesting of this suit is not to be required at all in the aforesaid cases, but they should proceed entirely without this to the very end of the cases. But we wish that the first act which usually happens after the contesting of the suit, like the reception of witnesses and other matters of this kind, should entirely exclude delaying exceptions, which the very contesting of the suit usually would exclude; and we wish that the first act have and obtain the force and effect of the very contesting of the suit even in all other matters.[250] ★

Fol. 168r
CONCERNING THE OATH
OF FALSE ACCUSATION

Chapter 1. Both The Plaintiff And The Defendant Should Take An Oath Against False Accusation At The Beginning Of The Suit[251]

Since we hate false accusations and avoid them with the greatest effort and care, desiring to repress completely the passion of those who proceed easily and rashly to litigation, we have deemed it necessary also to establish the present law through which we ordain that neither the plaintiff nor the defendant shall be admitted to contests of litigation in any ecclesiastical cases, for there frequently is calumny even in these cases, unless each submits to an oath against false accusation at the very beginning of the suit.

Chapter 2. When A Judge Is First Admitted To His Office, He Should Present An Oath Against False Accusation

Although the judge should not swear on false accusation in individual cases, still at the outset when he undertakes his office of judging he
Fol. 168v ought to take this kind of oath so as to cover ★ all cases in general that are handled by him.

---

[250]In the manuscript there follows a page that is blank except for John Foxe's notation, "Concerning judgements and perjury, see folio 103r."

[251]Again, none of the chapters in the manuscript are numbered and again, the titles are in Cranmer's hand. Chapter numbers are used here to aid the reader.

Chapter 3.   The Form Of An Oath Of False Accusation

Both plaintiff and defendant should testify, chiefly, to the following things when they take an oath against false accusation: that they think they have a just cause, that they do not wish in the whole action which will follow to make any false accusation, and that they have not given and will not give any gift, either personally or through others, either to corrupt the judge or to corrupt others through whom judgement is administered; that they do not want to make evasions or to contrive tricks in their proofs, or to seek delays, either to deceive the opponent or in order to prolong the suit, and finally that they will respond faithfully in all those matters which are required in court from them, provided the matters pertain to the case. ★

Chapter 4.   Oath Against Malice   Fol. 169r

Although an oath against false accusation is required, once with respect to the whole case after the contesting of the suit, still an oath against malice can be required from all parties to the suit when it seems good to the judge, and when manifest perjury is not feared.

Chapter 5.   The Difference Between The Oath Of Malice And
             That of False Accusation

The oath against malice differs from that against false accusation in this respect, namely that this oath does not refer, as that one does, to the whole suit but only to that matter which is presumed to be currently done with malice and the person from whom it is exacted ought to swear that he is not conscious of any malice or fraud by which he is seeking to defraud his opponent in what he proposes or does. This kind of oath can be exacted both before ★ and after the   169v
contesting of the suit, not only by the principals of the suit, but also by their procurators and substitutes, as they are called, as often as there is a presumption of malicious action.

Chapter 6.   The Oath Should Be Made Either Through The
             Principal Of The Suit Or Through His Procurator

The principal of a case ought to swear concerning false accusation whenever he can easily be reached, but the oath of the procurator will suffice, provided he has the special mandate to swear in this case concerning false accusation. But, if the procurator was placed entirely in charge of the principal's businesses before the latter's departure, there will be no need of a special mandate. If the principals of a suit have sworn concerning false accusation and then have appointed their

Fol. 170r procurator to prosecute the suit, the procurators ★ also will have to swear concerning false accusation, but for this a special mandate will not be necessary.

Chapter 7. The One Taking An Oath Ought Not To Have A Light Attitude Toward The Case

The agent or procurator or syndic who is to be admitted to swear concerning false accusation, ought to have a just and not light conception of the case.

Chapter 8. If One Party Dies, The Successor Himself Will Offer The Same Oath

When the man who had begun the case has died, his heir or successor, who will prosecute the suit, ought to offer an oath of false accusation, although the deceased had sworn.

Chapter 9. Oath In An Appeal

Also, in the case of an appeal there must be an oath concerning false accusation, although there was an oath at the beginning of the suit. ★

Fol. 170v ### Chapter 10. If A Man Refuses An Oath He will Drop Out Of The Case

If a man who is required to make an oath of false accusation or malice refuses to do this, he will drop out of the case whether he was a defendant[252] or plaintiff.

Chapter 11. The Oath Of False Accusation Must Not Be Omitted

But, because we fear that perhaps parties using a certain collusion may reciprocally omit a sacrament of this kind, and evade our penal clause in this way, we command, since we have made the present law not only for the convenience of individuals but also for the common good, that judges not either expressedly or tacitly allow this oath to be avoided but that they exact it completely as is ~~permitted~~, *stated*

---

[252]This was inserted by Cranmer for a word that is so thoroughly cancelled that it can't be identified.

above[253] ★ and not omit it in any way. For this oath of false accusation is numbered among the legitimate ~~observations~~ *customs*[254] of the courts. But, if the judge neglects it, especially when warned by a party, his sentence will be nullified by law. ★

CONCERNING DELAYS[255]

Chapter 1.   What Is A Delay

Delay is an opportunity of acting within a time prescribed by law or by the judge or by the agreement of the parties.

Chapter 2.   Kinds Of Delays

One type of delay is a legal delay which is defined by the laws; for a time is prescribed by the laws for appeal and for seeking restitution in full and similar acts. A judicial delay is one given at the discretion of the judge. A conventional delay is one which had its terminus from the agreement of parties. From the group of judicial delays, a citatory delay is given by the judge for the purpose of making an appearance; a deliberatory delay is given, once the writ had been offered, for deliberation on the matters ★ which are being sought whether concerning yielding or undertaking the litigation; a recusatory delay grants a time limit for proposing all exceptions, and for declining or deferring judgement; a probatory delay is given in order to offer proof and make allegations; a definitory delay is given in order to define the matter; a judicatory delay is given to the condemned to suffer the judgements or pay them; an appellatory delay ~~which~~ is given for appeal.[256]

Chapter 3.   Delays Must Be Limited As Much As Possible

We wish to limit the occasion for delays in every case, and for this reason we do not give judges as much power to grant delays as they

---

[253]In the text "permittitur" is lined out and "praemittitur" has been left. It could be that the scribe erroneously wrote both words and cancelled the wrong one since "praemittitur" makes no sense in this context.

[254]Cranmer lined out the one word and wrote in the other. It should be noted that the next page in the manuscript is blank with Foxe's notation at the top, "Concerning proofs, see folio 154."

[255]As in earlier chapters, the manuscript provides no numbers for the various sections of this chapter. Cranmer's hand again seems to have give titles to the various sections and for the reader's convenience, numbers have been put in.

[256]This word was lined out, perhaps by Cranmer.

might wish, but only as much as the urgency of the matter, and the necessity of the desired arrangements *requires*.[257] Therefore a delay

Fol. 173r ought not to be granted ★ except to one seeking it for a just reason and in good faith. Thereupon, if for the sake of delaying a solution, a crime of fraud is charged by a debtor, nevertheless, subject to the investigation of the crime, we wish the debtor to be compelled to make payment. *And*[258] we think there should be the same action in similar conditions.

Chapter 4.   Fixed Periods For Delays

Although it is a tradition from ancient law that any citation receives the space of ten days, and twenty days are given to deliberate, three months to produce witnesses and documents when they are in the province, six when they are in places contiguous to the province, nine when they are in overseas regions, but [only] thirty days for a

Fol. 173v contumacious plaintiff, still we wish these delays to be more or ★ less restricted at the discretion of the judges on the basis of persons, places and cases, but in no way to be further extended. And when the judge has restricted them much, he should express the reasons, which are inserted in the acts so that the matter of appeal may be exact. Still, an appellatory delay will not be changed at the discretion of the judge, for it will always be fifteen days, *which* will not be contracted or lengthened.[259]

Chapter 5.   Delays Which Pertain To The Knowledge Of The Case Should Be Done While The Judge Is Sitting And In The Presence Of The Opponent

Although citatory and deliberatory delays can be granted by a judge who is not sitting but walking in the place of judgement, still we wish those delays which require knowledge of the case to be given by a sitting judge, and while the adverse party is present, so that if he could make a counter charge and a question of this kind concerning

Fol. 174r delays ★ should emerge, the suit will be settled by sentence of the judge.

---

[257]Cranmer cancelled "flagiaverit" here and substituted "exegerit" but the translation remains the same in either instance.

[258]Here Cranmer cancelled "quodque" and inserted "Et" thus breaking one sentence into two but it does not seem to change the meaning. There are two other scribal corrections in this paragraph which do not alter the meaning.

[259]Someone, perhaps Cranmer, cancelled "quae" and inserted "qui" at this point in the sentence to correct an error of gender.

Chapter 6.   If The Judge Should Not Announce The Law
             Within The Time Prescribed For Proof, The Party
             Will Have The Lost Time Restored To It

However, if it is not a matter of the party's not being able to give its
proofs in the period of delay given to it but it is a matter of the judge's
fault, because he does not render judgement on that day, then a new
delay must not be given; but we wish the lost time to be restored to
the same party.

Chapter 7.   The End Of Delay Should Be The Same For Each
             Party

Whenever a delay is given by a judge, we have decreed that the same
time limit should be common to both parties, so that each party can
present its proof within it. But, if the one to whom the delay had been
granted renounces the delay while there is still time, we do not wish
the adversary to be able to provide proof by reason of the same delay.
★

Chapter 8.   A Delay Has To Prescribe A Fixed Period   Fol 174v

We wish a delay given by a judge to parties to be fixed either by a
number of days or to a certain date.

Chapter 9.   After A Delay Has Been Granted, The Duty Of
             The Judge Ceases While The Delay Lasts[260]

We decree that the office of the judge shall be inactive when a delay
has been given until the interval of time that has been sought runs
out. Holidays should not be excluded from this period but counted
in.

Chapter 10. The One Who Lost The Acts Should Not Be
             Admitted To Another Proof

If anyone proves his intention through witnesses or some similar
means, and afterwards loses the documents, even if he can prove that
it was an accident, we do not wish any further delay to be given to
him.

---

[260]It should be noted that in the titles of chapters 9 and 10, the scribe has made
changes which do not change the English translation.

Chapter 11. If A Writ Is Inserted In The Citation, It Excludes Delay For Deliberation

When a copy of a writ is transmitted to a defendant in citation, and he is called on to respond, deliberatory delays will not be given to Fol. 175r him, provided the citation contains ★ a just and proper time limit; otherwise he shall have delays to deliberate. ~~And we want this observed not only in civil judgement but also in criminal judgement.~~[261]

Chapter 12. At The Beginning Of A Case, Time Will Not Be Granted To The Plaintiff For Deliberation

Deliberatory delays will not be granted to the plaintiff at the beginning of the case, for he is considered to have come well informed, but if the defendant makes an objection or files a counter-suit, the plaintiff will rightfully have some delay for deliberations.

Chapter 13. Change Of Writ Does Not Always Require A New Delay In Order To Respond

If the writ is changed in that it does not alter the first petition in a way that the defendant would be less able to be certain about it, new deliberatory delays must not be granted. For, since someone could be Fol. 175v fully ★ informed by the first writ, it is permissible that something be added which does not change the nature of the business, and new delays must not be granted.

Chapter 14. Extension Of Delay

We do not wish more delays than our laws permit to be granted to anyone; still, we understand that these can be extended for good reason and these will not be new delays but former ones extended. An extension ought to be made before the first period of delay has expired. But, if the whole period has been complete, we do not wish the possibility of an extension to happen, but there will be a new delay.

Chapter 15. A Second Delay Can Be Granted For A Reason

We have decided that a second delay must be granted for a reason, and this only in respect to time in which someone was impeded, and Fol. 176r in respect to that matter ★ in which he was impeded. And so if someone was prevented from producing a witness, and he took care as soon as he could to produce this man within the first delay, a new delay will

---

[261]This sentence was lined out.

~~certainly~~[262] be granted to produce that witness, but not others whom he did not take pains to produce within the first delay.

Chapter 16. When A Delay Can Be Revoked

A delay which has been granted with the consent of the parties ought not be revoked without cause if one party is unwilling; but when the judge, by his authority, has limited the delay in advance, he can revoke it.

Chapter 17. Delay Given To A Defendant For An Oath Must Be Understood To Be Given To The Plaintiff For Proof

We understand that delay given ★ to a defendant for an oath ought Fol. 176v to be understood also as given to the plaintiff for proof through witnesses or documents.

Chapter 18. Delay When the Defendant Opposes Exceptions

We understand that delay ought to be given to either party from its laws when the defendant raises exceptions.

Chapter 19. Delay For Consultation

A delay can be sought from the beginning, in order to consult those whose advice the difficulty of the case requires, and whom the business concerns in some way, so that he who had been summoned may be informed by them. If, while the case is pending in regard to whose developments positions are offered, arguments are offered concerning some new point, a delay must be given to the procurator so that he can consult his principal party, if the new development is such that from the beginning his principal probably could not have known anything about it. ★ For, if it could have been foreseen from the Fol. 177r beginning and has an obvious connection with the principal issue, time will not be granted to him to consult his principal. For the principal must blame himself for not fully informing his procurator from the beginning as he should have done.

Chapter 20. Peremptory Summons

Too brief a limit should not be fixed for a peremptory citation unless the greatest necessity should suggest this. Otherwise, a party so summoned may appeal.

---

[262]Word cancelled by someone.

Chapter 21. One May Appeal Because Of Unjust Delays

If a judge either shortens or lengthens delays without cause and unjustly, one may appeal from him.

Chapter 22. A Third Summons

Fol. 177v Summoning delays should be listed as either three ★ or one peremptorily but one which concedes that space of time which can be equal to and appropriate to three. Beyond the first and second summoning delay, others are peremptory although perhaps they should not be listed as such.

Chapter 23. A Person Absent For Service To The State Will
　　　　　　 Be Excused From Judgement

A person absent for service to the state is excused from the limits set for him in court for as long a time as the ~~impediment~~ reason for the absence lasts. ~~Anyone who was despoiled and forcibly deprived of his goods cannot be compelled to respond to his adversaries in court unless restitution is first made. Once he has been restored in full, he will then have a four to six month delay for preparation.~~[263] ★

Fol. 178r Chapter 24. Removal From Administration

One who has been suspected of squandering and therefore has been removed from administration, although he has not yet been restored, is compelled to respond in court, and will not be restored unless the case has been investigated and he has been absolved.

Chapter 25. When The Same Limit Can Be Prescribed To Two
　　　　　　 Acts

It is permitted to set the same limit for two acts when they can concur at one and the same time, as to produce probatory witnesses and the rebuttal witnesses. ~~And if the acts are to be expounded in order of succession, the same limit [shall be set].~~[264] But, if the acts must be explained in successive order, they will not be able to have the same Fol. 178v common limit. ★ A judge giving a delay, or while one is pending which

---

[263]These last two crossed out sentences suggest in the spacing and style found in the manuscript that they were part of a different chapter that subsequently was cancelled. Since Cranmer titled all the sections, it could well be that it was his hand that cancelled this unnamed chapter.

[264]The cancelled sentence seems to be contradictory to the second following sentence. Perhaps this is why someone cancelled the sentence.

has already been given, may establish a terminal date one after another for the explication of another act as much for the same party as for the other, since no prejudice happens thus to a delay already granted. For example, if ten days are assigned to produce documents and five for witnesses, these acts do not mutually impede each other. But if one act depends on another, he may not do this. Indeed, it would be bad to give ten days to produce arguments and ten to prove intention, because arguments will perhaps be so clear that they may not need proof, or they will be so inept that they must be entirely repudiated.

Chapter 26. The Judge Cannot Spare One Party In Prejudice Against The Other

Although the judge can graciously spare a contumacious ★ defendant, Fol. 179r for example by waiting one day or so after that peremptory limit, still he should not do this in prejudice against a party, nor in such a way that he does not order expenses to be repaid.

Chapter 27. Judgements Should Not Occur On Holidays

We wish lawsuits and judgements to be avoided on holidays in honor of God, and all feast days as well; nor will witnesses give testimony at these times, and the process of a deed done then, and a sentence given then will not be valid.

Special holidays which are proclaimed by order of our royal majesty, either because of successful exploits or because of the inauguration of a reign or for public prayer, shall be equal to holidays instituted in honor of God, and for the same reason that court proceedings are not allowed on the former ★ days, even if the parties are willing, so Fol. 179v they are not allowed on the latter days.

Chapter 28. What Is Permissible On Holidays

We permit things which pertain to peace and concord, to be done ~~on special holidays not instituted to the glory of God~~ on holidays,[265] for example, oaths, pacts, transactions. It is also permissible to plead the cases of indigent persons on these days. ~~Also interrogations and punishments of brigands are not remitted on account of these holidays.~~[266]

---

[265]Cranmer has cancelled the passage to substitute in its place "on holidays."

[266]It would appear that Cranmer also lined out this sentence in his editing of this section.

Chapter 29. Summons Should Not Occur On Holidays

Summons which occur on a holiday are not valid; and when they expressly designate in advance a holiday for appearance, they are rash. The judge should then summon for a fixed date, and should add that if that date is a holiday, you should come on the next day. ★

Fol. 180r Chapter 30. The Harvest And The Vintage

Parties can make a renunciation on their own judgement on those holidays which have been instituted for the utility of men such, as the harvest feast or the vintage. If they should do this, both the judicial process and the sentence delivered will be valid. Still, the witnesses cannot be compelled to testify on these days if they do not want to.

On holidays, instituted on behalf of men, not only can the parties renounce, but for certain reasons they can be compelled to come into court; for instance if the matter should be about to perish because of time and it would not allow delay. For these reasons, a sentence which was brought prior to these holidays, can be entrusted to execution during them, and grave crimes against God can be acknowledged and punished.

Chapter 31. Fixed Holidays

Fol. 180v The courts should be quiet during the whole of Lent, ★ during the octave of Easter and the week before Christmas.[267]

Fol. 182r ★CONCERNING JUDGEMENTS AND WHEN ANYONE OUGHT TO BEGIN OR AGREE ON THEM

Chapter 1. What Is A Judgement[268]

A judgement is a lawful act of investigating and deciding, rightly and in due order, matters which are brought before a judge in a controversy.

---

[267]At the end of this chapter, Foxe has written this notation: "Concerning exceptions, see folio 202." There is no folio 181 in the microfilm copy of the manuscript.

[268]As in some earlier topics, no chapter numbers are in the manuscript. That is the case here. The titles for each chapter are in Cranmer's hand and numbers have been inserted for the reader's convenience.

Chapter 2.   ~~What Is An Ordinary Judgement~~ *On Ordinary Judgements*[269]

Ordinary judgements are those in which all those things are required which ought to be observed in the legal examination of cases. *For when the order of the law is not preserved, the process is rendered null if a judgement was ordinary.* [270]

Chapter 3.   ~~The Requirement For Pronouncing A Sentence In Ordinary Judgement~~[271]

In ordinary civil judgements, full examination of the case should suffice for pronouncing sentence. But in criminal judgements, the keenest investigation should be employed because of the danger, and there should be no pronouncement unless the fullest examination of the case is obtained, and the proofs were clearer than light itself. ★

Chapter 4.   Extraordinary Judgements   Fol. 182v

In extraordinary judgements the order of procedure is not observed in all respects. *But, they are divided into summary judgements given in chambers and without noise, and those lacking the forms and appearance of judgement.*[272]

Chapter 5.   Summary Judgements

In summary judgements, suits can be brought to conclusion without the completion of proof, for example, if the action is for the purpose of forcing someone to make appearance in court, and with regard to all those questions which arise concerning the investigation of the principal cause, they are only such that their resolution would not cause injury to the litigants in such a way that they would be unable to uphold their rights in another lawsuit. Also, summary judgements are [those] in which proofs against someone absent are admitted.

---

[269]This change was made by Cranmer.

[270]This sentence was added in Cranmer's hand.

[271]This title was cancelled in the manuscript with the same stroke as that used by Cranmer in the section above it. The Cardwell edition of 1851 considered this a distinct chapter as it is here.

[272]This sentence is in Cranmer's hand.

Chapter 6.   The ~~Judgement~~ *Process* Of Judgement In Chambers
And Noiselessly[273]

Whenever one can proceed in chambers, or as they say, without noise,
when, that is, the judge can proceed outside of the ordinary place
Fol. 183r while he is not sitting as a tribunal, and[274] ★ when holidays are not
observed, judgement is given by receiving a bill of action or letters of
appeal, and whatever does not cause injury to the adverse party.
Although we also wish that entire cases can be examined in chambers
sometimes summarily, as when minor offenses must be punished. Still
in this kind of judgement, we do not wish other observances of the
judicial process to be completely omitted.

Chapter 7.   Processes Without Form And Appearance Of
Judgement

A process is without form and appearance of judgement when only
those matters which are matters of natural law are kept in the process,
such as summons, legitimation of persons, by which for example,
those who wish to make any demand in the name of another person
show their mandate, petition, defense, and other things of this kind:
but those things which are a matter only of civil and positive law
Fol. 183v should be eliminated ★ like formal charges, holidays appointed on
account of the necessity of man, the contesting of the suit and similar
matters.

Chapter 8.   When One May Proceed Summarily And In
Chambers And Without Noise And Form Of
Judgement

~~An inferior judge~~ *A judge*[275] should never, at his own pleasure proceed
in the examination of a case summarily in chambers and without the
figure and form of judgement, but only when this is permitted expressly
by our laws. ~~or has been ordered by us in a delegation of the case.~~ *In
cases of benefices, matrimony, etc., as on the following folio,*[276] < wills, but
not in the cases of tithes and usury and cases touching these in any

---

[273]This change is in Cranmer's hand.

[274]Three words are lined out here and cannot be read.

[275]This change is in Cranmer's hand.

[276]Cranmer lined out the one passage and put in the other. The bracketed material
is not in the manuscript at this point but follows the Foxe-Cardwell version. Cranmer's
reference "to the following folio" is to the marked paragraph on folio 184v, which
turns out to be Cardwell's text. In the left margin on 183v, Foxe has written "In cases
etc." In the left margin of folio 184v, Cranmer wrote, "Let it be put in the preceding
folio."

way, the process should happen simply and in chambers and without noise and the form of judgement. However, in other civil judgements and criminal ones that are not notorious, we wish the order of judgements to be observed, unless something else is decided by a consensus of the parties or is prescribed by our royal commission. >

CONCERNING CRIMES

Chapter 1.   (No Title Is Given)[277]

Criminal judgements should be handled at a time when there is a treatment of the crime in the trial itself, so that they may be punished with juridical penalties. This should happen sometimes through accusers, official prosecutors, and sometimes through denouncers [police officials] who should refer to the judge about the crime. Sometimes the judge should inquire in his official capacity, without an accuser ★ or denouncer being involved; but sometimes through Fol. 184r exceptions raised by the litigants. But whether in these criminal cases, the judge ought to proceed ordinarily or extraordinarily, he should understand partly from the laws, and partly from the words of the commission appointed by us for him.

Chapter 2.   Notorious Crimes

When a crime is notorious, observance of the judicial order is not required but from the evidence (when it is already agreed by whom the crime was committed). Let it be sufficient for the culprit to be summoned to hear the sentence so that if he has any probable reasons, he should bring reasons why he ought not to be condemned to this, or that punishment. Although the crime is notorious, no one ought to be denied his legitimate defense. When a notorious crime is involved, whether the defendant comes when cited or does not come, ★ they Fol. 184v should proceed against him summarily.

Chapter 3.   Unnotorious Crime

If there is any doubt concerning the crime, when it is necessary that this doubt be removed by proofs, and indeed by proofs clearer than light, we wish the order of judgement to be preserved most strictly.

[277]Cranmer has written in "Concerning Crimes" but did not give the first paragraph a title. The manuscript again does not contain numbers for each section and they are supplied here to aid the reader.

Indeed, there can be no error in these matters without its being most harmful.[278]

Chapter 4.　Criminal Accusation

Fol. 185r　No one should be allowed to bring a criminal accusation ★ unless he previously has bound himself to undergo the penalty which the accused if convicted would have to suffer. If he should lose in the judgement, and unless he has given people as surety, he should beware of prosecuting the case.

If there is doubt about flight, [i.e., if it is thought they might flee], the accuser as well as the accused can be detained under custody until there is a settlement of the crime. As for those who either flee or hide because of offenses they have committed so they will not be drawn into judgement, when they have been summoned by the usual edict, their goods will be sequestered if they fail to appear. When this has been done, they should be called again by edicts and citations; and if they have not appeared thus, their goods will be confiscated and when they are able to be seized, they should be taken captive without delay.

Fol. 185v　　　　　★ The Age Of Judges

We do not permit the judge to be younger than eighteen years even if he is requested by agreement of the litigants. [279]

CONCERNING JUDGEMENTS

Chapter 1.　A Judge Who Is Not One's Own Becomes One's Own By Agreement

The jurisdiction of any judge who is not one's own, who is in charge of a tribunal or had another jurisdiction, can be substituted by agreement of the contending parties; but the agreement of the private parties does not make that man a judge who is not in charge of any jurisdiction, and whatever such a man has decreed does not have the authority of a judged case. A substitution can be made not only

---

[278]The next section in the manuscript is crossed out and is that section referred to earlier that Cranmer wanted transferred to Chapter 8, On Judgements.

[279]This section has been lined out. The quality of the "line" used is similar to that found in other places where one can be sure it was Cranmer who lined out a section. However here there is no way to prove Cranmer drew the line. This cancelled section was to be moved to folio 183v.

expressly but also tacitly. For, if contending parties have knowingly approached a judge who is not their own, they are understood to be substituting his jurisdiction. If anyone agrees on any judge in his presence and with ★ his adversary in regard to a certain case, he Fol. 186r cannot reject him for this case. A man does not seem to have agreed on a judge if he wants a type of action to be proclaimed for him by the same judge. ~~When the judge has died, a successor can proceed in his place according to retroactive form, just as the one to whom he has succeeded could have done.~~[280]

Chapter 2.   Delegated Judges

When an ordinary judge forbids one of several delegated judges to act as judge, he seems to commit this to the others.

Chapter 3.   Those Who Cannot Be Judges

~~But~~ Not all *men indiscriminately*[281] can be given as judges. For some are impeded by nature, like the deaf, the mute, and the perpetually mad, ~~and children [below the age of puberty]~~[282] since they are lacking judgement. Some are impeded by law (like the notorious), some by custom (like ★ women and slaves), not because they do not have Fol. 186v judgement, but because it is convention that they do not perform civil duties; *some, by age, as youths and minors under eighteen. For we do not permit such to be judges even if they are demanded by agreement of litigants.*[283]

Chapter 4.   The Refusal Of A Judge

A judge also can ordinarily be refused for any reason by which he is plausibly presumed to be inclined toward one of the parties. But, he who refuses ought to explain his reasons, and show the likelihood. If one of the litigants has made the judge sole heir, or partly heir or executor, another judge must necessarily be called in because it is unjust for someone to become judge in his own case. It must be observed that a man whom one party seeks by name should not be given as judge, for we judge this to be an example of injustice, unless this is permitted specially by us on account of the dignity of the judge who is asked for. ★

---

[280]This part of the manuscript which appears to be a chapter was crossed out by someone. Cardwell claims Cranmer but that is hard to determine.

[281]This was inserted into the text in Cranmer's hand.

[282]This was probably lined out by Cranmer.

[283]This sentence is in Cranmer's hand.

Fol. 187r   Chapter 5.   A Succeeding Judge Can Provide What His Predecessor Did Not Do. If The Judge Has Died, The Successor In His Position Can Proceed By Following Reverse Form [i.e., he can go back over or repeat earlier stages of the procedure], Just As The Judge Whom He Has Succeeded Could Have Done[284]

If a judge to whom a fixed term has been established dies, and another is put in his place, we will understand that as much time will be established afresh in his person as the previous judge, ~~at the time of his death~~ *who died had provided*[285] although the one delegating has not expressed this specifically in the subsequent grant. However, [this is to be done] in such a way that they do not exceed the legitimate terms. The man who is judge, in a case involving possession, ought to be the same in the petitory case lest the coherence of the case be divided.

Chapter 6.   Three Parts Of Judgement

A judgement has three parts, the beginning up to the contesting of the case, the middle up to the conclusion of the case, and the end
Fol. 187v   through the sentence. ★ ~~If the order of the law is not preserved, the process is rendered null if it was an ordinary trial.~~[286]

Chapter 7.   On Citation

The lawsuit is begun through citation, and the jurisdiction is acquired in perpetuity. The man to be called into judgement should be called not by three edicts but by one peremptory one in place of all, so that circuitousness may be avoided.

Chapter 8.   When Parties Can Send Procurators

It does not appear to be ambiguous in the law that the ordinary or delegated judge can not order either party to appear before him personally, unless there is a cause of correction or unless for the purpose of telling the truth or of taking an oath of calumny [false accusation], or unless some other legal necessity demands that the
Fol. 188r   parties be presented personally before him. ★ The principal parties

---

[284]This is at the very top of folio 187r and is in Cranmer's hand. Although the title is certainly long, it is as Cranmer wrote it. Again the editor is numbering the chapters for the ease of the reader.

[285]This substitution is in Cranmer's hand.

[286]This was lined out and is at the bottom of folio 187r and carries over to the top of folio 187v.

ought to respond not through procurators or advocates concerning the issue involved in the case but in person if the judge has decided that they should be interrogated or examined.

Chapter 9.   A Man When Cited Ought To Appear Before A
Judge, Even A Judge Who Is Not His Own

If one is called from another jurisdiction before a judge, he ought to come, for it is the job of the judge to determine whether it is his own jurisdiction, but it is not the job of the one called to despise the authority of the judge. For, even the privileged are obliged to come into court when called, with the purpose of alleging their privileges.

Chapter 10.   Change Of Locale After The Citation Does Not
Suffice For Refusal Of Jurisdiction

If anyone, after being called into court, begins to live within another jurisdiction, the exception of that jurisdiction will not be an obstacle as if *because* he was already called previously by the other.[287] ★

Chapter 11.   There Should Be Safe Access And Return For   Fol. 188v
Those Summoned Before A Judge

One who has been called before an ecclesiastical judge should not be molested or have his property seized by a secular judge, no matter what the latter's privilege may be, while going, remaining, or returning, subject to a penalty of ten pounds to be applied to the poor-box.

Chapter 12.   That The Costs Are To Be Paid By The
Defendant *Paying Court Costs*[288]

If a defendant is called to judgement and appears, and the plaintiff is absent *makes no objection,* the defendant after showing a copy of the citation and giving his pledge concerning the day of appearance, should be dismissed along with his expenses. The man who rashly has had his adversary called to judgement ought to give back to his adversary the travel costs and costs of litigation. *The judge shall compel the defeated party to pay the winning party's expenses unless for a just reason he grants help to the loser. It is the judge's responsibility to fix the expenses of the trial after the sentence is in execution and then to administer the oath over the truth of these same [expenses] to the winning party.*[289] ★

---

[287]The change is in Cranmer's hand.

[288]The change in the title is in Cranmer's hand.

[289]All the changes in this paragraph are in Cranmer's hand. The last two sentences were added by Cranmer at the bottom of the page

Fol. 189r Chapter 13. The Judicial Forum

It is the order of the law that the plaintiff should follow the jurisdiction of the defendant, and not the defendant that of the plaintiff.

Chapter 14. *A Defendant Can Be Allotted A Forum In Four Ways*

Defendants are allotted a forum in four ways in the section "Concerning The Office And Jurisdiction Of All Judges," and it is deleted there. When the defendant can be heard in several places, it is then placed in the hands of the plaintiff [to determine] where he wants to meet him. But a clergyman in a secular court, see in the following chapter. (If a clergyman has cited someone to appear in a secular jurisdiction, he can be cited by his adversary to appear in the [jurisdiction], and he shall be judged there, but not regarding criminal [charges]. Where a trial has once begun, it is required that the termination should also be had there.)[290]

Chapter 15. The Ordinary Judge Cannot Change The Usual Place

The ordinary judge ought to render justice in the place of the majority and ought to offer sentence in the same place unless another place is decided upon by agreement of the parties.

Chapter 16. Of Petition[291]

The plaintiff is not compelled to express the action in a written charge [petition], but it is sufficient to narrate the fact itself, and the truth of the case purely and simply so that the law of acting may be gathered from this. Whenever the judge agrees concerning the ineptitude of the petition, he ought to absolve the defendant, but still in such a Fol. 189v way that if ★ the plaintiff has presented a suitable and appropriate petition, the defendant would, nevertheless, be required to respond.

Chapter 17. When A Judgement Is Dissolved

A judgement is dissolved when the man who had ordered the judgement forbids it, or also when the man who has the greater power in the same jurisdiction forbids it, or also if the judge himself begins to be

---

[290]This entire chapter is in Cranmer's hand. The title and the first three sentences are found at the top of folio 189r. Cranmer's reference at the end of the third sentence is found on folio 190r and is bracketed there with Cranmer's own marginal note concerning the materials final location. The bracketed material on folio 190r is set off with parentheses above. The Cardwell edition contains here material that is not in the manuscript. See page 196, the section titled, "De foro judiciali."

[291]Cranmer wrote in a title that can't be translated now because he then lined out the title and thus obliterated some of the words. He then put in a new title that is above.

of the same power as the one who ordered the judgement. If one of the litigants who has a procurator dies after the case has been contested, the judgement is not dissolved. For the judge could proceed up to the sentence inclusively against the procurator, as against the principal of the suit: but execution will be made against the executor or the administrator of the goods of the deceased, and not against the procurator.[292] ★

On possessory Judgement   Fol. 190r

Let possessory be discussed before petitory in judgements. If there is a question concerning force and possession, we decree that determination concerning force takes precedence over possession of the property.[293]

Chapter 18. Of Incidental Cases

As often as another incidental or emerging case occurs simultaneously with a case and suit pending before a judge, nothing prevents a case of this kind from being determined before the same judge although he cannot examine the same cases principally in addition. ★ The Fol. 190v judgement is valid on an emerging case, even on one on which the judge does not pronounce but has proceeded beyond it.

A Judge Who Gives Offense By An Evil Fraud
Shall Pay The Damages Suffered By The Parties

Not everything is permitted to the power of a judge who is subjected to the requirements of the law. If a judge contrary to the precepts of the law in judging by an evil fraud neglected the law, he has given offense and shall pay the damages of the parties which perchance may result from that.[294]

Chapter 19. All Cases Should Be Terminated Within A Year

Since some suits are prolonged more than is just, through superfluous allegations and delays, so we want spiritual as well as ecclesiastical cases *all ecclesiastical cases*[295] to be terminated within a year after the

---

[292]At this point in the manuscript one comes to the section that Cranmer ordered to be moved to what here is chapter 14.

[293]This lined out part of the manuscript follows the bracketed material that was moved. It could well be that it was Cranmer's hand that cancelled this chapter but it is difficult to determine.

[294]Although Cardwell states that this was crossed out by Cranmer, it is hard to tell if this is so.

[295]This change is in Cranmer's hand.

suit was attested; otherwise, diligence will perish. If a negligent judge has not finished a case within a year by his own fault, he will be punished by a fine of twenty pounds payable to our treasury beyond

Fol. 191r ★ the interest of the parties: and nevertheless, unless the parties are in agreement among themselves, they should undertake to prosecute the suit by the form of process begun. If the case is not terminated within the appointed time, because of the negligence of one of the litigants, then the judge will fine the negligent party to restore the expenses and losses to his adversary, and to pay a ten-pound fine to our treasury, and unless the parties have reached agreement among themselves, they will prosecute the suit by the form of process begun.

Chapter 20. On The Duty Of The Judge

In order that all suspicion may be removed, the judge in a case (whose term in office has elapsed) *in an urgent case* is not permitted to receive

Fol. 191v witnesses and documents outside of his office.[296] ★

Judges, especially, must probe the quality of the matter by a full inquiry, and then must interrogate both parties rather often whether they wish anything new to be added: and then, from both allegations of fact and considerations of law, they should put forth their definitive sentence in writing. Concerning any matter which the judge has examined, he must also be compelled by a higher authority to pronounce on it.[297]

After the conclusion in the case, the judge cannot do anything

Fol. 192r outside of his office except ★ on matters previously treated prior if they were obscure.

Chapter 21. The Penalty For A Judge Who Knowingly
Renders An Unjust Sentence

~~A judge is understood to neglect a party's interest when with evil fraud he has pronounced a sentence at law. He seems to have committed evil fraud~~ The judge is held to pay damages for the party if his sentence is evidently accused of being produced with favoritism or hostility or

---

[296]The phrase bracketed by parentheses is not lined out in the manuscript but underlined and above it Cranmer has written the words translated, "in an urgent case."

[297]Right after this sentence in the manuscript, a chapter title and its contents have been struck out. That material is as follows: Title — "The Loser Pays Court Costs To The Winner — The judge shall condemn the loser to [pay] expenses to the winner, unless for just cause he may grant relief to him who lost. The judge after the sentence has the duty of assessing the expenses of the case after an investigation, and then of taking from the winning party an oath concerning their truth." Basically this material had appeared earlier on folio 187v and perhaps that explains the deletion here.

even avarice: then we wish him to be compelled to make good the true value of the lawsuit.[298]

Chapter 22. One Who Is Absent Contumaciously Must Not Be Heard If He Appeals

One should know peremptorily that an absent condemned man must not be heard if he appealed when he was absent only ~~for~~ through contumacy; otherwise he shall be heard.[299]

Chapter 23. Those Who Are Not Yet Adults

It is a matter of established law that a man who has arrived at adulthood, and has been freed from his guardians, begins to be under his own jurisdiction, and can undertake a lawsuit by himself, ★ or Fol. 192v through a procurator. But before this time, he will not be able to bring a case, or defend it on his own, but his suits, when they occur, will be conducted through his guardians.[300]

★CONCERNING CREDIBILITY OF DOCUMENTS[301] Fol. 194r

Chapter 1 Credibility of Documents

In pursuing suits the credibility of the documents and the testimony of witnesses should have the same force.

Chapter 2. ~~Division of Documents~~ Public Documents

Some documents are public, others private. Those are public which are made with the ~~subscription~~ subscription of witnesses by a notary appointed by our authority; but those of ourselves, or of any archbishop, bishop, archdeacon or his commissary or official, or any other person

---

[298]Although Cardwell stated that this was lined out by Cranmer and the stroke of the line is similar to other places where it is clear Cranmer lined out something, still it is difficult to determine who did it. Further, the paragraph is really not as clear as it could be and probably would have been edited further later.

[299]This is added in Cranmer's hand.

[300]In the margin of this folio, 192v, Foxe has written: "Concerning the office and jurisdiction of judges, see fol. 232."

[301]It needs to be noted that folio 193 is not found in the microfilm copy. Further, there are no numbers used to designate chapters in this section of the manuscript; they have been put in according to the divisions as designated by Cranmer's hand.

appointed by our authority; but those of ourselves, or of any archbishop, bishop, archdeacon or his commissary or official, or any other person holding public office are fortified by the affixing of a seal, and are rightly called authentic.[302]

Chapter 3.   Private Documents

We call writings private which are made by private persons and are not reinforced by any public or authentic *seal;*[303] we do not wish to give
Fol. 194v them credence unless ★ they are brought forth from a public archive, as completing the case in themselves, or have been otherwise proven.

Chapter 4.   Private Writings Are Not Valid Unless
Strengthened By The Subscription Of Three
Witnesses

Private writings in which something is agreed upon among some persons are valid in court, and have strength only if confirmed by the subscription of three witnesses, lest harm be done to both parties by the ambiguity of handwriting and the comparison of letters, and also lest an opportunity be given of denying perfidiously what has been transacted.

Chapter 5.   Books of Merchants

For example, it is pernicious to give credence to that writing by which each one by his own annotation has constituted someone a debtor to himself. Hence, no one must be allowed to furnish proof of debt from his own private records. Still, we wish full faith to be given to the
Fol. 195r books and accounts ★ of merchants, and others exercising some established trade, when these are supported by other corroborative evidence.

Chapter 6.   Means Of Completing Documents

In completing a document we wish this order to be observed, that the writer begin especially from the name of God, that he add the year of the Lord, the name of the king, ~~and the name of his reign~~ the title and year of the reign,[304] then the month and day and the name of the place where the contract is made. Then the matters to be expressed should be related, witnesses should be written down, or they should sign.

---

[302]The change in the title is in the scribe's hand as is the striking of the redundant "subscription."

[303]This is an insertion made by Cranmer.

[304]This change is in Cranmer's hand.

Also, the attestation of the notary should be added with the subscription and proper signature at the end. *But writing strengthened by someone else's signature receives no less faith than if it had been signed by the person himself, if this very fact and case is expressed in the same writing.*[305]

Chapter 7.   Preparation Of Writings

Writings prepared by legitimate means should make partial proof.

Chapter 8.   The Documents Themselves Must Be Shown In
                        Court

If one intends to prove his case by public document, ★ he should show it in court. Copies of course will accomplish nothing unless they have been written by authority of the appropriate judge. Once a document has been produced in court, seen and read, a true copy of it should suffice when compared faithfully with the original by the authority of the judge, and inserted in the acts of the court.   Fol. 195v

Chapter 9.   When Documents Must Be Shown

Everyone should have the opportunity of showing documents up to the *conclusion*[306] of a case, or in cases in which there is no conclusion up to the second assignment of a time-limit, for the purpose of hearing the sentence. And, not afterwards unless for a just reason it has seemed best otherwise to the judge who has examined the case. ★

Chapter 10.   Contrary Writings   Fol. 196r

Let him who has produced mutually contradictory writings in court, writings which mutually lessen credence in him, blame himself, since that was in his power which he preferred not to produce.

Chapter 11.   Public Documents Are Valid Even If The
                          Witnesses Are Dead

No reason permits that public writings lose effect because of the death of the witnesses whose testimony is recorded in these same writings.

Chapter 12.   Burned Or Lost Documents

As it is unjust for debtors to refuse payment when documents have been consumed by the force of fire, so one need not immediately believe

---

[305]This last sentence is squeezed in between the end of the chapter and the beginning of the next chapter by Cranmer.

[306]This was inserted by Cranmer but apparently to correct a scribal error.

easily those complaining about the accident. Therefore, you ought to understand that if documents do not survive, you ~~ought to~~ [307] prove with other arguments that credibility is present in the claims. Among those who are ignorant of the event, the witness from lost documents Fol. 196v cannot help at all★ to prove the truth.

Chapter 13. Suspect Document

If a document is erased in an unsuspicious place, it is not considered defective because of this, nor is it void from the breaking of the seal. If a document should have an erasure or a ~~letter~~ blot[308] in a suspicious place, or some other notable flaw, it is indeed corrupt and is disproved, but not *in toto,* only in that chapter where the flaw was detected. But one can give credence to the other chapters in it: we have decreed otherwise, however, when a false document is bound in some part of it, since then the whole is rendered suspect and can be rejected as false. If the engraving of the seal is not in agreement with the dignity Fol. 197r or office of the man who is said to have imposed it, the document ★ is rendered suspect.

~~A Written Document Sealed With A Different Seal~~

~~A written document provided with a different [i.e., non-standard] seal does not have less credibility than if it had been signed with the correct seal if this very fact and the reason for it are expressed in the document.~~[309]

When you see paper much older than the writing or dissimilarity in the wax, you should not undeservedly consider the document suspect. The credibility of a document in which one letter or syllable is put in place of another or is lacking, if the sense remains clear, does not become weak on this account. We do not wish to invalidate a document because of false Latin resulting from the placement of one letter, or Fol. 197v syllable in place of another, or from transposition of letters ★ or similar problems.

Chapter 14. Disproof Of A Document

If anyone wishes to prove some document false, first he shall bind himself by oath that he testifies that he will say nothing for the sake of calumny; otherwise he shall not be heard.

---

[307]This sentence had an insertion by Cranmer which was crossed out and is not unreadable.

[308]This change is in Cranmer's hand.

[309]After the first line on this folio (197r) which completes the last sentence of the preceding page, the above chapter was written and crossed out by someone.

To disprove some document, four or five witnesses at least are required who are of proved credibility, and seem altogether suitable to the judge.

~~Since even when documents are not involved, a sale remains settled; consequently, it is right for the substance of truth not to be invalidated even if [the documents] which had been involved have been lost,~~ ★ ~~that your standing is not diminished because you have lost~~   Fol. 198r the property to which you were born; if you can prove the same thing in another way, it is a certain point of law. If your adversary has declared in the acts of the presiding [judge], when the credibility of the document that he has brought forward is called in doubt, that he has not committed usury, you need not fear that the matter will be gone over once again on the basis of that document which even by his own declaration is acknowledged not to be genuine.[310]

Chapter 15. Keeping Documents

If there is a question of depositing the original of a will or other common documents, and there is a doubt in whose care it ought to be deposited, we will always prefer the older to the younger, the one of higher rank to the lower, and the male to the female. ★

Chapter 16. A Document Made By Different Scribes   Fol. 198v

A document begun by one scribe and not yet completed, either because of sudden death perhaps or some enduring impediment, can be completed by some other scribe with the permission of the ordinary and at the request of those whom it concerns, so that it may have lasting credibility.

Chapter 17. Transcription Of An Old Document

If a document is sought to be transcribed because of age or another just reason, it should be brought before the appropriate judge; if after diligent inspection he finds that it is not false in any part, he should order that it be transcribed by an official person, and this copy will have the same authority as the original.

---

[310]This section begins at the bottom of folio 197v and carries over to the top of 198r. According to Cardwell, Cranmer was the one who crossed it out, but there is no independence evidence of this.

Chapter 18. Proof Of Antiquity

We have decided to give full faith concerning ancient events and matters, which surpass the memory of man to old books and other Fol. 199r private writings of this kind kept faithfully ★ in public archives or elsewhere.

Chapter 19. The Credibility Of Authentic Writings Is Decreased[311]

We wish the usual credence to be shown to authentic seals and the documents to which these are appended or affixed until they are disproved by contrary proofs; and deservedly, the credibility of a particular document will be weakened if even one witness recorded in it has contradicted it.

Chapter 20. The Opponent Must Not Be Compelled To Bring Forward Something Which Counts Against Himself

A plaintiff must deliberate before action as to what proofs he wishes to use, and can prepare traps so that his opponent is compelled to bring forward something which counts against himself. We do not wish to detract from the regular disposition of the civil laws through this law, as regards the publication of invalidating matters.

Chapter 21. Accounts Of The Deceased[312]

Accounts of the deceased, which are found in his goods, cannot alone suffice for proof of the amount of money owed to him, not even if the deceased in his last will, signified that a fixed quantity of money or even certain things are owed to him.[313]

---

[311]This chapter and chapters 20 and 21 have been added by Cranmer and three chapters are in his handwriting.

[312]At the end of chapter 20, Cranmer wrote a new chapter title and a first line which he cancelled. Both cancelled lines are virtually impossible to decipher.

[313]Folio 199v is a blank page except for Foxe's notation at the top of the page which reads: "Concerning the crime of forgery, see fol. 112." It needs to be noted here that folios 200 and 201 are not found in the microfilm copy.

★CONCERNING EXCEPTIONS

Chapter 1.   What Is An Exception[314]

An exception is a defense by which a defendant tries in court to ward off the plaintiff from himself, and to exclude him from the action or from its effect.

Chapter 2.   Peremptory And Delaying Exceptions

If peremptory exceptions are proved, they completely remove legal action or suits that have been begun, but delaying exceptions only defer them. And some of the delaying exceptions are called declinatory, and are taken from observation of the courts, from reason of persons, place and time and rescript and they attempt to turn aside the judgments.

Chapter 3.   Real And Personal Exceptions

Real exceptions adhere so much to the matters about which the case is concerned that they apply to all those to whom the relevant matters are extended. For ★ an exception which is agreeable to the defendant, also is agreeable to the one who gives surety. But personal exceptions are so clearly unique to some one person that they do not carry over to others.

Chapter 4.   Peremptory Exceptions Can Always Be Objected
        To

Peremptory exceptions are perpetual, for they always oppose the plaintiffs, and there can be no exception to them by which they could not be raised against the plaintiff in every part of the judgment.

Chapter 5.   [Temporary Exceptions]

Delaying and declinatory exceptions are temporary. For they usually are caused for those who use them, because the time (either the time specified for payment or the time within which the laws prohibit action) has not yet elapsed, or because the appropriate condition no longer exists, or the judge is not competent, or some other reason of this kind. Exceptions of this kind do not forbid a plaintiff forever from acting, but it can easily ★ happen because of the change of

---

[314]Again the manuscript does not use any numbering system for the various parts that follow but Vermigli did write in the titles for the various parts. Numbers have been put in for the convenience of the reader.

circumstances and times that they may not have another opportunity. These exceptions are also temporary for this reason, since if anyone does not use them at the time prescribed by law, they will not be able to do so later.

Chapter 6. [When Declinatory Exceptions Should Be Opposed And When Approved]

But we wish all declinatory exceptions (since they impede the process of judgement but do not annihilate the case) to be proposed before the contesting of the case, or before the first act of the case if the case is not contested. If anyone has failed to raise them before the case has been contested, or before the first act, he may not use them afterwards, since by avoiding them he seems to have given consent Fol. 203v to the acts. When this kind of exceptions are raised, ★ we want them to be proved by the defendant before contestation of the suit, or the first act of the case has been reached.

Chapter 7. [When Delaying Exceptions Should Be Proposed And Proved]

But when delaying exceptions (by which the process of the judgment is not impeded, but rather the intention of the plaintiff) pertain to the business, and material under consideration, and these are proposed, prior to the contesting of the suit, no defendant is compelled to prove them before the plaintiff himself has begun to prove his charge. Yet, even if they should be proposed after the contesting of the suit, they must not be rejected by the court.

Chapter 8. [Declinatory Exceptions Against The Judge Must Be Proposed Before All Other Matters]

A declinatory exception which is against the judge not only ought to be proposed before contesting the suit but, before all other exceptions, Fol. 204r whether delaying or declinatory.★ For, if a defendant should begin to respond on other exceptions in court, it will seem that he approve the judge as his.

Chapter 9. [A Time-limit Must Be Proposed To The Judge Before The Contesting Of The Suit In Order To Propose All Delaying Exceptions]

In order that cases be not maliciously drawn out by delaying exceptions, we command the judge to prescribe some fixed final date before the contesting of the suit by which, if the defendant should not bring

forward all the delaying exceptions, after that he would not be heard
concerning them, unless perhaps some one should arise spontaneously
during the judicial process, or if it was prior, it was not known to the
defendant, or if it was known, then he did not have a means by which
he might prove it, a means which afterward occurred to him. Therefore,
before it is heard, he should impose an oath against malice. ★

Chapter 10. [The Time Of Proposing Peremptory Exceptions]   Fol. 204v

Peremptory exceptions which impede the trial and destroy the case,
like the exception of a case judged, settlement, or case closed, can be
opposed both before and after the contesting of the suit. But, exceptions
which only destroy the case and business, as is the exception of
agreement not to sue, and similar matters, are rightly raised after the
suit has been contested.

Chapter 11. [What Exceptions Can Be Objected To Through
             The Whole Case]

Exceptions of excommunication and false procurator can be raised
through the whole case.

Chapter 12. [The Exception Of Excommunication Must Be
             Proved Within Eight Days]

But in order that suits not be protracted more than is proper, we order
that the man who charges excommunication should specify its details
and the name of the excommunicator. He should know that this matter
ought to be brought to public notice, which he can prove with readily
available documents, within a space ★ of eight days (not counting the   Fol. 205r
day on which it was proposed.) But if he does not prove it, the judge
should not fail to proceed in the case, condemning the defendant to
pay the expenses which the plaintiff has shown by previous estimate
that he had during those days because of this.

Chapter 13. [Mixed Exceptions]

If mixed exceptions (as they are called in that they are partly delaying
and partly peremptory) are proposed after the contesting of the suit,
they will not have the power of delays but will only be considered
peremptory.

Chapter 14. [A Delaying Exception Impeding The Process Of
A Trial If Omitted In The First Instance, Cannot
Be Raised In An Appeal]

A delaying exception which impedes the process of trial cannot be
raised in an appeal if it was not brought up in the principal case. ★

Fol. 205v Chapter 15. [If Peremptory Exceptions Are Omitted In The
First Instance, They Can Be Objected To In An
Appeal]

If peremptory exceptions were omitted in the present, and indeed not
from malice nor to annoy the opponent, they will be able to be produced
in an appeal; but one may not raise those declinatory or delaying
exceptions which destroy the process of judgment, but only those
which deal with the business itself and the totality of the matter,
provided they have not been previously omitted out of malice.

Chapter 16. [What Is A Reply And When It Must Be Proven]

To the exceptions of the defendants, plaintiffs usually offer replies
which are nothing other than allegations of acts through which the
exception is resolved; and the plaintiff ought not to be compelled to
prove his own reply, unless the defendant has previously proved the
exception.

Chapter 17. [Whether A Judge Ought To Rule On Replies]

Fol. 206r It is not necessary that a judge rule on ★ replies, because their validity
can be well enough understood when the judge has decided on the
exceptions themselves, whether they should be admitted or rejected.

Chapter 18. [How Much A Reply Of Equivalent Crime Is
Worth]

A reply alleging equivalent crime injures the one who makes that
exception. For an exception, alleging some crime ought not be raised
by the person who is proved to be burdened by the same thing.

Chapter 19. [Neither The One Receiving Replies Nor The
Replier Confesses All Things Which He Says By
Receiving Or Replying]

The person taking exception is not to be thought to confess all things
which are included in his exception, just as the advocate, too, will not
be judged to confess all things which are contained in his reply.

Chapter 20. [On An Exception Against Witnesses, What Kind
Of Thing Is It And How Long It Is Valid]

Since an exception against witnesses is not delaying, it is indirectly
and obliquely peremptory. For it ★ looks to removing proof, and if Fol. 206v
this is removed, the authority of the plaintiff is destroyed. But the
proof is twofold. Exception is made either against the persons of
witnesses, as when they are called criminals or unsuitable for some
other reason, or against the statements of the witnesses, as when they
are accused of fraud. Therefore, an exception against the persons of
the witnesses can be raised and proved up to the sentencing. But,
afterward it will not be heard, unless there is an appeal. For there it
can be raised. But if it is learned that the witnesses spoke falsely, the
exception is allowable up to twenty years; yet not in an appeal, which
we nevertheless want to be accepted when it was not proposed in the
trial, for if it is raised then ★ and not proved, it will not retain its Fol. 207r
force for twenty years, but will be able to be sought again only in
appeal.

Chapter 21. [Exception Against Witnesses And Reply Of
Witnesses]

If a witness, against whom an exception is made, concerning a crime
replies against the objector concerning the same crime, he will not be
admitted to testimony for this reason, because the defendant is not
purged by relation of the crime, but if only he shows himself innocent.[315]

---

[315]Beginning with chapter five of this section, the brackets indicate that the
chapter titles are in the hand of Vermigli. At the bottom of this page, Foxe has written,
"Concerning the sentence and the matter adjudged, see folio 246. Folio 207v is not in
the microfilm copy of the manuscript.

Fol. 208r

★CONCERNING PRESCRIPTIONS

Chapter 1.   What Is A Prescription[316]

A prescription is a certain right agreeable for the time, having force by the authority of laws, imposing penalty on the negligent and imposing an end to suits, a law which does not derive entirely from natural law and does not conform to it in all respects. For as it is just by nature that no one ought to become rich at the expense of another, so it is congruent with natural reason both that a penalty be imposed on the negligent and that a limit be imposed on suits.

Chapter 2.   Prescription Of Tithes In Another's Parish

If one church has possessed tithes in another's parish for forty years, Fol. 208v we wish ★ the condition of the possessor be made better in law, because a forty-year prescription excludes all action completely.

Chapter 3.   A Possessor In Bad Faith Cannot Prescribe

No ancient possession of days helps any possessor in bad faith (unless he repent after he learned that he was possessing others' property)[317] when he could not be called a possessor in good faith. For what cannot be observed without mortal sin must detract from any law of custom. Therefore, it is necessary that the man who is claiming prescription at no moment of time be aware of the possession of another, and that he be constituted in good faith, without which no ecclesiastical prescription is valid. ★

Fol. 209r ### Chapter 4.   Interruption Removes Prescription

The prescription will not hold if the question of interruption of prescription was raised with witnesses or proofs presented, which ought to be received by both parties, and if the interruption was proved.

---

[316]There are no numbers used in this segment to designate chapters and they have been put in by the editor. The scribe has written the chapter titles and the entire chapter is in that person's hand except for some marginal comments by Vermigli and for a significant part of chapter seven which is written entirely in Vermigli's hand.

[317]The passage bracketed by parentheses is underlined, perhaps by Vermigli. In the margin in Vermigli's handwriting is the notation: "Those matters have nothing to do with the law." This notation is almost directly opposite the underlined passage.

Chapter 5. No One Can Prescribe Against Visitors

Because according to the Apostle, the man who sows spiritual things is not great if he reaps carnal things, since no one is compelled to fight at this own expense, ~~it is decreed~~ we have decreed[318] that one who is in subordinate status cannot establish for himself a right of prescription against his superior, visitation, or a procuration owed by reason of visitation.[319] Therefore, those alleging that they do not remember that they rendered the procuration or that it was sought, we think ★ ought not to be heard; but we have decided that those Fol. 209v who deny the above must be punished with a fitting punishment, and likewise must be subjected to make fitting satisfaction, despite any prescription of time.

Chapter 6. Prescription Of Churches Or Titles In Another's
            Diocese

A bishop who claims that he has lawfully gained prescriptive right to churches and titles in another's diocese, must allege the documentary proof of this type of prescription and prove it, since common law goes against him. ~~Although~~[320] good faith should be sufficient ★ for one who Fol. 210r claims his prescriptive right in ecclesiastical matters, if common law is not against him, or if there is not a presumption against him, or there is a presumption against him, good faith does not suffice but documentary proof is necessary which attributes to the possessor the cause of prescription, unless the prescription is alleged to be of such long standing that no memory exists to the contrary.

Chapter 7. Prescription Can Either Be Interrupted Or Cease
            Or Be Impeded

Prescription sometimes ceases, sometimes is interrupted; but cessation must not be considered to be the same thing as interruption. A prescription is said to cease when the prescription is not maintained because of some privilege of a person whose affairs are involved or because of a condition of the affairs themselves. ★ An impediment Fol. 210v can seem similar to this cessation when a prescription, as it were, is interrupted as when one is not permitted to initiate a lawsuit and demand one's legal rights because of some public interruption, or as

[318]This is in Cranmer's hand.

[319]In the margin Vermigli wrote the notation: "I think that nearly the same thing is found in [the section] on visitations."

[320]This is Cranmer's addition to the text.

in time of war, *or when justice is not rendered in a situation because of lack of a judge, or of the defendant and in time of pestilence.* [321]

In *these and similar cases*[322] a prescription is not absolutely dead but is at rest, impeded by a certain power, *and especially when a protestation of the plaintiff intercedes.*[323] But naturally, the prescription is said to be interrupted when what has begun is withdrawn and cannot go forward. But this happens when possession is snatched from us, not by legitimate power, which people call compulsory, but by violent power. The reason is that without possession, prescription does not proceed. ★

Fol. 211r   However, in a natural interruption there is this rule, that the prescription is of avail for all who have rights in the case.

[Also, a prescription is interrupted when the man whose case it is, repeats it by contesting a suit in court, although he does not complete the suit; likewise, by a flood of the sea or of a river, by payment of a pension or of part of something that is owed, by a second security bond made by a debtor. A prescription is also impeded from running when the man whose business it is cannot claim it, as is the case with minors who are still under the authority of another, and the mad, among whom you would also number the excommunicated; for while they are in such states, they are not heard when they claim their prescriptions. No one can with good faith renounce a conjoined prescription by his own agreement, since prescription was devised for the sake of the public good in order that ownership of property of course should not be uncertain, and a public right may not be given up by an agreement among private parties. Possession is not required in order to establish a prescriptive right in incorporeal matters, such as predial servitude, jurisdiction and similar matters—possession is not required by the knowledge and forbearance of the adversary. Prescription also is interrupted from running on by protestation before a judge, or if none is available, before a notary and witnesses. Princes employ this kind of protestation among themselves in order to impede prescription, since they cannot convene themselves under a judge who is common to each party.

One is said to possess quietly when one is not called into judgement, but sincerely when one is called with good faith. But good faith is presumed in cases of doubt even when knowledge of another's property is not had. But bad faith is proved in various ways: first, through

---

[321]This was written in Vermigli's hand and is found in the margin with a cross and a corresponding cross in the text to indicate where the marginal note is to be inserted.

[322]The manuscript originally used singular but it is shifted to plural by Vermigli's hand.

[323]This phrase is inserted in Vermigli's hand.

confession by the possessor himself; second, through common report which was in the neighborhood; third, through denunciation made at the time of the contract; finally, through incidental conjectures and if it was acquired contrary to the law and was not observed with the solemnity of the law. A prescription against the goods of the church or pious legacies does not run less than forty days, but after this time has elapsed, the church can be restored in full, provided restitution was sought within four years. After this time, it will not be heard. Bad faith impeded prescription before its time has expired. But when the prescription has been completed, and if it was finished in good faith, and if afterwards the thing prescribed is known to have been another's property, the one who established prescriptive right is not compelled to restore it. For when he knew that it had been another's, that it was now not another's, but his, he began to possess it as his own; for laws and right have decreed this. ★ The man who possesses ⠀⠀Fol. 211v in another's name does not gain prescriptive right. A space of three years of usucaption, taking by use, is assigned, but a period of prescription, up to ten years with regard to persons who are present, up to twenty years if absent, thirty years is longer, and forty years indeed is the longest. Thus usucaption pertains to personal property and prescription to real, immovable, property.][324]

★CONCERNING APPEALS ⠀⠀⠀Fol. 213r

Chapter 1. ⠀[What Is An Appeal][325]

An appeal, to begin with a definition, is a claim from a lesser to a greater, and through this, when legitimately interposed and pronounced, both the jurisdiction of the judge is suspended for the case and his investigation and examination is transferred to a higher [court]. There is a distinction, however, between judicial and extrajudicial.

Chapter 2. ⠀[Judicial Appeal]

An appeal is judicial when a claim is made in a judgement to a higher judge from a definitive sentence, from an interlocutory sentence, or

---

[324]In the middle of folio 211v, and after this section by Vermigli is completed, Foxe has written: "Concerning violent striking of clergyman, see folio 116." It must be noted that all the material above within the brackets is in Vermigli's hand. Folio 212 is blank.

[325]Chapter numbers have been put in for the reader's convenience. Chapter headings were inserted throughout this section by Vermigli

from grievances which are inflicted in pleading a case and when they are inflicted on parties: and when there is an appeal from a definitive sentence, it is sufficient to say, I appeal from this unjust sentence; Fol. 213v but where there is a claim from an interlocutory sentence ★ or some grievance, a cause must be assigned which is entirely true, just and explicit. And, if we wish to speak properly, there is no appeal unless in court, but what happens outside court can be called a claim.

Chapter 3.   [Extrajudicial Appeal]

An extrajudicial appeal is a claim from a present or likely future grievance to a higher court before it comes to judgement; in this case, a probable and likely reason ought to be assigned, and if this is given, it transfers the case to a higher judge. While an appeal of this kind is pending, nothing can be attempted to the disadvantage of the appellant by the judge from when the appeal has been made. ★

Fol. 214r   Chapter 4.   [Appeal Is Permitted Even In Extrajudicial Acts]

In extrajudicial acts appeal is permitted, as from elections, requests, provision and other matters of this kind. But it is necessary to interpose an appeal within ten days from the notification by which one has understood that he was aggrieved. For after a lapse of ten days, there will be no hearing by way of appeal; but through other remedies of the law one can make petition for full restitution and for redress of grievance.

Chapter 5.   [The Force Of Extrajudicial Appeal]

An extrajudicial appeal if imposed because of probable and likely causes so turns the case of a higher court, there is no valid act or motion against it. If anyone appeals from this, in order not be troubled regarding a possession when he suspects that he is probably going Fol. 214v to be troubled, if the [possession] is taken from him, ★ restitution is made above all things to the estate as it was at the time the appeal was issued.

In an extrajudicial appeal, if the one appealing and his adversary have different judges, the one appealing may make a claim to the one who corresponds to himself in rank, and his appeal will be valid.

Chapter 6.   [One May Not Appeal In Court From A Future Grievance]

One cannot appeal in court from a future grievance even conditionally, as if you would appeal in order not to be wronged; but one must await the wrong and appeal afterwards. For appealing from a future wrong can be allowed only out of court.

Chapter 7.   [If A Written Appeal Is Directed To The Judge,
             That Suffices. It Is Not Necessary That It Be
             Read In His Presence]

An appeal directed in writing to a judge cannot legitimately be ★ Fol. 215r
impugned because it was not read before him.

Chapter 8.   [What Must Be Done If A Just Fear Prevents An
             Appeal]

If a just fear, either of the judge or of an adversary or of municipal law which might prohibit appeal from some cases perhaps prevents someone from appealing, he will be excused; and we wish it to be as if he had appealed, provided this is attested before the judge by whom he was wronged from fear, if he should dare, and if it could be accomplished, and he should have his opportunity. But, if he did not dare and did not have this opportunity, if it could be accomplished before the judge to whom he decided to appeal, he should interpose his appeal. But if he should not succeed, it is sufficient then for him, before one or more good men, with a notary and witnesses present, to attest to this fear, to appeal, ★ and to express causes for the appeal; Fol. 215v
and to obtain from him or from them the proper designate before whom he may appeal. Care must be taken, however, that an appeal of this nature to a judge should in some way be announced within ten days of the grievance or the sentence. Otherwise, if he proceeds further in the case, what he does would not be invalid. But the presence of an adversary is not necessary while the appeal is thus being made. It suffices that the announcement be made to him. But, when no just fear impedes and there is an opportunity to have a judge, an appeal ought to be always judicial before the judge rather than extrajudicial, and it ought to be presented in writing unless the appeal from a definite sentence is made in person [viva voce] as they say.

Chapter 9.   [When An Appeal May Not Be Made Or Is Made
             In Vain]

One may not appeal from a correction or an executor unless moderation is ★ exceeded; and then the cause, and that indeed a true one, must Fol. 216r
be expressed. We also prohibit an appeal against accusations. Also, one may not appeal from penalty of the law: but appeal is made from sentence of the judge in which he has stated that the litigant has

become subject to the penalty of the law. In all cases in which laws prohibit appeal, the judge is not compelled to defer to this when it is imposed unless the cause is clearly expressed; and in appealing this case from a final sentence, it is necessary to express the cause, although it would not be required otherwise. Appeal should not be accepted for these matters in those cases which do not admit a delay of time. If an Fol. 216v appeal ★ is clearly frivolous, a judge does not act rightly by admitting it. One may not appeal a third time from the same article or from the same sentence. Also, one may not appeal from a judgement nor in an enormous and serious crime. Anyone appealing after ten days should not be heard by way of appeal, although he can make a complaint, and proceed with other pleas in order for restoration to be made entirely. In civil cases one does not appeal for another unless for his interest. When anyone has confessed in a judgment, his appeal is not admitted provided he has confessed on his own, not through an agent, and provided that the confession was not extorted through tortures or fear of them. And also, the following is required, namely, that he Fol. 217r has been convicted of the crime to which he confessed ★ in court. No injustice or iniquity must ever be charged against one who is supporting an appeal. And no appeal will be received when the case has been delegated from our royal majesty under condition that there would be no appeal from it.

Chapter 10. [When An Appeal Is Permitted In Ecclesiastical Cases Before The Final Sentence]

In ecclesiastical cases we prohibit appeal or complaint before the final sentence, unless from a sentence of censures or correction when moderation is exceeded, or whenever loss or burden brought by the final decision is not reparable by appeal. In these cases appeal, and even complaint before the final decision, will be permissible.

Chapter 11. [Order Of Appeal To Higher Judges]

It is permissible to appeal to the bishop from archdeacons, deans, and Fol. 217v ★ those below pontifical dignity who have ecclesiastical jurisdiction; and one may appeal from the bishop to the archbishop, and from the archbishop to our majesty. When the case has reached that level, we wish it to be determined either by a provincial council, if the case is serious, ~~otherwise by two or three~~ or by three or four[326] bishops, chosen by us for this purpose. When the matter has been determined and judged by these methods, nothing further can be known by appeal. Still we wish this observation to be made in addition that if the case

---

[326]The change is made in Cranmer's hand.

was subdelegated, there is always an appeal to the one subdelegating, and if it must be appealed again from him, the order already described should be preserved.

Chapter 12. [In A Case Common To Several Persons, The Appeal Of One Also Helps The Others] *[Manner Of Appeal Of Many Judges]*[327]

If several persons who are helped by the same law, and ★ who have Fol. 218r the same business and the same cause of defense were condemned by a single [judicial] decision, a successful appeal by one of them helps the rights and case of the others. *If there were several judges and a sentence was handed down from them or some burden inflicted, since all cannot be had simultaneously, one may appeal before the greater part of them and letters dismissory can be sought separately from them. However, the appeal itself, the referral to a specific judge, and the time-limit set, must be told to the adversary if he is not present.*

Chapter 13. [One Who Is Freed Through Appeal In One Case By His Own Judge Ought Still To Respond To Him In Other Cases]

A pending appeal is not a sufficient and suitable reason to reject the judge from whom the appeal has been made in other cases. Thus, when anyone has two distinct cases under the same judge, although he may have appealed one, he is, nevertheless, compelled to respond to the judge from whom he appealed concerning the other case.

Chapter 14. A[Prior Abandoned Appeal Should Be No Obstacle When A New Complaint Comes Before The Same Judge [Since] Appeal Can Be Made Again From That Judge]

One who has appealed and abandon the appeal and returned to the judge from whom he appealed, if he is wronged by him again, can again appeal. ★

---

[327]This title and the subsequent chapter are cancelled and in their place, Vermigli put a new chapter title and text which appear above. Part of the cancellation is on 217v and goes over to 218r. The next chapter, number 13, is on 218r.

Fol. 218v Chapter 15. [In A Common Cause Of Several Persons, An
Appeal By One Also Helps Others]

In the case of many condemned by one sentence who are helped by
common interest in a right, and have the same business and same
cause of defense, if one of them appeals, his victory will benefit the
others. And if by chance the one who has appealed, while the others
knew about it, and were silent, should abandon the appeal, another
of them will be able to carry out the appeal.[328]

Chapter 16. [Whether An Imposed Oath Might Prohibit
Appeal]

If anyone swears that he will stand by the matters judged and determined
in any case, since oaths must always be drawn up for honest cases
and cases thought out in a likely manner, if it should happen that a
sentence or a mandate of a judge exceeds the limits, both of honesty
and of justice, the one who has sworn can licitly appear since the oath
Fol. 219r should ★ not bind in these cases. But, if this should not happen, he
is bound by his own promise not to appeal.

Chapter 17. [One May Appeal Because Of A Suspected Place]

The place of trial to which the judge has issued summons ought to
be safe for the principal party and all those who come on his behalf
so that they can go to the place safely. Otherwise one may freely
appeal by an exception proposed concerning a suspected place.

Chapter 18. [It Is Permissible To Appeal As Much In Major
Cases As In Minor Ones]

The opportunity to appeal should not be denied either in major or
minor cases. For the judge ought not think that an injury is done to
him by the fact that the litigant appeals. for the size of the case does
not create the reason for the appeal, but the complaint of injustice
does. ★

Fol. 219v Chapter 19. [The Kind Of Case That Ought To Be Appealed]

When an appeal[329] occurs outside court, a case can be assigned which
is general and with respect to persons or complaint since the case
concerns most frequently the future, which cannot be known definitely.

---

[328]See chapter 12 above where a similar section had been cancelled, apparently
by Vermigli.

[329]This was inserted by Vermigli and is the correction of a scribal error.

But in a judicial appeal, when a case must be set forth, it is necessary that it be fixed and special since it almost always concerns a present or a past evil.[330] In addition, a case of appeal in court ought to be true. But, outside of court it is sufficient that a case be likely and probable, as, for example, I feared I would likely be wronged in the possession of something. Although up to now I have not been wronged, still I can appeal outside court. ★

Chapter 20. [When Appeal Is Made From A Final Sentence,   Fol. 220r
One Is Permitted To Act Otherwise Than In Other
Appeals]

Since it is not necessary to express the cause when appealing from a final sentence, because the appellant has set forth one cause in the trial, he can pursue another, and after that, still another as they come to mind. But in other appeals, since the cause ought to be expressed, it will not be possible to treat other matters beyond the cause, expressed in the prosecution.

Chapter 21. [In The Presence Of What Judge The Case Of
Appeal Must Be Put Forth And In Whose
Presence It Must Be Justified]

When the cause of appeal must be expressed, it will be put forth in the presence of a judge from whom it was appealed, unless fear prevents and if his presence can be had; but the justification will be rendered in the presence of the judge to whom appeal was made.

Chapter 22. [If Legitimate Exceptions Are Offered To The
Judge With Proofs, If They Are Rejected And
Licitly Appealed, The Appeal Is Justified]

When legitimate exceptions and their proofs have been offered to the judge, if he does not admit them, ★ one has a just cause for appeal. Fol. 220v
Indeed, for this reason the appeal is justified before the judge to whom it was referred, although the truth of the exception may not be proved. *Yet we do not wish*[331] that it be sufficient for the appellant to say that he proposed material or a legitimate and true exception, and made an

---

[330]The preceding sentence in the manuscript was combined to the following sentence via a line. There is enough space between the two sentences so that a chapter title could have been put it but was not.

[331]This change is in Vermigli's hand. At the end of chapter 22, there is a marginal note in Vermigli's hand marked by an asterisk: "Let there be inserted in this place the materials which are below this sign." This refers to a chapter at the top of folio 221v which is marked also with an asterisk. It now follows here as chapter 23.

appeal unless he demonstrates that he appeals because the exception was not admitted.

Chapter 23. [If An Appeal Is Justified, An Exception Is Not Proved Because Of It][332]

In addition, we have established that such an offering of proof should justify the appeal only as regards the development of [this] case, but should not be regarded as an exception for matters proved, to the prejudice of the opposing party.

Chapter 24. [For What Other Injuries And Sophistries Of The Judge One Is Permitted To Appeal]

In addition, if the judge should proceed to further matters, neglecting an exception or material, although he has not expressly rejected it, one can appeal from him. For these matters, if the judge should not proceed to further matters but should proceed by troubling the one Fol. 221r making the exception or proposing the material ★ which he often cites in order to hear his own deliberation, or often has assigned a final date for the same purpose, then we wish that one be able to appeal from this abuse if the judge, after being humbly requested twice, will not pronounce.

Chapter 25. [How The Process Is Justified In Divine Appeals]

And, although the process of first judges cannot be corrected if impugned when there is an appeal from an interlocutory sentence except from acts in appeal before him, nevertheless, *in an appeal*[333] from a final sentence, the judge to whom [the appeal was made] can correct his process from new acts held before him, and can pronounce a sentence contrary to the first one. Because it was not adduced or proved in the principal case, it can be charged and proved in the case of an appeal. ★

Fol. 221v ### Chapter 26. [For What Purposes Appeals Are Procured][334]

Appeals are procured not for the sake of oppressing anyone's justice, but so that imposed grievances inflicted may be repaired, and to correct injustice, and the unskillfulness of the judge, and sometimes to come

---

[332]The location of this chapter here is explained in footnote 331.

[333]This was inserted by Vermigli.

[334]It should be noted that this chapter is on fol. 221v and the material at the top of that page has been moved to an earlier page to become chapter 23 following Vermigli's instruction.

to the aid of the ignorance of the afflicted one himself. For in an appeal there is often room for boasts, I will prove what has not been proved, and I will oppose what has not been opposed. For what has been omitted in the first instance frequently has a place in the second.

Chapter 27. [In A Case Of Appeal Some Exceptions Can Be Repeated Which Did Not Have Place In The First Instance]

When a peremptory exception was not admitted in an instance, once an ★ appeal from a final sentence has been interposed in a case of Fol. 222r appeal, then it can be brought forth and proved. Likewise it is permissible, if the same peremptory exception was omitted in a prior instance, either by negligence or forgetfulness. But those exceptions which necessarily had to be opposed in a prior instance before the contesting of the suit cannot be brought forth in a case of appeal.

Chapter 28. [The Expiration Of A Time-limit And When It Is Not An Obstacle]

The expiration of a time limit for appeal or for completing an appeal, will not prejudice the appellant from being heard in a legitimate case, at least for the favor of restitution in full, and restitution will be made up to such time as was the length of the time of impediment. Because if there had not been an impediment, the appeal would have had its effect. Still, ★ we want the party to show his diligence within the time Fol. 222v of impediment, because otherwise he cannot establish that the impediment has proved the case; and it does not suffice to prove that there was an impediment unless one can show that this impediment was the cause of the failure to act. This is proved by proving one's diligence at that time.

Chapter 29. [The Limit For Appeal Is Ten Days]

We wish appeals and useful complaints of nullities to be made within ten working days from the time of notice of the sentence grievance. From this time, it is permitted by our constitutions to appeal, or make complaint before the judge from whom the appeal was made.

Chapter 30. [The Limits For Prosecuting And Completing A Case Of Appeal]

When anyone has appealed or made complaint of nullity, unless he has prosecuted the same within two months from the time of interposing appeal or ★ complaint; and unless, through summons or [a writ of] Fol. 223r prohibition from a higher court, he has informed the judge from whom he has appealed concerning a prosecution of this kind, and has brought it about that the said appeal or complaint has been completed within six months, counting from the end of the said two months, and will have been approved by the judge from whom he has appealed, subject to the cessation of any legal impediments, he will be compelled to abide by the sentence previously brought against him; and his appeal will have to be regarded as having been abandoned. Yet, we concede that the time limit given by law for prosecuting a case can be lessened not only by the judge, but also by the one appealing, but it cannot be extended.

Chapter 31. [A Final Sentence Must Not Be Entrusted To Execution Before Ten Days]

Within the days from the bringing of a sentence, during which appeal is allowed, the judged matter may not be entrusted to execution; we decree that this be observed not only civil cases but also in criminal Fol. 223v ones. ★ We also wish in criminal cases themselves, anyone else can appeal on behalf of the condemned, even if he is unwilling.

Chapter 32. [How The Time Limit May Slip By In An Extrajudicial Appeal]

In an extrajudicial appeal, because of an injury either future or already inflicted, the time limit either given by law, or set by the judge, or the appellant for prosecuting the case, will begin to run not from the day of appeal but from the day on which the aggrieved recognized that he was injured. Still, if this limit has passed, this will not prevent the aggrieved from being heard by a higher judge, not indeed by way of appeal but of complaint, since the appellant ought not to be heard any longer in an appeal as such once he has abandoned it. ★

Fol. 224r Chapter 33. [The Limit For Ending The Appeal Of A Case Cannot Be Changed By The Judge From Whom The Appeal Has Been Made]

Although the judge from whom the appeal has been made has the power to set the time limit for pursuing an appeal, still he cannot establish another limit for finishing the appeal different from that which the law allows.

Chapter 34. [The Limit Does Not Lapse If A Compromise Is
Reached]

If, once an appeal has been made, the parties agree on a compromise
limit for pursuing the appeal, we do not want it to be valid unless the
judge orders this procedure in the case, because he is aware that
danger threatens from too much delay.

Chapter 35. [Types Of Letters Of Appeal]

Letters of appeal are not all of the same type. Some are dismissory,
and these are given when[335] a judge defers to an appeal; some also
are refutatory letters and are given when appeal has not been admitted;
★ thirdly, others are called reverential, and these are given when appeal Fol. 224v
is made not because of the merit of the case but, because of the honor
of the judge to whom the appeal has been made. Finally, if sometimes
letters of appeal are given in an extrajudicial appeal, these are usually
called conventional or testimonial.

Chapter 36. [When Letters Of Appeal Are Needed And When
Not]

There is always need of letters of appeal in a judicial appeal, but not
likewise in an extrajudicial appeal.

Chapter 37. [When Letters Of Appeal Should Be Requested
And What Limit Of Requesting Them Should Be
Allowed]

When after an appeal has been made, the judge has set the day for
presenting letters of appeal, the appellant ought then to appear in
court to request them. If he should not do this, the sentence brought
against him can be entrusted to execution. And, since the length of
the limit set ★ for presenting letters of appeal is adequate, it will be Fol. 225r
sufficient for the appellant to appear at a suitable place and time to
request such letters urgently. But, if the judge has said openly that
he is unwilling to give them or if he has not given them within the
limit set, either out of malice or out of negligence, the litigants will
be able to prosecute the appeal without them. And if the judge, who
has not given them, attempts to proceed in the case, all his actions
will be invalid, and he will be punished by the judge to whom the
appeal was made with a penalty set at that judges' pleasure. But, we

[335]Perhaps Vermigli made an alteration here. The word "tum" has been replaced
with "tunc." Both words mean "then," and by a fluke of idiom, neither one gets
expressed in English.

wish the longest time for giving letters which cannot be extended to be thirty days, and if the appellant has not [requested][336] them urgently at the appropriate place and·time with this period, he will be deemed to have renounced his appeal. ★

Fol. 225v Chapter 38. [What Ought To Be Contained In The Letters]

In letters of appeal the case will be explained, and the letter will declare whether the appeal has been admitted or not. The signature of the one by whom the letters are presented must be affixed to them. And when the judge presents the letters, he will also decide the time limit for the appellant's prosecuting the appeal. But, from the presenting of the letters or the setting of the limit, the judge shall not be understood to have consented to the appeal that has been interposed. For with letters of appeal, it can easily happen that they may dwell on refutation, and a limit is set to constrain the malice of litigants, so that they may not draw out lawsuits of a superfluous sort.

Chapter 39. [It Is Not Wrong For The Appellant To Proceed To The Tribunal Of The Judge After Some Injury And He Is Not Thereby Impeded From Being Able To Appeal From This Within Ten Days]

When someone has been wronged in a judgment, although he comes to the judge who wronged him after the injury, and has carried on some business of his tribunal, the opportunity will not be taken from Fol. 226r him, because of acts ★ of this kind, to be able to appeal within ten days from the injury inflicted, especially since he did those things which he did after the injury not of his own accord, but compelled by the power of the judge.

Chapter 40. [If An Appellant Comes On Some Business With Protestation Before A Judge From Whom He Has Appealed, He Does Not Therefore Abandon His Appeal]

When anyone has appealed, although he comes to the judge from whom he made the appeal, after the interposition of the appeal, and carries on some business at his tribunal, provided that he protests that he does not therefore wish to abandon his appeal, he will not be judged to have renounced it.

---

[336]Vermigli here corrected a scribal error.

Chapter 41. [The Judge Ought To Withdraw From The Whole
Case After The Appeal Unless He Revokes An
Injury Inflicted]

Although an appeal sometimes pertains to some article of a cause,
still once it has been made, the judge from whom the appeal has been
made shall withdraw from the whole case itself. For, no one ought to
be compelled to respond to that judge in that case, in which he thinks
he has been wronged ★ by him; and he is not compelled further to Fol. 226v
appear before him to respond or to prove the injury, unless perchance
he is summoned to hear the revocation of the imposed injury. If the
judge makes this revocation, whether the appellant appears or not,
he has committed himself to pay the expenses, if the appellant had
any, and he must be summoned and must undergo this. For, he can
resume the case from which appeal was made, and can proceed further.
But this takes place when he has not deferred to the appeal, for if he
perchance upheld it, he can neither revoke the injury, nor resume the
case, for his jurisdiction in regard to that case has been transferred
entirely to a higher judge. ★ Still he will be able afterwards to make Fol. 227r
examination concerning the case, if the judge to whom appeal was
made has sent it back to him. Therefore, by deferring to an appeal,
the judge completely releases that case from himself unless the appeal
is abandoned, and the time limit set within which the appellant needed
to prosecute this appeal has elapsed. In that event, indeed, the case
returns to him again.

Chapter 42. [Attempts After Appeal Are Invalid]

Things attempted against and after appeal, whether judicial or
extrajudicial, are null by the law itself. But the judge from whom
appeal was made can, while the appeal is pending, do all those things
which tend towards an easier conclusion of it.

Chapter 43. [What Innovations After The Appeal Ought To Be
Released By The Judge Of Appeal, And What
Ones Ought Not]

Innovations after appeal from a final sentence, or between the sentence
and the appeal ought to be repealed before all things ★ by the judge Fol. 227v
of appeal. But innovations after the appeal from interlocutory sentence
or injury, until it is clear that the cause of appeal is true, ought not
to be repealed unless the lower judge has proceeded after a prohibition
ordering him not to proceed in the case imposed by a higher judge.
For, whatever is done after a prohibition is pointless and invalid.

Chapter 44. [How Much A Judge From Whom Appeal Is Made
             Can Learn About The Trial Of The Appeal]

The judge from whom appeal is made can learn about the trial of
appeal in order to instruct himself as to whether he must defer, not,
however, to the prejudice of the appeal. For this pertains to the judge
to whom appeal has been made.

Chapter 45. [When The Judge Of Appeal Ought To Send A
             Case Back To The Lower Judge]

When a lower judge has not deferred to an appeal, the superior judge
Fol. 228r ought ★ to send back the case of appeal to him, once his vanity or
malice has been recognized, and ought to fine the one who is appealing
unjustly on the same day for the expenses. But, when a lower judge
has deferred[337] to the appeal, it will be in the power of the higher judge
to send back the case to him or to retain it himself; and this must be
accepted, if the prosecution happens before the higher judge. Likewise
when a higher judge recognized that an appeal from an interlocutory
sentence or injury is frivolous, he should send back the case itself.[338]
But, if he recognized that the appeal itself was interposed for true and
just reasons, he will receive the main case into his power. He should
Fol. 228v ★ not send it back any further to a lower judge.

Chapter 46. [The Judge To Whom Appeal Was Made Should
             Not Prohibit A Lower Judge Unless It Is Clear To
             Him First That The Appeal Was Legitimate]

We prohibit a judge to whom an appeal or complaint is made from
prohibiting the judge from whom the appeal was made before he has
decided whether the appeal or complaint brought to him, was legitimate.
But, if it was an appeal or complaint from a final sentence with the
judge and the tribunal sitting *viva voce* on the spot close by the acts,
in this case, it will suffice for the judge to whom appeal was made to
reach agreement about this by oath of the appellant, or of a procurator
having his mandate.

---

[337]This reflects a change in mode which does not affect the translation.

[338]The sentence that begins "Likewise. ..." is actually a new paragraph with
enough space between it and the preceding sentence that a title could have been written
in. A line connects the two sentences with the instruction in Foxe's hand to combine
them into one paragraph.

Chapter 47. [Sentences Of Excommunication And Suspension
             Must Not Be Repealed By The Judge Of Appeal
             Unless The Parties Have Been Called In]

Not only have we decided that, if transferred business is denied through
appeal, the judge of appeal shall not prohibit the judge from whom
the appeal was made from proceeding in the case, unless there is
agreement concerning the transfer. But we by no means wish judges to
revoke or declare void sentences of suspension or ★ excommunication   Fol. 229v
promulgated against an appellant by him from whom the appeal was
proposed, unless the parties are summoned and agreement is reached
concerning the appeal.[339]

Chapter 48. [How A Judge Must Be Punished Who Has Not
             Deferred To A Just Appeal]

If a judge has not legitimately deferred to an appeal, he must be
punished; and if the cause was criminal, he will be deposed. But, if it
is civil, he will be punished by a higher authority with a penalty at
the superior's discretion.

Chapter 49. [A Summons Of The Parties Is Not Necessary In
             A Case Of Appeal]

In the examination of an appeal, first of all, care must be taken that
the parties are summoned in order to justify and impugn the appeal.
But, this is not necessarily required when they have a fixed period in
order to prosecute the appeal.

   When a judge from whom the appeal has been made must be
punished by the ★ judge to whom the case was taken, he ought to   Fol 229v
be summoned. But, also if he wishes, he can sit with the higher judge,
while he reviews the case which he had judged, so that nothing
prejudicial to him may be done.

Chapter 50. [The Judge From Whom The Appeal Was Made
             Will Not Be Punished By A Higher Judge Unless
             Summoned, And He Will Sit With Him In The
             Review Of The Case If It Seems Best]

When a judge to whom an appeal was made makes a judgment against
the sentence of the lower judge, because of new reasons brought
before him which were not involved in the prior judgment, he will not
simply say that the lower judge judged badly in the sentence, but with

---

[339]All the changes in this chapter are in Vermigli's hand.

the addition [that the reversal is made] because of the lack of proofs which had not then been brought forth.

Chapter 51. [A Judge To Whom An Appeal Is Made Cannot
 Arbitrarily Reject Or Admit An Appeal]

It is not in the power of the judge to whom an appeal is made either to accept or to reject the appeal; since if it is just, he is compelled to receive it. Indeed, the duty of judging is a public one and it cannot be renounced by the one, who has the duty of judging. ★

Fol. 230v Chapter 52. [When Parties Can Abandon An Appeal]

Parties by mutual consent are able to renounce an interposed appeal, and can return the case to the judge from whom the appeal has been made. The willingness of one party does not suffice to do this, and also it cannot be done if the judge has deferred to the appeal, because then he will no longer be able to judge this same case more fully unless, either the judge to whom appeal was made sends it back to him, or the limit established for prosecuting it has elapsed.

Chapter 53. [A Suspect Appellant Either Should Give Surety
 Or Be Guarded]

If an appellant was suspect of flight, either he should give men as surety that he will pursue the appeal or he should be guarded.

Chapter 54. [The Lower Judge Is Required To Execute A
 Sentence Given By Him If It Is Confirmed By A
 Higher Judge]

If a sentence that has been given is confirmed by the judge to whom the appeal has been made, it will be entrusted to execution by the judge from whom it was appealed.

Chapter 55. [In An Appeal From A Final Sentence, Any Injury
 Caused By An Interlocutory Decree Can Be
 Revoked By A Judge Of Appeal]

When there was an appeal from a final sentence or a complaint alleging
Fol. 230v ★ nullity, any injury which has been brought about by an interlocutory sentence can be licitly remedied by a judge of appeal.

Chapter 56. [When An Appellant Abandons An Appeal, He Is
Assessed For The Expenses Of His Prosecuting
Opponent]

When anyone abandons an appeal that he has interposed, and his
opponent pursues it, the person who abandons shall be assessed for
the other party's expenses.

Chapter 57. [Whoever Does Not Defer To Appeal Of His
Opponent Should Know That No One Need Defer
To His Appeal Either]

If anyone has not deferred to an appeal interposed by his ~~ordinary~~
~~opponent,~~[340] (the opponent) cannot be compelled to defer to his appeal
if later in the same case it should be interposed.

Chapter 58. [After An Appeal, Excommunication Ought Not
To Be Imposed]

If an appeal was interposed before excommunication was imposed, it
impedes his excommunication.

Chapter 59. [Excommunication After An Appeal Had Been
Brought Is Invalid]

And as excommunication, if imposed after a judicial appeal, does not
hold, so it does not hold after an extrajudicial appeal. Therefore, one
who fears being excommunicated unjustly, appeals outside of court
and [thus] suspends the jurisdiction of the judge. But, after the injury
has been inflicted, it is necessary to appeal. ★

Chapter 60. [Of What Great Moment The Revoking Of A Case   Fol. 231r
By A Bishop Or A Superior Judge Is]

A bishop can revoke to himself cases which are being tried before his
vicar, and the recall of some case made by a superior suspends the
jurisdiction of the lower judge more than an appeal does.

Chapter 61. [After A Legitimate Appeal From Sequestration of
Property, An Appellant Freely Receives The
Income]

If there is an appeal from sequestration of property and the appeal is
legitimately prosecuted, while it is pending, the possessors of the

---

[340]Vermigli inserted "opponent" here to correct an obvious scribal error.

De duabus Christi naturis post
resurrectionem ra 4   5

Credatur item, Dominus noster Jesus Christus _
etiam post resurrectionem dupliti natura constare,
Diuina quidem immensa, incircumscripta, et infinita
que vbique sit, et omnia impleat . Humana vero _
finita et descripta humani corporis terminis ac _
finibus ., qua postquam peccata nostra ppurgauisse
in celos ascendit, ibiqz ita sedet ad dextram patris
sz non vbiqz sit, quippe quem oportet in celo rema-
nere vsqz ad temporis restitutionis omnium, tum ad _
iudicandos viuos et mortuos venict, vt reddat vniqz
iupta opera sua .

De tribus symbolis . ra 5.

Et quomam omnia ferme, que ad fidem spectant
catholicam (tum quoad beatissimam trinitatem
tum quoad mysteria nre redemptionis) tribus symbolis
hoc est, apostolico, Niceno et Athanasy breuiter _
continentur . idcirco ista tria symbola sz fidei nre
compendia quedam retinimus et amplectimur , quod
firmissimis diuinarum et canonicarum scripturarum
testimonijs facile probari possunt .

Que sint canonice scripture.
quoad vetus testamentum . ra 6

Vt autem que sint scripture ille canonice
(ex quibus solis religionis, et fidei dogmata constare

Example of a scribal hand used

sequestered goods and others in their name may freely and with impunity enjoy these same goods.[341]

★CONCERNING THE DUTY AND JURISDICTION OF ALL JUDGES

Chapter 1.   Ordinary And Delegated Jurisdiction[342]

There is this difference between ordinary and delegated jurisdiction, namely, that ordinary jurisdiction is given and conceded by law or privilege, agreement or custom, while delegated is given and conceded by man.

Chapter 2.   Jurisdiction Of The King

The king has and can exercise the fullest jurisdiction, both civil and ecclesiastical, as much over archbishops, bishops, clerics, and other ministers as over laymen within his kingdom and dominions since all jurisdiction, both ecclesiastical and secular, is derived from him as the one and the same source.

Chapter 3.   Jurisdiction Of The Archbishop, Bishops, Archdeacons And Others

Archbishops and bishops have by law, ordinary jurisdiction within their ★ own dioceses, and the chapter[343] has it when the see is vacant; but archdeacons and other prelates of churches acquire and have jurisdiction only from privilege, agreement or prescriptive custom.

We judge that ordinary jurisdiction from privilege, agreement, or prescriptive custom which was acquired prior to these our ecclesiastical laws by any prelate of a church will remain in its own strength when it is not contrary to these laws of ours.

It has been agreed that jurisdiction from privilege, agreement or prescriptive custom, exercised previously by archbishops within their

---

[341]The next page in the manuscript is fol. 231v and it is blank except for Foxe's writing at the top which states: "Concerning the rules of law, see folio 260." Folio 231v is not in the microfilm copy.

[342]Cranmer wrote in the headings for each of these sections and they are numbered here for the readers convenience.

[343]Cranmer inserted "capitulum" but the word cancelled seems to be the same word and above the insertion is another perhaps earlier insertion so heavily cancelled it cannot be read.

provinces not only stands, unless contrary to these laws of ours, but also can be exercised by them in the future. ★

Chapter 4.   The Duty Of The Judge

It is agreeable that a good and serious judge sees to it in the exercise of his office that the jurisdiction over which he presides is peaceful and quiet and devoted to piety.[344] He will obtain this without difficulty, ~~if he carefully acts so that his jurisdiction lacks evil men and he seeks them out~~ *if he carefully seeks out information on evil men,*[345] and turns his attention to each one just as he has trespassed. And, the judge can get down to inquiry by reputation or by trials.

Chapter 5.   Delegated Jurisdiction

When jurisdiction has been given to someone, these [other powers] also seem to have been granted; and jurisdiction could not be exercised without them. Thus, the delegate can summon parties and coerce the obstinate with ecclesiastical ★ severity, even if the letter of commission does not contain this.

Chapter 6.   Jurisdiction Of Bishops And Prelates

Bishops should have in their dioceses, and other prelates of the churches in their jurisdictions, free power of inquiry, punishment and judgment of adulteries and crimes which pertain to their court, without impediment from anyone. And, when there is need, they should invoke secular judgment.

Chapter 7.   The Place Of Judgment

It has been agreed that the bishop in any place of his diocese and the archdeacon and other prelates, having jurisdiction in their usual places can sit by themselves or with another as a tribunal, and can hear ecclesiastical cases, correct the excesses of delinquents ★ and freely exercise other powers which pertain to their office. However, no one should be kept from sitting before the tribunal anywhere from the consensus of the ordinary of the place.

Chapter 8.   Privilege Of The Archbishop

The archbishop can be chosen as judge by subjects of suffragans although the suffragans are not aware.

---

[344]Inserted by Cranmer .
[345]Changed by Cranmer.

Chapter 9. Punishment For The Obstinate

Ecclesiastical judges should impose ecclesiastical penalties against the obstinate and the disobedient and should coerce those who despise ecclesiastical jurisdiction with penalties of this kind.

Chapter 10. The Chancellor

The vicar of the bishop is the ordinary judge, and he does not have delegated jurisdiction. The jurisdiction of the vicar lapses upon the death of the person who appointed him. ★

Chapter 11. The Age Of A Judge   Fol. 234v

A judge should not be appointed at less than the age of twenty-five years.

Chapter 12. When One Does Not Obey A Judge With
            Impunity

One cannot obey with impunity the one who pronounces on the law outside his territory. The same is true if he tried to pronounce on the law at a level above his jurisdiction.

Chapter 13. ~~Who Can Delegate Judges~~ On Delegation Of
            Jurisdiction[346]

By the custom of our ancestors, it is ~~ascertained~~ established[347] that only he can delegate jurisdiction who possesses it by his own right and not by a grant from someone else.

 The person to whom a case is delegated cannot subdelegate it to someone else, unless the case was committed to him by our royal majesty, for then, not only can he delegate but he can even compel others to accept a case which he has delegated to them. But, even if the diligence of that person who holds a commission to the case, ★ is found to be outstanding, he cannot delegate the whole matter. Fol. 235r Nevertheless, a person delegated by our majesty cannot give to his subdelegate the power of [further] subdelegation. Also, a person delegated by our majesty cannot make a subdelegation which adds this clause: "without possibility of appeal," not even if such power was delegated to him.[348]

---

[346]Cranmer replaced the one title with the other.

[347]This is Cranmer's change.

[348]This was added by Cranmer at the top of folio 235r.

There can be no doubt that a delegation is dissolved if he who delegated the power of jurisdiction has died before the case has begun to be treated by him to whom it was delegated.

An ordinary judge can delegate his jurisdiction, and he may delegate all of it or only one type. For, even he to whom the jurisdiction has been delegated acts by the authority of the person who delegated, not by his own authority.

A royal delegate acts in ~~His Royal Majesty's~~ our[349] [the King's] stead, and therefore, in that case is superior to those whose case he has undertaken to determine. So, if any of the litigants have been rebellious or contumacious, according to the seriousness of his action, he can be punished with ecclesiastical censures by the judge. ★

Fol. 235v   A judge delegated ~~by royal majesty~~[350] has power not only over the principal parties but also over others who may interfere with his jurisdiction, and he can punish them with ecclesiastical penalties.

A delegation made to an office, without specifying the name of the person, passes to his successor, unless perchance in the commission prior mention is made of experience, learning, or sagacity, and of similar characteristics which describe the person and not the office. But, if the delegation is made by the person's name, it expires upon the death of the appointee.

Delegation of a case can be made even to those persons who are[351] of a rank inferior to the parties to the litigation. ★

Fol. 236r   If a case is committed to two persons, even if it is not stated that one may proceed in it without the other, nevertheless, one of them can transfer his power either to his fellow judge or to another person.

If a case is committed to three persons, with a clause stipulating that if not all are able to be present, two may, nevertheless, proceed with the case, before the inability of the third one becomes evident, the two are powerless to do anything in the case. But, if one of the three refuses to be present when he could be, then the two others may proceed in the case. It is permitted for charges to be brought against the third [judge], because he has evaded or contemned the orders of their superior. We also declare that the same rule shall be followed in all respects in a case which is delegated to two [judges], with this addition, that if it is impossible for both of them to be present, one of them may, nevertheless, proceed. ★

Fol. 236v   [In the case of] jurisdiction delegated without conditions to several persons, if not all can be present, let those who can be present proceed. [But] if one of them has died, [their commission] expires.

---

[349]This change is in Cranmer's hand.

[350]Lined out by someone.

[351]An addition by an unknown had to correct a scribal error.

If several judges have been delegated, it is necessary for all of them to be present at the proceedings, unless it was expressed in the commission that in case some one or several of them could not be present, the rest should proceed in the case. But in that event, the colleague or colleagues should ascertain from the rest whether they are able or willing to be present.

Although a delegate of an inferior ordinary judge cannot subdelegate from the principal judge, still it is lawful to delegate one type or a particular part of the same case. ★

There is no doubt that a judge delegated by a lower-ranking Fol. 237r ordinary, from a principal case to the whole range of cases has the power to subdelegate, since the ordinary and a person delegated to the whole range of cases are almost identical in the eyes of the law. A delegate, if he is under the jurisdiction of the delegating [authority], is required to assume the burden of the commission, under penalty of contempt.

Chapter 14. The Jurisdiction Of A Delegate Expires In Its Entirety Upon The Death Of The Appointing Authority[352]

If anyone claims that he has been delegated by a principal judge, or has been sent with secret orders, let all persons know that no matter what his rank may be, he is not to be believed unless he has proved this with written evidence. ★

If a delegate has declared that he does not have jurisdiction, he Fol. 237v may not subsequently assume it even with the consent of the parties.

After a subdelegate has begun to examine a case, he cannot be removed by the delegating authority. But the vicar of a bishop can be removed whenever the bishop wishes because he is not his delegate.

~~A delegate of Our Royal Majesty cannot give the power of subdelegating to his subdelegate.~~[353]

~~Also a delegate of Our Royal Majesty cannot subdelegate with the addition of this clause, "without [right of] appeal, even though he himself was delegated with it.~~[354]

A person subdelegated by a principal judge of lower rank ★ can Fol. 238v

---

[352]Above the word "delegate" Foxe has written the word "Title" and in the 1571 edition and that of Cardwell of 1851, this became the title for a new chapter although in the manuscript there is no indication in Cranmer's hand or that of Vermigli that this is to be a title.

[353]This sentence was lined out by someone.

[354]The first two lines are lined out with a heavy stroke and then an X is drawn through them and the next three lines in a lighter stroke. There is no suggestion in the manuscript nor in the 1571 edition for the author of this deletion.

subdelegate an article of the case on different occasions, and what they call the presentation is not jurisdictional, as are citation and the like.

A case can be delegated to someone with this mandate, that he should not proceed to its determination unless he has received the advice either of the delegating authority or of some prudent man specified by name. If this is done, it will be necessary for the subdelegate to hear advice in accord with the mandate before he passes sentence, but he is not compelled to pass sentence in accord with that [advice]. For it could happen that it was unjust and contrary to the order of the law, and in that event the sentence must be given both in accord with his conscience and in accord with the laws.

The person who has been commissioned to excommunicate or Fol. 238v absolve ★ certain persons, or to impose penance for their sins, is permitted to request that not jurisdictional power but rather a certain ministry should be committed to him. Yet he can still excommunicate those who interfere with his exercise of the ministry entrusted to him, lest such a commission should be illusory and without effect.

There is no doubt that there ought to be a right of appeal from the delegate to the delegating authority.

It is established that if any person of higher or equal rank is made subject to the jurisdiction of another, law can be pronounced both for him and against him.

~~Every defendant ought to be given a hearing before his proper judge.~~[355] ★

Fol. 239r Chapter 15. A Judge Should Hear Only Those Matters Which Are Within His Jurisdiction

First of all, when a judge is approached, he ought to inquire whether jurisdiction over those things, persons, or offenses which are involved in the suit pertains to him. When it is established that they are within his jurisdiction, let him undertake the task of judging. But, if instead he determines that it does not pertain to his jurisdiction, let him remand the case to the proper judge, release the defendant from attendance upon his own court, and condemn the plaintiff to payment of costs (if any have been incurred).

[355]This is lined out at the bottom of the page, folio 238v.

Chapter 16   The Defendant Is Allotted A Forum By The
            Power Of The Judge[356]

Defendants are allotted a place for judgement for ~~five~~ four[357] reasons:
either because of domicile, that is to say, a person is to be judged by
the judge of the place where he lives; or because of the crime committed,
for anyone is judged in the place where he committed a crime and
was arrested; or because of the location of the thing which is the
object of the suit, for if the litigation is about an ★ ecclesiastical   Fol. 239v
benefice or ~~fields or houses~~ tithes of fields or houses,[358] the judge of the
place where those things are located should be approached; or because
of the place of contract, since where anyone has for the most part
contracted is where litigation should be conducted about the contract.
~~Finally, whenever they are given their [proper] court on account of~~
their [place of] origin, there it seems proper that anyone is judged
where he comes from, which reason moved Pilate to send Christ back
to Herod, namely having heard that he was a Galilean.
    ~~Let the plaintiff follow the jurisdiction of the defendant.~~
    ~~When the accused can be given a hearing in several places, then
it is left to the preference of the plaintiff where he wants to meet
him.~~[359]

Chapter 16. On Lawful Place of Trial

Clergy who are going to begin litigation should go to their bishop or
vicar, and without his consent and will, they should not accept any
other judge. ★   Fol. 240r
    ~~When the ordinary or the king has granted his office, it is necessary
to go to the delegate.~~[360]
    Concerning crimes which are purely ecclesiastical, no one should
make an agreement with anyone except before an ecclesiastical judge.

Chapter 17. Ecclesiastical Cases

The following are cases of ecclesiastical jurisdiction: benefices,
marriages, divorces, wills, administration of the goods of deceased
persons, withdrawal of legatees, mortuary dues, tithes, offerings and

[356]This chapter is marked off by a bracket with a marginal notation in Cranmer's
hand: "Let this be placed in the section 'On Judgements.'"
[357]This change is in Cranmer's hand.
[358]This change is in Cranmer's hand.
[359]Eight and a half lines at the end of this chapter have been crossed out, perhaps
by Cranmer, but one can't be sure.
[360]These two lines found at the top of folio 240r are lined out.

cases involving other ecclesiastical rights. Also, usury and heresies, incest, adultery, fornication, sacrilege, perjury, blasphemy, attack upon Fol. 240v a clergyman, accounts of churches and stewards, ★ cases of debt to churches and their ministers, repair and dilapidation of churches, cemeteries, and other ecclesiastical buildings; and generally in those cases with their incidents, origins, consequences, and any connections whatsoever. In all other cases which involve the correction of sin, an ecclesiastical judge, and no other, shall intervene, examine, and judge.

A case involving rights of patronage and annual ecclesiastical pensions is so joined and connected to spiritual causes that it can be determined only by an ecclesiastical judge.[361] ★

Fol. 241r Chapter 18. On Rejection Of A Judge

When the ordinary judge has been rejected as suspect, it is a sound and wise practice for him without delay to delegate the case to someone on whom the parties agree as not being suspect. If, moved by some just reason, he is unwilling to do this, let him order the causes of the suspicion to be declared in his presence by the rejecting party. Arbiters, chosen either by the litigants or by the judge and the defendant, if there is no plaintiff, shall investigate and pronounce whether these [reasons] are just. And so, that the affair may not be drawn out, a time limit is to be set in advance for the arbiters, within which they shall establish, concerning the causes of suspicion, whether they seem just or unjust. If these persons do not reach agreement, one party shall select one and the other another, who shall make a decision Fol. 241v within a fixed time. ★ But if they do not agree, they shall call to themselves a third person, and what two have determined shall be the judgment. If it is determined that the causes of suspicion are not just, then the ordinary shall discharge his duty. But if they are pronounced just, the ordinary or the litigants shall transmit the case to a superior judge, or he shall give them a delegate on whom they agree as not being suspect. But when the ordinary judge is the bishop's vicar, or inferior to the bishop, then the bishop himself shall judge concerning the causes of suspicion, and it will not be necessary to use arbiters unless perchance the bishop is away from the diocese, or is busy in a very distant place, for then arbiters shall be chosen as has been said.

Chapter 19. Causes of Rejection

Fol. 242r The causes for which a judge can be rejected are numerous. ★ For

---

[361]Four lines at the bottom of this page, folio 240v have been crossed out.

example: if the rejecting party has a legal dispute with the judge as with a private party; if the judge has a lawsuit with the office held by the rejecting party; if the judge was unwilling to admit the rejecting party to the kiss of peace or to show him the courtesies which are customarily offered to those who are of equal or similar rank; if the judge threatened the party that he wanted to harm him when an opportunity presented itself; if he was unwilling to greet him as a formerly [he] used to do; if the judge frequently associates with enemies of the refusing party; if he tried to inflict death or serious injuries on him; if he has brought criminal charges against him; if the judge is the lord of the opposing party; if he is his vassal; if he is his suffragan; if he is related to him; if he was the lawyer of the opposing[362] party in the same case; if the judge has a similar lawsuit with the other person. Finally, a judge can be ★ rejected if he is an associate of one of the Fol. 242v parties, or a fellow canon, or if he lives with him, or if he was the teacher or the pupil of the party, finally[363] and if any other causes similar to those are found.

Chapter 20. One Can Appeal From A Judge Justly Rejected

If a suspect judge who was rejected, justly and according to the form of our laws, did not allow the rejection, there can be no appeal from him.

No person shall be drawn unwillingly out of his diocese because of a legal action.[364]

Chapter 21. A Bishop Shall Not Delegate A Case Outside His Diocese

An ordinary shall not delegate cases pertaining to him to a place outside the diocese, unless perchance the parties are staying there at the time.

Chapter 22. The Archbishop Shall Take Action Against Negligent Bishops

If a bishop has been negligent in administering justice, it pertains to his archbishop to compel him to administer the law. He shall set a time limit for him, and if ★ without legitimate impediment he has not Fol 243v

---

[362]This change is in Cranmer's hand.

[363]Here a redundant word is lined out.

[364]This lined out sentence might have been struck by Cranmer but there is no way to be sure.

observed it, he [the archbishop] shall not only punish him with ecclesiastical censures, but also condemn him to [pay] the fair value of the case.

A negligent judge if he is challenged looks out only for his interests and will be condemned [to pay recompense] all the fair value of the case.

If any lay judge shall refuse to render justice to clergymen or ecclesiastical persons, if he is examined about this for a third time, he shall lose his judicial power.

An ecclesiastical judge can enjoin a lay judge from proceeding in a case which depends on one of which he himself presently has cognizance.[365]

Chapter 23. On Temporary Delegation

If his commission has expired, the judge in a case shall take no further action, but the things which have already been done will not be
Fol. 243v nullified ★ but shall serve to continue the case under another judge. But if any things are done after the commission has expired, they shall be regarded as null and void.

Concerning cases which are committed to be decided within a certain time, it is ordained that unless the established date has been extended by common consent of the parties, when that date has passed, the [court's] mandate expires.

Chapter 24. The Judge May Provide Counsel For Someone
Who Does Not Have Counsel

Since a party engaged in a lawsuit cannot be compelled to respond unless he has a lawyer, it is the responsibility of the judge to provide a legal counsel for that party who cannot find one; and if it seems advisable, he can give [him] a member of his own staff. He can also compel any other lawyer he wants to defend a needy person for a suitable fee which he can [afford to] pay him; and if he cannot pay at all, [that lawyer may be compelled] to defend him at no cost. ★

Fol. 244r Chapter 25. A Judge Can Demand The Return Of A Fugitive
From The Judge Of The Place To Which He Has
Fled

When a serious offense has been committed, the judge of the place from which an accused person fled *can seek from the judge of the place*[366] [to which he fled] that he be sent back to him.

---

[365]These nine lines are crossed out in the manuscript.
[366]This insertion is in Cranmer's hand.

Chapter 26. Judges Ought To Provide Mutual Support

When a sentence has been passed by the judge of the place where the crime was committed, or where the defendant has his domicile, in case of necessity, it may be mandated for execution by a judge in whose district the guilty person's properties are situated, provided this is requested by the who passed the sentence, since a judge of one diocese cannot execute judgment in another diocese.

Chapter 27. A Judge Can Commit To Others The Right Of Absolving An Excommunicated Person

A judge who can grant absolution from excommunication is permitted to delegate this kind of absolution to others.

~~One who is in charge of a jurisdiction ought not to pronounce judgment for himself or for his wife or others whom he has in his household.~~ ★   Fol. 244v

~~Although the prince is above the laws, still his delegate ought to follow and observe the laws in his procedure, and if his commission makes some mention of plenitude of power, this sort of commission, as one granted through deceit, shall not be valid.~~[367]

Chapter 28. Punishment At Discretion

When a fixed punishment is not found in the law, the ordinary judge or his delegate can impose an arbitrary one [i.e., a punishment at his own discretion].

Chapter 29. An Appellate Judge Shall Not Approve Wills Or Grant Administration Of Properties

If a question about the validity of a will or about granting administration of the properties of a decedent is before the ordinary judge, and in that case an appeal to a superior jurisdiction has been interposed, that superior judge has the power to pronounce on an issue involving ~~judge~~ justice[368] but the ordinary, to whom the right pertains ought to approve the will, or grant the administration ★ and do other requisite and Fol. 245r necessary things in that respect, into which the appellate judge shall, in no wise, intrude without the express consent of the ordinary.

[367]The first sentence at the bottom of folio 244r in the manuscript is lined out as well as the first five lines of folio 244v.

[368]Since "justice" immediately follows "judge" in the line, it would appear that this is a scribal error. The change appears to be the hand of the scribe.

Chapter 30. On Extension Of The Jurisdiction Of A Delegated Judge

The jurisdiction of a delegated judge cannot be extended from one matter to another by a procurator, who does not have a mandate, since a procurator is understood to be empowered only for those matters which are expressly found in his letters of commission, unless the lord [King?] knows and permits this.

Chapter 31. A Person Excommunicated By One Cannot Be Absolved By Another

A person excommunicated by his [proper] judge is to be avoided by other persons, and another judge cannot absolve him, unless he is a superior who has been approached by way of appeal or of complaint.

Fol. 245v ~~If a rescript concerning some ecclesiastical case has been acquired from His Royal Majesty and subsequently another in~~ ★ ~~the same case has appeared without mention of the previous rescript, the judges ought to suspend [action] in the execution of both of them until they may know the will of the prince more fully thereafter.~~[369]

Fol. 246r ## ★CONCERNING SENTENCE AND JUDGMENT

Chapter 1. When The Judge Can Follow Charges And Proofs Against Conscience

It is useful that precepts be given by learned and wise men, lest anyone follow some idea of his own in judging, an idea which he brought with him from home into the court; but that instead he will pronounce according to the charges and proofs. But, this rule ought to govern when a judge led by a certain frivolous arguments thinks that he understands the case otherwise than it has been proved. For in that eventuality, he ought to follow the charges and proofs, rather than his own opinion and conscience formed from some sort of imagination.

Fol. 246v But, if a judge has a clear conviction in regard to ★ the case, then he ought in no way, to decree something against it because of charges and proofs. But even in this case he ought again to make distinctions. For if a judge should have a conviction against the defendant, and

---

[369]This crossed out section is found at the bottom of folio 245r and the top of 245v. In addition, at the top of folio 245v, Foxe has written: "Concerning the commencing of a trial, see fol. 162."

yet in the trial the defendant is proved innocent, then he ought not to condemn the man because of his own conviction, by which he knows the man is guilty, but rather ought to absolve the man in accordance with that which was proved. Because even if he should do this, he [cannot,][370] nevertheless, be said to have acted against conscience, since he absolves the defendant not as innocent but only at the request of the court. But if the judge should have a conviction in favor of the defendant against the ★ charges and proofs, then he ought not to Fol. 247r decree against his clear conviction in the case, (because the judge must be believed who alleges conscience in the judgement of another if he can prove it.)[371]

Since the judge cannot supply matters omitted in the trial, it is necessary for him to declare how he can adduce his conviction in favor of the defendant against the charges and proofs, so that he may not impinge on the constitutions, by which he is forbidden to supply anything in the trial of facts. Therefore, in such a situation, the judge should declare his conviction through consultation of a higher judge. [Therefore, he should seek [assistance] from the plaintiff party and should insist with entreaties that opportunity be given to him to consult a higher judge. When he has explained his conviction to him, he gives him the authority to hear himself as a witness of truth and then may pronounce sentence according to the charges and proofs; and he does not supply the factual evidence as judge but rather as a minister of justice he takes care that the innocence of a neighbor may not be burdened by his fault.][372] ★

Chapter 2. The Judge Ought First To Require Specific Knowledge Of The Act

Fol. 247v

The judge should especially take care that he be sure, above all else, about the deed, and that especially in criminal cases he should hear anyone who can prove the innocence of anyone at all until he comes into full knowledge of the case. For in ordinary judgements, judges are ordered to search out the details of the case by full inquiry. But in criminal judgements, so clear a knowledge of the deed is required that delay of the oath is not permitted [in fact for lack][373] of open proofs as it is in civil cases.

---

[370]Vermigli has corrected "possit" to "potest" here.

[371]The material between the parentheses is underlined in the manuscript and in the margin in Vermigli's hand is this observation: "It seems redundant."

[372]This section has been added in a crabbed fashion at the bottom of folio 247r by Vermigli.

[373]Vermigli interlined and overwrote "in fact" which is an incorrect reading, and put in "for lack" which is correct in the context.

Chapter 3. When He Should Find Out What Is The Law In The Act

Fol. 248r After gaining certain {notice *knowledge*] of the act, it is his ★ next task that the sentence by which he will declare the law, be appropriate {and proved by act*for the proven act*] and for the law and custom which each region or state uses in this kind of act. But if the judge cannot establish either from law or from clear custom what he should consider as law in the proposed case, he must proceed from similar cases to similar laws until he can decide on the basis of some argument, taken from the law applied, what he ought to follow in pronouncing sentence.[374]

Chapter 4. If There Is Ambiguity, The Defendant Must Be Favored

But, if he cannot conclude this indeed by his own investigation or Fol. 248v from consultation with experts, ★ then in doubt concerning the law, he should pronounce in behalf of the defendant rather than the plaintiff [*unless the plaintiff develops a more favorable cause.*][375]

Chapter 5. What Is A Sentence

[Hitherto we have treated the things which a judge must consider before proceeding to pronounce sentence. Now we must decide about the sentence itself so that people can understand what pronouncement of the judge deserves to be called a sentence.][376] Only that pronouncement of the judge deserves to be called a sentence by which the end of the controversy is imposed by a legal disquisition conducted in court. [It remains now that the manner be indicated by which the sentence is duly brought.][377]

Chapter 6. How The Sentence Is Correctly Brought

Therefore, we have decreed that in observance of the *solemnity*[378] surrounding the giving of sentence, the parties should be summoned Fol. 249r ★ to hear the sentence. Otherwise, although it is a sentence of the

[374]Both of the changes in this paragraph are in Vermigli's hand.

[375]This addition is in Vermigli's hand.

[376]The material between the brackets is underlined in the text and in the margin Vermigli has written: "Redundant." It cannot be determined if the underlining means the material ought to be removed or not.

[377]The material between the brackets is underlined in the manuscript and in the margin Vermigli has written: "Redundant." This sentence was not included in the Cardwell 1851 edition but placed in a footnote.

[378]"Solemnitatus" was underlined and Vermigli wrote in "solemnitas" in the margin but in fact the text is correct.

greatest importance, we wish that the sentence be considered null if the parties are not summoned. Then we have decreed that the sentence should be promulgated by the judge sitting before his tribunal, or in some other honorable public place, with the parties present, or with one absent because of his contumacy; and that the draft of the sentence should be read aloud from a brief, in which it has been written down by the judge or a notary, with the judge clearly attesting that he pronounces according to the recital from the matter written about the case, [*unless the case is such that it is permissible to pronounce verbally without a brief.*][379]

If the contention between the contending parties is to be brought to an end (through)[380] the sentence, ★ it is necessary that [the judge's] Fol. 249v speech not be exegetical but definitive and decisive. In addition, it is not sufficient that the sentence be absolutory or condemnatory, unless the matters in this case are also clearly expressed, [also] unless it is clear what things he condemns the guilty party to do or undergo, and unless it is clear from what things he frees him. For the judge must try in every way to bring as clear a sentence as possible, [*and the clarity of the sentence must be especially shaped according to the petition of the written accusation.*][381]

Also, the judge must avoid a sentence *too abundant*[382] in reasons for the certitude which is required in the decision of a case, lest the sentence seem to have been given conditionally. It is not appropriate that the cause which moves the judge to give the sentence be expressed in the sentence itself. ★ But, if a sentence has been produced because Fol. 250r of the ineptitude of the written charges, then it is necessary that the cause of the ineptitude be inserted into the sentence by which the defendant is absolved from the effect of the sentence. [*But still it is necessary, in case of an appeal, that the judge to whom the appeal has been made always introduce the cause in the sentence. For, it is necessary that he demonstrate why he either approves or disapproves the sentence brought by the lower judge.*][383]

Chapter 7.   Types of Sentences

Now that we have finished the general form of sentences, we must finally turn to types of sentences, and first we must think about an

---

[379]The last sentence in this paragraph was added by Vermigli.

[380]This is a scribal change.

[381]This sentence was added by Vermigli

[382]This seems to have been inserted by Cranmer.

[383]The last sentence in this chapter has been added by Vermigli.

interlocutory sentence, because one comes to this first in the order of procedure in trials.[384]

Chapter 8.   An Interlocutory Sentence

Fol. 250v Therefore, we determine that that case is interlocutory ★ by which the approach to the examination of the principal case is prepared. This happens in two ways: for either the judge simply orders the litigants to do something, or by his pronouncement the delays of exceptions which either party has brought, so that he can come without obstacles to the decision of the principal case. Thus, we wish this kind of sentence to be so defined: an interlocutory sentence is one which is given between the beginning and end of a case about those matters which happen or come up which are beyond the knowledge of the principal case. Therefore, the force of such a sentence is not so great as in a final sentence. For this sentence, if given, can

Fol. 251r always be revoked by the judge unless through it he has ★ ordered that one party restore or give something to the other party. For then, the judge cannot revoke it because it has the appearance of a final sentence; as when, because of contumacy, one party is condemned to pay expenses to the other, [*or if it orders something finished to be restored into possession before due process is had in the case of a petition.*][385] Likewise decision must be made concerning all peremptory exceptions. For unless a sentence given concerning these matters were considered firm, but a judge were permitted to revoke it as often as it seems best to him, then progress toward the decision of the principal case would be quite uncertain.

Chapter 9.   Final Sentence

But, we ordain that assistance be rendered more zealously in a final sentence, by which pronouncement is given on the principal case. For if there is any omission from those things, [without which][386] we have

Fol. 251v judged must be observed [without regarding][387] the solemnity ★ of the trial or regarding the very form of speech, we wish the sentence to be rejected as unlawful.

---

[384]The text of this chapter has been underlined and in the left margin Vermigli has written "redundant." In the text there is a sentence effectively scratched out which is basically identical to the following uncancelled clause which begins "... but first we must think. ..." The scratched-out sentence is interlined.

[385]This is an insertion found in the left margin in Vermigli's hand.

[386]This change is in Vermigli's hand.

[387]This change is in Vermigli's hand.

Chapter 10. A Final Sentence Cannot Be Retracted Unless It Is Given Against Divine Law

Moreover, if nothing of such matters is lacking in a final sentence so that it can be considered null because [it is] *[brought]* in an unlawful way, and there has been no appeal from it within the time allotted for appeal, then we wish the sentence to become *res judicata,* that is, *[to acquire]* such authority that no one can controvert it. Indeed, the judge may not revoke it, change it or remove some part of it, or emend it, whether he has well or badly performed his duty in pronouncing it. But, ★ great care must be taken in observing this rule that a sentence Fol. 252r badly given against the right of the litigants should become *res judicata* provided there has been no appeal from it. But, we have ordained that it be otherwise, if sentence has been given contrary to divine or natural law. For a sentence containing obvious injustice is null by the law itself, and no one ought to be compelled by law to stand by it, even if appeal from it has been prohibited. In like manner, a sentence which cannot be kept without mortal sin is rightly revoked by a judge and is neglected by the litigants as null, ★ because it cannot become *res* Fol. 252v *judicata* because of the offense to conscience, *[licitly also the judge will change the sentence if he sees it is an obstacle to the commonwealth.]*[388]

Chapter 11. When A Judge May Change, Add To Or Diminish A Sentence

If there is any grammatical error in the words of the sentence, the judge may remove it. Also, the judge may not only change a final sentence that has been brought, but also may add to it in pronouncing on the addition and diminution of actions, provided he does this on the very day on which he passes sentence and provided it was sought before it was entered in the official record. For it seems wrong, once the judgement has been completed, to permit again a new suit concerning *[additions]* ★ and diminutions of actions to be moved from Fol. 253r a suit that has been resolved.[389]

Chapter 12. Impugning A Sentence

(Now we must proceed to decide about impugning interlocutory and definitive sentences.)[390] Since [it] is quite easy to pass a false sentence, [it] is good

---

[388]The changes indicated in this paragraph are all in Vermigli's hand.

[389]The word "additions" was inserted by Vermigli.

[390]Apparently Vermigli underlined this first sentence and in the left margin wrote "Redundant."

to have certain methods by which [it] can be remedied, so that [its]³⁹¹ ratification or our indolence in admitting it does not involve us in fraud. But before anyone tries to impugn a sentence, he ought to see whether it has been pronounced in accord with the allegations and proofs, and as laws and custom require, and in lawful form with observation of the formalities. For, it should appear that any such

Fol. 253v matter has not been observed ★ in regard to it, there is no need to impugn it, because by the law itself we wish it to be considered null, as containing a manifest error of the law, so that it does not become *res judicata* even if no appeal is made from it or an appeal made from it has been abandoned. Therefore, anyone against whom such a sentence has been given can defend himself by an exception of nullity, if there is agreement on this; and such an exception invalidates it forever, that is, for forty years, the period after which all action and obligation are removed.

Fol. 254r   In cases in which a judge can revoke his own sentence, it ★ should suffice that his emendation of the sentence be simply sought, because in such cases either the (cause)³⁹² of his revoking it is evident, or the formality of the judiciary process is not required. But if one seeks to change or correct a sentence by claim of nullity, it is necessary that the error, or fraud of the judge be cleared by legitimate documents, so that the reason why it is claimed (to be null)³⁹³ becomes clear. [*And it will have to be proved*] whether the judge [*neglected*]³⁹⁴ any of those things which are necessarily required for legitimate examination, as for example, if the citation of the parties has been omitted or a formal written accusation not offered, or the suit not contested or no oath

Fol. 254v on calumny, or the sentence has not been pronounced according ★ to the legitimate form described above. Then this sentence ought to be called null, because these things are ordered to be observed for the purpose of rightly making judgements, so that the judge can rightly and in an orderly way arrive at the knowledge of the case.

But as often as a case requires that there should be a pronouncement on the nullity of the sentence, the case must be tried not before another higher judge, as in appeal cases, but before the same judge who judged the principal case. But this only happens when the case has been tried before the ordinary judge, not when it has been tried by a delegated judge. For his jurisdiction is ended when he has judged badly [*in regard to the definitive sentence; and he cannot revoke*

---

³⁹¹Vermigli changed the pronouns from plural to singular in this sentence.

³⁹²This appears to be underlined by the scribal hand.

³⁹³The words contained within the parentheses are underlined in the text.

³⁹⁴This word and the phrase marked in brackets were inserted in Vermigli's hand.

an interlocutory sentence, or be discharged from his office because of it. But if he has judged badly in a final sentence.][395] Appeal and petition ★ can be made Fol. 255r from him to the person who delegated [authority to him], so that either he himself may examine the case or he may ask that it be examined by the other.

Chapter 13. Supplement On The Impugning Of A Sentence

It remains for us to decree something about the supplement on impugning which it seems should be given in this case, namely, concerning fraud. For also that supplement concerns, in general all those who can show that they have fallen under judgement through the authority and instigation of false instruments or witnesses. If in the investigation of the case there was not an examination of the crime of fraud, and it appears that the judge was deceived by ★ the appearance Fol. 255v of such proofs, then because of the odium of this crime we not only order that the sentence be rescinded before appeal is made from it, but we wish that after it has become *res judicata,* the person harmed by it should be restored in full so that the case can be [*tried again.*][396] And if anything has been paid in accordance with this [sentence], it is permissible for the party to ask for it back.

Chapter 14. *Res Judicata*

The decision of a suit is *res judicata,* the thing that judges, but that which is established in this decision becomes the *res judicata* if it has been done duly and legitimately in such a way that it cannot be assailed as null and appeal cannot[397] be made from it. ★

Chapter 15. When A Matter That Has Been Judged Among   Fol. 256r
Certain People Is Prejudicial To Others.

(And since the force of *res judicata* is so great, it must be considered incidentally whether it is harmful only to those between whom the judgement [was] passed or also to those touched by the issue about which the judgement was made, either by reason of a common subject, or by reason of a contact. Therefore, one must see how broadly the law of sentence extends to harm others or to help them.)[398] And, it is the general rule that a matter performed among certain people does

---

[395]This is added in Vermigli's hand. Vermigli made other changes in the paragraph which changed it from passive to active voice.

[396]This is Vermigli's correction of a grammatical error.

[397]"non" has been enclosed in a box in the text.

[398]The sentence bracketed by parenthesis was underlined by Vermigli [?] and in the left margin Vermigli wrote: "Redundant."

not harm others. And, this rule has place whether something has been tried in court or outside of court. But, in a matter tried in court, this
Fol. 256v ★ addition must be made to the rule: that not even then are the acts of others prejudicial to us if they have done something in our name provided they have done this without our permission or ratification. (Although this rule may be general,)[399] still if anything is done without my prohibition, by the one who has common right with me, in this matter concerning which the trial has occurred, since I could have prohibited him, the sentence brought against him begets prejudice for me. It is otherwise as if I did not know his plan and had no power of prohibiting him. ★

Fol. 257r   There are also cases in which a sentence is simply prejudicial to all in whose interest it is, that it not be so judged if it becomes *res judicata*. For example, if a testament has been rescinded by the complaint of neglect of obligations to a family, those things which were owed by disposition in the name of the legatees cannot be sought if it had not been judged against this. Indeed, even the things paid out are sought back. Where there is the greater danger, there the matter must be tried the more cautiously, and since the tribunal of the eternal judge is sure not to have that man as a defendant, whom the judge condemns unjustly, great care must be taken by ecclesiastical
Fol. 257v ★ judges ~~and all others~~,[400] and there must be prudent attention so that in any trials of cases, hatred not win out or favor usurp, but fear should suffer exile, reward or expectation of reward should not overturn justice; but those who do not show regard of persons are the ones who hold the scales of justice in their hands, brandishing yardsticks [for][401] just measure, so that in all proceedings they must conduct cases, especially in conceiving and giving sentences, as if they have their eyes set only upon God, imitating the example of him who, bringing complaints of the people into the tabernacle, referred them
Fol. 258r to God so that ★ he could judge according to his power. For whatever ordinary or even delegated judge, wasteful of his reputation and persecutor of his own honor, does anything in judgement for favor or in meanness, against conscience and against justice, to the harm of another party, knows that within a year he will be removed from the execution of his office, and will be also condemned to [indemnify]

---

[399]The phrase bracketed by parenthesis was underlined and in the margin Vermigli wrote: "Redundant."

[400]This phrase was cancelled by someone.

[401]Vermigli underlined "just" and wrote above it: "for."

the party whom he has harmed according to the value of the lawsuit, even though he was not at all condemned.[402]

★CONCERNING RULES OF LAW[403]

Necessity makes permissible that which was not permitted in the law.

Those matters which were introduced because of necessity ought not be drawn into argument.

A man who is once evil is always presumed to be evil.

That which touches everyone ought to be approved by everyone.

What is done in public affairs by the majority is attributed to all.

When time is added in a will, it must be believed that it has been added on behalf of the heir unless there was another intention in the testator. ★

Those things in the will which were written in such a way that Fol. 260v they cannot be understood are just as if they had not been written.

Penal cases must be interpreted more benignly.

In almost all penal cases help is given to both age and imprudence.

Inexperience is counted as a fault,.

Outward appearance derogates from the race.

Special things are always inherent in general.

The part is contained in the whole.

It is fitting for the accessory to follow the nature of the principal.

When the principal case is not sound, those that follow do not hold their place. ★

The one to whom more is permitted ought not permit that which Fol. 261r is less.

The man who does not comply with the authority of the magistrate cannot be without guile.

Heredity is succession into the whole right which the deceased had at the time of death.

Those who are put in charge of the personal property by the will of the deceased are called testamentary heirs or executors.

---

[402]At the bottom of the page, Foxe wrote: "The defendant can get a jurisdiction in four ways. Defendants get a jurisdiction for four reasons, either on account of residence, etc. see folio" At the top of folio 258v he wrote: "Concerning Appeals see folio 213." Folio 258v is a blank page, as is folio 259.

[403]In Cranmer's hand in the left margin throughout this section, he has written in references to Canon law by title and number. All of the references as given by Cranmer have been duly noted by Cardwell and the reader is referred to that Latin edition for the references.

It must be believed that all by the name of heirs are signified to

Fol. 261v be successors. ★

No delay is intelligible in a case where there is no petition.

One who has ceased to possess because of trickery is condemned in favor of the possessor.

Whatever is either done or said in the heat of anger, is not thought to have been a judgement of the mind previously unless it appeared with perseverance.

As often as the same conversation expresses two opinions, that opinion should most especially be accepted which is more suitable for performing the deed.

In cases of doubt the more benign [things] must be preferred.

In cases of obscurity that which is least must be followed. ★

Fol. 262r   It is in accordance with nature that the advantages of anything follow him who is followed by the disadvantages.

There is no just excuse for empty fear.

Ratification is withdrawn and is made equivalent to the mandate.

One cannot have a share which was carried on in his name.

When the rights of the parties are obscure, the defendant rather than the plaintiff must be favored.

Ignorance of the deed, but not of the law, is an excuse.

It is agreeable for hatred to be restrained and favors increased.

It is proper that a benefice granted by a prince should remain. ★

Fol. 262v   An indult from the law is not a benefit that may be taken away by anyone.

No one is prohibited from using several defenses.

What was pleasing once cannot be displeasing later.

No one ought to be weighted down by hatred of another.

No one must be punished without fault unless there is an underlying cause.

Neither injury nor trickery is done to one who is aware and agrees.

The useful ought not to be nullified by the useless.

No one ought to pursue rewards from that which he seems to impugn. ★

Fol. 263r   When anything is prohibited, all things which follow from it are prohibited.

Plural speech is content with the number of two.

One ought not to impute fault to a man who lacks firmness as he does not do what he had agreed to do.

One who is silent seems to consent.

One who is silent does not confess but neither does he seem to deny.

Ignorance is presumed when knowledge is not demonstrated. ★

Fol. 263v What does not obtain an effect by law does not constitute an impediment.

He who is prior in time is more powerful in law.

What is granted because of someone's kindness must not be twisted to his loss.

No one is obliged from a deliberation, provided there is no deceit.

He who raises an exception does not seem to confess the claim of his opponent.

What is not permitted in one's own name will not be permitted in another's.

One can do through another what one can do through oneself.★

Fol. 264r What is freely granted to one person ought not to be used as an example by others.

The sin of a person ought not redound to the detriment of the church.

Those matters which one would not be likely concede in particular are not conceded in a general concessions.

Good faith does not allow that the same thing be twice exacted.

When anything is prohibited to anyone by one way, it ought not be admitted by another.

The gates of dignity are not open to the infamous.

Whoever embraces the words of the law and struggles against the will of the law commits an offense against the law.★

Fol. 264v Whatever is permitted to the power of the court is not subjected to the necessity of law.

The judge is also compelled to pronounce on that of which he has knowledge.

No one must be thought to have said that which has not previously come to his mind.

The pronouncing of a conversation in the masculine sex is often extended to both sexes.

Whatever things are necessary for food, drink, care of the body, and things of this kind that are necessary for living, and also clothing and coverings, and other things we use for the purpose of living and caring for our body: [all these] are included in the word sustenance.★

Fol 265r Father, grandfather, great-grandfather, and all superiors are contained in the name of parent, but also mother, grandmother, and great-grandmother.

Grandchildren and great-grandchildren and other descendants from them are contained in the name of children.

So a daughter and grandson is included in the name of sons.

One is intestate not only if one does not have a will but also if there has been no entry into inheritance from his will. ★

Fol. 265v   Expenditures are necessary if the estate will either perish or deteriorate if they were not made; payments are useful if they make the estate better; they are pleasurable if they only decorate outward appearance.

Interest on money is not income because it is not from the principal sum itself but from another cause, namely, from a new obligation.

Those who are born dead or are aborted before the seventh or eighth month are seen as neither born nor begotten.

That mother is believed to have a son when she dies if she could give birth to the child from her cut womb. However it is false to say she has given birth if the son was cut from her after she died. ★

Fol. 266r   There is no doubt that the female as well as the male is contained in the term "men."

Also a girl is signified by the term boy.

It is proper that every satisfaction that a creditor is willing to accept is called a payment.

One who is in the womb is considered as already born when there is question concerning the baby's advantage.

The law as it were permits more with two negative words than it prohibits.[404]

Fol. 268r   ★CONCERNING DEFAMATION

Chapter 1.   That Detractors Are To Be Punished By Laws

Because all Christians ought to show by mutual charity that they are true disciples of Christ, the ill-will of certain wicked persons is to be constrained. [These are] those who assail their brothers with such lethal hatred that they are willing to crush them calumniously with false accusations. Thus it happens, that we consider that the restraints of laws are to be cast upon the license of those whose feelings cannot be mitigated by Christian charity, which is absolutely not present in them. Those, then, whom duty itself does not move by its power, will be subdued by the severity of the law.

Chapter 2.   When And How Detractors Should Be Punished

First, therefore, let the following be established: whoever in wicked deceit, with purpose and knowingly have violated anyone's reputation

---

[404]Folios 266v and 267r-v are missing from the microfilm copy of the manuscript.

by means of a fictitious and fabricated accusation, or in any way have caused it to be violated, or use abusive speech against anyone, or either compile or write an infamous libel themselves, *or when they have discovered one* compiled or written by others, *do not immediately either tear it up*[405] or consume it with flames, but divulge it either by bringing it to light, or seeing that it is brought to light are first, surely to be led away by him to whom this injury has been done, provided that he wishes to prosecute the injury, to the pastor and elders of the Church, so that they may thoroughly terrify the unfitness of such detractors with a harsh and forceful ★ lecture. If they are willing to give assent   Fol. 268v to the authority of those men and are prepared to gather up and restore, as far as they are able, the reputation of the man whom they had previously attacked with false accusations, the case, by that very fact, will be closed, and he who was assaulted with false accusations will not cause any other trouble for his detractors, nor drag them before ordinary judges. For there should always be a special concern for the salvation of souls, and charges not necessary, as far as it is permissible, are to be dismissed. But, if calumniators and detractors of this type are unwilling to be brought around by the beneficial precepts of the pastors and elders, then at length let their names be referred to the ecclesiastical judges themselves before whom, when their acts of calumny and detraction have been fully established by clear proofs, they will be condemned by the sentence of the judges to deposit into the poor boxes, which are the property of their own churches, those sums of money which their resources will appear able to bear conveniently. Also let them be stricken with the penalty of excommunication from which we do not want them to be freed in any respect until, in the opinion of the ecclesiastical judge, satisfaction has been made to the man who was injured and also until they have carried out those penances which will seem fitting for such a crime.

Chapter 3.   They Who Prove An Exposed Crime Are Not To Be Punished

Because it is greatly to the interest of the commonwealth that crimes be restrained by penalties and that one's own just defense be reserved for each person, we establish the ★ following: if anyone makes someone   Fol. 269r else a defendant by an accusation, denunciation or exception, or by any other legitimate and solemn method, and has established his good faith with the judge of the accusation brought forward, he ought to be freed from every penalty of that law, because he pursued not

---

[405]The changes indicated in this paragraph have been made in the hand of the scribe. The "or" was inserted and the next two phrases were written in between the lines.

calumny but truth. If, however, the accuser has failed in his case, let him be bound by the penalties of the law, unless he is able to show that he has been led to this design, not for the purpose of speaking evil nor by the desire of making false accusations, but by some just reason.[406]

Fol. 270r

★CONCERNING DILAPIDATIONS

Chapter 1.   Owners Ought To Provide Homes For A Vicar In Their Own Churches.[407]

If a church, which has someone fixed as a hereditary possessor, should not have a building in which the vicar can locate and does not have a convenient area in which a house was placed previously, if the hereditary possessor was equipped with either another building or some farms pertaining to the right of the church, or some building, or ground on which a home could be built, the bishop shall set it aside by his own authority for the vicar, providing in this way that the vicar may live suitably and conveniently in all respects. ★

Fol. 270v   Indeed this habitation of the vicar should come from the expenses of the hereditary possessor of the church so that, within three years after he was warned by the bishops, it should be completely built. If the bishop sees that the possessor resists in this and if he [the bishop] believes it is a case of hard dealing, either he should see to it that the church revenues are held back from him or he should bind him with ecclesiastical penalties. But, if perchance the proper bishop himself is not vigilant enough, the prime bishop whom people call metropolitan should investigate and judge this case when it is brought to him.

Chapter 2.   How Ruinous Houses Must Be Restored

Fol. 271r Moreover, in those parishes in which houses were once ★ provided for the pastors and their vicars, but they have either fallen fully to the ground because of the neglect of previous ministers or because of emptiness, or they are beginning to collapse because of length of

---

[406]At the bottom of the page in Foxe's writing is this: "Concerning delays, see folio 172." Folio 269v is blank except that in a scribal hand the following is written: "Concerning squandering [property]; Concerning alienation and renting out; Concerning election."

[407]The titles for the chapters in this section have been written in by Cranmer but no numbers assigned to the sections. Numbers have been put in for the reader's convenience.

time, and there is nothing left in the fortunes of the previous ministers by which they can be rebuilt, the bishop should see that a seventh part of the annual revenue be set aside as a deposit until either a new house is constructed suited to all the needs of the minister, or the dilapidated house is put into good condition.

Chapter 3.   The Manner of Correcting Those Who Devastate
             The Woodlands Of The Churches

If anyone without the agreement of the bishop of that district sells, cuts down, lops off, removes, or in any way destroys or devastates the trees, bushes, groves, woodlands, woods, brush, thickets, or any source of wood pertaining by right of any ecclesiastical benefice to himself ★ more freely than necessary, he will bring the full price andFJ Fol. 271v worth of all the wood of this kind cut down and removed into the box attributed to the poor. In addition, he will make as much satisfaction in this matter to his successor as the bishop thinks is just; and the method followed in this case will be the same as was previously established by us for rebuilding buildings.

Chapter 4.   Those Who Leave Buildings Dilapidated Or In
             Ruin At Their Death

Likewise, when the present incumbent of the church dies, if he has left dilapidated, or in poor repair, or completely in ruin the upper part of the church which people call the chancel, or ★ any other houses Fol. 272r pertaining to the property of the church, his successor will have permission to sue the heirs or administrators of goods, by whatever name they are called, for the losses of such damage and faults. However, the length of possession will have to be considered. But if a whole year has not passed, nothing will be demanded; however, in proportion to the time over a year, the equity of the ecclesiastical judges will devise a plan of satisfaction for this. Finally, if anything was collected for the expense of such buildings for any reason, and the minister never expended that on them, the heirs or administrators should grant this to the successor so that he can free the good name of the former minister in such a good case. ★

Chapter 5.   How The Ruins Of Buildings Belonging To   Fol. 272v
             Churches, Cathedrals, Colleges, And Guest
             Houses Must Be Repaired

Also, the law is the same concerning the rebuilding and repair of houses which are assigned to those beneficiaries of the churches, whom people commonly call deans, prebendaries, and masters of colleges, or hospitals, whether these houses are situated in cities or in the country. However, we do not want them to be limited to the rebuilding or repair of buildings situated in the country, which have not been inhabited within the past twenty years.

Fol. 273v   ★CONCERNING THE ALIENATION AND RENTING
OUT OF ECCLESIASTICAL GOODS

Chapter 1.   Nothing Can Be Alienated From A Church
Without The Agreement Of The Ordinary And
Patron.[408]

Those who are involved in governing churches shall not sell, exchange, give away or by any kind of contract or agreement alienate for all time houses or fields or any possession or revenues of the churches unless the patron and the bishop gave their agreement.

Chapter 2.   How Renting Ought To Be Effected

Every rental of ecclesiastical benefits should expire within ten years, or should not run beyond the tenth year and should not occupy the
Fol. 274r time of successors. For ★ experience most often has condemned such rentals because the right of the successor in them is openly violated by those who were formerly involved in that office, unless perchance there was a necessary, or useful reason for renting, because of the ruinous condition of the buildings, or the sterility of the fields and the tenants have obligated themselves to rebuild the houses and cultivate the fields. And in the meantime they shall pay to the church the whole annual rent which used to be paid in earlier times. But, not even these arrangements should proceed in any way unless the patron and bishop consent to them.

Chapter 3.   Four Causes Of Alienation

We do not wish recourse to be taken to the alienation of ecclesiastical goods unless there is one of the four following causes which imposes
Fol. 274v the necessity of alienation. ★ The first cause arises when the church is so ruined by debt that it cannot sustain itself by the annual lawful taxes. Next, if a great and evident utility invites, for we readily allow

---

[408]There is no folio 273r in the microfilm copy. The titles of the chapters of this section are in Cranmer's hand. The numbers of the chapter are given in the manuscript.

Chapter 3.   Four Causes Of Alienation

We do not wish recourse to be taken to the alienation of ecclesiastical goods unless there is one of the four following causes which imposes the necessity of alienation. ★ The first cause arises when the church Fol. 274v is so ruined by debt that it cannot sustain itself by the annual lawful taxes. Next, if a great and evident utility invites, for we readily allow the state of the churches to be made better. A third cause follows, the pious act of freeing Christian peoples from slavery of tyrannical peoples, when they have fallen into the power of enemies of our religion. A fourth and last reason for alienation is, when something of this kind is cut off in which the church was being harmed rather than helped. However, it is not desirable for alienation of church goods to follow even these reasons unless the bishop and the patron agree to it. ★

Chapter 4.   Punishment Of Those Who Alienate Contrary To   Fol 275r
                      Law

Moreover, as often as exchange, renting or alienation of church goods is begun, contrary to the provisions of these laws of ours, first of all we wish all such agreements to be nullified. Next, it is our pleasure that the clerics themselves, who for any reason, take part in agreements of this kind should be excluded from their ministries.[409]

★CONCERNING ELECTIONS   Fol. 276v

Absolutely the same formula of elections should obtain in the leading churches which people call cathedrals, or in colleges and gatherings of academic institutions, which has been sanctioned in internal practices of individual colleges, unless perchance anything be found in these which is at variance with the reformed religion in this our kingdom or with our constitutions.[410]

[409]Folio 275v is missing from the microfilm copy of the manuscript.
[410]Folio 276v is missing from the microfilm copy of the manuscript.

★CONCERNING WILLS

Chapter 1. What Is A Will[411]

A will is the definitive expression of our desire and final decision concerning the disposal of our affairs after death. It names and establishes a certain heir who now is commonly called the executor. But, whoever alters either whole wills or any part thereof, knowingly for whatever reason, commits a violation and should be struck with anathema and should be driven from the community of Christian people.

Chapter 2. Furnishing Witnesses

A will should be protected by legal witnesses, < and as far as it can be conveniently done, > [412] they should be listed by name, [such as] the minister himself and the [officials][413] of the church whom they call wardens, < so that the authenticity of the wills may be greater, and if these perchance cannot be used, either > [414] two or three men should give acknowledgment who are outstanding for probity, and tested credibility, or finally the will itself should be signed by the hand of the testator and of two or three witnesses.

Chapter 3. Nuncupatory Wills

If anyone dies suddenly, the agreement of three witnesses of proved credibility will be accepted, even though the will was not entrusted to writing. And, in both kinds of will, in the written or in the expressed word of the testator, which is called nuncupatory, it will suffice if the testator names the heir of his will. ★

Chapter 4. That A Will Should Be Valid

It is always appropriate that this [principle] be held, that every authority should be accorded to the most recent will, and that any antecedent wills be considered null unless the testator, in certain clauses placed in former wills, openly orders that this clause be kept in the last will.

---

[411]From this point to the end in the manuscript, one finds a different scribal hand than earlier. In the preceding pages there were two distinct hands used. Here a "new" third hand is found.

[412]The phrase bracketed by carets is missing in the Latin text printed by Cardwell.

[413]There is a blank space here in the manuscript where apparently someone was to later fill in the missing word.

[414]The phrase bracketed by carets is missing in the Latin text printed by Cardwell.

If this happens, then those clauses only will stand, concerning which the testator has decreed item by item.

Chapter 5.   Concerning Codicils

Since it often happens that once the will has been finished and concluded, many things come into the mind of the testator concerning which he made no provision in the will, and which he very much wants added to it; for this reason we concede that those later additions have no less binding power than those placed in the will, if he provides by a letter that those things should be taken care of, or if he seeks that these be attested by two or three witnesses of proven reliability.

Chapter 6.   The Time Allowed To Plead A Case Against A Will

If anyone wants to bring anything against the will in court, either he should bring it up when the will is probated, or within the following year. But, if he waits longer, the case should be thrown out unless perchance he can offer and prove the excuse either of age or of long journey, so that he heard nothing about the will, < [or unless] he alleges ignorance of the matter in his behalf. > [415] ★ Moreover, we Fol. 278r wish these excuses to be defined thus: first, in which age is an impediment; then finally it is pleasing that these be heard when they are grown up and old enough to plead the case. First, however, they should attain the years of legal age: if they omit any [years], they should lose the whole right of pleading the case. But, to those who have crossed the sea, we will allow six months after return; if they do not use the benefit of this, also no action will be left to them. < Ignorance of the event, since sometimes it deserves pardon if fraud is absent, will be allowed a month, in which if the plaintiff does not pursue his rights, afterwards he will have no standing in the case. > [416]

Chapter 7.   Who Is Permitted And Who Is Not Permitted To Make A Will

All people of whatever sex or condition will have the power of making wills, unless there is something in them which is contrary to these present laws of ours. However, we except those, first of all, who are not independent, but are held in the power of another such as are, namely, wife, slave, minor children under fourteen. Next, we do not admit the mad, nor those bereft of their senses unless perchance some

---

[415]This phrase is not included in the Cardwell edition.

[416]This phrase is not included in the Cardwell edition.

periods of sanity of this kind are intermittent in which they can regulate their own affairs reasonably. In addition those who cannot themselves speak, or understand the words of others, or entrust their thoughts to writing, should be excluded unless they use nods and signs so evident and clear that suitable witnesses can be produced Fol. 278v who are certain of their will and undoubted ★ opinions. Also, we do not concede freedom of making wills to heretics, nor to those who have received sentence of death, or perpetual exile, or perpetual imprisonment. Let those lack also this advantage who have not dismissed concubines before their last days. There should be a similar punishment of women on the other hand, as often as there is a similar cause. There should be added to these persons people who have had two wives at the same time, or women with two husbands, unless a legitimate divorce in the former person occurred previously and thus provided a firm basis for the later condition. Also, those would be dismissed who have practiced prostitution, or pandering, unless they have undergone public penance for their public crimes. Also, money lenders or, to speak most crassly in a vulgar way, usurers, unless perchance they either have given back the money, or have taken full precautions about refunding, or have wholly made satisfaction in some other way for their usury. Therefore, none of these specified people will have the right of making a will, or of appointing an heir. And, this will have to be generally understood, that the condition of testators must be scrutinized and followed, the condition of those now dying, not of those making out wills a long time ago.

Chapter 8.   How Those Who Cannot Make A Will By
             Common Law Still May Leave Legacies To Pious
             Causes

At the end of life, those who have practiced concubinage or have two Fol. 279r wives, likewise women of similar depravity, ★ can apply their goods to pious causes. Similarly, those who have practiced prostitution or pandering publicly, or were userers and have never been converted to good behavior, still if by pious duties they lay out something in their last will, it is pleasing that these honorable thoughts even in bad people should be of value.

Chapter 9.   Pious Causes

Moreover, these are numbered among pious causes: when something is brought to the relief of prisoners, to the refreshment of the poor, to the maintenance of orphans, widows, and afflicted persons of any kind, particularly and especially when something is designated by will for the marriage of poor girls, to cover the nakedness of needy students living in the academies, for the repair of public roads. However, when anything has been willed superstitiously, rather than piously, the bishop should interpose his authority, in order that the legacy be distributed to pious causes.

Chapter 10. What Kind Of Distribution Of Goods There Ought
To Be Either From A Will Or An Intestate Person

The distribution of goods left by will or without a will should be as follows: A man who has a wife and children should put aside a third part of this goods for his wife, then a third for his children and should place the remaining third according to his own discretion. But, if he dies intestate, his wife first and then his children will have their equal thirds, but the administrators shall distribute the remaining third. But, if the testator has no child, a half of the goods should ★ remain with Fol. 279v the wife, and the man should decide concerning the remainder as he wishes. And if he dies without a will, only this same remainder will be in the power of the administrators, and the wife will also have her portion safe and untouched. But, if the testator has a child from his wife and the wife dies with the child surviving, then it pleases us that half of all the goods go to this child, but the remainder should be referred to the will of the testator; and if by chance the man dies intestate, the right of the child will be inviolate and the remainder will be disposed according to the authority of the administrators. However, such a plan disposing of property ought to be initiated always in such a way that debts, and all funeral expenses should be deducted. But the right of children, since it can be uncertain because of the various number of them, should be defined by a perpetual rule of equality, so that however many there are, each should have his own share in the accounting of the property, unless perchance the father makes some other disposal in the will by name. And, since the condition of the parents is more tenuous, the parents will be permitted to deduct as much as they think best from the third part of the goods to which the children have a right. In order to facilitate these matters, it is agreed that the remaining portions, which we have reserved for wives and children, can be added to the parents' wealth, if their place is empty. Finally, if death also takes away the son of a testator, who dies either with or without a will, and this son should have children, as much of the grandfather's goods as would have come to the son should accrue to the grandchildren, so that the humanity of our laws can diffuse itself most broadly to all.★

Fol. 280r Chapter 11. Which Children Can Be Cut Out Of Their Legal
Portion

No son ought to be passed over in the will of his father, unless the
father has disinherited him with clear words either before the drawing
up of the will, or at the very time of the drawing up of the will.
However, the disinheritance itself will not be valid unless he has some
just cause spelled out; in order that these causes may be clearly known
we have listed them here in order. Thus, the first and most important
is, if the son has assaulted his father; and then, if he has willfully and
knowingly injured him with any other serious and notable injury; if
he openly has proved him guilty of crime, not for the sake of the state
but out of malice or inner hatred; if he was familiar with enchanters
or witches; if he has committed incest with his step-mother or his
father's concubine; if he has attacked his father's reputation with
slander, or has harmed his estate; if he has refused when requested
to be surety for his father or to provide bail for him; if he should be
a hindrance to his father's making a will or for any reason amending
one. A daughter is certainly without benefit in a will, if she has lived
by the custom of harlots or prostituted her body, when in the meantime
her father has offered honest provisions for marriage. For, if the father
has neglected the daughter to her twenty-fifth year, and has not
arranged a marriage, the neglect of the father released the daughter
from blame or at least he cannot exclude from his family, or his will
Fol. 280v her whom ★ he himself by his own fault has held back for himself in
virginity until she is old. The ingratitude of children who do not
support mad or mentally deranged fathers, in so far as their means
permit, is also punished by the penalty of disinheriting; the same holds
if they do not find some way of freeing their captive fathers; if they
slip into heresy and remain in it; if they have practiced pandering or
prostitution.

Chapter 12. Why Even Poor Parents Can Be Passed Over By
Children In Wills

Parents, on the other hand, can be passed over by their children in
their wills if they shamefully desert their children, or cast them out
from themselves because of some terrible and monstrous hatred, or
drive them away from themselves in great danger to life. If they plot
to inflict loss of safety on their children by poisons, or any magic arts,
or attack the chastity of their wives, likewise if they have hindered
their children's freedom in drawing up wills; if they have not cared
for their mad children; if they have been convicted of heresy and have
refused to repudiate it; children can use all these reasons for omitting

parents in wills, provided always in these two chapters that the mother also is understood under the name of the father.

Chapter 13. Why Wives Can Be Passed Over In Wills

Always, also, husbands ought to make provision for their wives in their wills, unless a just cause of offense can be brought forth, which we do not want admitted, unless it is supported by strong arguments. For their rights ought not to be snatched away from them by ★ calumny. We wish equity to be observed both in the case of children, and in the case of feeble parents, lest they lose their right through any neglect. However, husbands can exclude wives < from their wills > for the following reasons: if they attack the husband with force; if they have planned their husband's destruction by any machinations; if they have contaminated themselves by any evil or magic arts; if a wife with foresight and knowingly has defamed her husband's good name or fortunes by calumny or false accusation; if she hinders her husband from making or emending his will or changing it in any way; or if she has not cherished him when mad, delirious or gravely ill; if she has betrayed his safety for any reason except for the country's welfare; if she has not rescued him when captive either by money or other means as much as she could; if she embraces heresy and refuses to give it up; if she has exposed or charged a daughter or any servant maid for any passion; finally if she has left her husband and cannot be called back to him.

Fol. 281r

Chapter 14. Those Who Cannot Be Constituted Heirs Or
            Participants Of Legacies

The following will not be constituted heirs or enjoy any benefit of wills: those who are persistent heretics, those who have received sentence of death or of perpetual exile, or of life imprisonment, those who have defiled themselves by concubinage, those who maintain two wives at one time against all right and law, women whose guilt is the same for the same crime. There will be numbered here those who have been condemned for any kind of procuring ★ or disseminating of infamous writings which the civil law calls notorious, those who openly live by pandering or prostitution. Also, usurers will be excluded from all benefits of wills. Moreover, that time at which the will was executed, or at which he died shall not be taken into account, but rather the morals of persons shall be evaluated at that time, in which either an inheritance is to be received by them, or things willed to them become payable.

Fol. 281v

Chapter 15. Unjust Or Impossible Conditions Of Legacy

If anyone leaves to anyone in a will a fixed amount, adding a condition that is either unfair or impious, the legatee will lose the amount unless he swears that he will repudiate the condition. If he should refuse to be brought to this action, the legacy at the discretion of the bishop shall be bestowed upon some pious institution. But, if the condition was such that it can not be fulfilled, it ought to be seen as a vain addition. Therefore conditions of this kind will not hinder the rights of heirs or legatees, especially if they show the following: that they indeed have worked out the conditions for proceeding as well as they could, and that they have not spared any personal diligence [in the matter].

Chapter 16. When Heirs Can Take The Goods Of The Testator

Heirs will not have access to the goods of the deceased except for the purpose of completing a certain study which they call "inventory" and in order to pay the funeral expenses, until the wills have been fully Fol. 282r probated either by the bishop or by the proper judge ★ of that district, whom we most frequently call by the common name "ordinary," and until the obligatory bond has been given by the heirs in the presence of the ordinary, that they will proceed honestly and sincerely in this whole business of the goods entrusted to them, and that they will render and account to him of their trust, when the ordinary demands it, and that they will always hold the ordinary himself safe and quiet in the whole transaction. For, it is the proper < right > of bishops to confirm wills, and < of granting power by authority of their writs > [417] and also to appoint the administration of property, if wills of the deceased do not exist. Therefore, we refuse to remove this right of theirs, unless a singular privilege occurs, or it has been otherwise decided by some lawful agreement, or unless some good custom, or a space of time defined by law which people call "prescription" transfers this authority to other men or places.

Chapter 17. The Payment Of Judges And Ministers

When the goods of testators do not exceed five pounds total, nothing will be paid either to the judge or his assistants for the confirmation of the wills; the scribe will receive only six pence, because he has recorded the decisions of the judge, and the copy of the will into the records. However, the judge when he has established that a will of

---

[417]These phrases are missing in Cardwell's edition.

this kind is firm and solid, shall confirm it by adding his seal at no
charge; but ★ the expenditure for parchment, the wax, and the writing Fol. 282v
is to be divided equally among those for whom profit will come from
these same materials. But if the goods of the testators exceed five
pounds, but are less than forty pounds, forty pence will be put aside
for the judge and his assistants and of this amount twelve will be paid
to the scribes and the rest will remain for the judge and his assistants.
But, when the wealth of the testator exceeds forty pounds, five shillings
will be given to the judge and his assistants, and half of this will go
to the scribe; but if he is not satisfied with this, he will accept this
condition, that he should receive a penny in return for every tenth
line of the will, provided that each line has a width of ten inches.

Chapter 18. Heirs And Administrators Will Render An Account
         of Goods

We do not want anyone to be in so privileged a position that either
the heirs, whom people call "executors," or the administrators would
be absolved of rendering account of the legacies. It is agreed that such
an accounting should be made in all cases whether the testators died
with or without wills. Therefore, as to those who have been provided
with such privileges, unless they lay aside and repudiate their favored
position, we do not want them to have any right in the business of
handling the goods, or to be employed in any way in administering
them. ★

Chapter 19. The Seal Of The Deceased   Fol. 283r

Since many clever tricks often happen when the signet of the deceased
is intercepted, we order that as soon as a man dies, whatever his signet
is which he used to affix to his writings, should be placed in a certain
chest or purse where it can be kept safe, and in addition this chest
or purse will be affirmed by the signature of three honorable men, so
that thus the signet of the testator may be brought safely to the judge
at some early time. But, when heirs or executors have brought the
signet to the judge, he immediately should destroy and demolish the
image and form of the signet, and should restore the material to them
and not keep it in any way for himself.

Chapter 20. Completing The Inventories Of Goods

The heirs or administrators, shall call to themselves two persons who
either owed something to the testator or will receive something from
his will, or if, these men are not present, then they shall choose two
men of honorable reputation who were relatives of the deceased, or,

if all such men are absent, two men of whatever condition provided they are honorable and are men of integrity; and these should see to it fully and perfectly that the accounts of all matters be entrusted to writing; they shall keep for themselves one copy of these writings, commonly called inventories, and should entrust another to the safe-keeping of the judge, who when he has demanded, and received

Fol 283v oaths from them concerning the ★ faithfulness and honesty of these writings, will promptly take these writings, approve them and keep them in a safe place. For we command that the copies of the wills and indices, or inventories, as people call them, should be diligently kept by the judge, or by the judge's assistants, so that those concerned will immediately have access to them as often as they seek them. Moreover, whenever these writings are demanded, it is agreed that they be shown, immediately and quickly, and the fee for transcribing these things should be that which we have established above; or if the scribe wishes to be paid according to the number of lines, he may receive a penny for each ten, and the lengths of the lines should be as we prescribed above. But, if avarice of either the judge or his assistants should insist on more than we have assigned, and the fee itself is levied in advance on all persons, then they shall be subject to a penalty of ten pounds, of which one half will go into the poor box and the rest will go to him whose business it was, if he wishes to, make accusations and to pursue the case juridically.

Chapter 21. Heirs And Administrators Ought To Seek Only The Truthfulness Of The Inventories

It is not fair that either the heirs, or administrators of goods be compelled to show more than is found in those writings which we call inventories; if however belief in the inventories themselves has remained firm. ★

Fol. 284r ### Chapter 22. Action To Be Taken When Doubt Occurs Concerning The Will Or Heirs

When in an ecclesiastical court there can by law be confidence neither concerning the authority of the will nor concerning the people who are to be employed in the administration of the goods, the judge, in order that in the meantime the property many not be lost, will commit the resources to the care of reliable trustees. However, if the heir has taken time for planning and does not immediately believe that the business ought to be begun because it is so complicated, the ordinary should see that a letter is drawn up for him by the authority of which he can collect the scattered resources of the testator; provided that

in the letter there is legal notice that the heir, within a space of the
next six months must render an accounting of all things collected by
him by any right of the testator, and that he shall not otherwise enter
into possession of the wealth of the testator, until a true and honest
inventory of all the goods has been completed, as has been prescribed
a little before. Administrators, who are put in charge of the property
of men without wills, shall follow this same accounting.

Chapter 23. The Penalty Of Heirs Who Refuse

Those who by name are constituted heirs in a will, when the ordinary
has advised them and has set a fixed time within which they must
undertake the administration of the will, or if the warnings of the
ordinary may not have happened and no one has done anything in
this matter with them, if after receiving word of the death of the
testator they allow six whole months ★ to pass without undertaking Fol. 284v
the administration of the will, and without giving a just reason which
compels their absence, immediately the ordinary shall exclude them
from the will, and should not allow any profit to go to them from it.
However, they should restore and replace fully and completely anything
they took from the will before hand; and this business shall be entrusted
by the judge to relatives of the deceased.

Chapter 24. Distribution of the Goods Among Heirs And
Administrators

When there are several heirs or administrators, they should receive
equal parts of the goods, so that one, if there is unfair treatment of
individuals by the other, can be on the way to recovering his right.
Therefore, the ordinary will see to it very carefully that this equality
of goods always be kept among them, unless perchance they themselves,
have decided differently among themselves or unless the ordinary
thinks another plan ought to be made for the sake of the widow and
children.

Chapter 25. When Payments Of Bequests To Pious Causes
Should Be Made

As soon as the debts have been paid, immediately, that which the
testator bestowed upon pious causes should be allocated. In this
matter, if those whose interest it is should delay longer than six
months from the approval of the will, the bishop or the ordinary, by
their authority of ecclesiastical censure, ★ should see to it that not Fol. 285r

only the share, but also whatever additions [there may be] shall be collected together and made to conform to the will of the testator, unless the time of paying the legacies is clearly specified in the will.

Chapter 26. When A Dying Legatee Transmits A Legacy To The Heir

If a legatee dies after the bequest falls due, but before the heredity has been taken possession of, the heir of the legatee will succeed to the right of the legatee. But, the bequest can not be handed over until the will is confirmed by the judge.

Chapter 27. When A Legacy Is Not Paid By The Heir

An heir is not held to the obligation to pay a bequest when it, having previously come to the legatee as a gift or in some other gainful way, subsequently should be put into the possession of the same legatee, for no one ought to be helped twice by the same favor; but as regards that thing which the legatee previously acquired for a price, if it is proved that he gave it for a reduced price. The purchase does not impede his benevolence, since not profit but a burden seems to be inherent in it.

Chapter 28. When The Bequest Is Not Valid

Bequests cannot be valid, and ought not to be executed, where the legatee departs from the purpose of the testator; or if the condition does not exist for which the bequest was made;or if the thing bequeathed passes away and is dissolved by some accident, or change, or calamity before the inheritance is entered upon; or if the legacies were attached to buildings, unless the buildings were dilapidated or destroyed. ★

Fol. 285v ## Chapter 29. When Legacies Ought To Be Lessened

When the inheritance was so small, that if all the legacies were fully represented, the full right could not be left to the wife or children, we want as much to be taken from it as is sufficient to fill out the share of the wife and children.

Chapter 30. What Must Be Promised By Legatees

Whatever has been expressly bequeathed to each one should not be given to each, unless he has legally guaranteed that he will restore what he receives if the inheritance was defective, and could not sustain the burden.

Chapter 31. On Matters Entrusted to Guaranty

As often as either an inheritance or legacies are entrusted in a will to the guaranty of a certain person, that is, they are so entrusted to a man for the interim that the same things afterwards are transferred to another by the will of the testator, these trustees ought not to be admitted to inheritances in any way or to legacies, until they have provided, either by suitable sureties, or even by bonds that they will keep the inheritance safe, and the legacies inviolate with precisely the same conditions which the testator signified, or expressed legitimately in his last will.

Chapter 32. How The Goods Of The Deceased Must Be Used

Heirs should set aside nothing from the goods of the testator for themselves even as a reward, nor should they distribute mutual gifts among themselves nor should they take possession of anything of this kind in any way and as if it were assumed it is their own unless, either something was openly given to them in the will or for something they have paid a fair price in the presence of suitable witnesses. It is agreed that administrators also should use the same rule regarding property.
★

Chapter 33. Nothing Must Be Given To Another Without Consent

Fol. 286r

We allow nothing to be taken from the goods of the testator, or given to another, no thing or possession of any kind; and we do not allow anything to be recorded in the books as something received, or, as they commonly say, any quittance to be given, either by the heirs, or by the administrators of the goods, unless there is common consent in this of all who have previously obliged themselves by oath; and we wish those who have done otherwise to be coerced under pain of excommunication.

Chapter 34. A Will Ought To Be Carried Out In A Space Of A Year

When heirs or administrators have once applied themselves to the settlement of wills, within the space of the year next following or, to speak more plainly, within twelve months from the time when they took on the administration of the will, they will review all the particulars of the things willed and will complete most fully the whole business entrusted to them as much as the desire of the testator, and the reckoning of the inheritance allows. But, if they do not finish this duty of theirs in the time defined, although the ordinary has incited them to diligence, if when he asks for a just reason for their delay they show none, they should be subjected to ecclesiastical punishments, and also should lose all profits which would have accrued to them from the will.

Chapter 35. When Heirs Can Act Separately In A Will

If several heirs or administrators were constituted by the same law, and if it should happen that one of them either died or was away for a necessary reason or was so impeded that he either refused within Fol. 286v six months, or could not share in the work ★ with others, the others will be permitted to handle the whole will and to bring all matters to conclusion. For, it is not safe or fair that the desire of the testators, fettered by one person, should be suspended for a long time and that his effects should be left uncertain.

Chapter 36. The Successors Of The Heirs And Administrators

When a solitary woman, whom we call a widow, has been made either heir or administratrix of the goods, and has taken these same goods after her husband, a man, whether his wife is dead or survives, will be pushed by the judge, who entrusted that administration or execution, to fulfill the whole desire of the testator. And so we wish this to be held in all legitimate successors of heirs, and administrators, so that whatever burdens of wills the predecessors knew, their successor should understand that these same things pertain to them, as much as the limitations of the goods and inheritances brought to them by any means allows.

Chapter 37. How Heirs Of Different Dioceses Are Brought Together By Law

When several heirs for one will have come together, although they are situated in different regions and dioceses, as they call them, still they shall be called together by that judge who confirmed the will, and by his authority they shall receive all duties which pertain to the trust and duty of heirs. We also wish that the same be understood concerning the administrators of goods. ★

Fol. 287r Chapter 38. How An Account Must Be Rendered By The Heirs

The ordinaries, or whatever other judges may confirm and register wills, and to whom has been entrusted the authority of directing the administration of goods left without a will, can and ought to demand an account of the duty performed by the heirs and administrators after a year. If they see that these men have conducted themselves with integrity, and without corruption in the matter, they should give them full and permanent discharge. However, we make this reservation: that if by chance something from the fortune of the deceased was not distributed as it should have been, and has not yet been settled, either it should be given to those who have a right to it or the heirs or administrators, at the will of the judge should apply it to some holy purpose.

Chapter 39. Penalty For Those Who Violate Wills

Forgers of wills who have brought forward or affixed their seal to false wills, or have by any means perverted a will, that in itself is genuine, either by adding or subtracting or changing or making erasures or by using any kind of fraud or depravity, if they should be convicted clearly of such terrible wickedness, they should be expelled as forgers from all the duties conceded to them by law, and they should be without every benefit of the corrupted wills.

Chapter 40. Those Who Are Without A Will

Those are said not to leave a will, first of all, who do not entrust it to writing, unless a sudden death overtakes them; those who do not name anyone heir; or if the heirs who are left reject it ★ and refuse Fol. 287v to accept the responsibility or are of such a kind that they cannot undertake it. And those must be judged to be without will when the will has been prepared so poorly that it cannot be confirmed by a legitimate judge.

Chapter 41. A Defective Will Ought To Be Carried Out

When a will is judged worthless, and the property must be distributed by the administrators, the judge ought especially to see to it that, insofar as he has an understanding of the wishes of the testator, this should be all important. For, although the will was not legitimate, still, we gladly follow the humanity of the civil laws to the effect that we should preserve the last wishes of men in regard to their own goods, and should [ensure] that the judgements which they would never reverse should be firm and inviolate as far as that can be done.

Chapter 42. To Whom The Administration Of Goods Should Be Committed And What Payment They Should Receive

As often as anyone dies intestate, his wife should be put in first place for the administration of his goods, the closest relatives in the second place, or if the judge so decides, he can join them in this duty along with the wife. However, let it always be clear that whoever has received the duty of administration should bring guarantors beforehand or even should post bond by which it can be fully and lawfully ensured that in this business they will proceed honestly and without any fraud, because the ordinaries will guarantee security to all parties, and finally because they will render an accounting of their actions whenever the judge legitimately requires it. ★ But, if by chance it sometimes should happen that because there are many equally close relatives, since they have equal claims to equal rights, then the judge should determine the case as honorable arbiter, and by his own decision should assign this duty of administration to one, or several of them. However, when some one in a relationship equally shared by many stands out who seeks the privilege of administration, or if many in an unequal degree of relationship, desire to be given this task, the judge can join together in this duty the wife of the deceased, and either one single man, if he wishes, or can designate whichever ones he chooses at this pleasure from the others, provided no gain comes about in this matter. And, no pay ought to be given to the judge from the designation of administrators unless the goods exceed five pounds; but the scribe even in those fortunes which do not come to five pounds will receive six pence. But, if the goods exceed in worth five pounds, and still are less than forty pounds, thirty pence will accrue to the judge and his assistants.

Fol. 288r

Chapter 43. Solutions For Matters Not Mentioned In This Chapter

Since heaps of doubts and controversies usually are focused on this chapter on wills, as long as the infinite avarice of men, plots to circumvent the wishes of the dead, it is wise to obviate the perversity of all parties. Therefore, those matters whose remedy or cure cannot be found in the constitutions, should be taken to the authority of Roman law; ★ with this exception however, that nothing should be taken from it of such a nature as would be at variance with these decrees of ours, or would not agree with the common law of our kingdom.

Fol. 288v

ordo titulorum in Codice D. Mat. Cant.

Vid. fol. 6. b.

Table of contents of 1571 edition in John Foxe's hand

De testamentis

Quid sit testamentum. Cap:

Testamentum est iustæ voluntatis et perfectæ mentis definita sententia, de re mea post mortem restauratione, quod notat et instituit rerum heredes, qui iure executor vulgo dicitur. Testamenta vero quisquis vel universa rescixerit, vel una illorum partium quarum ratione scient violat anathema, male pœnitat, et ex communibus Christianæ sanctitatibus expungetur.

De testibus adscribendis. Cap: 2:

Testamentum legitimis testibus communitum sit, et si nominatim ponat quatenus quidem communde fiert potest, ipse minister et cætera quos Guardianos appellant, ut maior testamentorum autoritas et existat, qui iure fortis sine iure non possit, aut duo vel tres assistant una spectatæ probitatis, et explorate fidei, dum denique testamentum ipsius manu testatoris vel dictante vel scribente resignetur.

De Testamento nuncupativo Cap: 3:

Si quis ex vita subito migraverit trium probata fidei testium consensibus accipiet, licet testamentum scriptis mandatum non sit, et in utroque testamenti genere tam scripto quam sumendo testatoris exemplo quid nuncupativum vocatur satis erit si ista mente sua testator heredem nominaverit.

Example of one scribal hand used

Reformation
of Ecclesiastical Laws First Begun By Authority of King Henry
8th: Then Continued and Augmented Through King Edward
6th Into This Form; and now Published For Fuller
Reformation of These Laws.

London
Publisher: John Day
1571
April

PREFACE TO THE LEARNED CANDID READER

There is nothing more important for the community as a whole and the private salvation of each one than the retention of the correct doctrine of religion in each constituent group of the Commonwealth. Moreover, proper discipline according to the best laws is extremely important for the best religion. The one should lead us to piety; the other should arrange the external life and manners of men in interpersonal relations. These two forces of law and true doctrine joined hand in hand are the most powerful means of administering the entire Commonwealth. Moreover, the proper practice of the one benefits the practice of the other. If they should be divided, like a ship cut into two halves, I do not see that the one without the other can achieve very much, particularly in these times. On the one hand, no state or kingdom, however well behaved, can be suitably controlled if the rule of religion is absent or if religion deviates from the truth. On the other hand, if the care for morality is not cherished and scrupulous judgements are not rendered, religious worship alone cannot accomplish the perfection of happiness. Augustine perceptively said as much when he wrote in *The City of God* that the state cannot be happy "when the morals suffer ruination even though the walls still remain standing." Also, I think our very wise ancestors recognized this when they balanced rewards equally with punishments and brought together the institutions both of laws and religion. Also, they believed that provision must be made for every constituent section of the Commonwealth so that good people should have something by which they might be encouraged to virtue and to the genuine worship of God. They saw to it that the fear of punishment would remain for the wicked to recall them from their vice, and that by the same means any controversies over any injuries that might arise could be removed and brought to an end.

But diligent and manifold caution must be displayed especially in this matter of arousing virtues and the genuine worship of God. For just as every religion ought not to be admitted into political union unless it corresponds as closely as possible to the expressed norm of the divine will, so also I think one should be especially prudent in choosing foundational laws so that they be suited to the Commonwealth. Moreover, no rashness of any kind should thoughtlessly come forth from them, nor tyranny impose itself upon them, but the laws should approach as closely as possible the archetypal rule of equal, honest and perfect reason. Next, care must be taken that the laws do not smell of the ruler's greed or taste of private privilege. People say that such was the case with the laws of Epitades who, when he had made a law that each man be free to leave his possessions to the person of his choice, was in reality simply making it legal to disinherit his son whom he hated. Further, laws should not breathe inhumanity such as was true of the laws of Draco and Phalaris of Agrigentum, and you may add to them the case of the Roman bishop. It would be of advantage, moreover, to beware that the laws do not, with a multitude of decrees and provisions, deface rather than decorate the Commonwealth.

It would be much the best hope, to be wished for in all prayers, that the life and manners of all Christians be such that there would be need not for a few moderate laws, but rather for none at all, and that there be such strength of religion among all that the Pauline statement truly could be affirmed of us: "The Law has not been instituted for the just man, etc." (I Tim. 1:9) However, it is not possible to attain to this in the weakness of this life, and I do not know whether one may even hope for it in this visible Church. The evil there is so promiscuously intermingled with the good that the worse part of the Church usually overshadows the better part. Therefore, laws have necessarily been prepared as a safeguard so that the coercion of discipline and laws may at least contain those whom religion cannot direct.

Without laws it is agreed that there can be no government of human society. Everywhere the examples of history prove this, not only the example of more recent times but also of the oldest antiquity, whether we look first at the Attic republic or at the Spartan republic. After various civil conflicts, finally the one republic received laws from Solon and other from Lycurgus. From then on each was much more pacified and enlarged. For it is agreed about Athens that when three factions mutually and simultaneously contended without any fixed law, when hatreds grew greater, and when this dissension threatened destruction for everyone, the republic was entrusted to Solon. He made laws by which he restored liberty and tranquility to this state for five hundred years after him. Moreover, it did not shame the Athenians to borrow certain Egyptian laws at this time and to transfer them into their own state (as Herodotus bears witness). The same practice of borrowing laws later came into use among the Romans. When public necessity compelled them to write laws for their own state, the Roman Council of Ten was sent into Greece to collect established codes of law from the Athenian laws of Solon, from the laws of Zaleucus among the Locri, from the laws of Charondas among the Thurini, from the laws of Lycurgus among the Spartans, and from the laws of Phoroneus among the Argives, and to consult the foremost men in Greece about instituting a republic.

And from these laws, at length, the twelve Tables of law were drawn up. Cicero has attributed such value to these that somewhere, while discussing the ideal condition of the state, he said that anyone at variance with Roman laws was going against nature. In brief, no race, no state, no nation was ever so savage or barbaric as not to have some laws (even though they were not always similar to one another) by which the state would retain at least some moral honesty, even if those laws did not drive out all vices. Thus also our English of time past were not without decretals of laws wisely constituted by our most prudent ancestors. Henry of Bracton's law book declares this referring to the sanctions instituted under the auspices of King Ine, Edward the Elder, Aethelstane, Edmund, Edgar, Alfred, Ethelred, Canute, and other princes. As long as these laws could maintain their authority, at least some discipline of life and manners flourished in this kingdom.

However, not long after this, the pope of the city of Rome, that wholly theatrical contriver, descended into the orchestra for the purpose of dancing his drama. While the other actors were driven off the stage little by little, he wished to keep the stage alone and to keep up all of the roles of everyone. First of all, leaving to secular magistrates only those matters which seemed secular, he transferred to himself and to his ecclesiastical people, with a most clever lie, all that was left regarding life and manners, while he fashioned himself as the vicar of Christ on earth and as the designated successor of the apostolic chair. As soon as he sensed that he had persuaded the princes of this, he gained a base from which to try even greater tricks. And indeed, he did not lack boldness when the opportunity presented itself. Therefore, when this remarkable actor set out with this preliminary narrative, and afterwards saw that the introduction had proceeded so beautifully for his ends, he prepared himself similarly for the remaining scenes of the action, scenes which he managed not less skillfully. As soon as he had obtained access to the kings themselves and to the highest monarchs, he tried to pluck at their authority little by little and soon sought to equal it, then even to surpass it, and then he sought to put the authority which he had surpassed under his yoke. When he perceived that this, too, was successful, he assumed greater confidence and proceeded to spread out farther and to extend greater wings from the nest with no longer any humble or plebeian thought about himself. He who formerly used to walk in the lowly comic slipper now strutted in the high tragic buskin, having become the fully tragic king instead of pope. Indeed, he who was ordered by Christ not to lord it over his own people no longer recognized the name of "subordinate." Finally this ecclesiarch swelled to such magnitude that he who was accustomed formerly to receive laws from others and to be kept in rank now reversed the tables and personally imposed laws on others and prescribed legal decrees for all. What he prescribed we now call canon law. In this very law, however, his impudence does not practice any moderation but accumulates laws upon laws, decrees upon decrees, and in addition other decretals and others and others. Moreover, even before he has established any end of accumulation, he has so loaded down the world with his Clementines and Sextines, Intravagantes and Extravagantes, Provincial Constitutions and Synodal Constitutions, Paleae, Glosses, Sentences, Chapters, Summaries, Rescripts, Briefs, Long and Short Cases, and infinite Rhapsodies, that Mount Atlas, by which supposedly the heaven is sustained, would hardly be able to bear this burden if it were imposed on it.

And indeed, a certain disorderly and extraordinary superstitious veneration of this pontifical fable kept him developing this way. It was remarkable what crowds he gathered, what tricks he performed for the world, and how he contrived to mislead by means of this veneration. He indeed put forward to the world some appearance of religion, but in such a way that it would not be difficult for the close observer to see that he contemplated a far different mystery, which was, of course, to raise up an ecclesiastical empire of unheard of power and glory in this world. Not content with this, he did not stop extending the law of his court until he had brought also the entire civil sword with its full power into his possession. He did not do this with the intention of strengthening the discipline of life and manners (this perhaps was never a serious consideration for him). Instead, he did this partly in order to stabilize the dignity of his position by fortifying it with every means [possible], and partly in order to garner as much wealth as possible from every place to satisfy his avarice. In doing this, he was not much unlike the example that Plutarch records of Dionysius of Syracuse who had imposed as many laws as possible with an insidious purpose, adding laws upon laws, and then allowing these same laws to be neglected by the people again. His neglect of the laws was carried out with as much craftiness as his promulgation of the laws, so that he might thereby make everyone liable to himself. The plan of the pope seems not to have been otherwise, for he added together such a patchwork quilt of laws in order to hold most people ensnared by these canonical articles so that greater gain would come to him from dispensations and condemnations. And consider that this is the denouement of the drama of this troupe-leader. For as old comedies almost always ended in a wedding, so all the efforts of the pope almost always ended in money. Briefly, under the papacy ecclesiastical affairs have been so governed that they never were nor ever could be in worse condition. Indeed, there was left almost nothing true in religion, nothing healthy in morality, nothing free in consciences, nothing genuine or sincere in worship, and nothing in laws except that which pertained to certain useless ceremonies or absurd dogmas or to the preservation of the privileges of rank. And if some shadow of justice and scrutiny of morals perhaps was shown in consistories, nevertheless things were so conducted that anyone could buy exemption from punishment. Also, there is this unsuitable added factor, that since all political power was far removed from these church courts, all the business of these tribunals was reviewed in the meantime by various canonists and other officials of the same sort. Of these persons, a great percentage who lived off the suits had more of an eye toward their own advantage than toward the rectitude of virtue and morality. For the sake of modesty, I would here suppress many things that perhaps ought not to be passed over. But it would be better to avoid scandal than to indulge the pen in this place.

Such a great extravagance of this sort of thing necessarily demands correction. Divine providence did not fail his Church. Indeed, by the singular kindness of divine providence the church finally began to shine. Coming out from under a dense cloud, it shone forth with the aura of true religion during the reign of King Henry VIII of most auspicious memory. It was during his reign that he became the first of all kings to strike completely from the boundaries of his kingdom the name of this pontiff, along with the haughtiest symbols of authority. He did this for the great good of the Commonwealth. Not content merely to drive away the name and the empty titles from himself and from his possessions, the prudent king also was intent on shattering all the laws and decrees by which the Church previously was constricted in order to establish full freedom for the entire Commonwealth along with himself. Therefore, both by his decree and by the public decree of Parliament, several men, thirty-two in number, were chosen who were outstanding in experience and in education. These men entirely abolished pontifical law (which we call canon law) with all that authority of decrees and decretals, and they substituted new laws, under the name and authority of the king, which would rule over the judgments made over controversies and morals. That which is evidenced in the king's own letter, which we have added as a preface to this book, should also reveal his serious interest in this matter and his pious will. The proposition of the king indeed must be praised, and perhaps the attempts of those who had written those former laws, although so dissimilar to these present laws, should also be praised. But the former undertaking lacked both the means and the occasion for success, perhaps because of the impropriety of the times or perhaps due to the lack of perseverance of those to whom the business was then entrusted.

Following all this came the death of King Henry — a death that struck the huts of the poor and the towers of kings with equal force. After him there came into the reign of the kingdom his son whom he had left behind, Edward VI, whose renown has never sufficiently been praised. Above all else, he supplied a greater impetus and vigor to the correction of religion which his father had just begun, and he had some success in his undertakings. The result was that the fountains of religion were cleansed much more thoroughly than before and were restored to a certain natural beauty. But the evil morals of those times were far removed from what people professed. They afflicted sound religion with decay and all good men with no small sorrow. In this case it is believed that while doctrine was reformed, there were not suitable restraints of law employed to check the unbridled lawlessness of the multitude. For these very practices and provincial constitutions which reign today in the courts and consistories of papal law were still continuing even then. These practices were practically nothing but a verbose assemblage of ceremonials, that is, nothing which would be greatly conducive to the correction of Christian life. In the meantime, because of his own divine genius, our Edward was not without knowledge of all this. Therefore, he soon gathered Parliament and Convocation into frequent meetings. Following his father's example, Edward completed with diligent haste what his father had formerly intended with regard to the reforming of papal canons.

What need is there of many words? From a common voting of all ranks this business was entrusted to a committee of thirty-two, not to the same men as under Henry VIII but nevertheless to the same number and of course to men endowed with equal excellence. These men were partly from the episcopacy, partly from the theological profession, partly from the profession of civil law, and partly from the profession of common law. There were eight men in each of these four classes. This committee was created for the purpose of fixing and enacting, at its discretion, certain chapters of sanctions into legal formulae which would suffice in place of the Roman constitutions. These new formulae were proposed as being better for the Commonwealth and especially salutary for morals.

It was not long before the king's will was carried out. The matter was completed with felicity and speed, for responsibilities were distributed into various tasks and the following organization was adopted: the thirty-two were divided into four groups of equal proportion so that in each group of eight there were two bishops, two theologians, two common lawyers, and two civil lawyers. And it was finally agreed that what was concluded and defined in each individual group should be transmitted to the remaining groups for their consideration and inspection. Moreover, from the total committee, eight persons were especially selected to whom were entrusted the first pre-arrangement of the work and the virtual preparation of the material. The names of these eight are contained in the letter of King Edward.

In this manner these laws were completed, whether one chooses to call them ecclesiastical or political. The material for these laws seems to have been sought from the best laws everywhere, not only from ecclesiastical laws but also from civil laws from the hoary antiquity of ancient Rome. Thomas Cranmer, Archbishop of Canterbury, was in charge of the entire work. Walter Haddon, an eloquent man with legal talents, added clarity and good rhetoric. I do not know if the hand of John Cheke, an outstanding man, was added to this undertaking. Because of these endeavors, the laws were fashioned in a more cultivated style than is the usual custom for other laws. As of me, if I might accomplish anything by my prayers, I would willingly pray that someone with a style and rhetoric like that of Haddon might forge ahead to polish our common laws and thus complete the same thing with them as Haddon, of most outstanding memory, did with the ecclesiastical laws.

But leaving these matters to the consideration of others, I return to our ecclesiastical laws. We have already stated how they were elaborated and by what authors they were written. It only remains for me now to discuss something of their dignity and value. Because I do not wish to run ahead of others in my judgment, I leave each one free to judge for himself. It will be enough for us merely to present these matters to eager readers, for these have been long since promised in our earlier documents. We do not intend that they should assume the force and authority of law here, but we want only to exhibit a sample of what is possible, as it were, for those having the inclination to read these things. When they have read them, each one may freely decide for himself on the basis of his own inquiry what he thinks must now be decided concerning these matters. As there is nothing and never was anything so felicitously worked out by human nature that no prejudice was inherent in it, so perhaps there will be matters here which will seem to demand either "second thoughts" or a more discriminating reflection on the reader's part. In this area, except for certain matters which I am compelled to skip over for the sake of brevity, there is one matter that I may not at all pass over and assume to be admissible to learned judgment. I refer to chapter sixteen, under the title "Concerning Services", which forbids that anything be done [as part of a service of public worship] beyond the directions and the rules of that book written in our common language, the book which has been established to be the proper and perfect teacher of all divine worship. But we acknowledge that the word of God alone is the perfect teacher of all divine worship. It is agreed in the time intervening, that in the prayerbook there are some things which seem not to square exactly with ecclesiastical reformation and which should be changed in a straightforward way. However, others will be able to perceive these things more clearly than I am able to advise against them.

In the meantime I can never sufficiently praise the pious and truly Christian concern of our most illustrious Prince Edward. Nor do I consider to be any less outstanding the diligence of the learned men who were in charge of gathering these laws which, it is agreed, were received with the greatest approval and applause in their time. There is no doubt but that these same sanctions would have been ratified by parliamentary authority and decreed for public use if life had been spared to the king a little longer. Indeed, as we must grieve that this did not happen, so now we, in turn, must hope that what was denied to the happiness of the Church through the premature death of that illustrious king, King Edward, may be supplied in the more fortunate times of our most serene Queen Elizabeth. Indeed, we hope for public authorization by this present parliament as well as for the approving votes of learned men. We earnestly ask them that they judge kindly our boldness which is manifest in our publishing these laws.

KING HENRY THE EIGHTH

Henry the Eighth by grace of God king of England and France, defender of the faith and lord of Ireland and supreme head on earth under God over the English provinces (of the Church); greetings and an increase of evangelical truth to all the archbishops, bishops, abbots, clerics, earls, marquises, counts, barons, soldiers, gentlemen, and other men of whatever rank, our subjects and our lieges wherever you may be throughout our kingdom and our dominion. Since you, my very fine citizens and citizens most dear to me, acknowledge me as the one and only ruler of this kingdom now, as the unique and supreme head of this Anglican Church over these lands according to God (as the plan of divine and human law demand) and you acknowledge that the power both of ecclesiastical and worldly polity has been granted to me and my predecessors by divine law itself (but which was snatched during many centuries by the malice, fraud, trickery and cunning of the one Roman bishop) and that it pertains to me and my successors by the unanimous consent of all; I cannot neglect making a calculating of my duty and my office more and more each day; and I cannot be without the greatest concern of mind and thought in magnifying the glory of God and propagating true doctrine of Christian piety and maintaining the safety and peace of this empire. For then those words come to my mind which are contained in the sixth chapter of the book of Wisdom to the effect: "Hear, oh kings and understand since power has been given to you by the Lord, and power from the Most High who will question your words and scrutinize your thoughts. To you therefore, oh kings, are these words of mine that you should learn wisdom and not destroy. For those who safeguard justice will be judged justly and those who have learned justice will find what they should respond to etc." From these words one can easily see that a reckoning of one's power must be most exactly rendered by kings and that those most severe punishments remain if they have not conducted themselves as they should have in administering the republic.

But if there is need of such great care and solicitude on the part of any kings whatsoever, then how anxious and solicitous one must believe that Christian kings must be since not only civil polity has been given to them but also ecclesiastical power! For they must concern themselves not only with those things which pertain to human society but also with those which are consistent especially with the divine Christian religion: it is right that Christian princes so estimate the present felicity of this world that they use this power of theirs to spread the worship of God, that they strive towards the following, namely that correct doctrine may be propagated and the glory of God may be enhanced.

Therefore, when I was noting that justice towards the republic and care for guarding the peace, and piety and an eagerness to increase and enhance the Christian religion, that all these are exacted from Christian kings, I was judging that I ought to do nothing less than under take all plans needed in this kingdom of mine and as much as I could I ought to satisfy the charge laid upon me. To be able to accomplish this more easily and expediently, you are quite aware of how much care I have shown in promoting and protecting those programs which seemed especially conducive and helpful for this task; and as for those programs which seemed to impede and stand in the way of this goal, you know how eagerly I have tried to remove and destroy them and still assiduously try to. For it was previously declared to you sufficiently how in this Britain of ours for many centuries past how inimical was the unjust and intolerable power of the Roman Bishop to God's most holy will, how it was opposed to propagating the Christian religion of true doctrine; how greatly and very often it disturbed the peace of this republic and its tranquility; and it dared by destroying the divinely constituted royal power to transfer to itself the owed obedience of all from the true and just power of the prince against all divine and human law. When by God's grace the power of this man was clearly removed hence, we have considered that all laws, decrees and institutes which were authorized by the Roman bishop must be forthwith abrogated lest any remnant should survive by which it might be that his power has not been wholly broken. In place of these laws, in order that the glory of the greatest and best God might be more easily illumined in the future and that the true Christian philosophy and the reign of Christ might grow and that all things in this church of Christ might be handled properly and correctly, we give laws published for you by our authority which we wish to be accepted, cherished, and observed by you all; and under penalty of our indignation we command you that your piety towards God, your law towards your fatherland and your obedience towards your prince should be conspicuous to all not without immense glory of the divine name and you should show yourselves not less concerned for your accounts than I have been concerning my duty in your cause; these accounts strictly command that you, all and each, use these constitutions of ours as much in the courts as in the schools and they severely prohibit anyone of you from presuming to admit other laws beyond these and the laws of our kingdom. Farewell.

KING EDWARD SIXTH

Edward Sixth, by grace of God, king of England, France and Ireland, defender of the faith, and supreme head on earth of the English and Irish Church sends greetings to the most reverend father in Christ, Thomas Archbishop of Canterbury by the same grace, primate and metropolitan of all England, and to the reverend father in Christ, Thomas, bishop of Ely, and to our beloved in Christ Richard Cox our Almoner and Peter Martyr, professors of sacred theology, to the doctors of laws William May and Rowland Taylor of Hadley, and also to our beloved faithful, John Lucas and Richard Gooderike esquires: Since we propose in a short time to assign and depute you thirty-two men to choose and compose our ecclesiastical laws according to the power, form and effect of the same act of parliament made in the third year of our reign at Westminster and since that number seems too large for handling of prenaming, describing and composing laws, although this then has to be held because of the consultation and judgment about this, then also it remains as very expedient because of the perfection and fullness of the same laws, it seems more agreeable to us, with the agreement of our Privy Council, to commit the beginning, entrance, first form and outline of this matter to a group of eight who will be a portion of the thirty [sic] doctors; of course they will be as it were a preparation for the larger number.

Therefore with greatest confidence in your prudence, knowledge and diligence,we have named and established, with the opinion of the council, you as our commissaries and impart to you authority by these presents that you may come together at convenient and opportune places and times with as great speed as possible at once and you may diligently read, consider and ponder the course of ecclesiastical laws existing in use within our kingdom or previously used; then having done this you may find, make and put into writing in place and instead of these former laws a collection, compilation and ordering of such ecclesiastical laws as you have decided would be especially expedient, because of your knowledge, wisdom and judgment to be practiced in use and to be proposed and published in whatever courts and ecclesiastical jurisdictions of ours within this kingdom of ours and our other dominions: having consideration and respect owed to the course of previously named statute, for the preservation of our common laws that do retain their vigor and for all other articles and branches of the named statute and as soon as the proclaimed laws have invented, formed, described and compiled by you, we wish these same laws to be immediately shown to us and written down so that we may transmit them for the opinion of our council and that of the rest of the thirty-two along with you for the further ratification and completion of the proclaimed ecclesiastical laws as it were of naming our commissioners jointly according to the form of the proclaimed statute.

And although we know you are gifted with such modesty and wisdom because you consider that burdens imposed and committed to your shoulders are of great moment and weight; still wondering that our proposal is nothing other than that which is rendered effective by you thanks to the same preparation; so because a greater number is able to proceed more certainly and in a more ordered way for the consultation and perfection of the same, we wish you to be more certain that your actions and studies in this effort will not only be most pleasing to us but also will be received with the most kind and favorable interpretation.

And in addition we wish that you come together immediately after the reception of these presents and that you use that speed and celerity in this matter that the cause demands; commanding and strictly demanding all and singular persons whose counsel, opinion and help you need in this undertaking and that those asked by you offer help, consultation, and aid as they desire to please us. In witness whereof we have caused to these our letters patent. Witness myself, at Westminster, on the 11th day of November in the 5th year of the king's reign.

Marton

By the king himself
and by the aforementioned authorization of Parliament.

Index

Index by RVS